Guide Through
The Romantic Movement

GUIDE THROUGH
THE ROMANTIC
MOVEMENT

By

ERNEST BERNBAUM

UNIVERSITY OF ILLINOIS

SECOND EDITION
REVISED AND ENLARGED

A COMPANION VOLUME TO THE
ANTHOLOGY OF ROMANTICISM

THE RONALD PRESS COMPANY ⟊ NEW YORK

Library of Congress Catalog Card Number: 49-8022
PRINTED IN THE UNITED STATES OF AMERICA

PREFACE TO FIRST EDITION

During the last ten or fifteen years great progress has been made in the study of the Romantic Movement. Many of the views formerly current as to the lives and works of the Romantics are no longer tenable. The discoveries of the specialists have not yet, however, been incorporated in textbooks covering the subject; and it is to supply the need for such a work that I have composed this *Guide* and *Anthology*. Feeling that too many books on the subject have been written primarily to express their author's personal opinions rather than to give an objective account of the matter, I have tried, so far as is humanly possible, to keep my own opinions under restraint. What I have chiefly attempted to do is to make accessible to students in colleges and graduate schools those facts, judgments, and documents that recent research and controversy have brought to light. I acknowledge with gratitude my constant indebtedness to those scholars whose works are listed at the end of each chapter in the *Guide*.

Any rudiments of originality that may appear in the *Guide* probably arise out of the fact that I have systematically sought to answer, with respect to each Romantic, these questions: (a) what relation was there between his life (outward and inner), his personality, and his ideas? (b) in what kind of life did he find happiness? and (c) what was his relation to other Romantics?

I recommend that the chapter on the Pre-Romantic Movement be studied after the chapters on the great Romantics, though in deference to convention I have placed it before them. I believe that, in the case of college students, the study of what the great works were should always take precedence over the causes which perhaps originated them.

In the Selected Bibliographies I have tried to discriminate between matters of elementary and of advanced character. The works listed under "Of First Importance" should be in the library of any college which desires to give a course in the subject that good students will derive profit and pleasure from.

E. B.

v

PREFACE TO SECOND EDITION

As nineteen years have passed since the first edition was published, the author may perhaps be allowed to point out that it not only synthesized the materials found in the works of other scholars and critics but also contained a few original contributions, a fact which he at that time refrained from mentioning. These new ideas or topics included the following, which were then either much neglected or wholly ignored:

1) the influence of the School of Sensibility on the Romantic Movement.

2) the systematic comparison of the sixteen chief Romantics with one another; their likeness and their differences.

3) the placing of Blake, not among the Pre-Romantics, but in the forefront of the Romantics.

4) an analysis of the philosophy, ethics, and literary principles of Wordsworth which gave equal place to its realistic and its idealistic tendencies.

5) coherent surveys of the philosophical ideas and literary theories of

Lamb
Hazlitt
Landor
and De Quincey

together with a rejection of the then prevailing assumption that those authors were important chiefly for their styles.

6) the exposition of what was original in the theory and methodology of the historical novel as re-created by Scott.

7) for Byron and for Landor a different kind of explanation than the prevailing ones, of their respective relationship to the Romantic Movement.

8) the incorporation of the young Carlyle among the great Romantics.

9) the significance for Romanticism of the modern revolution in the philosophy of natural science.

10) the survey of the history of the subject to 1930.

As explained in Chapter 22, "The History of the Study of the Subject" (p. 343), although there has been since 1930 a huge accumula-

tion of new facts and interpretations, there has been among scholars no
revolutionary change in general views about the Romantic Movement;
accordingly I have not found it necessary to introduce in this edition
any radical modifications of my previous attitudes toward the subject
as a whole. Nevertheless every sentence of the first edition has been
reweighed and reconsidered in the light of the newest discoveries and
the most recent opinions; many corrections and additions have been
made in matters of detail, and not a few passages of considerable length
have been modified or entirely recast. The chief improvement, I venture to hope, will be found in the various sections dealing with the philosophy and the aesthetics of some of the Romantics, and with the effect
of modern science on the status of Romanticism, topics of great difficulty which I have tried to treat with greater precision than formerly.

Chapter 20, "The Imagination: Romantic Concepts of Its Nature,
Function, and Powers," and Chapter 21, "What Kinds of Modern Prose
Fiction Would the Romantics Admire?: An Essay in Speculative Criticism," are entirely new. They will, I believe, be found useful supplements to the general chapter on the Romantic Movement: the first, as
giving a more precise interpretation (as recent scholarship discloses it)
of the central point in the romantic doctrines; the second, as showing
what conclusions romantic principles of criticism would reach if they
were applied to the most popular literature of our own day.

Since 1930 there has been a vast increase of serious interest in the
Romantic Movement. Scholarly research and controversies and critical
re-interpretations have become so extensive and recondite that it has
become increasingly difficult to survey the field as a whole. Most of its
leading scholars are therefore specialists in one or two Romantics or in
some particular branch of the subject. The outpouring of learned books
and articles from year to year waxes greater and greater; concerning
Wordsworth alone during the last ten years there appeared no less than
fifty volumes and one hundred and thirty articles of a scholarly character. Hence I have found it very difficult indeed to choose the items that
ought to be included in the *Selected Bibliographies* of the *Guide*. I have
tried to admit nothing that is not in some way of substantial importance,
and I have regretfully omitted many items that have some value, but not
sufficient for inclusion in my limited space. Nevertheless the Bibliographies in this edition are at least twice as extensive as in the previous
one, the writings of some eight or nine hundred scholars, editors, and
critics being listed. It would have been easy, but not really serviceable
to students, to quadruple the length of the Bibliographies. No doubt I
have inadvertently omitted some items that by my own standards should
have been included; and I shall thank anyone who calls such to my attention. It is almost impossible to be "selective" without occasionally being
unjust; even as it is impossible to make characterizations of the works
as brief as mine are without occasionally being unfair.

The Bibliographies are intended not only to help the student who
wishes to explore the field further, but also to take the place of foot-

notes for the chapters to which they are appended. As in the first edition, I gratefully acknowledge my indebtedness to the authors named in the Bibliographies for those facts and opinions which I have utilized in my discussion. To have given a footnote reference for each borrowing would have increased the size of this volume by probably one-quarter. And, in this respect as in others, brevity has been one of my main practical objectives.

A *Key to the Abbreviations* used in the Bibliographies will be found on page 349.

In the text of the chapters, cross-references are regularly given to the copious selections from the Pre-Romantics and the Romantics in my *Anthology of Romanticism* (Third Edition), so that whenever the reader of the *Guide* comes upon an allusion to some important work of those authors he is enabled to turn readily to the pertinent passage. Furthermore, the annotations in the *Anthology* provide additional information, and also suggestions for further inquiry and for class discussions.

It is hoped that another edition of the *Guide* may be issued in due course, in order to keep it abreast of the progress of research and of new developments in criticism. I shall be grateful to readers who send me corrections, or suggestions for improvements.

E. B.

Freedom's Haven
Jaffrey, New Hampshire
January, 1949

CONTENTS

GUIDE THROUGH THE
ROMANTIC MOVEMENT

CHAPTER 1

THE APPROACH TO THE SUBJECT

The importance of that change in men's feelings, thoughts, and tastes which is called the Romantic Movement is universally admitted. With the exception of Shakspeare and Milton, no English authors outrank such great Romantics as Wordsworth, Coleridge, Scott, Byron, Keats, Shelley, and Carlyle; and the combined effect of the group is the most powerful of any of the literary influences that mold our civilization. The Romantics may nowadays be ᵔdmired or detested, but no one who is mentally or aesthetically awake can ignore them. They have produced or affected every conspicuous phase of nineteenth-century and twentieth-century thought and action, from Emersonianism and Whitmanism in America to the Oxford Movement in Great Britain, from realism to naturalism, from nationalism to socialism, from the philosophy of Hegel to the philosophy of Nietzsche. For better or worse, the modern outlook is chiefly the creation of the Romantics—most English and American literature of the last hundred years being either an application of the romantic principles to new themes or a hostile reaction against those principles. To understand our present-day cultural heritage, we must know the Romantics.

Most college students, through no fault of their own, are, however, not in the right frame of mind to profit from the reading of the Romantics. Owing to the fact that our largest national business, education, is the worst conducted, students in school and college have the impression that a cultural subject is something to be learned from a book or a teacher and rendered back to that teacher in recitations or examinations more or less accurately—the process leaving little impression upon their attitudes toward life or upon character. The student to whom real life is one thing, and his studies quite a separate and secondary matter, should take up some other subject than the Romantic Movement. It may be possible to study profitably in that fashion The Pottery of the Hopi Indians or The Recessive Accent in Greek (though I doubt it), but it is an utterly preposterous self-deception to suppose that one can derive anything of value from the Romantics until one shakes off such indifference.

The Romantics do not give one merely a pleasant and decorative addition to one's knowledge; rightly studied, they shake the very foundations of one's former beliefs, likings, and assumptions. That is why they are educative. They fulfill, to an extraordinary degree, that true ideal of

3

education voiced by President Robert Maynard Hutchins of the University of Chicago when he said:

> Among all sorts of people and in all kinds of places, it has become the fashion to attack American education. One criticism is that it upsets and disturbs young people. The conception of education as a process of settling, or hardening, of the fixation of sound principles and righteous dogma in the youth of America, brings me at once to state my own view of university training. It is that the purpose of higher education is to unsettle the minds of young men [and, presumably one may add, of young women], to widen their horizon, to inflame their intellects. It is not to reform them, or amuse them, or to make them expert technicians in any field. It is to teach them to think, to think straight, if possible; but to think always for themselves.

Those are sentiments which the Romantics would applaud, and which their works are peculiarly well fitted to help one carry into realization.

The Romantics may prove desirably unsettling because they suggest a multitude of reasons why the views current among us today, in a time when the practical, scientific, and material achievements of our country overshadow every other activity, are not as sound as we suppose them. The Romantics raise the question whether those common-sense notions and purposes which tyrannically direct most of us are leading us to happiness or to bitter disappointment. To every human being, that is a fateful question which only cowardice or folly will contentedly leave unanswered. The Romantics are not dogmatists. They do not furnish cut-and-dried formulae which we can readily apply to those problems peculiar to our individual lives or to our generation as a whole. But by sympathetically following their lives and observing how they gradually found their way through problems which are akin to our own, though not identical therewith, we shall discover much that illumines our experience and clarifies our future purposes. This end, however, will not be attained unless we first patiently try to understand just why our authors came to believe as they did, exactly what it was that they believed, and just how their beliefs and preferences would work out when applied to our own life and environment. "We read fine things," says Keats, "but never feel them to the full until we have gone the same steps as the author." This method of study and attitude of mind the *Guide* and my *Anthology of Romanticism,* with the Topics for Discussion contained in the latter, are intended to serve; but the volumes will not achieve their aim unless he who reads them will try seriously to consider how the romantic ideas as to what is true, good, and beautiful, affect his own life and views.

Only a fatuous refusal to pay attention to the lessons of the recent past would induce anyone today to take the same attitude toward the Romantic Movement as was customary in the earlier half of the twentieth century. In that period few people made the right kind of approach to the study of romantic literature. The majority were prejudiced against Romanticism from the outset. The dominating influences of the times were anti-romantic—materialistic, prosaic, scientific, technological, and secular. The world was ruled by the "practical" man, and obsessed by his idols. Religion and philosophy were feeble and confused; the new forces in politics, whether Fascist or Communist, were anti-democratic; poetry whimpered in its darkness; and fiction floundered in sophisticated hopelessness. The inevitable outcome was universal distrust and hatred, the brutalities of genocide, the savagery of biological and atomic warfare, and the paralysis of any confidence in the future of mankind. Everything that the Romantics believed in had been ignored or despised. And the result was the greatest moral failure, and the closest approach to total ruin, that civilization had ever experienced. The lesson is indeed obvious. The right way to approach the Romantics today is with the knowledge that those who neglected or derided them have proved false prophets and fatal guides; and that perhaps if we were to understand the grounds of their faith, and were to recover it, we might find a way out of the inferno of evil and fear into which the anti-romantics have misled us.

CHAPTER 2

THE PRE–ROMANTIC MOVEMENT

CHRONOLOGICAL TABLE OF THE CHIEF PRE-ROMANTIC WORKS

1696 ff.		Beginnings of Sentimental Comedy
1706		The Arabian Nights, transl.
1709		Beginnings of the Sentimental Tale
1709	Shaftesbury	Virtue or Merit
1711	Shaftesbury	The Moralists
1719	Winchilsea	Nocturnal Reverie
1719 ff.		Ballad Collections and Imitations
1726	Dyer	Grongar Hill
1726–30	Thomson	The Seasons
1735	Brooke	Universal Beauty
1740	Richardson	Pamela
1742–44	Young	Night Thoughts
1743	Blair	The Grave
1744	Akenside	Pleasures of Imagination
1744 ff.	Collins	Poems
1744	J. Warton	The Enthusiast
1747	T. Warton	Pleasures of Melancholy
1748	Richardson	Clarissa Harlowe
1748	Thomson	The Castle of Indolence
1748	Gray	Hymn to Adversity
wr. 1749	Collins	Popular Superstitions of the Highlands of Scotland (publ. 1788)
1749	Hartley	Observations on Man
1751	Gray	Elegy in a Country Churchyard
1754	T. Warton	On the Fairy Queen
1756	J. Warton	Essay on Pope
1756	Amory	John Buncle
1757	Gray	Progress of Poesy
1757	Gray	The Bard
1757	Burke	The Sublime and Beautiful
1759	Young	On Original Composition
1759–65	Sterne	Tristram Shandy
1760–63	Macpherson	Ossian
1762	Hurd	Chivalry and Romance
1763	Smart	A Song to David
1764	Walpole	Castle of Otranto
1764	Evans	Ancient Welsh Bards
1765	Percy	Reliques of Poetry
1766	Goldsmith	The Vicar of Wakefield
1766	Brooke	Fool of Quality
1768	Gray	Fatal Sisters, etc.

1768	Sterne	Sentimental Journey
1770	Percy	Northern Antiquities
1770	Goldsmith	The Deserted Village
1771	Mackenzie	Man of Feeling
1771	Beattie	The Minstrel
1777	Day	Desolation of America
1777	Chatterton	"Rowley" Poems
1777	Morgann	On Falstaff
1782	Cowper	To a Young Lady
1785	Cowper	The Task
1786 ff.	Burns	Poems
1786	Beckford	Vathek
1789	Bowles	Sonnets
1789	White	Selborne
1789–92	Darwin	Botanic Garden
1789	Blake	Songs of Innocence
1791	Gilpin	Picturesque Beauty
1792	Bartram	Incidents and Scenes in Florida
1792	Wollstonecraft	Rights of Woman
1793	Godwin	Political Justice
1794	Godwin	Caleb Williams
1794	Radcliffe	Mysteries of Udolpho
1795	Lewis	The Monk
1796	Taylor	Lenore, transl.
1798	Cowper	On the Receipt of My Mother's Picture
1803	Cowper	To Mary
1803	Cowper	The Castaway

Meaning of "Pre-Romantic."—The term "Pre-Romantic Movement" is used to designate the development during the eighteenth century of literary tendencies which resemble, or which influenced, those of the Romantic Movement of the nineteenth century. It is a convenient term, although not strictly definable and although applied to different works for different reasons. Some of the works usually included in the Pre-Romantic Movement, e.g., the poems of Burns, are thus included merely because they appeared before Wordsworth's and Coleridge's *Lyrical Ballads* of 1798, and not because any deficiency in their romantic quality is implied. In other cases, however, such as the writings of Godwin, the term comprises works which are not at all romantic in themselves but which for one reason or another facilitated the coming of Romanticism. Inasmuch as some sort of connection may by an ingenious historian be plausibly discerned between *all* the works of any period, it is to be feared that in the course of time each and every piece of eighteenth-century literature may be found pre-romantic; in other words, that the term, ceasing to mean anything distinctive, may become useless. But at present it serves passably well, since it is by general custom confined to certain authors and types, such as those represented in the "Selections from the Pre-Romantic Movement" in my *Anthology of Romanticism,* whose relation to later Romanticism is considered peculiarly close.

Difficulty of the Subject.—It used to be supposed that the differences between the age of Pope and the age of Wordsworth were clear and distinct, and that the passage from the earlier age to the later was abrupt and revolutionary. It was assumed that the individual authors of both periods were consistent with themselves, and with the particular school to which they adhered; and that they never wrote anything consciously or unconsciously out of accord with their other writings or with those of their group. On these assumptions, students felt that they were mastering the subject when they had learned certain sharp contrasts between the "neo-classic" and the "romantic." Closer examination, however, has shown that the true history of the matter is far more complex—that many features formerly believed to be confined to the romantic period are found also in the neo-classic, and that many authors definitively classified in one of the hostile schools now and then displayed astonishing inclinations to desert to the enemy. Often, although one passage of an eighteenth-century poem will appear obviously romantic, another just as obviously will seem neo-classic. An author may sympathize with one tenet of the pre-romantic faith, and logically ought to sympathize with another, but will disagree therewith—apparently quite unembarrassed by his vagaries. To suppose that the pre-romantic writers deliberately set out to prepare the way for the Romantics, that they clearly and fully knew to what goal their tendencies would lead, and that they held undeviatingly thereto, would be to misconceive the situation. In actual occurrence the pre-romantic phenomena were often confused, disassociated, and illogical. Yet, if one is to set them forth in a few pages, and if one is to bring out their significance clearly enough to be intelligible, one is forced to simplify and systematize a little too much a movement which was frequently blind and groping. Mankind usually advances by steps which are hesitant and meandering.

It has been said by historians of literature that the romantic spirit had two notable manifestations before the Romantic Movement of the early nineteenth century—one in Palestine in the days of Christ, another in England in the days of Shakspeare; and it is undeniable that, not only in those periods but in others, many anticipations of modern Romanticism may be found. The Pre-Romanticism of the eighteenth century, however, was the most directly influential upon its immediate successor. Yet few of the Pre-Romantics understood fully in what directions they were tending. They rarely used the word "Romanticism"; and each of them promoted the rise of Romanticism only partially, or superficially, or with respect to merely one or two restricted subjects or phases. The great Romantics were to go further and deeper than these predecessors; they were to see more clearly their objective, and its universal relationships. In the case of some of the eighteenth-century authors the fact that they are now regarded as Pre-Romantics is not the most important or admirable aspect of their work—e.g., in the cases of Gray and Burns; while in other instances—e.g., Macpherson, or "Ossian," and Chatterton—that fact is probably the chief reason why they are still read. In this chapter, all of them are considered only with respect to the part some of their works played in the new movement.

THE FIRST QUARTER OF THE CENTURY

The Neo-Classic Dominance.—The neo-classic spirit dominated the age of Pope. After the political and religious unrest of the seventeenth century, the majority longed for peace, moderation, and the reign of common sense. In poetry and prose, they were tired of the fantastical, the irregular, and the hazy. They demanded correctness, and adherence to literary rules which were clear and reasonable. They loved the polite and the witty. They were chiefly interested in the urban rather than the rustic, in maturity rather than in youth, in the civilized present rather than the ruder past, in an age of Stoical rationality like the Augustan Age of Rome, rather than in an age of faith, like the medieval. In persons, in historical epochs, and in literature and art, they valued the typically human more than the individually peculiar; and they assumed that they themselves were typical. Thus in all things they tended to confuse contemporaneous conventions with permanent laws. The proper study of mankind was Man—a dualistic creature, capable of virtue and reason, but addicted to vice and folly and therefore requiring for his salvation much discipline. It was well that the State disciplined him by force; the Church, through prohibitions and through the terrors of eternal punishment; and Literature, through satire. Such were the views of men in other respects as different as Pope, Swift, and Addison; and they were the most admired and influential writers of the age.

The School of Sensibility.—The opposition to Neo-Classicism during the first quarter of the century arose in many different quarters, some of the authors being personally not known to each other, and probably not conscious of any similarity between their tendencies. Chronologically the first pre-romantic indications appeared in the drama, but the character of the new movement will be better understood by observing first its appearance in philosophy.

At least as early as 1709, and possibly ten years earlier, there appeared the *Inquiry Concerning Virtue or Merit* (*Anth.*, 4) by the amiable young idealist, Anthony Ashley Cooper, third Earl of Shaftesbury, in which was asserted a fundamental tenet of the School of Sensibility, viz., that orthodoxy drew too black a picture of man's nature, and that man instinctively and without instruction or discipline had a "moral sense" which recognized virtuous conduct and delighted in it. Nothing except "force of custom and education in opposition to Nature" stood in the way of morality. Two years later, in *The Moralists* (*Anth.*, 5), appropriately given the subtitle *A Rhapsody*, this ethical optimism was supplemented with a natural religion, called "romantic," in which Shaftesbury declared that man would find the response to his own instinctive goodness, its sanction and support, in the Genius of Nature, the beauty and harmony of which assured him that the Universe was the best of all possible worlds. A quarter of a century later, Pope, in his *Essay on Man,* tried to engraft some of this sentimental optimism upon his own orthodox ethics; but there could hardly be a greater contrast than that between his argumentative attempt to prove his religion by an appeal to the understanding, and Shaftesbury's enthusiastic attempt to persuade by an appeal to the heart and the instinctive sense of beauty. In the latter half of the century, Shaftesbury's *Hymn to Nature* was translated by the pioneer German Romantic, Johann G. von Herder (*Naturhymnus von Shaftesburi*), and it became famous throughout the literatures of Europe.

The influence of Shaftesbury upon *belles-lettres* was not immediate, and before it became effective there had already developed tendencies in the drama which unintentionally moved in the same direction. On neoclassical principles, comedy, when dealing with everyday contemporary life, was supposed to be satirical throughout, chastising evils and follies by laughing them to scorn. To introduce pathos or tears was to bring about a confusion of genres. If sympathy was to be appealed to, or a sense of admiration for man's nobler qualities was to be aroused, the proper place for it was not a comedy, but perhaps a romantic drama in verse, or an heroic romance in prose, or something similarly remote from the life of the despicable and ridiculous ordinary human being. To the consternation of the neo-classic critics, however, there began to appear from 1696 onwards a steadily increasing stream of comedies which were not wholly satirical but in the main sentimental. Colley Cibber in 1696 produced his *Love's Last Shift,* and in 1704 his *Careless Husband;* Richard Steele followed in 1705, with his *Tender Husband,* and in 1722 with his *Conscious Lovers.* Critics like Dennis protested that these dramatists "knew nothing of the nature of comedy," but the public thought otherwise; and thence onwards down the century sentimental comedies grew more numerous than satirical high comedies.

The sentimental comedy was an unwitting ally of Shaftesburian philosophy in basing its plot upon faith in the goodness of the human heart, and upon an aesthetic appeal to instinctive sympathy for that goodness. Its plot usually approximated the following: the faultless heroine is wronged by her lover or husband, not because he is wicked (he is really "good at heart") but because he is misled by worldly follies. Near the end of the play, in as dramatic a scene as contrivable, he is confronted with the pitiable consequences of his errors. He beholds the heroine as "virtue in distress," his moral sense is awakened, he melts into tears, instantly reforms, and makes amends.

The counterpart of sentimental comedy was domestic tragedy. This differed from the other branch of the drama of sensibility chiefly in avoiding a happy ending; for here again both the hero and the heroine were essentially good, and the erring hero, before his lamented death, was brought to repentance. Far fewer domestic tragedies appeared than sentimental comedies. Aaron Hill produced one, *The Fatal Extravagance,* in 1721; and George Lillo another, *The London Merchant, or the History of George Barnwell,* ten years later. Both of these were based upon Elizabethan originals; but whereas the Elizabethan authors made no attempt to gloss over the deliberate wickedness of the wrongdoers, Hill and Lillo exculpated them and threw the responsibility for their crimes upon unfortunate accidental circumstances. The same method was employed in the best-written tragedy of this kind, Edward Moore's *The Gamester* (1753). From the neo-classic point of view, all such tragedies violated the principle that the hero of a tragedy should at least partly contribute to his downfall through some defect in his character.

Although Richard Steele did not write domestic tragedy, he considered it a legitimate form, which ought to move the ordinary human being more powerfully than tragedies dealing with persons of high estate. In prefaces to sentimental comedies, Steele and his fellow innovators defended them; and some of his essays in *The Tatler* and *The Spectator* likewise supported principles in harmony with them. Thus by the end of the first quarter of the century not only had the drama of sensibility begun its career, but there had been some attempts to support it with a literary theory.

In the same period there appeared in *The Tatler* and its successors short tales which may fairly be described as domestic tragedies and sentimental comedies converted into prose narratives. They centered about the distresses of the virtuous, and, as one reader says, were "wept over with great pleasure." One of the best of these stories was that of Amanda (*Spectator,* May 10, 1712) by John Hughes, who was, albeit somewhat timidly, elsewhere venturing to commend the poet Spenser (*Remarks on the Fairie Queen,* 1715).

Other Pre-Romantic Works.—Not every pre-romantic work of 1700–1725 is, like sentimental philosophy, sentimental drama, and sentimental tale, to be associated with the School of Sensibility. Some have little or no connection with faith in humanity or with a pathetic appeal to the moral sense. In 1706, an attempt was made to translate *The Arabian Nights* from that French version by Antoine Galland (1704–17) which was beginning to give Western Europe a hint of the exotic beauty of this masterpiece. If the first English translation had been worthy of the Arabian original, or even of the French intermediary, the Pre-Romantic Movement might have been accelerated by contact with a world so different from the neo-classic, so unrationalistic, so colorful in its imaginative freedom, sensuousness, and fatalism. Decades were to pass before the real qualities of *The Arabian Nights* were felt, the crude prosaic style of the translation almost destroying them; nevertheless a few of its most obvious marvels were perceived and imitated.

Some works that were subsequently to affect the pre-romantic current had their origin not in a literary purpose but in a scholarly or antiquarian one. Of this the first example is George Hickes' *Linguarum Veterum Septentrionalium Thesaurus* (1703), a learned collection of Old Norse literature. Here appeared in the original and in translation the weird incantation of Hervor, the kind of passage which was to awaken interest in the gloomy superstitions of the northern world. It was later repeatedly versified.

More important than such exotic influences was the publication of ballads, collected or composed, by Lady Elizabeth Wardlaw, William Hamilton, Allan Ramsay, and David Mallet. Here was the revival (or, better, the maintenance) of traditions native to the British Isles, "not pilfered," as Ramsay said, "and spoiled in transportation from abroad," and not trimmed with "foreign embroidery" (Preface to his collection entitled *The Evergreen*, 1724). Their motives for editing ballads or imitating them were various—a mere craving for change, for something as different as possible from the current neo-classic verse; or a kind of literary patriotism, proud of the allusions to local history and scenes, and glad to give the native dialect a literary standing; or a genuinely historical curiosity; or a half-reluctant admiration for the simpler manners and more vigorous life of their forebears. It is not to be supposed that the Neo-Classicists always regarded ballads with aversion; indeed in two celebrated *Spectator* papers (May 21 and 25, 1711) Addison, albeit in a rather apologetic manner, had expressed his fondness for *Chevy Chase*. Nevertheless those who looked upon earlier ages and manners as the Neo-Classicists did, could hardly be expected to feel the finer qualities of the best ballads nor to value them at their true worth. Such appreciation was a slow development. Ramsay himself, like other early editors, did not have a scrupulous respect for the texts; he modernized and altered expressions which might offend his age. And Lady Wardlaw, who published her imitation as an original, lapsed into anachronisms which nowadays seem absurd. But such defects were natural in inexperienced pioneers.

Finally, there appeared during 1700–1725 a considerably larger amount of nature poetry than might be expected. Poets such as John Pomfret, in *The Choice* (1700), and John Gay, in *Rural Sports* (1713), praised country life, its quietude, and its opportunities for leisurely contemplation. Frequently, however, poetry of this kind seems to us to betray such superficial observation as to imply a lack of real interest in the theme, and it is only in comparatively few cases where the fidelity to the objects and the warmth of the feelings seem evident, that such poems are considered pre-romantic, e.g., Lady Winchelsea's *Nocturnal Reverie,* Croxall's *Vision,* and especially Dyer's charming *Grongar Hill.*

THE SECOND QUARTER OF THE CENTURY

James Thomson.—The nature poetry of the first quarter of the century is not comparable in importance with Thomson's *Seasons* (*Anth.,* 7). In length, in closeness of observation, in fullness of detail, in affectionate delight in the smaller elements of nature, and in awe and enthusiasm for the greater, it surpassed its predecessors. His diction was somewhat conventional; yet, by using blank verse rather than the Popean couplet, he showed not only a spirit of independence but also an artistic sense for harmony between substance and form that, as we shall see, was to be lamentably rare among writers of the pre-romantic kind.[1] In some respects Thomson was affected by the School of Sensibility. He rebuked the world of wealth and fashion. He had his scenes and sketches of humble virtue in distress, his touches of humanitarianism and pathos, which suggested a kinship between his spirit and that of Steele's sentimental tales. Moreover he sometimes combined with such feelings (as Steele did not) rhapsodic exaltations like those of Shaftesbury, for example in part of the Hymn concluding the *Seasons*. Thomson knew Shaftesbury's work, but, unlike him, he desired to be orthodox in his religion; and his views were based largely upon those of Isaac Newton. Newton's scientific doctrines concerning the regularity of natural law could be, and were, harmonized with Christian faith and ethics into an imposing system which seemed more reasonable, and was less aesthetic or mystical, than Shaftesbury's.

The Poetry of Sensibility.—Lesser poets than Thomson show the Shaftesburian influence clearly enough—a poetaster like Jenyns, for example, with his protests against pessimistic conceptions of God and man (*An Essay on Virtue*). Henry Brooke, although he likewise mistakenly kept to the heroic couplet, was a more vigorous follower, unmistakably sincere. He gloried in the presence of God in nature, seeing Him "in every atom," and notably in such marvelous instincts as are shown in the migration of birds; and he delighted to describe what seemed to him the complete contrast between the evils of civilization and the goodness of nature (*Universal Beauty*). In the Prologue of his *Gustavus Vasa* he applied the same idea to the political field. The explosive corollaries of Shaftesbury's theories were beginning to be drawn.

In 1744 the young Joseph Warton published *The Enthusiast; or, the Lover of Nature* (*Anth.,* 24). In this short blank-verse poem, he contrived to touch upon a larger number of the commonplaces of his school than any previous devotee. On the one hand he expressed the contempt for cities, formal gardens, conventional society, business, law courts, and Augustan style; on the other, the love for the simple life, solitude, mountains, stormy oceans, instinctively noble savages, untutored poets who "warbled wildly," and tragedies of terror. A year later another young disciple, John Gilbert Cooper, versified Shaftesbury's cosmogony in *The Power of Harmony*.

The true poet in this group was William Collins (*Anth.,* 28). His difficult *Ode on the Poetical Character* (*Anth.,* 30) inclines as far in the direction of rhapsody and wonder as Pope's *Essay on Criticism* leans toward common sense. His *Ode on the Popular Superstitions of the Highlands of Scotland* (*Anth.,* 34), a singularly prophetic utterance, combines two motifs dear to the School of Sensibility—the moral interest in the "blameless manners" of the peasant with the aesthetic interest in his folklore. The emotional and lyric power of Collins was such that the

---

[1] It failed him when, in *The Castle of Indolence* (*Anth.,* 16), he used the Spenserian stanza to express an un-Spenserian mood.

too early ending of his career by insanity and death meant a great loss to the new school.

The Poetry of Melancholy and Death.—In the 1740's there arose a vogue of poems that were mournful in tone, and by some scholars these are associated with the sentimental school. Since that school trusted the emotions, it might readily induce indulgence in emotions for their own sake; and in so far as this indulgence motivated the writing of melancholy poems, the influence of the School of Sensibility upon them may be granted. It should be added, however, that several of the writers of those poems were far from adhering to the main tenets of that school, and that they held much gloomier views of God and man. Edward Young's *Night Thoughts (Anth.,* 18) is one of the most important poetical treatments of the theme of immortality between Davies' *Nosce Teipsum* (1599) and Tennyson's *In Memoriam* (1850). The *Night Thoughts* may rightly claim a place in Pre-Romanticism by its impressively emotional tone, but its theology and ethics were as orthodox as they were somber. Much the same may be said of Robert Blair's *The Grave,* the title of which gave rise to the nickname "the Graveyard School." But in the case of *The Pleasures of Melancholy (Anth.,* 39) by Thomas Warton, the brother of Joseph, we have a clear connection between the sentimentalists and this elegiac fashion.

New Literary Theories and Standards.—The neo-classic delight in satire found an enemy in William Whitehead, whose *On Ridicule* urged that satire was futile, and pleaded the cause of humane kindness. The aesthetics of the School of Sensibility were versified by Mark Akenside in his lengthy *Pleasures of Imagination (Anth.,* 22). Developing Shaftesbury's conception of the harmony of the universe, Akenside taught that the instinctive perception thereof was the essential trait of poetic genius. Good taste or the capacity for appreciating beauty were, like the moral sense, innate rather than acquired by schooling or culture: the farm laborer would delight in a beautiful sunset. This theory harmonized with Joseph Warton's conception that Shakspeare's only education was through contact with Nature and that he "warbled wildly," i.e., extemporaneously *(Anth.,* 24); and with Thomas Warton's preference of Milton and of "magic Spenser's wildly-warbled song" to Pope's artful lines *(Anth.,* 26).

The Novel of Sensibility.—The sensationally popular works of the new school during the second quarter of the century were the novels of Samuel Richardson, *Pamela* (1740) and *Clarissa Harlowe* (1748). A prosperous middle-aged printer in London, he touched the sentimental movement on only one of its sides. He had none of that enthusiasm for nature which Shaftesbury and the poets had expressed. But he was in deep accord with the spirit manifested in the dramas of sensibility and the sentimental tales, and they doubtless influenced his novels. The tale of Amanda, by John Hughes, is, indeed, an anticipation of the main plot of Richardson's *Pamela;* and when dramatizations of his novels were made in

England and on the continent they proved to be typical sentimental comedies (*Pamela*) or domestic tragedies (*Clarissa Harlowe*). Richardson, however, in his long novels, made a much deeper and more prolonged impression than his predecessors. With him the mood of sensibility was not a matter of a few minutes or hours but of days. To read *Clarissa Harlowe* (especially, as was commonly done, to read it aloud) was so prolonged an experience of that mood as to leave an indelible impression. Many sentimentalists before him had valued the emotions highly and had appealed to them, but none had traced the life of the emotions, especially in women, with such patience, sympathy, and knowledge, as he displayed. In power over pathos, he was unrivalled. Popular with all classes, his novels did more to extend the taste for sensibility than all the other sentimental works of this quarter of a century.

THE THIRD QUARTER OF THE CENTURY

The Novel of Sensibility.—Even as Neo-Classicism tended toward the uniform, sensibility encouraged the individual and the odd. One of the oddest works of the century appeared in 1756, Thomas Amory's *Life and Opinions of John Buncle*. Professing to be an autobiography but usually regarded as a work of fiction, it introduces us to a unique character who was cheerfully devoted to many inconsistent opinions. He achieved consistency in only one respect—his opposition to the orthodox and conventional. For the rest, he was by turns rationalistic and sentimental. On the one hand, he was devoted to mathematics, especially to algebra, and to an argumentative Deism which conceived of religion as something to be proved by evidences. On the other hand, he rhapsodized over the beauty of women (his hero marries seven times in the course of the story) and over the delights of pedestrian wanderings among the hills of northern England, which he describes as if they had the altitude and grandeur of mountains. The latter trait, at a time when sentimental vagabondage was unusual, is historically noteworthy. Most significant, however, is the mental unbalance, the incoherence—symptom of a soul which has lost its old system of beliefs and had not yet found a coherent new one.

Three years later, in 1759, appeared the very genius of incoherence and sensibility, Laurence Sterne. The Neo-Classicists had preached the control of the feelings and imagination by the judgment. They (even the liberal-minded Fielding) were concerned about the proper relationship between the beginning, the middle, and the end of a plot, and about the depiction of general types. Sterne boasted that his pen governed him, not he it; and, though the boast was not quite true, his *Tristram Shandy* began at the end and had no discernible middle. Alone among those eighteenth-century novelists who had a theory about their art, he believed that no one theory could cover its potentialities and that each novelist should be a law unto himself. For his own part (and this was a natural outgrowth of the sentimental movement), he wished to relate not so much what his characters did, but precisely what, when things happened to them, their mental and emotional reactions were. The story was next to nothing; the individual characters (few of them were typical, many were odd "originals") and their feelings were all in all. This implied that it is not the general laws of life that matter, but an individual's own sensations in the course of his personal life—an assumption which would antagonize a Neo-Classicist. It was a theory and a kind of prose fiction not fully understood and carried into practice by anyone except Sterne, until our own century.

The leering obscenity of Sterne, which seemed to belong to that rakish social world against which the sentimentalists were revolting, was the chief point of difference between him and his school; it shocked or grieved them, Richardson especially. In other respects he was consistently their ally, ever preferring the natural to the conventional; taking a foreign tour not to instruct his mind or polish his manners but to vary and refresh his sensations—a "sentimental" journey; identifying amatory experiences with spiritual; sympathizing with the unfortunate without stopping to inquire whether they were responsible for their misfortune; weeping indiscriminately over distressed human beings and distressed animals; and everywhere finding the source of all virtue and joy in his "dear Sensibility."

Sterne had a talented disciple in Henry Mackenzie, who did not attempt to imitate his whimsicality and irregularities of form, but who in *The Man of Feeling* cultivated sentimentalism with fine delicacy. He gave his hero such extremely modest and sensitive traits as to make him seem effeminate. In *Julia de Roubigné* he illustrated the kinship between sensibility and humanitarianism by an outburst against negro slavery.

A reaction against the formlessness of Sterne was shown in Goldsmith's *Vicar of Wakefield*. Here, although the interpretation of life is akin to that of the sentimental school, extravagance was held in check by Goldsmith's exquisite sense of humor and by his love of balanced form and purity of style. The result was one of the most beautiful of prose idylls.

The Poetry of Sensibility.—In both prose and verse, Goldsmith, unlike most of his contemporaries, succeeded in expressing sentimental views in a classical style. In *The Deserted Village* (*Anth.*, 63), he employed the heroic couplet and the antithetical manner so admired by the Neo-Classicists to convey a message congenial to their opponents. He evoked sympathy for the decline of the country villages, "bowers of innocence and ease," with their lovable and virtuous inhabitants, and attributed their passing to the growth of luxurious and profligate cities. His theory and his descriptions were somewhat out of accord with the actual contemporary economic facts. Nevertheless the warning was justifiable in those days, and became more and more so in later times. Goldsmith was a pioneer in the romantic revolt against the spoliation of the countryside and the degenerative urbanization of man.

Incomparably inferior to Goldsmith were such other poets of the new school as Richard Jago and John Langhorne. Jago, with ludicrous ineptitude, pleaded for a humaner attitude towards animals; and Langhorne, in a stilted manner, recommended a kinder and more lenient treatment of the poor and unfortunate.

Literary Theories and Standards.—Besides Sterne's utterly ignored theory about the novel, there appeared in the period Joseph Warton's *Essay on the Genius and Writings of Pope (Anth., 26)*. Warton granted that Pope was the supreme master of one kind of poetry, but maintained that the kind was second-rate, because confined to contemporaneous life and not so imaginatively sublime and pathetic as the poetry of Shakspeare, Milton, and Spenser. Perhaps the most daring sally in this militant defiance was the passage in which he asserted that Horace himself, lawgiver to the Neo-Classicists, had declared that satirical and didactic verse was not the most poetical.

A year later, in 1754, Thomas Warton produced his *Observations on the Fairy Queen of Spenser (Anth., 40)*. Here Chaucer was praised as well as Spenser; and the criterion of poetry was declared to be its appeal not to the intellect but to the feelings and imagination. More than any previous pre-romantic critic, Thomas Warton emphasized the need of the historical method in criticism. Neo-Classicism tended to judge all authors by a universal standard which ignored differences between historical periods, and which too often assumed that the universal was identical with the then customary. Thus whatever in Chaucer, Spenser, or Shakspeare seemed strange because it was not an act, a sentiment, or an expression common in the eighteenth century, was apt to be judged unnatural and therefore faulty or ugly. Against this narrow view, Thomas Warton urged that first of all "we should endeavor to place ourselves in the writer's situation and circumstances," bearing in mind the manners and beliefs of the poet's own age, as well as his own purposes and aims, and not trying to judge his work by its conformity to narrow standards. By contending for these principles, Warton, who twenty years later produced a *History of English Poetry*, the first extensive treatment of the subject from that point of view, performed a permanently valuable service, not much impaired by the fact that like his fellow sentimentalists he erroneously supposed that Spenser wrote without premeditation, artlessly, and merely to please the fancy with charming images.

In 1759, Edward Young's *Conjectures on Original Composition (Anth., 20)* attacked Pope's translation of Homer on the grounds that it was untrue to the virile temper of the Homeric age, and that it should have been written in blank verse. Pope and his school were also censured for being too sedulous in the imitation of authors, whereas a true genius, like Shakspeare, was uninfluenced by previous writers and looked for inspiration only to life and nature. In 1762, Bishop Richard Hurd published his *Letters on Chivalry and Romance*. By this time the conflict had tended to become one between admirers of Homer, Virgil, and Horace, and admirers of Shakspeare, Milton, and Spenser. The qualities of the latter group which chiefly distinguished them from the former were of Chris-

tian or medieval origin.   To the Neo-Classicist the medieval, or "Gothic,"
age seemed semi-barbarous.   Hurd boldly defended it, and the works influenced by it, as superior to the classical and pagan.   He declared that
Christianity, with its medieval institution, chivalry, had introduced into
life and literature, and notably into the "system of gallantry," i.e., the
relations between men and women, a spirit much more gentle and humane than pagan ages conceived.   Moreover, the religion, and even the
superstitions, of the despised Gothic era were much more solemn and awe-
inspiring than those of Homer and Virgil.   With this proposition, the
assembling of the chief argumentative weapons in the arsenal of the
School of Sensibility may be said to have been completed.

Macpherson's "Ossian."—In 1760, James Macpherson, a young Scotchman, published *Fragments of Ancient Poetry Collected in the Highlands
of Scotland, and Translated from the Gaelic or Erse Language,* with a
preface by Dr. Hugh Blair, a celebrated professor of rhetoric, assuring
the public that these were "genuine remains of ancient Scottish poetry."
In 1762 Macpherson produced a much longer work, *Fingal, an Ancient
Epic Poem, by Ossian the Son of Fingal, Translated from the Gaelic,* with
a dissertation in which he defended himself against charges of forgery.
The last of the Ossianic poems, *Temora, an Ancient Epic Poem,* appeared
in 1763.   The acclaim with which *Ossian* (*Anth.,* 53) was welcomed, not
only in England but also on the continent, can hardly be exaggerated.

To understand the sensational popularity of *Ossian* in its day, one must
take into account the point at which, c. 1760, the literature of sensibility
had arrived.   By that time the new school had engaged in two major efforts.   One of those had been, as we have seen, to depict in dramas, tales,
and novels, contemporary life in such a way as to arouse faith in the
goodness of human nature.   To too many people, however, the contrast
between actual life and the rose-colored world depicted in such literature
seemed too obvious; and when Dr. Johnson denounced sentimental optimism as cant, or Henry Fielding in his novels cast ridicule upon Richardson's characters as unreal, it was clear that this interpretation of life had
not proved altogether convincing.   The other main effort of the School
of Sensibility had been to build up, in sentimental philosophy and in
sentimental criticism, a doctrine that, inasmuch as the instinctive was
the good, literature would be the better the less contact it had with the
artificial and civilized and the closer it kept to the simple and natural.
The more nearly primitive a people were, the more beautiful should be
their poetry.   The weakness of this theory lay in the fact that it *was*
merely a theory.   So far as known, the masterpieces of the world's literature were not products of uncivilized epochs.   Where, a sentimentalist
might be asked, can you show us this supposedly superior poetry written among a people living in a state of nature?   Hence the timeliness of
Ossian, which, after 1760, was the answer to that challenge.

Macpherson seemed to bring forward not only the evidence that was
needed to prove the literary theory of the sentimental school, but at the

same time the evidence for its theory as to the state of nature. The warriors of Fingal he depicted as leading the simple life, knowing nothing of money or luxuries, awed by the wild grandeur of nature, sentimental and melancholy in mood, and, although brave in battle, merciful to their enemies. In point of fact, this was a misrepresentation of the actual life and manners of the third-century Celt, who was a joyous and manly barbarian; but Macpherson insisted upon the authenticity of the work. He had the effrontery to point out the superiority of Ossian to Homer on the ground that in Ossian the warriors were never revengeful or inhumane, but always lived up to their "disinterested and generous sentiments." To the delight of his school, he made evident the contrast between the Celts, a nature people, and their foes, the "civilized" Romans —a contrast which Edward Gibbon, a decade later, ironically commented upon in his *History of the Decline and Fall of the Roman Empire,* as follows:

> Something of a doubtful mist still hangs over these Highland traditions; nor can it be entirely dispelled by the most ingenious researches of modern criticism: [1] but if we could with safety indulge the pleasing supposition that Fingal lived, and that Ossian sung, the striking contrast of the situation and manners of the contending nations might amuse a philosophic mind. The parallel would be little to the advantage of the more civilized people, if we compared the unrelenting revenge of Severus with the generous clemency of Fingal; the timid and brutal cruelty of Caracalla, with the bravery, the tenderness, the elegant genius of Ossian: the mercenary chiefs who, from motives of fear or interest, served under the Imperial standard, with the free-born warriors who started to arms at the voice of the king of Morven; if, in a word, we contemplated the untutored Caledonians, glowing with the warm virtues of nature, and the degenerate Romans, polluted with the mean vices of wealth and slavery.—*History of the Decline and Fall,* ch. 6.

Thomas Gray.—Among the many who were deeply stirred by Ossian's mountain monotones was Thomas Gray. His earlier poetry was classical in temper and style, and he was of too academic and critical a nature ever to be swept away into the more extravagant and sentimental enthusiasms; but his later work shows a growing interest in various pre-romantic movements. His *Elegy Written in a Country Churchyard* (1751; *Anth.,* 42) perhaps the most beautiful lyric in our language, was in the fashion of the Graveyard School, though intrinsically superior to any other poem of that kind. Pre-romantic too were his *Progress of Poesy* (1757; *Anth.,* 45) with its emphasis upon feeling and sublimity; and *The Bard* (1757; *Anth.,* 47), a clear anticipation of Macpherson's epics. It is therefore

---

[1] That the Caricul of Ossian is the Caracalla of the Roman history, is, perhaps, the only point of British antiquity in which Mr. Macpherson and Mr. Whitaker are of the same opinion, and yet the opinion is not without difficulty. In the Caledonian war, the son of Severus was known only by the appellation of Antoninus; and it may seem strange that the Highland bard should describe him by a nickname invented four years afterwards, scarcely used by the Romans till after the death of that emperor, and seldom employed by the most ancient historians.—Gibbon's note.

not surprising to note in Gray's letters after the appearance of *Ossian* that if he believed anyone then living capable of composing the work he would undergo the hardships of a journey to the Scotch Highlands to behold such a genius. As his later poems show *(Anth., 50)*, he continued to be interested in Celtic and Scandinavian antiquity, but he never gave a sentimental interpretation to such themes. In other words, he did not overidealize the past.

Revival of the Past.—Likewise pre-romantic, but not motivated like *Ossian* by sentimentalism, were the publications of Evan Evans and of Bishop Thomas Percy. Evans, a clergyman and antiquary, published his small collection, *Some Specimens of the Poetry of the Ancient Welsh Bards, Translated into English* in 1764, "in order to give the curious some idea of the taste and sentiments of our ancestors." The same scholarly purpose predominated in the publication of the more extensive and very celebrated collection, Percy's *Reliques of Ancient English Poetry* (1765; *Anth.*, 59). Percy was a true antiquary and virtuoso, loving to collect things old and strange—Chinese, Scandinavian, American, Indian, medieval, Elizabethan, and what not. He had rescued a mid-seventeenth-century manuscript of medieval ballads, and had gathered many others from different sources. From our modern point of view, he modernized his texts too freely, and was neo-classic in apologizing for qualities in the ballads that "would require great allowances to be made for them in a polished age like the present." But to his diligence the world is indebted for the preservation of many precious treasures. The effect of the *Reliques* in gradually developing a taste for the ballad style was very great. The *Reliques* gave a basis for the theories of Herder. Percy also, by his translation of Paul Henri Mallet's *Northern Antiquities* (1770; *Anth.*, 62), fostered the notion that the nature-worship of the ancient Norse was a kind of divine revelation to primitive "Gothic" peoples, a notion which a generation later seemed attractive to Carlyle and other Romantics.

The Gothic Novel.—Readers of Richardson or Sterne naturally developed a taste for the pleasures of emotion, which craved stronger and stronger stimulus. Presently the sentimental novel of contemporaneous life seemed to them stale and tame, because modern conditions, being comparatively peaceful and prosaic, afforded too few situations of a violently exciting kind. It was natural therefore that novelists should turn back to more spacious days. Sometimes the attempt was inept, as, for example, in Thomas Leland's historical novel, *Longsword* (1762). Two years later, however, the ingenious Horace Walpole managed to unite in *The Castle of Otranto* (1764; *Anth.*, 56) characters like those in the sentimental novels with a plot as full of mystery, surprise, and horror as those of the romances. To this type of romance, because its action was usually laid in medieval times, was given the absurd name of "Gothic." Walpole was not its only begetter. Decades earlier than *The Castle of Otranto*, a Frenchman, the Abbé Prévost, whose novels were well known and imitated in England, had begun to spice the sentimental domestic novel by the addition of such stagey properties as romantic castles, ruins, dungeons, ghosts, and supernatural occurrences; and even the rugged realist Tobias Smollett had introduced two "Gothic" episodes in *Ferdinand, Count Fathom* (1753). It is important to note that the employment in the Gothic novels of these new means of arousing emotion did not change the fundamental point of view, and that the conception of human character usually remained that of the School of Sensibility.

Chinese Gardening and Gothic Architecture.—During the first half of the century, in the arts of architecture and of gardening as in literature, the predominant aim had been balance and regularity. But from the fifth decade onwards, Gothic architecture came increasingly to be favored instead of classical; and an interest arose in Chinese gardening ("sharawadgi"). It began to be generally recognized that Nature was varied and complex rather than simple and uniform. Edmund Burke, in the same essay, *On the Sublime and Beautiful* (1759), in which he justified freedom of the feelings, and even the use of terror, as an element of the sublime, expressed his pleasure in the fact that landscape gardening was escaping from rigidly geometrical formalism. The lovely grace of Chinese gardens, the bold aspirations of Gothic architecture, and the daring "irregularities" of Shakspeare, were felt to be part of one and the same new insight and taste. The arts were still to "imitate" Nature, but a Nature conceived more rich in variety, energy, and the wonderful.

The Noble Savage.—From the very beginning, the principles of the School of Sensibility had carried the implication that "civilized" people had no ground except vanity for considering themselves superior to those nature people whom they called "uncivilized." In the 1770's there were a number of curious developments of this idea. Lord Monboddo, an eccentric propounder of paradoxes, would arouse Dr. Johnson's indignation by maintaining that the life of a savage was nobler and happier than that of a London shopkeeper; and in his *Origin and Progress of Language* (1773) he asserted that to behold the ideal conditions of existence one must go to the South Seas, "where the inhabitants live without toil or labor upon the bounty of nature." In 1774 an anonymous poem, *Otaheite* (i.e., Tahiti) described "the gentle tribes" who dwelt in a perfect climate and knew none of the ills of civilization—neither toil, nor anxiety, nor false modesty, nor constraint:

> Their evening hours successive sports prolong
> The wanton dance, the love-inspiring song.
> Impetuous wishes no concealment know,
> As the heart prompts the melting members flow.
> Each Oberea [queen] feels the lawless flame
> Nor checks desires she does not blush to name.

A South Sea Islander named Omai, who was brought to London in 1774, became the rage in society; nothing but gentleness and charm was perceived in him, and Sir Joshua Reynolds portrayed him as if he were an incarnation of dignity and virtue. At first glance the interest in contemporaneous South Sea Islanders and the interest in third-century Celts may seem to have nothing in common, but both were manifestations of a yearning to find somewhere, whether in man's past or present, an actual state wherein his circumstances and his character were ideal.

The Last Quarter of the Century

The Cult of the Past.—In the last quarter of the century the cult of the past continued to take two forms—one, antiquarian and in the main faithful to the historic facts; the other, sentimental and anachronistic. Of the latter type, Thomas Chatterton's work was the most astonishing because of the precocity of its author. The son of a Bristol schoolmaster, he developed in childhood an interest in old manuscripts and books, and from the age of sixteen began to compose imitations of medieval writings. He borrowed words from Chaucer, and from Percy's *Reliques,* but chiefly from Spenser—sometimes mistaking their sense. Many of his fabrications he ascribed to one Thomas Rowley, a fifteenth-century monk. He sent some of his forgeries to Horace Walpole, who, on consulting Thomas Gray and William Mason, discovered the imposture. The unfortunate youth had lost his position in a lawyer's office, was unable to find another, and finally, destitute and starving, committed suicide at the age of eighteen. In the later romantic movement he was depicted by Wordsworth, Shelley, and others, as the most pathetic illustration of the world's inhospitality to poetic genius, and of the failure of the poetic temperament to adjust itself to the actual conditions of life. As may be seen in his *Boddynge Flourettes* and *Balade of Charitie (Anth.,* 70), Chatterton dealt with the fifteenth century as Macpherson had dealt with the third. He interpreted the Middle Ages as an age of simplicity, in which there flourished benevolence and the love of nature.

The revival of the past by antiquarian methods continued vigorously. There was much collecting of ballads, re-editing of medieval and Elizabethan English works, and translation of foreign literature. One illustration of the general extension of such knowledge is the steadily increasing adaptations and translations of Scandinavian literature, among the chief translators being Mathias, Downman, Johnstone, Jerningham, Sterling, Hole, Sayers, Amos Cottle, and Joseph Cottle—the last being a contemporary and friend of Coleridge, Southey, and Wordsworth. In 1787 the most celebrated monument of Old Norse Literature, the poetic *Edda,* was translated. It was described at great length, and quoted from in the *Analytical Review,* the reviewer recalling Thomas Gray's earlier version based upon it, the *Descent of Odin (Anth.,* 50).

Cowper and Bowles.—One of the most pleasing achievements of the sentimental movement was the poetry of William Cowper—especially pleasing to those who were frightened by the more violent emotional developments of the school but who loved its quieter moods. In his youth Cowper had been engaged in professional life in London, and had written satiric verse; but he found himself temperamentally unsuited to an active career, and, after an attack of madness, withdrew to a retired life in the country. His poem in blank verse, *The Task* (*Anth.*, 73) (so called because its composition was enjoined upon him by a friend), describes the small incidents of daily life in such circumstances, and their significance to a reflective mind. The newspaper brings him its burden of strife and oppression from the outside world, and he laments the existence of war, tyranny, crime and brutal punishment, negro slavery, and cruelty to animals. The consolations of life he finds in friendship and the family affections, and in meditation among familiar country scenes. His lines *On the Receipt of My Mother's Picture* (*Anth.*, 77) and *To Mary* (*Anth.*, 79) are models of affectionate tenderness. A deeply religious spirit moves through Cowper's poetry, expressing the Methodist (Wesleyan) reaction against the rationalism and formalism of the Anglican church. He loves a Christianity which is sincerely personal, deeply emotional, and actively democratic and humanitarian. He was tragically afflicted with the notion that he himself had committed the unpardonable sin against the Holy Spirit, and was therefore doomed to a dreadful fate, as *The Castaway* (*Anth.*, 79) shows; but this illusion did not mar the serenity of the main body of his work. He said that his purpose was "to discountenance the modern enthusiasm after a London life, and to recommend rural ease and leisure, as friendly to the cause of piety and virtue." He was in his generation the favorite poet of the gentler votaries of sentimentalism, of those who were alarmed by the virility of Burns or horrified by the excesses of melodramas or novels of terror. Thus the young lady who represents the sentimental school in Jane Austen's *Sense and Sensibility* is especially fond of Cowper.

William Lisle Bowles in 1789 published a small volume containing fourteen sonnets (*Anth.*, 95). He seems a disciple of Cowper, somewhat more plaintive in tone. His sonnets were praised by the young Coleridge as

> those soft strains
> Whose sadness soothes me like the murmuring
> Of wild bees in the sunny showers of spring.
> *Poems,* 1796

Writers on Nature and on Travel.—A place in the Pre-Romantic Movement, though not in the School of Sensibility, must be given to those who were faithfully studying aspects of nature at home and abroad. Among these was Gilbert White, author of *The Natural History and Antiquities of Selborne* (*Anth.*, 95), whose accurate and loving observation of the fauna and flora of his small Hampshire parish made him one of the most celebrated of naturalists as well as one of the most delightful. —Erasmus Darwin, a physician and scientist of Lichfield, whose hobby was the cultivation of a botanical garden, tried to cast his observations of the wonders of nature into verse *(Anth.,* 97). His *Botanic Garden* consisted of two parts, *The Loves of the Plants* and *The Economy of Vegetation.* His poetic diction was neo-classic, and his metre the heroic couplet. It would be hard to find a more amusing illustration of the truth that the old style and form were unsuited to the expression of the new themes, than Darwin's well-meant labors.—A growing body of literature concerned itself with the beauty of landscape, in nature, in painting, and in landscape gardening, and with the principles of such beauty. A representative of this tendency was William Gilpin *(Anth.,* 98) who wrote descriptions of the Lake District, the Scottish Highlands, and other lovely regions, as well as *Remarks on Forest Scenery.* His careful observations and analysis of the elements of "the picturesque" showed the way to the great romantic nature writers, and was to culminate in Ruskin's *Modern Painters* (1843 ff.).

The travelers also contributed to an increasing knowledge of the wonders of nature. In 1770 the Scottish explorer, James Bruce, who dwelt in Abyssinia two years, had at last discovered the source of the Blue Nile, and his popular account, *Travels to Discover the Source of the Nile,* was rich in adventures that stimulated the imagination. Another representative work of this kind was that of William Bartram *(Anth.,* 98), an adventurous Quaker of percipient imagination, who described his lonely journeys through the southern parts of the United States, and had many marvels to relate. Such books of travel were widely read, and exercised a considerable influence upon Wordsworth, Coleridge, and other Romantics of the next generation.

Aesthetic and Literary Theories.—There was much argumentation, so complex and confused that it is impossible to summarize it briefly, on aesthetics and literary criticism. It abounded in self-contradictions. There were pleas for originality, but disagreements about what it consisted in and how it might be fostered. Other issues were: what is taste? and how important, relatively, are unity, proportion, variety, novelty, and sublimity? The debates were on two levels of intelligence and difficulty. On the philosophical level, as has lately become clearer through the researches of Bate and others, there were profound speculations which were in the next century to become influential upon Coleridge and Hazlitt. Aesthetic criticism, formerly based upon neo-classical confidence in the reason and in the reason's power to excogitate the ideal, was given by the rise of associationist psychology a new basis in empirical experience. Feeling and intuition were gradually acknowledged to be more important in grasping the meanings of experience—in capturing qualities and interrelationships, and at the same time giving them organic form and thereby communicating their significance to readers or beholders. But this admirable effort to think through to the fundamentals of aesthetics was confined to intellectual circles, and had at the time little effect upon current literary criticism, which dealt with less abstruse problems.

Blair, an admirer of *Ossian,* turned his attention to the pastoral, and suggested that the neo-classical type be reformed by ceasing to imitate the conventions of the Greek and Roman pastoral and reflecting instead the actual life of rural England—sound advice which was soon to be followed.

A remarkable critical study appeared in 1777, Maurice Morgann's *Essay on the Dramatic Character of Sir John Falstaff.* This is probably the boldest and most original of several noteworthy contemporaneous discussions of Shakspeare. When neo-classic critics discussed Shakspeare's characters at any length (they were more inclined to criticize his plots), they discussed them as if they were artificial contrivances constructed by Shakspeare's intellect and completely analysable by the intellect of his readers. Upon the minds of Morgann and a few others at this time— such as William Richardson, in his *Philosophical Analysis of Shakspere's Remarkable Characters* (1774–89)—it began to dawn that this prosaic conception of Shakspeare's method was inadequate to explain the extraordinary effect of vitality conveyed by his great characters. They felt that one could not completely *understand* or explain those characters, but that one did *feel* them and their motives to be consistent and human. In other words, the characters appealed to our imagination as real, because it was imagination rather than the calculating intellect which had created them. To study them profitably the critic should think of them not as mechanically made puppets whose complete nature was limited to what they had been made to do or say, but as complex living beings, whose conduct was intelligible only by taking into account their fundamental character, "their latent motives and their unavowed policies." It followed, as Henry Mackenzie (*Lounger,* Nos. 68–69; 1786) as well as Morgann asserted, that Shakspeare was a creative artist who had much more method in his seeming madness than either the Neo-Classicists with their talk about his "irregular genius" or the sentimentalists with theirs about his "warbling wildly" had perceived. In these critical essays lay the germs of a new and profounder interpretation of Shakspeare; but it was not until the days of Coleridge, Hazlitt, and De Quincey that they came to rich fruition.

Meanwhile the School of Sensibility continued to cherish its theory that poetic originality was wholly a product of nature. James Beattie, in *The Minstrel; or the Progress of Genius,* using the stanza of Spenser but not imitating his diction, told the tale of a poet who was "a poor villager," knowing little or nothing of urban luxury or worldly ways, and having next to no formal schooling, but gifted with sensibility, devoted to Nature, and moved to the depths of his soul by her grandeur and mystery. In the course of the century there had been a number of attempts to discover real poets in several farm laborers, bricklayers, or shoemakers (Stephen Duck, Henry Jones, James Woodhouse, etc.), but such attempts had collapsed ridiculously. Academic skepticism might therefore reasonably ask Beattie and his school: "Where in the actual history of literature can you point to anyone reared like your minstrel who is a true genius?" But when, in 1786, there burst upon the world the poems of the Ayrshire ploughman, Robert Burns, the School of Sensibility seemed at first glance to be triumphantly justified.

Robert Burns.—That Burns was a true poet, and one of the greatest, was soon recognized: the sincerity and force of his feelings, his graphic power, his command over different moods, his ease and apparent spontaneity, and his closeness to the fundamentally human, aroused general admiration. His poetic genius was immediately ascribed to his supposed lack of culture. Upon the appearance of his first volume of poems, Henry Mackenzie introduced him to the world as "this heaven-sent ploughman, from his humble and unlettered station," and attributed his powers to intuition merely. Mackenzie was mistaken. Although Burns had had little formal schooling, he had something which is often far better—an interest in reading. Self-educated he was, but far from uneducated. At an early age he had thoughtfully read many substantial works, and by 1786 his knowledge of literature was remarkably wide. He drew from both Scotch and English sources. He was familiar with the dialect verse which is so important a strand in the Pre-Romantic Movement—including the verse of Jane Elliot, Jean Adams, Anne Lindsay, Robert Ferguson, and John Mayne. In English literature, he of course knew Pope; but his favorite poet was Goldsmith, as *The Cotter's Saturday Night* (*Anth.,* 83) would suggest, and he delighted in Thomson, Young, Gray, Collins, Beattie, and Cowper. He was enthusiastic over *Ossian.* Among novelists, his "bosom favorites" were Sterne and Mackenzie. The similarity between his chief themes and those of the School of Sensibility is too obvious to require illustration, but in powers of expression he was incomparably superior to most of his predecessors. Occasionally he fell into some of the sentimental excesses, and exalted indiscriminately every kind of natural ebullition; but for the most part his sense of humor saved him from too extravagant enthusiasms. Later Romantics like Wordsworth were to surpass him in the range and depth of their interests, but they too loved him and did not question the fellowship, in the movement to which they belonged, of him who had shown them

> How Verse may build a princely throne
> On humble Truth.
>
> Wordsworth, *Grave of Burns; Anth.,* 293

His champions against those who tried to blacken his character and belittle his work were Scott, Wordsworth, Hazlitt (whose "On Burns and the Old English Ballads" was an especially valuable defense) , and Carlyle.

The American Revolution.—As shown in the cases of *Ossian* and of Burns, the School of Sensibility was desirous of finding evidence to support its ideas, in actual events, past or present. Another event which the sentimentalists thus interpreted was the American Revolution. They took the American side in the dispute with the colonies, not because, like

Edmund Burke, they looked upon the colonists as Englishmen whose constitutional rights were being invaded, but because they regarded them as a people happily different from Englishmen or any other decadent Europeans. A half-century earlier the idealist George Berkeley had described them as a nature people, dwelling

> In happy climes, the seat of innocence,
>   Where nature guides and virtue rules,
> Where men shall not impose for truth and sense
>   The pedantry of courts and schools.

When it appeared that Great Britain would endeavor to suppress the revolution, Richard Price, a London clergyman, predicted that all the colonists would spring to arms at the magic word of liberty and under the leadership of invincible freeborn heroes win immediate victory over the effete mercenaries of a tyrant.

In 1777, i.e., when the English were at war with the Americans, Thomas Day, an amiable young sentimentalist, published his poem, *The Desolation of America*. Upon most of his readers it must have had an effect as infuriating as would have been produced during World War II by an American poem extolling the virtues of Germany and denouncing the wickedness of the United States. When America won her independence, seven years later than Price had prophesied, that optimistic champion of liberty hailed the event as, next to the introduction of Christianity, the greatest forward step in history and as likely to result everywhere in the freeing of mankind from political bondage. Enthusiasts of this sort raised expectations concerning a free people in an unsullied wilderness which Americans found it difficult to live up to. A half-century later Emerson regretfully wrote:

> This country has not fulfilled what seemed the reasonable expectation of mankind. Men looked, when all feudal straps and bandages were snapped asunder, that Nature, too long the mother of dwarfs, should reimburse itself by a brood of Titans, who should laugh and leap in the continent, and run up the mountains of the West with the errand of genius and love.
> *The Conduct of Life.*

The French Revolution.—An even greater hope was created by the outbreak of the French Revolution in 1789. "How much the greatest event it is," exclaimed the liberal statesman Charles James Fox, "that ever happened in the world, and how much the best!" At last it seemed as if even an old nation could rid itself of an evil régime and of an unrighteous system of privileges. The early leaders of the Revolution, many of them inspired by French authors whose spirit was akin to that of the English School of Sensibility, proclaimed an intention to foster liberty, equality, and fraternity throughout the world. It was to be a new era of universal benevolence and peace. In England this program was greeted with immense enthusiasm. Characteristic of the spirit of the times was Richard Price's exultant declaration:

I have lived to see the rights of men better understood than ever, and nations panting for liberty which seemed to have lost the idea of it; I have lived to see thirty millions of people, indignant and resolute, spurning at slavery and demanding liberty with an irresistible voice; their king led in triumph and an arbitrary monarch surrendering himself to his subjects. After sharing in the benefits of one [1] revolution I have been spared to be a witness to two [2] other revolutions, both glorious. And now, methinks, I see the ardor for liberty catching and spreading; a general amendment beginning in human affairs; the dominion of kings changed for the dominion of laws, and the dominion of priests giving way to the dominion of reason and conscience.—*Discourse on the Love of Our Country.*

With the astonishing exception of Burke, who disapproved of a political reorganization which flouted historical considerations, every important man of letters was temporarily a sympathizer with the Revolution. The following list, which includes only the most prominent out of scores of sympathizers, may suggest how favorably the Revolution was looked upon by leading authors, orators, and publicists:

Age in 1789	*Name*	*Class*
66	Richard Price	Clergyman and Reformer
61	Robert Bage	Novelist
58	Mrs. Macaulay	Historian
56	Joseph Priestley	Scientist and Philosopher
53	John Horne Tooke	Philologist
52	Thomas Paine	Pamphleteer
52	Alexander Geddes	Liberal Theologian
51	Joseph Johnson	Publisher
48	Henry Fuseli	Artist
44	Thomas Holcroft	Dramatist and Novelist
40	Charles James Fox	Orator
40	Charlotte Smith	Novelist
39	Thomas Erskine	Advocate
38	Richard Brinsley Sheridan	Dramatist and Orator
33	Gilbert Wakefield	Liberal Theologian
33	William Godwin	Reformer and Novelist
32	William Blake	Poet and Artist
31	Joseph Fawcett	Clergyman
30	Mary Wollstonecraft	Reformer and Pamphleteer
30	Robert Burns	Poet
27	Helen Maria Williams	Journalist
24	James Mackintosh	Lawyer
19	William Wordsworth	Poet
17	Samuel Taylor Coleridge	Poet
15	Robert Southey	Poet
14	Walter Savage Landor	Poet

[1] The English Revolution of 1688.
[2] The American and the French.

The fact that Wordsworth, Coleridge, and Southey, during several of their most impressionable years, were among these sympathizers with the French Revolution was to have important effects upon the Romantic Movement.

For the first two or three years nothing occurred in France that was very disturbing to the friends of the Revolution. When Burke attacked it in his *Reflections* (1790), sentiment was overwhelmingly against him, as shown in pamphlets by Thomas Paine, Mary Wollstonecraft, James Mackintosh, and many others, as well as in speeches by Fox and Sheridan. His warnings were laughed to scorn. But by 1792, when France began to make war upon her neighbors, the feeling grew less confident; and upon the execution of the French king in 1793 and the outbreak of her war with England, the apprehensions became still greater. The next three years were for most of the sympathizers a period of agitation—doubts and hopes rapidly alternating. The ideals which they had expected the French to realize were so true and noble that to turn against that nation seemed to be to despair of humanity itself. But the sanguinary Reign of Terror (1793–94), the French aggressions upon neighboring nations like Holland and Switzerland, and the rise of a military dictatorship under Napoleon (1796 ff.), ultimately disillusioned most of them.

William Godwin.—During the earlier and happier years of the Revolution, when the notion seemed plausible that a new reorganization of society can be effected without paying any regard to the historical circumstances under which society and human nature have developed, William Godwin excogitated that system which he set forth in *Political Justice* (*Anth.*, 102). Like the School of Sensibility, Godwin was opposed to the orthodox conceptions of psychology and ethics and to the institutions based upon their assumptions; but he was opposed to them for reasons contrary to those of the sentimentalists. The latter wished to trust the instincts and emotions more than the conservatives did; whereas Godwin, going to the opposite extreme, despised the emotions and wished the calmly reasoning intellect to be the sole guide of life. In the Pre-Romantic Movement, he was—with the exception of David Hartley, the psychologist (*Anth.*, 52)—the first important writer who had a materialistic or mechanistic conception of the universe. Man, in his opinion, had no soul but was wholly a product and portion of a physical universe, and his conduct was necessarily determined thereby. Man's only hope lay in his sharpening his intelligence and power of reasoning in order that he might fully understand the circumstances in which he found himself and act accordingly. All customs, laws, and institutions which interfered with an individual thus adjusting himself to his own environment and problems, were evil. Since the entire present structure of society was built on a false conception of man's nature, it should be entirely reformed. No force of any kind should be employed; there should be no war, no courts, no jails, no laws, no personal property, no marriage bond; for only in complete freedom of action could the individual reason and act rightly. But once thus freed, man would see the truth, follow it, and attain perfection. In this state of philosophical anarchy, there would be no disease, no anguish, no harassing emotions; the intellect would be supreme, and mind would master matter.

Godwin's sincerity and benevolism were unquestionable; and his argument, once his premises were granted, was convincingly clear and logical, especially to young seekers after a millennium. Coleridge and Wordsworth, and later Shelley, fell for shorter or longer periods under the spell of Godwin's courageous optimism. "Godwin," says De Quincey, "carried one single shock into the bosom of English society, fearful but momentary." Hazlitt, who thought his popularity "sultry and unwholesome," nevertheless admitted that no one "was more talked of, more sought after; and wherever liberty, truth, and justice was the theme, his name was not far off . . . Tom Paine was for the time considered as Tom Fool to him, . . . and Edmund Burke a flashy sophist."

A controversial tract based upon the same materialistic and rationalistic assumptions as Godwin's treatise was Mary Wollstonecraft's *Rights of Woman* (*Anth.*, 101). In this, the position, the training, and the character of women were bitterly denounced. The faults of woman were ascribed to the fact that her education was an education of the feelings or sensibilities, so that she might be nothing better than the dependant of man, his plaything or solace. Justice would never be done her, and she never could develop real virtues, until she was brought up on the principle of ignoring sex and sentiment, and of giving her exactly the same mental training which man in some degree enjoyed and which made him her superior. To become his equal, she should secure economic independence and be guided solely by her intellect.

Mary Wollstonecraft's life was more agitated than one should expect in the case of such an advocate of rational conduct. She became the mistress of an American, Capt. Gilbert Imlay, who deserted her despite her passionate devotion to him. (Their daughter, Fanny Imlay, committed suicide in 1816.) After Imlay left her, Mary Wollstonecraft lived with William Godwin in a happier union, which was regularized by a marriage ceremony before her death in 1797. It was with her second daughter, Mary Godwin, that Shelley, deserting his wife Harriet, eloped in 1814. Godwin married again—a Mrs. Clairmont, a widow, whose daughter Jane Clairmont was at one time the mistress of Byron. These rather complicated relationships, not without importance in the history of the Romantic Movement, may perhaps be made clearer by the following table, in which the sign ∽ signifies a *liaison* and the — a marriage:

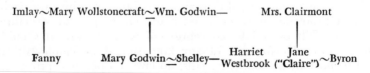

Imlay∽Mary Wollstonecraft∽Wm. Godwin—   Mrs. Clairmont

Fanny   Mary Godwin∽Shelley—Harriet   Jane
Westbrook ("Claire")∽Byron

The Novel of Purpose.—Godwin, who was not without his share of imagination, though it was a power that theoretically he distrusted, illustrated some of his doctrines in a novel, *Things As They Are, or The Adventures of Caleb Williams* (1794). The chief character, Falkland, lives as gentlemen do, according to an inflexible code of honor, rather than, as Godwin thought men should, according to whatever his reason may find correct in each particular situation. By blind loyalty to his formal code, Falkland is led into revenge and murder. Other frightful events follow, all calculated to show the irrationality of codes, laws, and penal systems.

Because of its author's fame, and because the story has melodramatic power, *Caleb Williams* is still read, or at least remembered by title. It was only one of many novels of purpose, the others now forgotten, which flourished in those years when there was much enthusiasm for radical projects of social, educational, economic, and political reform. What had been the novel of contemporary manners thus became doctrinaire. Two years prior to Godwin, his friend Thomas Holcroft (to whom Godwin was indebted for not a few ideas) had set the fashion with his *Anna St. Ives* (1792), to be followed by *Hugh Trevor* (1794–97). Other noteworthy novels of purpose were Charlotte Smith's *Desmond* (1792), Robert Bage's *Hermsprong, or Man As He Is Not* (1796), Mary Hays's *Emma Courtney* (1796), and Mrs. Elizabeth Inchbald's less violently revolutionary *Nature and Art* (1796). In several of these, the theory of the noble savage, or that of education according to nature, was influential. Their general tendency was to associate with the established order everything that was wicked, cruel, stupid, or senile, and to show youth and enlightenment advocating the overthrow of things-as-they-were and believing in the speedy attainment of perfection. James Lawrence's *Empire of the Nairs,* originally written in German in 1793, with its advocacy of free love, belongs in this group.

Pantisocracy.—In the novels of purpose the heroes and heroines are frequently depicted as engaging in lengthy discussions of social and economic problems—discussions which strike the modern reader as tiresome and unreal. That they were not entirely without counterpart in the actual life of young people at that time is shown in the enterprise called Pantisocracy, in which Coleridge and Southey were the leaders. They had met in 1794, when Coleridge was twenty-two and Southey twenty. Both were beginning to suspect that the millennium was not to be achieved in France as promptly as they had hoped. "I look around the world," Southey said, "and everywhere find the same spectacle—the strong tyrannizing over the weak, man and beast. . . . There is no place for virtue." Yet both, at that time devotees of Hartley and Godwin, believed that men and women would be "necessarily virtuous" provided they might live in the right environment. France now looked dubious, likewise the settled parts of the United States—but there were the unspoiled American solitudes. Hence arose the scheme which Coleridge described as "trying the experiment of perfectibility on the banks of the Susquehanna." He hoped that the second generation of the Pantisocrats would combine "the innocence of the patriarchal age with the knowledge and genuine refinements of European culture." The Susquehanna Valley, an American realtor had truthfully informed them, was excessively beautiful; and, as he somewhat overconfidently added, it was secure from hostile Indians.

Civilization, then, in so far as it meant rulers and prisons, social classes and personal property, traditional religion and education, was to be left behind. Twelve young couples were to constitute the Pantisocracy, all, as the term signified, to be equal and all to rule. One of the points left unsettled was whether the marriage contract might be dissolved if either party desired it. The men were to till the fields and produce sufficient means of support in two or three hours a day, and the women were to perform the domestic duties (presumably in the same brief time). All products were to be shared in common. The abundant leisure hours were to be devoted to reading and discussion. Under such ideal conditions, they felt certain, man's instinctive goodness and natural intelligence would assert itself triumphantly, and virtue and happiness would at last be attained.

Coleridge was to have expounded Pantisocracy in a book, which he characteristically speaks of as if it existed, but which he never produced. Three of the required twelve couples were in view—all of them related, or about to be related, by marriage—Robert Lovell, a young Quaker and poet, and his wife Mary Fricker; Southey and Edith Fricker; and Coleridge and Sara Fricker. But lack of money, and disagreements over some points in the theory, prevented the realization of the Pantisocratic dream. Not a few such perfectionist communities were actually settled in America, e.g., at Oneida, New York, and have proved highly interesting as social experiments. But if Coleridge and Southey had established theirs, the probabilities are that whatever improvement in the condition of society might have resulted, it would have been bought at the heavy price of our loss of their literary works.

The Romance of Sentimental Adventure and the Tale of Terror.— Side by side with the novel of purpose which aimed at reform, there flourished the romance which strove to be entertaining and which was therefore more popular. It may be divided into two not absolutely separate types; first, the romance of sentimental adventure which grew out of Prévost's modification of the earlier novels of sensibility; and, secondly, the tale of terror.

It is perhaps illuminating that the authors of the chief romances of sentimental adventure, which were not as unrestrained in their sensationalism as the tales of terror, were women. Clara Reeve, with her *Old English Baron* (1777), originally and more significantly entitled *The Champion of Virtue*, was the first of this group. She was followed by Sophia Lee, with *The Recess* (1783); and by Charlotte Smith, with

Emmeline, or the Orphan of the Castle (1788), *Ethelinde, or the Recluse of the Lake* (1789) and *Celestina* (1791). Mrs. Smith made much use of descriptions of picturesque landscapes, as did her successor, Mrs. Radcliffe (*Anth.*, 105). The best of Mrs. Radcliffe's works, which were the most popular of their kind, and were admired by Scott for their exciting incidents and lavish descriptions, are *The Romance of the Forest* (1791), *The Mysteries of Udolpho* (1794), and *The Italian* (1797). The fundamental motif—virtue in distress—was retained in the novels of these four ladies; but there was a steady increase in the exciting circumstances devised to agitate the innocent and gentle heroines. The villains became more and more dreadful, the sights more appalling, the suspense and mystery more intense. The time came when it was not considered hysterical for a heroine to say, "I love to weep, I joy to grieve; it is my happiness, my delight, to have my heart broken to pieces." The remoteness from reality was, to be sure, often great (it is characteristic that Mrs. Radcliffe had led a very secluded life, and had never seen even the romantic scenery her fancy reveled in, to say nothing of villains or dungeons); but some concessions to the probable were made. When the ghostly apparitions or seemingly supernatural phenomena had served their melodramatic purpose, it was explained that some entirely natural causes accounted for the appearances—and thus the reader was comfortably back in his rationalistic eighteenth-century world again.

The tales of terror, often similar to the sentimental romances in incidents and settings, were bolder in spirit. In them, the supernatural remained supernatural to the end, their world being one in which moved dreadful forces that were inexplicable but nevertheless real to the imagination. The tale of terror was likewise more daring in its depiction of physical tortures and other horrors, in its sensualism, and sometimes in its defiant impiety ("Satanism"). Its authors were less concerned with the pathos of innocence in distress than with the supposed sublimity of passionate wickedness in its extremest forms. If their world, too, was unreal, it did not err on the side of the effeminate or of the prosaic.

To write a successful tale of terror was a difficult task; and of the many attempted in this period only two have survived. One is William Beckford's *Vathek* (1786), which, after seeming in danger of falling into oblivion, has of late years won the position of a minor classic. Beckford, who had inherited a huge fortune, lived in a grandiose manner, indulging in ambitious architectural enterprises, purchasing Gibbon's whole library, and amassing costly furniture, jewels, and treasures of art. The gorgeousness of the East strongly appealed to him, and he drew from the *Arabian Nights* the setting of his *History of the Caliph Vathek* (*Anth.*, 92). He related the caliph's insatiable pursuit of wealth and power, his acceptance of the aid of a fiendish Giaour, his impiety, his barbarous cruelties, his sensual lusts, and—most impressively of all—his ghastly punishment, "his grief without end, and remorse without mitigation." Beckford became one of Byron's masters.

The other noteworthy tale of terror was *The Monk* (1795) by Matthew Gregory Lewis *(Anth.,* 107). It was even more sensational than *Vathek,* and less artistic, the author being more concerned to outdo his predecessors and shock his readers than to create the illusion of reality. He borrowed very freely from other adepts in creating horror, including the minor German romanticists, and made his villainous monk Ambrosio the perpetrator of revolting atrocities.

The Melodrama of Terror and Revolt.—Some of the most extreme tales of terror were, like the *Horrid Mysteries* (1796) which Jane Austen mentioned in her *Northanger Abbey,* translations from the German. Upon the drama, this kind of German influence was also strong. The most prolific German writer of melodrama, August Friedrich Kotzebue, who wrote some two hundred plays, was frequently translated, a score of his works being acted in London between 1796 and 1801. Mrs. Inchbald, "Monk" Lewis, and even the rather fastidious Sheridan adapted them to the English stage. Their popularity was intensified by the fact that they not only were very skilful in producing melodramatic thrills but they also intermingled therewith appeals to current sentimental and radical notions about the iniquity of things-as-they-were and the glory of the natural and the free. It was all very superficial and inconsistent, but it appealed to that overwrought and disorganized state of mind which marks the end of the century.

Retrospect.—The eighteenth century, which had begun in a mood of peace and self-confidence, ended in one of violence and perplexity. The most consistent single factor in the change was the School of Sensibility, waxing emotionally stronger and stronger through sentimental philosophy, drama, tale, novel, poetry, and romance. In the course of time it felt the need for more congenial forms of expression, and these were furnished to it by various pre-romantic revivals of blank verse, Spenserian stanza, ode, dialect verse, ballad forms, etc. In its effort to demonstrate convincingly its belief that virtue and happiness were the natural state of man, it turned from ordinary contemporary life to a supposedly happy past *(Ossian,* Chatterton, etc.), or to a future which promised to achieve perfection (Revolutionary America and Revolutionary France). But some of the literary inventions turned out to be forgeries, and the political results fell far short of what had been hoped. The fact that Romantics like Coleridge, Wordsworth, and Southey, passed in their youth through a period of enthusiastic optimism ending in bitter disappointment, is, to the student who is chiefly concerned with the main Romantic Movement, perhaps the most important fact concerning Pre-Romanticism. For the various philosophies of life which such Romantics finally constructed were deeply affected by what they had learned in the intellectual and aesthetic turmoil of the previous epoch.

The following list of tendencies, or features, which are commonly regarded as characteristic of the Pre-Romantic Movement, may be useful as (a) a topical summary of the above chapter, and also as (b) a means of grouping together under topical headings the bibliographical references given chronologically below.

1. Faith in the instinctive goodness of human beings

2. Faith in the relatively high moral and religious value of sympathy or benevolence (School of Sensibility)

3. Accurate observation of nature, though without mysticism

4. The same as (3), with the suggestion that nature has a religious significance

5. Elegiac interest: in death, mutability, mourning, melancholy (Graveyard School)

6. Interest in humanitarian movements and reforms

7. Interest in kindness toward animals

8. A democratic attitude: insistence on the rights and dignity of man, and on the freedom of the individual socially and politically

9. Attacks upon wrongs in the established order or in conventional usages; political, economic, social, or educational

10. Interest in the state-of-nature; the "noble savage," preference for the simple life of earlier ages, primitive religions, folk-poetry

11. Interest in the medieval period; as an age of faith, chivalry, and poetry

12. Attacks on Pope and other neo-classical authors

13. Revival or imitation of older forms of verse; ballads, sonnets, blank verse, Spenserian stanzas, etc.

14. Use of local dialects and color

15. Translation or imitation of Oriental tales

16. Translation or imitation of old Scandinavian literature

17. Translation or imitation of old Celtic literature

18. Development of the historical novel, the Gothic School, and the School of Terror

19. Development of literary theories and literary criticism stressing the relatively greater importance (over the rational and formal) of the imaginative, emotional, intuitive, free, individual, and particular (rather than general)

20. Exaltation of Shakspeare, Spenser, and Milton

SELECTED BIBLIOGRAPHY OF THE PRE-ROMANTIC MOVEMENT *

The following lists of books and articles, and the comments upon them, deal *only with their bearing upon Romanticism.* For a general introduction to eighteenth-century literature, see the admirable handbook by A. D. McKillop, *English Literature from Dryden to Burns,* 1948; and the selections and notes in *Eighteenth Century Poetry and Prose,* 1939, edited by L. I. Bredvold, A. D. McKillop, and Lois Whitney.

* For explanation of the abbreviations, see page 349.

OF FIRST IMPORTANCE

There is no up-to-date scholarly book on the Pre-Romantic Movement as a whole. Since W. L. Phelps's pioneering book surveyed the field in 1893, scholarly research has been centered upon special topics or individual authors. In the absence of a good monograph on the subject, one may turn to sections in general literary histories, such as "The Pre-Romantic Period" in Legouis and Cazamian's *History of English Literature,* 1929, Book IV; or "Romanticism and Changing Taste," "Sentimentalism," "Medieval Revival," and "Primitivism" in McKillop's handbook, listed above, pp. 213, 258, 365, and 367.

The following bibliographies are arranged chronologically (except for a section on the French Revolution), in order to show through what phases the study of the subject has passed, and what aspects of it have from time to time received special attention.

Phelps, William Lyon; *The Beginnings of the English Romantic Movement,* 1893. — Though out-of-date, especially in factual errors and omissions, this remains an illuminating introductory survey of the general nature of Pre-Romanticism and of some of its more interesting manifestations.

Elton, Oliver; *A Survey of English Literature: 1730–80,* 2 vols., 1928; *A Survey of English Literature: 1780–1830,* 2 vols., 1912. — A general history, but stresses the preromantic features.

Allen, B. Sprague; *Tides in English Taste: 1619–1800,* 2 vols., 1937. — The new movement in art, decoration, gardens, etc.

Willey, Basil; *The Eighteenth Century Background: Studies on the Idea of Nature in the Thought of the Period,* 1940. — "I have tried to indicate some stages in that divinization of 'Nature' which culminates in Wordsworth." Important on Newton, Hartley, Priestley, etc.; cf. TLS, June 22, 1940. In opposition to Willey's theory of nature, see Bernbaum, ELH, VII, 333; 1940.

Bate, W. J.; *From Classic to Romantic: Premises of Taste in Eighteenth-Century England,* 1946. — The history of aesthetic judgment and theory, from neo-classic intellectualism toward intuitive assimilation of experience and romantic expression thereof. Of basic importance. Rev. ELH, XIV, 6; 1947.

FOR ADVANCED STUDENTS

Stephen, Leslie; *History of English Thought in the Eighteenth Century,* 2 vols., 1876. — Hostile to sentimentalism, friendly to rationalism.

Texte, Joseph; *Rousseau et les Origines du Cosmopolitisme Littéraire,* 1895; transl. J. W. Matthews, 1899. — Relations between English and French schools of sensibility.

Reynolds, Myra; *The Treatment of Nature in Poetry between Pope and Wordsworth,* 1896. — First to call attention to the numerosity of nature poems.

Beers, Henry A.; *A History of English Romanticism in the Eighteenth Century,* 1898. — Emphasizes the revival of the medieval. Includes a chapter on "The German Tributary."

Farley, Frank E.; *Scandinavian Influence on the English Romantic Movement* (Harvard Studies and Notes in Philol. and Lit., IX), 1903. — Authoritative. Cf. Hustvedt, below, 1916.

Conant, Martha P.; *The Oriental Tale in England,* 1908.

Havens, R. D.; "Romantic Aspects of the Age of Pope," PMLA, XXVII, 297 (1912); "Thomas Warton and the Eighteenth Century Dilemma," SP, XXV, 36 (1928); "Changing Taste: A Study of Dryden's and Dodsley's Miscellanies," PMLA, XLIV, 501 (1929). — Warns against too rigid classification of authors as "classical" or "romantic."

Scarborough, Dorothy; *The Supernatural in Modern English Fiction*, 1917.

Bernbaum, Ernest; *The Drama of Sensibility: A Sketch of the History of English Sentimental Comedy and Domestic Tragedy: 1696–1780*, 1915.

Killen, A. M.; *Le Roman Terrifiant ou Roman Noir de Walpole à Anne Radcliffe*, 1915. — Also traces the influence of Gothic romance on French literature.

Hustvedt, Sigurd B.; *Ballad Criticism in Scandinavia and Great Britain During the Eighteenth Century*, 1916. — See Farley, above, 1903.

Moore, C. A.; "Shaftesbury and the Ethical Poets," PMLA, xxxi, 2 (1916); "The Return to Nature in English Poetry," SP, xiv, 243 (1917); "Whig Panegyric Verse: A Phase of Sentimentalism," PMLA, xli, 362 (1926).

Bernbaum, Ernest; Introduction to *English Poets of the Eighteenth Century*, 1918. — Brief sketch of the conflict between the classical poets and the pre-romantic.

Birkhead, Edith; *The Tale of Terror*, 1921. — On Walpole, Reeve, Radcliffe, Lewis, Beckford, etc. Cf. Scarborough, above, 1917; and Foster, below, 1927.

Doughty, Oswald; *English Lyric in the Age of Reason*, 1922. — Distinguishes four phases: The Citadel of Reason, 1700–45; Disillusion, 1745–80; New Ideals, (1745–80?); and the Rise of Humanism (Cowper) and Mysticism (Blake). — Readable.

Tinker, Chauncey B.; *Nature's Simple Plan: A Phase of Radical Thought in the Mid-Eighteenth Century*, 1922. — On theories about the state of nature, freedom, primitive bards, and inspired peasants. See, below, Fairchild, 1928; and Whitney, 1934.

Snyder, Edward D.; *The Celtic Revival in English Literature: 1760–1800*, 1923. — Complements Farley, above, 1903.

Robertson, John G.; *Studies in the Genesis of Romantic Theory in the Eighteenth Century*, 1923. — Traces romantic aesthetics back to critics of the Italian Renaissance.

Longueil, Alfred E.; "The Word 'Gothic' in Eighteenth Century Criticism," MLN, xxxviii, 453; 1923.

Van Tieghem, Paul; *Le Pré-Romantisme*, 2 vols., Paris, 1924–30. — On themes of poetry, the Scandinavian revival, Ossianism, etc.; based on wide knowledge of European literature.

Reed, Amy Louise; *The Background of Gray's Elegy: A Study in the Taste for Melancholy Poetry, 1700–1751*, 1924. — Traces varieties of melancholy from Burton and Milton down to Gray. See, below, Draper, 1929; and Sickels, 1932.

Folkierski, W.; *Entre le Classicisme et le Romantisme*, Cracow, 1925.

Birkhead, Edith; "Sentiment and Sensibility in the Eighteenth Century Novel," Engl. Asso. — *Essays and Studies*, xi, 1925. See, below, Wright, 1937.

Van Tieghem, Paul; "La Sensibilité et la Passion dans le Roman Européen au Dixhuitième Siècle," RLC, vi, 424; 1926. — On the revolt of love against conventional worldly standards.

Kaufman, Paul; "Heralds of Original Genius," *Essays in Memory of Barrett Wendell*, 1926. Traces the significant changes in the meaning of "genius." Cf. Hans Thüme. *Beiträge zur Geschichte des Geniebegriffs in England* (Halle, Niemeyer), 1927.

Foster, James R.; "The Abbé Prévost and the English Novel," PMLA, xlii, 443; 1927. — On the novel of sentimental adventure (Sophia Lee, Clara Reeve, Mrs. Radcliffe, Charlotte Smith, etc.). Cf. Paul Hazard, "L'Abbé Prévost et l'Angleterre," *Etude Critique sur Manon Lescaut*, 1929; and Hazard, below, 1937; also Foster, 1948.

Railo, Eino; *The Haunted Castle: A Study of the Elements of English Romanticism*, 1927 (transl. from Finnish). — The "elements" are castles, ghosts, the Wandering Jew, etc. The history of each topic set forth in detail. Much on Walpole, Ann Radcliffe,

Monk Lewis, and Maturin. Copious bibliographical references. Rev., MLN, XLIII, 423; 1928.

Sadleir, Michael; "The Northanger Novels," *Edinburgh Rev.*, July, 1927. — Cf. TLS, Aug. 11, 1927.

Wood, Paul S.; "The Opposition to Neo-Classicism in England between 1660 and 1700," PMLA, XLIII, 182; 1928. — Holds that such opposition should not be termed romantic.

Smith, David Nichol; *Shakespeare in the Eighteenth Century*, 1928. — Cf. R. W. Babcock, *The Genesis of Shakespeare Idolatry*, 1931; and Augustus Ralli, *A History of Shakespearian Criticism*, 1932, esp. vol. II.

Brauchli, Jakob; *Der Englische Schauer-roman um 1800*, 1928. — Comprehensive survey, with long classified lists of novels of terror.

Fairchild, Hoxie N.; *The Noble Savage: A Study in Romantic Naturalism*, 1928. See Tinker, above, 1922.

Clark, Kenneth; *The Gothic Revival*, 1928. — Interrelations between art and literature. Cf. Elizabeth Manwaring, *Italian Landscape in Eighteenth Century England*, 1926; Christopher Hussey, *The Picturesque*, 1927; and especially B. Sprague Allen, *Tides in English Taste*, 2 vols., 1937.

Viatte, Auguste; *Les Sources Occultes du Romantisme: Illuminisme-Théosophie, 1770–1820*; Paris, 2 vols., 1928. — The secretive heresies and black arts which played an important evil role.

Stockley, V.; *German Literature as Known in England: 1750–1830*, 1929. — Systematic account of the translations. Not concerned with influences, which are left to F. W. Stokoe's (rather unsatisfactory) *German Influence in the English Romantic Period*, 1926.

Draper, J. W.; *The Funeral Elegy and the Rise of English Romanticism*, 1929. — Detailed study of middle-class laments. See Reed, above, 1924, also review by R. S. Crane, PQ, IX, 173; 1930.

Drennon, Herbert; *James Thomson and Newtonianism* (Univ. of Chicago *Abstr. of Theses*, Humanistic Ser., VII, 523) , 1929. Stresses Newton's influence as more important than Shaftesbury's. Cf. Drennon in PMLA, XLIX, 71 (1934) , and in SP, XXI, 453 (1934) ; also, below, Nicolson (1945) . — Rev. of Drennon by Bredvold, PQ, XIV, 175; 1935.

Baker, Ernest A.; *The History of the English Novel*, vol. IV, 1930 (Sterne) ; vol. v, 1934 (The Novel of Sentiment and the Gothic Romance) .

Warner, W. J.; *The Wesleyan Movement and the Industrial Revolution*, 1930. — Cf. Umphrey Lee, *The Historical Background of Early Methodist Enthusiasm*, 1931; and HJ, July, 1933.

Williams, George G.; "The Beginnings of Nature Poetry in the Eighteenth Century," SP, XXVII, 583; 1930.

Yvon, Paul; *Le Gothique et la Renaissance Gothique en Angleterre: 1750–1880*, 1931. — Cf. TLS, Feb. 11, 1932.

Sickels, Eleanor M.; *The Gloomy Egoist: Moods and Themes of Melancholy from Gray to Keats*, 1932. — See above, A. L. Reed, 1924.

Lovejoy, A. O.; "The First Gothic Revival and the Return to Nature," MLN, XLVII, 419; 1932. — "The Chinese Origin of a Romanticism," JEGP, XXXII, 1; 1933. — Cf. Shan y Chan on Chinese Gardening, Univ. of Chicago *Abstracts of Theses*, VII, 537; 1932.

Frantz, R. W.; *The English Traveller and the Movement of Ideas* (Univ. of Nebr. Studies) , 1932–33.

Harrison, A. W.; "Romanticism in Religious Revivals," HJ, July, 1933. — On Methodism; see below, Gill, 1937.

McKillop, A. D.; "A Critic of 1741 on Early Poetry," SP, xxx, 504; 1933.

Rose, Ruth O.; "Poetic Hero-Worship in the Late Eighteenth Century," PMLA, XLVIII, 1182; 1933.

Harder, Johannes H.; *Observations on Some Tendencies of Sentiment and Ethics, Chiefly in Minor Poetry and Essay (until 1777)*, 1933.

Whitney, Lois; *Primitivism and the Idea of Progress in English Popular Literature of the Eighteenth Century*, 1934. — Cf. R. S. Crane; "Anglican Apologists and the Idea of Progress," MP, xxxi, 273 and 349; 1934.

Crane, R. S.; "Suggestions Towards a Genealogy of the 'Man of Feeling,'" ELH, I, 205; 1934.

Bredvold, L. I.; "The Tendency Towards Platonism in Neo-Classical Esthetics," ELH, I, 91; 1934.

Hooker, E. N.; "The Discussion of Taste: 1750–70," PMLA, XLIX, 577; 1934. — Cf. PQ, XII, 189; 1934.

Creed, John M.; *Religious Thought in the Eighteenth Century: Illustrated from Writers of the Period*, 1934.

Monk, Samuel H.; *The Sublime: A Study of Critical Theories in Eighteenth-Century England: 1674–1800*, 1935. — Admiration for the Sublime as inimical to Neo-Classicism, and as stimulating interest in vastness and irregularity in Nature.

Lovett, David; "Shakespeare as a Poet of Realism," ELH, II, 267; 1935.

Thorpe, Clarence D.; "Addison and Hutcheson on the Imagination," ELH, II, 215; 1935.

Sherwood, Margaret P.; *Undercurrents of Influence in English Romantic Poetry*, 1935. — From Herder to the young Browning.

Steegman, John; *The Rule of Taste: From George I to George IV*, 1936. — Successive rebellions against classic correctness. See below, B. S. Allen, 1937.

Aubin, R. A.; *Topographical Poetry in Eighteenth-Century England*, 1936.

Lovejoy, A. O.; *The Great Chain of Being*, 1936. — From the idea of Unity to that of Diversity.

Brown, Wallace C.; "The Popularity of English Travel Books about the Near East: 1775–1825," PQ, xv, 70; 1936.

Scheffer, John D.; "The Idea of Decline in Literature and the Fine Arts in Eighteenth-Century England," MP, xxxiv, 155; 1936. — Cult of the primitive bard.

Wright, Walter F.; *Sensibility in English Prose Fiction, 1760–1814: A Reinterpretation*, 1937.

Gill, Frederick C.; *The Romantic Movement and Methodism*, 1937. — Cf. T. D. Shepherd; *Methodism and the Literature of the Eighteenth Century*, 1940; and Robert F. Wearmouth; *Methodism and the Common People*, 1945.

Hazard, Paul; "Un Romantique de 1730: l'Abbé Prévost," in *Authority and the Individual* (Harv. Terc. Publ.), 1937.

Meinecke, Friedrich; "Klassizismus, Romantizismus und Historisches Denken im 18. Jahrhundert," in *Authority and the Individual* (Harv. Terc. Publ.), 1937.

Draper, John W.; "The Metrical Tale in Eighteenth-Century England," PMLA, LII, 390; 1937.

Bond, Donald F.; "The Neo-Classical Psychology of the Imagination," ELH, IV, 245; 1937.

Williams, G. S.; "On Sentimentality," *Readings for Creative Writers,* 1938.

Shapiro, Leo; "Lucretian Domestic Melancholy," PMLA, LIII, 1088; 1938. — Thomson, Gray, Collins.

Summers, Montague;
    The Gothic Quest: a History of the Gothic Novel, 1938.
    A Gothic Bibliography, 1941.
Less than 1,000 copies published. "Gothic" is used in a very broad sense; thousands of sensational novels are covered, including nineteenth-century ones. Important on Monk Lewis. Cf. above, Railo (1927) and Brauchli (1928) ; and see my review, MLQ, III, 486; 1942. — Cf. Mary M. Tarr; *Catholicism in Gothic Fiction,* 1946.

Tillotson, Geoffrey; "Eighteenth-Century Poetic Diction," Engl. Asso. *Essays and Studies,* XXV, 1939. — A strong defense. — Cf. his *Essays in Criticism and Research,* 1942; and René Wellek's attack, MP, XLI, 261; 1944.

Fairchild, Hoxie N.; *Religious Trends in English Poetry.* (Vol. I: 1700–1740, *Protestantism and the Cult of Sentiment,* 1939. — Vol. II: 1740–1780, *Religious Sentimentalism in the Age of Johnson,* 1942). "The romanticism of the 1780–1830 period is simply Protestant Christianity in a more or less delightfully phosphorescent state of decay," I, 538. — Cf. TLS, Jan. 20, 1940; and May 15, 1943.

Whitney, Edward A.; "Humanitarianism and Romanticism," *Huntington Libr. Quart.,* XI, 159; 1939.

Stern, Bernard H.; *The Rise of Romantic Hellenism in English Literature: 1732–86,* 1940.

Wasserman, Earl R.; "The Return of the Enjambed Couplet," ELH, VII, 239; 1940. — Predecessors of Leigh Hunt.

Larrabee, Stephen A.; *"Il Poco Più* and the School of Taste," ELH, VIII, 47; 1941. — The nameless grace, the "je ne sais quoi."

Wellek, René; *The Rise of English Literary History,* 1941. — Ch. 6 on Thomas Warton.

Sypher, Wylie; *Guinea's Captive Kings: British Anti-Slavery Literature of the Eighteenth Century,* 1942. — Detailed survey; includes pro-slavery writings. — Cf. Earl L. Griggs; *Thomas Clarkson: the Friend of Slaves,* 1936.

Warner, James H.; " 'Education of the Heart': Observations on the Sentimental Movement," *Papers of the Mich. Acad. of Science, Arts, and Letters,* 1943.

Brett, R. L.; "The Aesthetic Sense and Taste in the Literary Criticism of the Early Eighteenth Century," RES, XX; 1944.

Burgum, E. B.; "The Neoclassical Period in English Literature: A Psychological Definition," *Sewanee Review,* Spring, 1944. — Its relation to the class struggle.

Nicolson, Marjorie H.; *Newton Demands the Muse,* 1945. — Effect of his discoveries on the critical theories of Addison and Burke, and on the imagination of Thomson, Akenside, Young, etc. "Epilogue" on Blake.

Kallich, Martin; "The Association of Ideas and Critical Theory," ELH, XII, 290; 1945.

Bullitt, John, and Bate, W. J.; "The Distinction Between Fancy and Imagination in Eighteenth-Century English Criticism," MLN, LX, 8; 1945.

Clark, R. T., Jr.; "Herder, Percy, and the Song of Songs," PMLA, LXI, 1087; 1946. — On the theory that the perfection of poetry had been attained in primitive times.

Foerster, Donald M.; *Homer in English Criticism: The Historical Approach in the Eighteenth Century* (Yale Studies), 1947. — Cf. R. H. Pearce, "The Eighteenth-Century Scottish Primitivists," ELH, XII, 203; 1945.

Kliger, Samuel; "The Gothic Revival and the German *Translatio*," MP, xlv, 73; 1947. — The tradition that the "Goths" were bearers of enlightenment and reformation.

Wasserman, Earl R.; *Elizabethan Poetry in the Eighteenth Century*, 1947. — Cf. ELH, iv, 213; 1937.

Foster, James R.; *History of the Pre-Romantic Novel in England* (MLA Monograph Series, xvii), 1948.

THE RELATION OF THE FRENCH REVOLUTION
TO ENGLISH ROMANTICISM

Dowden, Edward; *The French Revolution and English Literature*, 1897. — More genial and masterly than the following study, but Hancock contains matter of value not found in Dowden.

Hancock, A. E.; *The French Revolution and the English Poets*, 1899.

Gregory, Allene; *The French Revolution and the English Novel*, 1915. — Sympathetic toward the radical revolutionary novelists.

Allen, B. Sprague; "Minor Disciples of Radicalism in the Revolutionary Era," MP, xxi, 277; 1923. — Also his "Analogues of Wordsworth's 'The Borderers,'" PMLA, xxxviii, 267; 1923.

Brinton, Crane; "The Membership of the Jacobin Clubs," *Am. Hist. Rev.*, xxiv; 1929.

Thompson, J. M., ed.; *English Witnesses of the French Revolution*, 1938. — Narratives of fifty witnesses, including Mary Wollstonecraft, Tom Paine, Samuel Rogers, and Wordsworth.

Adams, M. Ray; *Studies in the Literary Backgrounds of English Radicalism, with Special Reference to the French Revolution* (Franklin & Marshall College Studies), 1947.

Anthology

Grigson, Geoffrey, ed.; *Before the Romantics*, 1947. — Selections from poetry and prose of c. 1650–1750, with lively comments.

Bibliography

For new books and articles, consult *English Literature, 1660–1800: A Current Bibliography*, annually in the April issue of the *Philological Quarterly* (includes Blake).

CHAPTER 3

WILLIAM BLAKE

(November 28, 1757–August 12, 1827)

1783 Poetical Sketches	1794 Songs of Experience
1789 Songs of Innocence	wr. c. 1803 The Mental Traveller
1789 The Book of Thel	Auguries of Innocence
wr. 1791 The French Revolution	1804–08 Milton
c. 1793 The Marriage of Heaven and Hell	1804–20 Jerusalem
c. 1793 A Song of Liberty	c. 1818 The Everlasting Gospel

Early Life.—William Blake was primarily an engraver and painter. Born in London, the son of a shopkeeper in modest circumstances, he received, from the age of ten, training under a drawing master and under the engraver, James Basire. Thus his only systematic instruction was technical. None of the other great Romantics, not even Keats, had so little scholastic or literary training as Blake; and none of them began in so unbookish an environment. To him this proved a disadvantage as well as an advantage; but he saw only the latter, saying:

> Thank Heaven, I never was sent to school
> To be flogged into following the style of a fool!

He was deeply impressed by his father's religion—Swedenborgianism, a new interpretation of Christianity. It belittled church organization and the priesthood, rejected stern or terrifying dogmas, and emphasized the gentle and mystical. Its founder (see Emerson's essay on Swedenborg in *Representative Men*) beheld spiritual beings within all material things; he preferred those books of the Bible which, like *The Revelation of St. John,* were visionary; and he believed that he held intercourse with the souls of the departed, with angels, and with God. In later life, Blake rejected some of the new prophet's doctrines (e.g., predestination), but he remained under the spell of his mysticism and allegorizing. "Daily and nightly," he likewise was "under the direction of messengers from Heaven." These visitations began in his childhood; and the older biographies of Blake are rich in anecdotes, of doubtful accuracy, concerning them, and also concerning his alleged gift of second sight.

Such visualization of his inward experiences was stimulated by the loneliness of his occupation and by its solemn surroundings. To Westminster Abbey and other medieval sanctuaries he was sent by his master to make drawings. Here his love for Gothic art developed. "Greek form," he asserts, "is permanent in the mathematical memory: Gothic is living form."

Having completed his apprenticeship, he tried to earn a living in various ways—as an engraver, as a dealer in engravings, and as a teacher of drawing. Some of his work was done on illustrations for books issued by Joseph Johnson, a publisher of radical tendencies. At twenty-five, he married Catherine Boucher, the illiterate daughter of a market-gardener. During their married life of forty-five years, she proved a perfect help-mate to him, patient in their poverty, skilful in assisting his labors, unswerving in her faith in his genius. On his deathbed his last effort was to draw the portrait of her whom he called his "angel."

Earlier Literary Period.—The early reading of Blake included, in a desultory way, the Bible, Swedenborg, the German mystic Jacob Boehme, Shakspeare's lyrics, Spenser and his eighteenth-century imitators, Milton, seventeenth-century minor poets, Thomson, Chatterton, *The Castle of Otranto,* and *Ossian.* By some of the lyrical pieces he had been inspired to write poems himself, but without intention of publishing them. Their publication as *Poetical Sketches* was, however, undertaken by a Rev. Mr. Matthews, whose wife aspired to be a leader in "literary society." The kind intention of this patronage was, in Blake's opinion, defeated by the condescending tone which Mr. Matthews took in his introduction to the volume, where he spoke of the poems as "the products of untutored youth." Blake tolerated neither condescension nor criticism; he was, moreover, unfitted for association with conventional society by his out-spoken anti-aristocratic sentiments. His intercourse was henceforth al-most entirely with artists like John Flaxman, Thomas Stothard, and Henry Fuseli, with his few patrons, and with those authors who were attached to the publisher Joseph Johnson. Among the latter were Wil-liam Godwin, Mary Wollstonecraft, and Thomas Paine—all of them en-thusiasts for political and social revolution, although for reasons quite different from those of Blake.

Earning his meager living as an artisan, Blake was closer to the work-ing classes than most of the other Romantics, and keenly felt the iniqui-ties of the economic conditions of his times. Though in his later works he hid his political views under the disguise of allegories, he always advo-cated radical reforms in church and state. The "Blake of *this* world" was a revolutionary as well as a pietist.

It was between his thirty-first and thirty-seventh year, and during the period when England was intensely agitated by the progress of the French Revolution, that Blake composed most of his best-known works. Unable to get them published in the ordinary way, he was inspired (by the spirit, he averred, of his dead brother Robert) to invent a new method of printing. Its essential feature was that both the words and the pictures or marginal designs of every page were engraved in relief upon copper, and the printed sheets partly colored by hand. In this manner were pro-duced the *Songs of Innocence* and his subsequent works, first editions of which are now valued at several thousand times their original modest price. The loving artistic care which Blake, assisted by his wife, bestowed upon his volumes entitles him to be regarded as the pioneer in the modern craftmanship of beautiful books. And since he sang his songs to his own music, his completeness and independence as an artist were extraordinary.

Later Literary Period.—Since the literary works of Blake were not a popular success, his main occupation continued to be that of an artist. He was engaged by William Hayley, a wealthy poetaster, to illustrate a *Life of Cowper.* He was settled in a cottage near Hayley's estate, at Felpham, Sussex, this being his first close acquaintance with country life, the beauty and peace of which delighted him. But even here there were troubles. One morning when he stepped out into his garden he found a red-coated dragoon standing in it as if he owned it, and profanely refusing to leave it. The pacific Blake promptly ejected him. The soldier, one Scolfield haled him into court, charging that he had cursed the King and all soldiers; but Blake was acquitted. Less dramatic but more tiresome were the patronlike demands of the commonplace Hayley, which, after three years' endurance, he found intolerable. He returned to London, after what had been for him an unusually discontented period. Doubtless his unhappiness was increased by the fact that his literary efforts had been failures.

Then suddenly, in his forty-seventh year, he climbed out of his Valley of Doubt. A visit to a picture gallery, the Truchsessian, in 1804 left him, as he said, "enlightened with the light I enjoyed in my youth, and which has for exactly twenty years been closed from me." It had been closed for him by "the spectre"—the rationalistic skepticism dominant in his time. Henceforth he would not cater to contemporaries, but design and write in the service of the Eternal. This sublime resolution had two different results. It preserved the individuality of his genius as an artist and engraver; but, in the judgment of the best critics, it inhibited his effectiveness as a poet. As an artist, trained in the traditions of Raphael, Michelangelo, and Dürer, he continued to speak, not in the jargon of the hour, but in a form of expression intelligibly beautiful to broadly cultured perception. His greatest drawings—"When the Morning Stars Sang Together," "Elohim Creating Adam," "Elijah," "The Nativity," "The Wise and the Foolish Virgins," "Pity," "The Spiritual Form of Pitt Guiding the Behemoth," "The Spiritual Form of Nelson Guiding the Leviathan," his illustrations of Young's *Night Thoughts* and of Blair's *Grave* and, above all, his illustrations of the *Book of Job*—are acclaimed as among the masterpieces of modern engraving, unsurpassed in grandeur of invention and concentrated force of expression. In the medium in which he had been trained, he was a superb craftsman. In his later literary work there appeared more and more the influence of his wide reading in little known authors—writers even more occult and esoteric than Boehme and Swedenborg—Pythagoreans, neo-Platonists, Gnostics, alchemists, and mythologists with fanciful theories about the prehistoric ages of mankind. He based the myths and symbolisms of his Prophetic Books, such as *Milton, Jerusalem,* etc., upon religious and speculative traditions which had developed half-surreptitiously during more than two thousand years, side by side with the commonly accepted religious faiths, and which were not altogether heretical but were partly heterodox and therefore to most of his contemporaries unfamiliar and confusing. Some of Blake's disciples today praise these mystical poems as his highest achievements, but their value is strongly disputed. Charles Lamb wrote:

> Blake is a real name, I assure you, and a most extraordinary man, if he be still living. . . . He paints in water-colors marvelous strange pictures, visions of his brain, which he asserts he has seen. . . . His poems have been sold hitherto only in manuscript. I never read them, but a friend at my desire procured the "Sweep Song." There is one to a tiger, which I have heard recited, beginning:
>
> > Tyger, Tyger, burning bright,
> > Thro' the desarts of the night,
>
> which is glorious, but alas! I have not the book; for the man is flown, whither I know not—to Hades or a Mad House—but I must look on him as one of the most extraordinary persons of his age.
> > To Bernard Barton; May 15, 1824.

And even Leigh Hunt, who was usually so quick to recognize new merit, condemned Blake's Descriptive Catalogue of his exhibition of pictures as "a wild farrago of nonsense."

In the last years of his life, Blake watched the growing fame of Wordsworth, Coleridge, Byron, Shelley, and Keats (he drew striking sketches of several of them) ; but he could hardly have supposed that after a century the poetry of his younger and simpler period would have been held worthy of a place beside theirs. His death was almost unnoticed. So narrow were his means that he was buried in a general grave in Bunhill Fields; and when, in 1927, men sought to honor the spot with a memorial tablet, his precise resting place could not be found.

His Character.—Blake's chief faults were arrogant self-confidence, and furious contempt for any whose opinions differed from his own. In other ways he did not possess what is ignorantly called "the artistic temperament"; for he was not capricious, nor disorderly, nor attitudinizing, nor egotistic, nor lazy and talkative. He was a genuine artist, in his sincerity and in his self-forgetful and diligent devotion to his calling. Should he, because of his visionary habits or for other reasons, be considered insane?[1] His nervous system was not perfectly healthy, and physicians would probably diagnose his condition as "manic-depressive" in tendency; but to call him "insane" in the ordinary sense of the term would be misleading. If you make the criterion of sanity conformity to worldly stand-

[1] See Havelock Ellis, *The Fountain of Life* (1924), p. 403 ff. (In the Index wrongly "Robert" Blake.)

ards and opinions, you may think Blake mad; but if you make it conformity to religious and aesthetic ideals, it is the worldly wise and the
merely practical who are the true madmen. Blake conducted his life
rationally enough. He gave up the pursuit of wealth; but he did enough
remunerative drudgery to supply his simple wants, and he was never a
burden upon his friends or upon society. Refusing to slave for super-
fluities, or to imitate what seemed to him inane conventions, he secured
freedom for his soul. This "affectionate, enthusiastic, hope-fostered
visionary," as he called himself, managed (more successfully than many
tiresomely sane people) to find happiness. He spoke sincerely and truly
in these doggerel lines:

> I've Mental Joy and Mental Health,
> And Mental Friends and Mental Wealth.
> I've a Wife I love and what loves me:
> I've all but Riches bodily!

His Ideas.—The views of Blake combined those of the School of
Sensibility with those of Swedenborg. He attacked the neo-classic, the
rationalistic, the skeptical, and the scientific. He accepted the individual
inner light and the mystical vision. The imagination was the guide to
truth. It revealed to him principles of startling character—theological,
political, ethical, and literary. There was no distinction between the
divine and the *fully* human. Jesus was divine, but so are you and I.

> Thou art a Man, God is no more:
> Thy own humanity learn to adore.

To rationalize religion was to destroy its essence; accordingly, in opposition to Hume's *Natural Religion* (1779), he wrote *There Is No Natural
Religion*. But Calvinism was as bad as skepticism: "every religion that
preaches vengeance for sin is the religion of the Enemy." To exercise the
imagination was a religious act, was the true worship; for it meant to behold the universe truly, to behold the eternal values. Jesus was the
Divine Imagination.

The beginning and the end of true reality was divine spiritual power
(Los, creative energy, imagination, poetic genius). It was in the first of
men (Albion, the Druids, Adam, etc.). But there had been a Fall, an
imperfect finite world detached from the divine spirit; this was evilly
dominated and limited by Reason (Urizen). By assuming that we could
understand this imperfect natural world through experience and rationalizing, we were deluded. The true quality of the Universe was not
disclosed by scientific analysis but through direct spiritual revelation.
To redeem the world and mankind, Reason (Urizen) must be reunited
with Imagination (Los) and Love (Luvah); whereupon Man in his
divine completeness (Albion) will arise again, as in Jesus Christ.

The first commandment of the Religion of Imagination was to free
ourselves from all inhibitions, without and within. Since the essentially

human was divine, attempts by the State or the Church to force men into conformity with political, social, or moral laws or institutions were evil. Were mankind completely free, it would become completely good. The abolition of the marriage bond would not result in an orgy of sensualism but in true fidelity and spiritualized love. The use of compulsion in education, of force in any way (as in the slaying of animals) was inhuman.

Even higher than the principle of Liberty was that of Love—the bond of universal sympathy. Love and Imagination were virtually synonymous. "God becomes as we are," said Blake, "that we may be as he is." (*There Is No Natural Religion.*) The purpose of the creation was the reproduction of imaginatively creative minds. The true Man, who can be freed in body and soul only by the self-annihilation of the unregenerate worldly or merely rationalistic man, is the Poetic Genius. Blake is thus the apostle of the Religion of Art. In some of his ideas, modern critics maintain, he anticipated the psychology of Freud or of Jung— the division between the Id and the Ego, etc.

Since classical pagan literature fostered views hostile to some of Blake's, he maintained that it should not be admired and imitated as much as it had been. Even his beloved Shakspeare and Milton had been "curbed by the general malady and infection from the silly Greek and Latin slaves of the Sword." Henceforth the true literary model was to be, not Homer or Virgil, but the Bible.

His Works.—In his first poems, *Poetical Sketches* (*Anth.*, 112), Blake yearned for the rebirth of poesy and melody, and sang of love and nature. In *Songs of Innocence* (*Anth.*, 114), today his most popular volume, he revealed glimpses of life as it appears to innocent childhood, full of charm, and joy, and trust—the piper, the gentle shepherd, the beloved lamb, the angels guarding all creatures, the glow-worm piloting the emmet, the laughing countryside, the sports on the echoing green, the little lost boy whose tears banish the vapor of night and who is found by his father, the little black boy who will be radiant in Heaven, the charity children who are the flowers of London town—and over all the pity of God and the peace that passes all understanding.

Unlike the merely sentimental, however, Blake did not shut his eyes to the apparent evils and sorrows of life. In *Songs of Experience* (*Anth.*, 125), probably the most powerful expression of his genius, childhood is passed, and maturity is grieved and alarmed by painful and terrifying things. Blake intimates, however, as in *The Tiger*, that in even the most forbidding appearances of God's universe there is a beauty and probably an inscrutable justice. *The Book of Thel* (*Anth.*, 117), the first important symbolic poem, hints a similar faith: Thel, on the threshold of life in this world, beholding its pains and ultimate death, would remain in Eternity; but other existences disclose to her the beauty and comfort of the mutual self-sacrifice which unites all creatures.

In *The French Revolution* (*Anth.*, 120), Blake voiced his democratic and pacifist feelings; and in the paradoxes of *The Marriage of Heaven and Hell* (*Anth.*, 122), he attacked a theology which seemed to him to have perversely misrepresented the will of God by placing the energetic and the free in Hell and the slavish in Heaven.

The rest of his writings were chiefly the Prophetic Books, of which *Milton* and *Jerusalem* (*Anth.*, 131) were the most important. For many years the symbolism of these poems was not understood, but recently the key to the significance of the various allegorical personages has been discovered. To the advanced student of Blake, the Prophetic Books are of fascinating interest and delight. But to the general reader, though he now and then comes upon passages of startling vividness and beauty, the plan as a whole is bewildering, and the mythological characters too rarely become alive.

His Style.—Since the lyricists of the seventeenth century, no one had sung in more exquisitely melodious strains than Blake in his earlier poems. In the best of them everything was pictorial and musical. Unlike many Pre-Romantics, he did not make the mistake of trying to express new and revolutionary sentiments in diction and metre associated with literary conservatism. The form of such poems as *The Book of Thel* was as unusual as their substance.

Blake showed, almost from the outset, two stylistic tendencies. One was toward the simple, direct, and clear—applying, as it were, to literature his maxim regarding pictures: "The more distinct, sharp, and wiry the bounding line, the more perfect the work of art." The other tendency was toward the indirect, the symbolical, the portentous, perhaps the sublime, and certainly the obscure. He believed that only in this latter manner could he express the profounder aspects of his faith. His devotees agree with him. But others, though they love his earlier poems, and though they have learned the key to his allegorical system, are unable to derive from the Prophetic Books sufficient additional values to compensate for the effort. To some it seems that Blake was too often straining to reach the lofty and collapsing into vacuity. Moreover, in some of the allegories Blake himself did not arrive at a decision as to the basic plan. His theory that he was "writing in and for Eternity" led him to disregard the fact that in this world some approach to orderly arrangement in space and time (i.e., in setting and plot) is a condition of intelligibility. The earlier poems are therefore the more admired, not because of any superiority in their substance, but because to them he succeeded in giving a finished and beautiful form.

His Relation to Other Romantics.—When one considers both the sentiments and the style of Blake's *Poetical Sketches* (1783), *Songs of Innocence* (1789), and *Songs of Experience* (1794), one is inclined to maintain that the beginnings of the Romantic Movement may be seen in these poems quite as clearly as in Wordsworth's and Coleridge's *Lyrical Ballads* (1798). But even at his best, Blake did not cover as wide a range as some of his successors. His interpretations of Nature were limited to a few lovely aspects; and his conception of mankind seemed visionary, because he proffered no suggestions as to how the chasm between actual conditions and his paradise of complete freedom might be bridged. His idealism was too often an abstract idealism. Too rarely concerned with actual life, he failed to stir certain human emotions that the later Romantics appealed to. Yet his pioneer work helped to clear the way: he attacked philosophical and religious bigotry; he pointed to beauty and truth in unexpected places; and he gave a new value to the imaginative, the childlike, and the humane.

"There is something," said Henry Crabb Robinson, "in the madness of this man which interests me more than the sanity of Lord Byron and Walter Scott," and he tells us that Wordsworth likewise was keenly excited over Blake's works. Blake loved many of Wordsworth's poems, especially the *Ode on Intimations of Immortality,* but he deplored the baldly realistic passages in some of the other poems, and he denounced Wordsworth's theories about nature and "natural piety" as dangerously wrong. "There is no such thing as natural piety," said Blake, "the natural man is at enmity with God." Blake was somewhat eccentric to the main development of English religious thought, while Wordsworth was one of its chief conduits of inspiration. Blake's dogma, "Imagination has nothing to do with memory" also contradicts Wordsworth's theories and practice. On the other hand, some of Blake's ideas about the nature and function of the imagination are similar to Coleridge's, and to those of the Romantics in general. "Blake and Coleridge," wrote a contemporary, "when in company, seemed like congenial beings of another sphere, breathing for a while on our earth."— Among the authors of the latter part of the nineteenth century whom Blake influenced were Swinburne, the poets of the Irish Renaissance, particularly W. B. Yeats, A. E. Housman (stylistically), some of the Imagists, and Havelock Ellis.

SELECTED BIBLIOGRAPHY

OF FIRST IMPORTANCE

Selections

Selected Poems (World's Classics), ed. Basil De Selincourt, 1927.
Poems, chosen by Laurence Binyon, 1931.
The Portable Blake, ed. Alfred Kazin, 1946.

Texts

Poetry and Prose of William Blake, ed. Geoffrey Keynes (Nonesuch).— Text of the 3 vol. ed., omitting variant readings. Strongly recommended. If this is not obtainable, use the *Poems* (Oxford), ed. John Sampson, 1921; or *Poems and Prophecies* (Everyman's Libr.), ed. Max Plowman, 1927.

A facsimile reproduction of the *Songs of Innocence,* e.g., William Muir's, 1884; J. H. Wicksteed's, 1928; or Ruthven Todd's (Falcon Press), 1948.

Standard Biography

Wilson, Mona; *Life of William Blake,* 1927; 2nd ed., 1932.

The Best Introductory Critical Discussions

Yeats, W. B.; "William Blake and the Imagination," 1897; rptd. in *Essays,* 1924. — See also his *Ideas of Good and Evil,* 1903.

Damon, S. Foster; *William Blake: His Philosophy and Symbols,* 1924; rptd., 1947. — First good interpretation and commentary. Overlooks some influences upon him; see Saurat, 1929, et al., below.

Plowman, Max; *Introduction to the Study of Blake,* 1927. — Enthusiastic, but clear. Inexpensive.

De Selincourt, Basil; Introduction to *Selected Poems,* 1927. — Good on Blake's poetic style.

Percival, Milton O.; *William Blake's Circle of Destiny,* 1938. — His system "logical and coherent," and the culmination of a long tradition. — Good review, TLS, Aug. 27, 1938.

Schorer, Mark; *William Blake: The Politics of Vision,* 1946. — Blake a rebel against inner and outer repressions; for individual self-fulfillment through imaginative intuition and love.

FOR ADVANCED STUDENTS

Important Additional Texts

The Writings of William Blake, ed. Geoffrey Keynes (Nonesuch), 3 vols., 1925. — Standard, beautiful, costly.

Among the many facsimile reproductions, the following are noteworthy (besides those listed above):

Poetical Sketches (Facsimile Text Soc.), 1934.

Illustrations of the Book of Job, ed. Binyon and Keynes, Pierpont Morgan Libr., 1935. — Costly.

Blake's Note-Books (the "Rossetti MS"), ed. Keynes (Nonesuch), 1935.

The Prophetic Writings of William Blake, ed. D. J. Sloss and J. P. R. Wallis, 2 vols., 1926. — Valuable Commentary and Index of Symbols.
Helpful in beginning the study of these more difficult works of Blake (besides Mona Wilson) are: Frederick E. Pierce's *Selections from the Symbolical Poems,* 1915; and the Introduction to Joseph Wicksteed's *Blake's Vision of the Book of Job,* 2nd ed., 1924.

Biography and Criticism

Gilchrist, Alexander; *Life of Blake,* 2 vols., 1863; 2nd enlarged ed., 1880; in Everyman's Libr., 1942. — Still an indispensable biographical source.

Swinburne, A. C.; *William Blake,* 1868; new ed., 1906. — Enthusiastic.

More, Paul Elmer; *Shelburne Essays,* IV, 1906. — The best of the unsympathetic "humanistic" criticisms.

Symons, Arthur; *William Blake,* 1907. — A step forward, both biographically and critically.

Ellis, Edwin J.; *The Real Blake,* 1907. — Supplied new materials, but credulous and uncritical. "A piece of fantasy" (Schorer).

Chesterton, Gilbert K.; *William Blake,* 1910. — Vivacious interpretation by an orthodox Christian; neglects the revolutionary intent.

Berger, Pierre; *William Blake: Poet and Mystic,* 1914 (orig. French, 1907; new ed., 1936).

Gardner, Charles; *Vision and Vesture: Blake in Modern Thought,* 1916; 2nd ed., 1929. — "The most creative and most religious genius." — Gardner's *Blake, the Man,* 1919, has a chapter on his relations with "The Rebels," Godwin, Mary Wollstonecraft, Paine, etc.

Pierce, F. E.; "Blake and Seventeenth Century Authors," MLN, xxxix, 150; 1924.

Bruce, Harold L.; *William Blake in This World,* 1925. — The emphasis is on "this" — i.e., on persistent purpose to reform.

White, Helen C.; *The Mysticism of William Blake,* 1927. — Cf. C. H. Herford, *Hibbert Journal,* xxvi, Oct., 1927.

Binyon, Laurence; Introduction to *Poems,* 1931. — Admirable. Cf. E. M. Forster, "An Approach to Blake," *Spectator,* cxlviii, 474; 1932.

Murry, John Middleton; *William Blake,* 1933. — Subjective. "In his Christo-Marxian mood" (Schorer).

De Selincourt, Ernest; *Oxford Lectures on Poetry,* 1934. — Condemns the Prophetic Books — the visions not successfully communicated.

Saurat, Denis; *Blake and Milton,* 1935. — Confusing. Cf. R. F. Schaupp's "Blake's 'Correction' of Milton," *Ohio State Univ. Abstracts: 1934;* 1935.

Quinn, Kerker; "Blake and the New Age," *Virg. Quart. Rev.,* xiii, 271; 1937. — Cf. Grace Jameson, "Irish Poets of Today," PMLA, liii, 575; 1938.

Lowery, Margaret R.; *Windows of the Morning: A Critical Study of the "Poetical Sketches,"* 1940. — Includes a critical survey of the most important biographies.

Bronowski, Jacob; *A Man Without a Mask:* 1943. — His personal position economically and politically; his rebellion against an industrial age. — "Excellent" (Schorer); but cf. TLS, Apr. 22, 1944.

Preston, Kerrison; *Blake and Rossetti,* 1944. — See Witcutt, below.

Cheney, Sheldon; *Men Who Have Walked with God,* 1945. — The last chapter compares Blake with other great mystics, ancient, medieval, and modern.

Nicolson, Marjorie H.; "Epilogue on Blake," *Newton Demands the Muse,* 1946. His reaction against eighteenth-century admiration of Newton's system.

Witcutt, W. P.; *Blake: A Psychological Study,* 1946. — Striking similarities between Blake's four Zoas and Jung's four psychological functions are disclosed — and somewhat exaggerated. — See controversy with Preston et al., TLS, July 22, Aug. 5, 19, Sept. 2, 1944; also the rev., TLS, Feb. 15, 1947.

Todd, Ruthven; *Tracks in the Snow,* 1946. — Blake's relation to eccentric mythologists and artists (Fuseli, Martin, etc.).

Frye, Northrup; *Fearful Symmetry,* 1947. — Elaborate exposition of Blake's mythology by a zealous admirer. Not as clear as Percival and Schorer. "A magnificent book; fiery understanding" (Edith Sitwell).

Kennedy, Wilma L.; *The English Heritage of Coleridge,* 1947. — Ch. 5, "A Mystic's Conception," shows agreement between Blake and Coleridge on Imagination.

Davies, J. G.; *The Theology of William Blake,* 1948.

On Blake as an Artist

Figgis, Darrell; *The Paintings of William Blake,* 1925.

Binyon, Laurence; *The Engraved Designs of William Blake,* 1926.

Sitwell, Sacheverell; *The Hunters and the Hunted,* 1948. — On the pastoral school influenced by Blake.

Bibliographies

As Blake is not included in the *Romantic Movement Bibliography,* ELH, consult for new works on him *English Literature, 1660–1800,* PQ, annually, April.

Keynes, Geoffrey; *Bibliography of Blake,* Grolier Club, N. Y., 1921. — Rare. — Cf. Keynes's bibl. in *The Cambridge Bibliography of English Literature,* II, 347; 1941, which lists MSS, Blake's own etched works, facsimiles, etc.

CHAPTER 4

SAMUEL TAYLOR COLERIDGE

(October 21, 1772–July 25, 1834)

1798 France: An Ode	1809–10 The Friend (revised, 1818)
1798 The Ancient Mariner	1817 Biographia Literaria
1799 Love	1808–18 Lectures (delivered)
1816 Christabel	1825 Aids to Reflection
1816 Kubla Khan	

His Early Life.—Coleridge's father was a clergyman and schoolmaster in Devonshire—"a perfect Parson Adams in learning, goodheartedness, absentness of mind, and excessive ignorance of the world"—who understood his son's love of reading, introspection, reverie, and solitude. When his father told him how vastly greater the stars and planets were than they seemed to be, the lad was not amazed; for, as he characteristically said in later years, he did not even then regard his senses as the criteria of his belief. "I regulated all my creeds by my conceptions, not by my sight." Before the age of ten he was sent to Christ's Hospital, London, an ascetic and severe school, where he received a classical and orthodox education and won high scholastic honors. Here Charles Lamb, his schoolmate and lifelong friend, describes him as "alone among six hundred playmates." But both at school and at Cambridge University, which he entered at nineteen, he made friends with a few who like himself were literary and idealistic.

In his college days he was a radical of the sentimental school, a dissenter from the doctrines of the Church of England, an admirer of the materialistic psychology of David Hartley and of some of the teachings of Godwin, a sympathizer with the French Revolution, and a pacifist, denouncing England's war against France. He loved the sonnets of Bowles, a poet of sensibility. His radicalism was tempered, however, by other addictions which, sooner or later, were to conflict therewith: he retained his belief in God; he pored over Milton and the Bible; and he was fascinated by the mysticism of Plotinus and the faith of the seventeenth-century Cambridge Platonists. For the time being he was nevertheless almost as unhesitant a reformer as Godwin or Paine or Blake. This tendency was encouraged by Robert Southey, then an undergraduate at Oxford, whom Coleridge met in 1794, and with whom he collaborated in a play, *The Fall of Robespierre,* and in that socialistic scheme which they called Pantisocracy.[1]

[1] See above, p. 31.

53

After little more than two years at the university, Coleridge left without a degree. He had drifted into an engagement with Sarah Fricker, Southey's sister-in-law; and, not without some pressure on Southey's part, married her. He was not yet twenty-three, and his only prospects lay in assurances that his friend Joseph Cottle would publish whatever poetry Coleridge might write. For the rest of his life Coleridge was mostly or wholly dependent upon others. He might have supported himself and his family if he had been willing to do hack work diligently, but in point of fact he was largely or wholly supported by a series of patrons and friends. The charge of supporting his wife and children often fell upon Southey, whose own loyalty to duty made it difficult for him to judge Coleridge's shiftlessness leniently.

The library record of Coleridge's reading during the years immediately after his marriage, and the jottings in his notebook during that period, show that his intellectual growth was proceeding at least as rapidly as during his attendance at the university. His curiosity was that of a philosopher rather than that of a mere *littérateur;* he read books of science and of exploration as well as *belles lettres,* and he pursued the ramifications of a subject in the manner of a scholar. He was intensely interested in so many things that he would not confine himself to a particular vocation. He wrote verses of humanitarian tendency, such as *To a Young Ass (Anth.,* 137) , in which, after the fashion of Sterne, he exclaimed

> Innocent foal! thou poor despised forlorn!
> I hail thee *Brother*—spite of the fool's scorn!

In *The Destiny of Nations* he indulged the absurd fancy that what Joan of Arc's Voices communed with her about were such conceptions as the Protoplast and the Leviathan. As late as 1798, in *The Wanderings of Cain,* he attributed to the first murderer sentiments of the tenderest and most domestic character. To the most liberal of the newspapers, *The Morning Chronicle,* he contributed poems attacking Burke and glorifying such heroes of liberty as Godwin, Erskine, Priestley, Lafayette, Kosciusko, and Schiller. But, like Blake, he abhorred Voltaire as "in the service of the dark master."

He lectured on contemporaneous political and other problems, and issued a short-lived periodical, *The Watchman* (1796) , in advocacy of his ideas. On Sundays he preached in Unitarian pulpits, without recompense—one of his engagements leading to that first meeting with young Hazlitt which the latter so brilliantly described.[2] Indeed he was on the point of entering the ministry, when an annuity from the Wedgwood brothers saved him for literature. He bestowed some time upon the tutoring of a young disciple, Charles Lloyd. He even tried to cultivate the acre or two behind his cottage, saying, "I would rather be an expert self-maintaining gardener than a Milton if I could not unite both."

---

[2] See the selection, *Anth.,* 395.

Thus, at twenty-four, although well-intentioned and busy, he had arrived nowhere.

His Poetical Period.—It was between the ages of twenty-five and twenty-nine that Coleridge wrote nearly all the poetry that was to make him immortal. The drifter became a master. Two causes chiefly aided in the transformation. One was the painful but salutary correction of his optimistic sentimentalism by the imperialistic results of the French Revolution. The French invasion of the republic of Switzerland led Coleridge to write his *Recantation* (Feb., 1798), later entitled *France: An Ode (Anth.,* 160). Here for the first time he succeeded in uttering deep and significant feeling in sublime style.

The second influence was that of Wordsworth, whom Coleridge had known since his college days, but whom he did not associate with closely until the Wordsworths settled near him in the west of England in 1797. Coleridge, though conscious of his own powers, looked up to Wordsworth (a man who, with even deeper passions than himself, had won self-mastery) as his superior, and as the greatest personality he had ever known. Precisely what each gave to the other has never been fully and clearly set forth, and may be unascertainable, but the poems which Coleridge wrote while in frequent intercourse with Wordsworth show a mastery over style and form superior to his other work. Nothing is more unlike Wordsworth than *The Ancient Mariner;* nothing is more genuinely Coleridgean: yet it is clear that Coleridge would never have found himself in this masterpiece without the wise encouragement and counsel of his fellow-poet.[3] He also began *Christabel* at this time under the same stimulating and benign influence. It was the only really happy period of his life, when, as Wordsworth later reminded him:

> Thou, in bewitching words, with happy heart,
> Didst chaunt the vision of that Ancient Man,
> The bright-eyed Mariner, and rueful woes
> Didst utter of the Lady Christabel.
> Conclusion of *The Prelude*

Already in this period, however, there were signs of danger. When his pupil Charles Lloyd deserted him, Coleridge tried to forget his worries by leaving home and by taking opium. As a mere child he had run away from home; when his engagement to Sarah Fricker caused him misgivings, he had long absented himself; and now again he fled. Hitherto he had taken opium only a few times, as an apparently necessary anodyne when in very great pain. Now in his despondency he overindulged in it —the dream-fragment *Kubla Khan* being the first fruit. During the next eighteen years this vice (for about half that time a secret even to his intimate friends) laid increasing hold upon him, despite his repeated efforts to throw it off.

---

[3] For the details of their collaboration, see the notes on *The Ancient Mariner, Anth.,* 1095.

After *The Ancient Mariner* had been published in the *Lyrical Ballads,* Coleridge went with the Wordsworths to Germany. There during nine months he studied science, philology, and especially the German language and literature, and laid the foundation of one of his most important intellectual resources. He interested himself in German criticism and aesthetics, in the new philosophy, and in the Romantic Movement which was at this time (1798–99) at full flood. He hoped to make speedy use of his "endless transcription" from these sources of inspiration, but it was not until ten years later that much resulted therefrom. The only immediate result was his translation of Schiller's tragedy, *Wallenstein.*

On his return he settled, in order to be near Wordsworth, at Keswick, Cumberland, in the north of England; but he often wandered away to London and elsewhere. Such was his literary and intellectual reputation that he might have achieved speedy success, for editors and publishers were more than ready to accept whatever he might offer them. He did some political writing for the *Morning Post,* but failed to persevere in anything—except in his metaphysical studies and meditations.

Coleridge had shown little sense of responsibility toward his wife and family in leaving them for so long a sojourn in Germany, and in that respect his removal in 1800 from Nether Stowey to Keswick was also regrettable, Mrs. Coleridge feeling that William and Dorothy Wordsworth absorbed his interest and were biased against her. Wordsworth was then engaged to Mary Hutchinson (whom he married in 1802), who had a sister, Sara. Sara Hutchinson and Coleridge, already estranged from his wife, had fallen in love with each other by the end of 1799. This was the great passion of Coleridge's life. His notebooks contain glowing and mournful passages concerning it; and it inspired his poem *Love,* which is partly autobiographical, the statue of the armed knight and other particulars in it referring to objects near Sara's home. The original version of *Dejection: An Ode* (not published until 1937) clearly revealed it; and when that version was read by Coleridge to William and Dorothy, it of course deeply disturbed them. For at least ten years, until c. 1811, this hopeless love (divorce from Mrs. Coleridge being impossible in the then state of the laws) dominated Coleridge's feelings. It helped to render him year by year more wretched, unsettled, and ineffective.

His intellectual activity was often of greater service to others than to his own creative work. In 1802, for example, he helped Wordsworth by furnishing him with those neo-Platonic ideas about pre-existence which constitute such a striking feature of the *Ode on Intimations of Immortality* (stanzas v–viii). The extent to which his conversation and letters assisted other Romantics is insufficiently known. He succeeded in writing the second part of *Christabel* at this time, but he felt that his poetic power was dying away. His chronic ailments, his estrangement from his wife, and the impossibility of his marrying Sara Hutchinson, contributed to that melancholy state of mind which he voiced in his *Ode to Dejection* (April 4, 1802). Herein he lamented that his loss of inward happiness had resulted in the extinction of

What nature gave me at my birth,
My shaping spirit of Imagination.

It was his farewell to the writing of great poetry. Some of his friends hoped he would recover his poetical powers; and, as if to encourage them, he pathetically pretended that his last notable poem, the *Hymn Before Sunrise* (*Anth.*, 179), was wholly original, when it actually was an expanded version of a German poem by Fredericke Brun.

His Period as a Critic.—Coleridge's life from the age of thirty to forty-three was, in point of conduct, the most reprehensible part of his existence. He neglected his family more than ever, and failed to communicate with them for long periods. For some months in 1811–12 he even became estranged from the Wordsworths. The too obvious fondness between him and Sara Hutchinson had long been a source of pain and worry to them; so likewise had been his irregular habits. Wordsworth's complaints, confidentially uttered, were indiscreetly repeated in a distorted form to Coleridge; and it was not without difficulty that the latter was induced to make friends with Wordsworth again. His association with Sara was not thereafter renewed.

He now sank into humiliating dependence upon benefactors, and made less and less effort to struggle against his evil habits. "He is going to turn sober," said the faithful Charles Lamb, "but his hour has not struck yet; meantime he pours out goblet after goblet." It should give pause to persons prone to snap judgments upon moral questions that from this wretched man, at the nadir of his physical and moral being, there issued some of the loftiest, wisest, and most humane criticism of literature and life that has ever been bestowed upon the world. It was given in the form of public lectures—in 1808, on poetry and the fine arts; in 1811–12, on Shakspeare and Milton; and in 1818–19, on philosophy. The audiences often included eminent men of letters, and were usually enthusiastic if not awestruck; but the attendance was small. Coleridge lectured extemporaneously, and sometimes departed from his announced subject. Unfortunately the only records we have of some of his lectures are merely the notes jotted down by a listener, such as Henry Crabb Robinson.

Coleridge had not become callous to the suffering and disgrace which his bad habits entailed. Here is a letter written by him at this time:

My entreaties for your forgiveness, and for your prayers. Conceive a poor miserable wretch, who for many years has been attempting to beat off pain, by a constant recurrence to the vice that reproduces it. Conceive a spirit in hell employed in tracing out for others the road to that heaven from which his crimes exclude him. In short, conceive whatever is most wretched, helpless, and hopeless. . . . In the one crime of opium, what crimes have I not made myself guilty of!—ingratitude to my Maker! and to my benefactors—injustice! and unnatural cruelty to my poor children! self-contempt for my repeated promise—breach, nay, too often, actual falsehood! After my death I earnestly entreat that a full and unqualified narration of my wretchedness and of its guilty cause may be made public, that at least some little good may be effected by the direful example.

Not long afterwards, at the age of forty-three, Coleridge resolved to take the step which saved him. He placed himself under the direction of a physician, James Gillman, whose residence at Highgate, London, became his home for the rest of his life.

His Philosophical Period.—Under Gillman's regimen Coleridge improved physically, and succeeded in making ready for publication what was for him no small quantity of work. In 1816, he published *Christabel* and *Kubla Khan;* in 1817, *Biographia Literaria;* in 1818, a revised edition of his periodical essays, *The Friend;* in 1825, *Aids to Reflection in the Formation of a Manly Character;* and in 1830, *On the Constitution of Church and State.* Those, therefore, are misleading who imply that in these years he was a mere talker. It is true that he wrote less than he intended to. He tried to produce a comprehensive work setting forth his entire philosophic system, and he begrudged every hour given to lecturing or other remunerative work as an hour lost "from the Permanent." But he composed only portions of this *magnum opus,* and the incoherence of his literary remains left his editors perplexed.

In his last years he suffered from the neglectful or hostile reception of *Christabel* and *Biographia Literaria,* and from bitter attacks, such as those of his former disciple Hazlitt, upon his now conservative political and religious views. But he was consoled by the loyalty of some old friends and the devotion of new adherents. His talk was an inexhaustible marvel.

> Great in his writings [said Charles Lamb], he was greatest in his conversation. In him was disproved that old maxim that we should allow every one his share of talk. He would talk from morn to dewy eve, nor cease till far midnight, yet who ever would interrupt him,—who would obstruct that continuous flow of converse, fetched from Helicon or Zion? He had the tact of making the unintelligible seem plain.

Even the dour young Carlyle reluctantly paid homage to his power, saying:

> A sublime man; who, alone in those dark days, had saved his crown of spiritual manhood; escaping from the black materialisms, and revolutionary deluges, with 'God, Freedom, Immortality' still his: a king of men. The practical intellects of the world did not much heed him, or carelessly reckoned him a metaphysical dreamer; but to the rising spirits of the young generation he had this dusky sublime character; and sat there as a kind of *Magus,* girt in mystery and enigma. (*Life of Sterling,* ch. 8; 1851.)

Among the many distinguished admirers who paid visits to Coleridge were Landor and Emerson. His disciples included John Sterling, to whose intelligent appreciation he owed what was (with the possible exception of Leigh Hunt's) the first worthy critique of *Christabel;* and his nephew and son-in-law, Henry Nelson Coleridge, who wrote the first competent general review of his poetry (1834) and who edited many of his posthumously published writings. His insistence that Reason and Faith need not be hostile made him a guiding light to the liberal thinkers in the Church of England, the so-called "Broad Church" group—Arnold of Rugby, Julius Charles Hare, and Frederick Denison Maurice.—When Coleridge died, Charles Lamb said:

> His great and dear spirit haunts me. I cannot think a thought, I cannot make a criticism on men or books, without an ineffectual turning and reference to him. He was the proof and touchstone of all my cogitations.

And Wordsworth mourned him as "the most *wonderful* man he had ever known."

His Character.—The lower part of Coleridge's countenance was fat, flabby, and inexpressive; his lips thick; but his eyes and forehead noble. His mental energy was too fiery for his bodily strength. His health was congenitally poor: he suffered increasingly from dental sepsis, neuralgia, rheumatism, and swellings of the knees. He could not breathe through his nose, presumably because of adenoids. It is lamentable to think what he suffered that modern medical science could have saved him from, but that the science of his time only rendered worse. It was to gain respite from his pains that he took laudanum, a tincture of opium—only to find the habit more terrible than the disease. Again and again he tried to free himself. While in Germany he abstained totally from opium and alcoholic beverages for three months, and almost entirely from protein food; but the result was that he raised up another demon—insomnia. The wretchedness of his health accounts largely, though not wholly, for the errors of his ways—for his greatest sins, sloth and intemperance; for his fleeing from troublesome practical responsibilities; and for his disorderly methods of work.

He was vacillating of purpose, and endeavored to play too many parts. He attempted to be a farmer, tutor, preacher, reporter, political writer, reviewer, editor, translator, lecturer, dramatist, poet, and philosopher. His inner life showed a similar lack of concentration. He had a professorial passion for omniscience, a receptive mind, a scholarly curiosity to understand all sides of controversial questions, and a time-consuming ambition to try to reconcile opposites. "My mind," he said, "is of too general an affinity with all things; and though it perceives the *difference* of things, yet it is eternally pursuing the *likeness,* or, rather, that which is common between them." Every phenomenon suggested to him a general principle and infinite connections; rarely could he force the flood of his thoughts into a discernible direction. To paraphrase what he said of another, "The man was a chaos of truths, but forgot that God was a God of order."

His natural disposition was cheerful, humorous, and sensitively imaginative to an extraordinary degree. Weak of will, he had a strong conscience, which made him sincerely remorseful, and which ultimately brought about the reform of some of his moral habits, although it was too late to reform his methods of work. He was deeply affectionate; and. though he estranged his friends temporarily, he lost few permanently. For us, who never knew him, to condemn him severely seems fatuous when so many of his contemporaries who knew him best, including those who were hurt by his conduct, persisted in loving and revering him. They accepted the paradox that this exasperating sinner was a true poet, philosopher, and lover of mankind. Gladly would he learn, and gladly teach. In letters to his friends he squandered a wealth of thought that, hoarded and copyrighted, would have brought fame and fortune to an astute man of letters. His redeeming virtue was self-forgetful devotion to the quest of the divinely true.

His Chief Poems.—The greatest of Coleridge's poems were composed after he had reformed his early views upon man and society. The first of them, *France: An Ode* (*Anth.*, 160), is the noblest expression of his feeling of tragic disappointment over the failure of his former political hopes. The contrast between his attitude therein, and that of his *Ode to the Departing Year* (1796; *Anth.*, 142), written not much more than a year earlier, is striking. In the earlier ode he still regarded those European nations that opposed France as foul oppressors of Liberty, and Great Britain, their ally, as accursed by Heaven. In style and content it seemed of the Pre-Romantic Movement—the sort of outburst that, in similar circumstances, might have been uttered by Henry Brooke, Thomas Warton, or Thomas Day. In *France: An Ode*, with its climax

> The Sensual and the Dark rebel in vain,
> Slaves by their own compulsion!

it is Milton that is largely influential upon his thought and diction. Here Coleridge's sentiments were no longer so youthfully simple and one-sided. He voices not only his new enmity to imperialistic France but also his still persistent love of Liberty and Nature. In short, he sees complexities and depths in his subject, as he did not see them in the subjects he had previously attempted. Unlike the typically second-rate minds which pass from a superficial liberalism in youth to a superficial conservatism in maturity, from one thoughtless extreme to another, Coleridge held fast by whatever was good in his earlier conceptions. He did not cease to see those aspects of life to which alone he was percipient before 1798, but henceforth he saw others also, some of which were in conflict with them; and he tried to rise to a higher view, which should reconcile the visions of his youth with the experiences of his maturity.

In *Love* (*Anth.*, 168), he retained unusually much from his first period, which may explain why it enjoyed among his contemporaries exceptional popularity. The older elements in it were its sensibility, its gentleness, its representing love less as a passion than as a tender affection and worship, and its plaintive strain. The new element, the touch of genius, was its subtle delineation of the way in which love was awakened in the innocent Genevieve by her following sympathetically another's tale and suddenly recognizing her own feelings in another's heart.

The Ancient Mariner (Anth., 146) and Christabel bore the same relation to previous verse-tales of terror that France: An Ode bore to Coleridge's previous political verse. In his earlier writings the relation between Good and Evil had been presented, after the sentimental fashion, as excessively simple. Evil was portrayed so obviously evil that men ought to have found it easy to do good and think justly. Into the world of The Ancient Mariner and Christabel (Anth., 169), though Good remains, Evil has entered as a veiled yet dreadful power, half-repellant, half-fascinating, seizing upon us when least expected, and visiting consequences upon us that are unforeseen. It is a vision of Evil perfectly true to life. A vision of Evil, I say—not an analysis of it, nor a sermon upon it. In these two poems Coleridge sought the golden mean between the kind of romance which is invented to point a moral, and the kind which is invented merely to entertain and which sheds no illumination upon life. Of course there were those who discovered the moral of the poem in the good Mariner's sentiment

> He prayeth well, who loveth well
> Both man and bird and beast,

and thereupon conceived of it, as has been wittily said, as a tract for the prevention of cruelty to albatrosses. Others, however, thought that Coleridge had not included enough moralizing in the poem, lines like the foregoing being distressingly few, and by far the greater portion of the poem having to their minds no discernible edification whatever. Among such critics was the celebrated Mrs. Anna Letitia Barbauld, author of a Life of Richardson and of Early Lessons for Children, admired by some for "her uncommon powers of mind, cultivated by a thorough English and classical education," but odious to Charles Lamb, who spoke most disrespectfully of what he termed "the cursed Barbauld crew, those Blights and Blasts of all that is Human in man and child."

> Mrs. Barbauld [Coleridge says] once told me that she admired the Ancient Mariner very much, but that there were two faults in it,—it was improbable and had no moral. As for the probability, I owned that that might admit some question; but as to the want of a moral, I told her that in my own judgment the poem had too much; and that the only, or chief, fault, if I might say so, was the obtrusion of the moral sentiment so openly on the reader as a principle or cause of action in a work of such pure imagination. It ought to have had no more moral than the Arabian Nights' tale of the merchants sitting down to eat dates by the side of a well, and throwing the shells aside, and lo! a genie starts up, and says he must kill the aforesaid merchant, because one of the date shells had, it seems, put out the eye of the genie's son (Table Talk; May 31, 1830).

This passage is easily misunderstood, especially by those to whom "pure imagination" means free invention without any regard whatever for truth of any kind. And Coleridge, in his eagerness to protest against moralistic interpreters, increased the danger of misunderstanding by giving *The Ancient Mariner* in its second edition the subtitle "A Poet's Reverie." (On second thought, he cancelled this subtitle.) "Reverie" implies a daydream, a drifting course of fanciful notions not checked by any consideration of whether they have a relation to reality. And this was as far in one direction from what Coleridge intended to create, as a moralizing story was in the other.—The moral life and the aesthetic should not be dissevered; they should be cooperating activities of one and the same human mind. The themes of *The Ancient Mariner* (rather than its "moral") are such impercipient and proud callousness as leads to the slaying of the albatross, and the aesthetic sensitivity and creative imagination which saves by engendering love of Nature and of Man, i.e., by accepting the oneness of all life.

Precisely what Coleridge intended may best be discovered by considering certain reviews, which he wrote shortly before *The Ancient Mariner*, of Mrs. Radcliffe's *Italian* and Lewis's *Monk*. The kind of romance-writing which they exemplified he condemned on several grounds. In the first place, however ingenious, it "attempted to please by what was unnatural, and by a departure from that observance of real life" which was requisite. Secondly, it was not content with its freedom to invent marvelous incidents, but it ventured mistakenly to indulge in fantastic characterization:

> The romance-writer possesses an unlimited power over situations; but he must scrupulously make his characters act in congruity with them. Let him work *physical* wonders only, and we will be content to dream with him for a while; but by the first *moral* miracle which he attempts he disgusts and awakens us.

Thirdly, it introduced supernatural beings or agencies which in no way suggested the real forces of the universe, and thus it rendered itself "incapable of exemplifying a moral truth."

Coleridge's aim in *The Ancient Mariner* and *Christabel,* therefore, was neither to produce maxims for the practical guidance of life nor to entertain us with strange fancies. He removed the incidents, variations of the perpetual conflicts between good and evil, out of the commonplace conditions of ordinary life, into realms where the forces of good and evil seemed invested with supernatural qualities. The preternatural or supernatural in these worlds of his, however, was not arbitrary but seemed in harmony with universal laws, and thus bore the marks of authenticity. It suggested the eternal mystery of the interpenetration throughout universal life of spirit and matter, of good and evil. And even more clearly, the human in these poems was true to permanent laws; what the Ancient Mariner felt in his circumstances, what Christabel felt in hers, was unerringly in accord with our common human nature. That is what Coleridge had in mind when he stated his purpose as follows:

My endeavors should be directed to persons and characters supernatural, or at least romantic; yet so as to transfer from our inward nature a human interest and a semblance of truth.

He had a percipient understanding of the emotional complexities of human nature (even of his own self, as his letters show), and hence could create, e.g., in *Christabel,* complex but true characters in his poetry, and interpret them rightly, as in his criticisms of Shakspeare. He often anticipates the disclosures of modern psychology, so much so that it has been plausibly suggested that he left *Christabel* unfinished because its explorations into the depths of human nature would have been considered too sensational to publish.

The Style and Form of the Poems.—In his best poems he had the power to evoke an atmosphere of mystery, wonder, and pathos; and his command over the appropriate diction, rhythm, and harmony was complete. "Of pure poetry," said Leigh Hunt, "strictly so called, that is to say, consisting of nothing but its essential self, without conventional and perishing helps, he was the greatest master of his time. If you would see it in a phial, like a distillation of roses, it would be found without a speck" (*Anth.,* 1012). The quantity of his best work is smaller than that of any other poet of equal power, but in quality he was in his own domain unsurpassed. Rare indeed was his command of rhythm and harmony; rarer still his power to evoke an atmosphere of mystery, wonder, and pathos, and to give to the unearthly a universal appeal. The fame of these poems is one of the evidences that the soul of man craves realities that are inaccessible by the pathways of common sense, and can only be reached by those of imagination, poetry, and religion.

To disembarrass his themes from contemporaneous or commonplace associations, Coleridge resorted to the unusual in metre and diction. In *Christabel* the measure consisted, not of an equal number of syllables in each line, but of an equal number of accents (four)—a form which gave him greater freedom for modulating the rhythm in accordance with changes in content and feeling. In *The Ancient Mariner* he used the ballad form, but introduced new features into it. He avoided those crudities and ineffective simplicities which were apt to appear in even the most beautiful ancient ballads, and he far surpassed most of them in subtle artistry and spiritual elevation. In his first version, overanxious to employ all means of rising above realism, he introduced too many archaisms into the diction; later he skillfully removed those that were unnecessary or disturbing. The addition of the marginal gloss was also an artistic improvement.

But his highest artistic achievements in this poem were, as has been brilliantly disclosed by Professor Lowes, his conduct of the action and his treatment of the supernatural. In the plot there is nothing "romantic" in the bad sense of the term, nothing meandering, digressive, episodic; all is balance and order. Details drawn from amazingly numerous and varied sources, he reduced to such unity that they seem always to have been associated. He sailed indeed, as the contemporaneous critic, John Wilson said, "a rich-freighted Argosy, tilting over Imagination's seas"; but he steered its course with a master hand. As for the supernatural elements, he made the suspension of disbelief as easy as possible by introducing only such supernatural beings and incidents as had long been believed in by former generations and appealed for faith to a kind of hereditary memory. Rationalism, unable to account for the fascination of the poem, and hating anything that suggests the intermingling of the human and the mystic, has attacked the poem again and again; but to the spirit of mankind it has remained "a warm poetic joy."

His Philosophy.[4]—The system which Coleridge throughout his life tried to excogitate and explain was a dynamic philosophy of life as an organic process of development toward higher levels of existence. There were insoluble mysteries; but in large degree the Universe was knowable, first through the activities of our senses and our understanding, next, on a higher level, through the Reason and Imagination, and finally, on a still higher level, by means of Faith. These different means were not necessarily antagonistic to one another. "One light," as a Cambridge Platonist had said, "does not oppose another; the light of faith and reason may shine together though with far different brightness." It is a philosophy somewhat resembling Goethe's, and still more Hegel's, though of the latter Coleridge knew little. He hoped to set it forth in one great comprehensive work, but never succeeded in composing it. The fragments which he left, however, enable us approximately to trace its general outlines.

The principle which was basic in his thought was that the human mind could not attain complete truth suddenly but could rise toward it only by constant effort and gradual stages. First one idea would seem true, and then facts or reflections would arise that seemed to deny it. If the mind were really progressing toward the light, it would not utterly reject the first idea nor wholly surrender to the second, but would excogitate a third which should include whatever was sound in the two former. The third idea would, in due course, meet with some fact or principle which challenged it; and thus the really intellectual life became an arduous but stimulating reconciliation of opposites.

The opposites, which in his younger days had pulled him first in one direction and then in the other, were sentimentalism and materialism. Each seemed presently incomplete. Sentimentalism was too idyllic and subjective to interpret life in its actuality. Materialism had its strong claims: he was for a time profoundly interested in scientists like Hunter and Hartley, and in mechanistic philosophers like Godwin. At one stage of his development he could even assert: "I am a complete necessitarian, and believe in the corporeality of thought." But this, too, presently failed to account adequately for the whole of his experience. Its chief

[4] This section, and the next (on his principles of criticism), may be postponed until Coleridge's *prose* is studied (*Anth.,* 329).

error was its assumption that everything in the universe could be ascertained by observation of the environment; and, to Coleridge, looking inward was as revealing as looking outward. As he said,

> I may not hope from outward forms to win
> The passion and the life whose fountains are within.

How did it become possible for him to give due recognition to those empirical phenomena that the materialists harped upon, and yet satisfy the cravings of his inner nature? The answer lies in his distinction between the understanding and the reason. "Until you have mastered the fundamental difference in kind," he declared, "between the reason and the understanding as faculties of the human mind, you cannot escape a thousand difficulties in philosophy." Whenever we use our minds to understand, we observe particular things and draw common sense inferences concerning them; and thus we may get on practically. But we never rise thereby to universal truths and values; for the mind, confining itself to understanding, submits itself to the environment, to things as they appear to be. By the understanding we can never attain to knowledge of God, free will, immortality, or conceptions of similar value.

But it is a materialistic fallacy to assume that the mind in its pursuit of truth is wholly dependent upon sense-impressions. It should look within, become self-conscious, and discern the real nature of the universe through its own being and powers. The mind can arrive at valid syntheses, as in mathematics, which are not wholly generalizations from experience. *Conceptions* are derivable by the understanding from phenomenal experience, but the Reason arrives at genuine *Ideas,* which are also constitutive of experience. Ideas unite the outer and the inner— deep calling to deep in the self-evolution of truth. The Reason, thus functioning, is a spark of the divine (of the Logos) in Man; by it he recognizes genuine universals, or eternal verities.

It is sometimes supposed that Coleridge derived these ideas from the great German philosopher, Immanuel Kant, to whom likewise the distinction between the understanding and the reason was fundamental; and it is true that his study of Kant's terminology influenced his own. But there remains an essential difference between Kant's philosophy and Coleridge's. To Kant the human mind could not rise to a knowledge of God, that is to a knowledge of him in any normal sense of the word; whereas to Coleridge God was a certainty of the most absolute and highest kind of knowledge. Coleridge's philosophy, in this important respect, was derived not from Kant but from the seventeenth-century English Platonists, who leaned strongly toward a religious or mystical interpretation of the universe. To Coleridge, moreover, Christianity, "rightly understood," harmonized with the soundest philosophy, and its essential doctrines were eternal truths of the reason. This did not imply a literal acceptance of every statement in the Scriptures.

The human mind, Coleridge maintained, discerns at the heart of the universe an Infinite Power, active in ways that transcend the merely mechanical:

> And what, if all of animated nature
> Be but organic harps diversely framed,
> That tremble into thought as o'er them sweeps,
> Plastic and vast, one intellectual breeze,
> At once the soul of each, and God of all?
> *The Æolian Harp.*

God had created in everything—in Nature, in Man, in Society, past and present—its essential idea and therewith its purpose and destiny. To the mere understanding, however, these inner and essential qualities were hidden behind the obvious outward appearances; and therefore the practical man was unwittingly violating truly rational principles, was blind to the relation between Nature and himself, was pursuing aims not ultimately satisfying to the real character of Man, and was adhering to conventions and institutions (political, ecclesiastical, educational, and social) not entirely in harmony with the true purpose of Society.

To know the Universe as it really is Man needed to attain within himself an emotional and intellectual life and integrity similar to that of the Universe itself; in other words, Man needed to become attuned to its harmony; hence Coleridge said: "My observation is that deep thinking is only attainable by a man of deep feeling," and "all truth is a species of revelation." Correspondingly, Man's individual freedom of will was at its highest when it worked in obedience and cooperation with the will of God; this was self-realization without selfishness.

It was disciples of Coleridge—Thomas Arnold of Rugby, J. C. Hare, and especially F. D. Maurice—who led the liberal or "Broad Church" movement, which held it possible to reconcile traditional Christian beliefs with new scientific discoveries and social developments, and which welcomed rather than feared diversity of opinions within the same spiritual brotherhood. They agreed with Coleridge that the best Christianity begins by loving truth wherever found.

Coleridge's politics, after he was disillusioned by the outcome of the French Revolution, became the politics of the unpolitical. He was the strongest influence against Bentham's utilitarian party with its goal of a radically reformed constitution and a governmentally managed economy. Reconstructing the political framework was to Coleridge less important than raising the intellectual, moral, and religious tone of the nation, and fostering the patriotic unity of the people. Every political issue should be brought to the test of moral principle; far more important than reform by legislation were moral improvement and the encouragement of a learned "clerisy" in church and school instilling culture and unselfish public spirit. He became the philosophic guide of the Conservative Party in Disraeli's day, not merely because he had opined that only educated men were fit to have political power, and that the encouragement of worthy leaders was more advantageous than universal suffrage, but also because he had, like Burke, insisted that some of the ancient institutions and ways were based on permanently true ideals. His ultimate desire was the highest welfare of the common people, and he leavened the program of the Conservatives by his liberal social idealism.

His Literary Principles.—Although the form and style of Coleridge's critical writings sometimes show obvious flaws, such as carelessness and digression, and although his prose is frequently prolix and too involved, he is one of the very greatest critics, partly because his criticism had a philosophical foundation. He affirmed that literature should give us a vision of life, not as it appeared to the understanding, but as it was revealed to the reason. The mere fancy, which corresponded to the understanding and was skillful only in collecting and combining particulars, was inferior to the genuine imagination, which was an ally, or even a form, of the reason and discerned the general and the permanent. True art and literature partook rather of the supernatural than of the natural. He declared:

> I adopt with full faith the principle of Aristotle, that poetry as poetry is essentially *ideal,* that it avoids and excludes all accident; that its apparent individualities of rank, character, or occupation must be *representative* of a class; and that the *persons* of poetry must be clothed with *generic* attributes, with the *common* attributes of the class; not with such as one gifted individual might *possibly* possess, but such as from his situation it is most probable beforehand that he *would* possess.
>
> *Biographia Literaria,* xvii

But his plea for the ideal, it is important to bear in mind, did not imply that the poet was to turn away from the actual and indulge his personal fancy in the making of the prettily idyllic. If he was a poet of genuine imagination, he would keep in contact with the actual, but would dissever from its representation any features which were accidental, temporary, contingent, and irregular, retaining only what disclosed its permanent nature and its essential relations to the universe.

This attitude explains why Coleridge disagreed with some of the theories that Wordsworth had advanced in the preface to the *Lyrical Ballads.* He protested that, however laudable was Wordsworth's desire to delineate rustic character faithfully, it was not necessarily best to confine oneself to the vocabulary of the rustics. The best part of language, the most expressive of human nature, originated *within* the mind and was not natural to the uneducated. When Wordsworth was at his best, as in *Michael,* he chose characters that had in a considerable degree a sound and religious education, and the diction he then employed was far above what might be called in any usual sense of the terms, "low or rustic." Those poems which actually kept to the primitive or vulgar were of little value. To profit by contact with nature there was necessary either extraordinary sensibility, or education, or both.

Imagination in its primary degree, Coleridge said, is active in that ordinary perception by which the outer world enters our consciousness. In its higher degree, "it dissolves, diffuses, dissipates, in order to *recreate;* . . . it struggles to idealize [i.e., to discern the underlying idea] and to unify; it is essentially *vital,* even as all objects (*as* objects) are essentially fixed and dead" (*Biog. Lit.,* xiii). This fusion by the imagination of the knower with the knowable object is the highest psychological experience of man; it creates all true art and literature. By imagination the senses are raised to their full powers; when Milton rightly termed poetry more "sensuous" than rhetoric he meant sense-experience that was imaginatively realized. By imagination man had his deepest insights into reality; by it he saw in the universe the moral and spiritual principles, and in Nature its symbolisms. Literature and art used their own special forms of expression which were not paraphrasable in unimaginative prose; but their style was a necessary means, not an end in itself; it was requisite for the peculiar kinds of truths they alone could communicate. Imaginative literature and art are the highest revelation of those qualities of the universe which civilized man values most.

To Coleridge that literature was the greatest which was most revelatory of the infinite within the finite. The noblest prose work was the Bible, which, though not verbally inspired, was at its best the sublimest revelation of spiritual truths. The most fruitful and most celebrated application of his critical principles, however, is found in his lectures on Shakspeare. His Shakspearian criticism has, to be sure, its limitations. He knew or cared little about the actual conditions of the theatre and drama in Shakspeare's day, and he cared still less about the accuracy of the Shakspearian texts; hence he occasionally misunderstood or misinterpreted passages. Nevertheless the general value of his criticisms can hardly be exaggerated. To this day it remains true that no one can fully appreciate the essence of Shakspeare who has not read the lectures of Coleridge upon him.

Coleridge accepted and heightened that new valuation of Shakspeare as the supreme poet which pre-romantic critics had introduced, but he broke away from the pre-romantic attempt to account for that superiority on the ground that Shakspeare was a child of nature, happily ignorant of rules of art, inspired with original genius, and achieving perfection without premeditation. To Coleridge Shakspeare was consciously and purposively a poet. His art was not the extemporaneous outpouring of instinct, but the deliberate employment of the technical means which were the most appropriate for the expression of his thoughts and feelings. Those thoughts and feelings were too complex to embody in dramas having a mechanical simplicity of form; hence he gave to them not a chaotic and capricious freedom (as some neo-classicists supposed), but a unity which was subtly organic.

The test of greatness which Coleridge chose to apply to Shakspeare and other authors was derived from his growing sense that life, with its interplay of matter, mind, and spirit, was not as simple as ordinarily represented, and yet was not utterly puzzling. Hence he asked: what proportion of the marvelous wealth and complexity of universal experience has this poet succeeded in controlling, in harmonizing? By this criterion, Shakspeare had no equal among poets. His reach was gigantic, but so was his grasp. Indeed, though he did not cast his thoughts into a philosophic system, he comprehended so much that the system-makers ignored, that he was not only the sovereign among poets but also the sage among philosophers. His wisdom was especially shown in the living truth of his characters, which were more real than most actual persons, and in his attitude toward them. Coleridge delighted to recognize in Shakspeare one of his own favorite principles, that of the need of reconciling opposites; and never was he more brilliant than when he traced the weaknesses of Hamlet and other tragic heroes to the fatal predominance in them of some one passion. By discussing such characters as if they had been created by Wisdom itself, as if every word and deed of theirs were profoundly significant, he bestowed upon them a new glory and a new lease upon immortality. Extraordinarily illuminating was his response to the subtler emanations from Shakspeare's poetry, and to such moral delicacy as is discernible in some of Shakspeare's portraiture of women; in those respects, many learned Shakspearian critics of today fall far short of his percipience.

The sources of Coleridge's philosophical and literary principles were very numerous. His indebtednesses for particular passages to various authors are difficult to ascertain. English writers of the seventeenth and eighteenth centuries, especially the Cambridge Platonists and William Law, gave him many of his basic critical views; but as he reconsidered them in relation to the literary movements of his own times he found much that was congenial to his own tastes and reflections in such German writers as Herder, Kant, Schiller, Jean Paul Richter, August Wilhelm Schlegel, Schelling, and Jacobi. But on important points he differed from each of them. In his lectures he often introduced passages which he had translated from the German philosophers and critics without properly acknowledging that they were not his own; but the fact that these were not original does not of course impair their intrinsic value. In his less formal criticisms—for example, in the too much neglected comments in his *Anima Poetae*—his originality is unclouded and his astuteness remarkable.

His Relation to Other Romantics.—If English literary life had been as addicted as French to the formation of literary schools, organizing themselves, concocting catchwords, issuing concerted proclamations, engaging in public demonstrations against *l'infame,* etc., there is little doubt that Coleridge would have been the recognized leader of the Romantics, for he comprehended what was common in their individual views more philosophically than anyone else, and he was the peer of any of them in the quality of his poetical work. His most important influence was upon Wordsworth; as Garrod says, in a facetious half-truth, "perhaps Coleridge's greatest work is Wordsworth,—and, like all his other work, Coleridge left it unfinished."

Late in his life, he became acquainted with Blake, and they are said to have talked together "like congenial beings of another sphere," which is credible in view of the resemblances in theme, spirit, and form, of some of their poems; though they would have differed sharply on theology and aesthetics.—As a poet, Coleridge influenced Scott in *The Lay of the Last Minstrel,* and Keats and Shelley repeatedly. As a critic, especially of Shakspeare, his work is the keystone of the interpretations of Lamb, Hazlitt, Leigh Hunt, De Quincey, and Carlyle; but Hazlitt insisted that he was a more realistic critic than his master. In social and political attitudes, he strongly influenced the young Carlyle and John Stuart Mill. As a philosopher, he was an exceptionally stimulating influence, even upon those who could not understand or would not accept his system. The present progress of knowledge concerning his work makes it seem likely that his position in the Romantic Movement will in the future appear even more nearly central than it does now.

SELECTED BIBLIOGRAPHY

OF FIRST IMPORTANCE

Selections

Garrod, H. W., ed.; *Coleridge: Poetry and Prose* (Oxford), 1925.
With essays by Hazlitt, Jeffrey, De Quincey, Carlyle, etc.

Potter, Stephen, ed.; *Coleridge: Select Poetry and Prose* (Nonesuch), 1933.

Griggs, E. L., ed.; *The Best of Coleridge* (Ronald), 1934.

Texts

Poetical Works, ed. James D. Campbell (Macmillan), 1893.—Nearly complete, and satisfactory for ordinary purposes, especially because of the superior value of its biographical introduction and notes.

Complete Poetical Works, ed. Ernest H. Coleridge, 2 vols. (Oxford), 1912.—Textually the best, with variant readings, etc. Of this there is a one-volume edition, with some omissions; but to this latter the Campbell edition seems preferable for the reason stated above.

Biographia Literaria, ed. John Shawcross, 2 vols. (Oxford), 1907.—The best edition.—An inexpensive ed. in Modern Readers' Series (Macmillan).

The nearest approaches to *complete editions* of both the poetry and the prose are:
ed. William G. T. Shedd, 7 vols., 1853, 1884.
ed. Thomas Ashe, 8 vols. (Bohn's Libr.), 1865, 1884–85.

The Best Biography

On the period to June, 1800, Lawrence Hanson's *Life of S. T. Coleridge: The Early Years,* 1938. If and when it is completed it will probably be the standard Life. It is more percipient and judicious than E. K. Chambers' *S. T. Coleridge: A Biographical Study,* 1938, which is factually thorough, but preferable only because it covers Coleridge's whole career (has been justly called "Coleridge, with the Coleridge that matters left out"). The best comparison of Hanson and Chambers is Thorpe's, in *College English,* May, 1940; see also TLS, Jan. 7, 1939.

The Best Introductory Critical Discussions

Hazlitt, William; *On the Living Poets*, 1818; *My First Acquaintance with Poets*, 1823 (*Anth.*, 395) ; and *Mr. Coleridge*, 1825. — In Hazlitt's *Works*, v, xii, and iv.

Pater, Walter; "Coleridge," in *Appreciations*, 1889.

Watts-Dunton, W. T.; "The Renascence of Wonder," in *Chambers's Cyclopædia of English Literature*, iii, 1–10 (1903) .

Gingerich, S. F.; "Coleridge," in *Essays in the Romantic Poets*, 1924. — Good elementary introduction to his ideas.

Lowes, John Livingston; *The Road to Xanadu: A Study in the Ways of the Imagination*, 1927; enlarged, 1930. — Primarily on the sources and the composition of *The Ancient Mariner* and *Kubla Khan*, but passes far beyond those topics and reaches conclusions of wide importance on the subject indicated in the subtitle. The elaborate Index has general usefulness.

Richards, I. A.; *Coleridge on Imagination*, 1934. — Asserts that his terms must be re-examined, and their meaning clarified. Like most New Critics, implies that Coleridge emphasizes synthesis too much, and that the discordant is the real. — For rebuttals of Richards, see D. J. James, *Scepticism and Poetry*, 1937; and Stephen Potter, Appendix of *Coleridge and S. T. C.*, 1935.

FOR ADVANCED STUDENTS

Important Additional Texts

The original form of *Dejection: An Ode*, ed. Ernest De Selincourt, Engl. Asso. *Essays and Studies*, 1937. — Addressed to Sara Hutchinson.

Christabel, ed. E. H. Coleridge, 1907. "His great edition" (J. L. Lowes) . — Illustrated by a facsimile.

The Political Thought of Coleridge: A Selection, ed. R. J. White, 1938. — Rev. TLS, July 9, 1938.

Anima Poetae, ed. E. H. Coleridge, 1895.

Logic, etc., in *Coleridge on Logic and Learning*, 1929, and *Coleridge's Treatise on Method*, 1934, ed. Alice D. Snyder.

Shakespearian Criticism, ed. T. M. Raysor, 2 vols., 1930. — Vol. i from the MSS.

Miscellaneous Criticism, ed. T. M. Raysor, 1936.

Philosophical Lectures: 1818–1819, ed. Kathleen Coburn, 1948.

Four early *Reviews*, previously unidentified, in Garland Greever, *A Wiltshire Parson: W. L. Bowles*, 1926.

Coleridge's *Marginalia* (on Kant, Schelling, Schiller, Bruno, Descartes, Milton, Shakspeare, etc.) , more important in his case than in that of most authors, are dispersed in publications too numerous to be recorded here. They are discussed by J. L. Haney, "The Marginalia," *Schelling Anniversary Papers*, 1923, and "Coleridge the Commentator," in Blunden and Griggs, *Coleridge Studies*, 1934; by Alice D. Snyder, "Coleridgeana," RES, iv, 432 (1928) , and by Henri Nidecker, "Notes Marginales," RCL, vii–xiii (1927–33) . Cf. also Kathleen Coburn, "Unpublished Coleridge Notebooks." *Victoria Libr. Bulletin* (Toronto) , March, 1938.

Letters

Letters of Coleridge, ed. E. H. Coleridge, 2 vols., 1895.

Unpublished Letters of Coleridge, ed. E. L. Griggs, 2 vols., 1932. — The editor is preparing an edition of the complete correspondence (TLS, July 19, 1947) .

Biographical

For biographical information and interpretation (besides Hanson, Chambers, Campbell, and Hazlitt, above) consult:

Minnow Among Tritons: Mrs. S. T. Coleridge's Letters to Thomas Poole, ed. Stephen Potter, 1934. — His wife's revelatory letters.

Cottle, Joseph; *Early Recollections,* 2 vols., 1837–39; enlarged as *Reminiscences,* 1847.

Sandford, M. E. (Mrs. Henry); *Thomas Poole and His Friends,* 2 vols., 1888. — One of his early friends and benefactors.

Gillman, James; *Life of Coleridge,* 1838. — By his physician. Cf. Lucy E. Gillman Watson, *Coleridge at Highgate,* 1925. On Gillman's limitations, see B. R. McElderry, Jr., PMLA, LII, 412; 1937.

Knight, W. A.; *Coleridge and Wordsworth in the West Country. Their Friendship, Work, and Surroundings,* 1913.

Kaufman, Paul; "The Reading of Southey and Coleridge," MP, XXI, 317 (1924). — Their borrowings from the Bristol Library, 1793–98. Cf. Alice D. Snyder on borrowings at Göttingen in 1799, MP, XXV, 377; 1928.

Raysor, T. M.; "Coleridge and 'Asra,'" SP, XXVI, 305 (1929). — The first clear and documented account of his love for Sara Hutchinson. Cf., above, De Selincourt's ed. of *Dejection.*

Griggs, E. L.; *Hartley Coleridge,* 1929. —Revelatory on Coleridge as a father. Cf. H. W. Hartman, *Hartley Coleridge,* 1931.

Rea, J. D.; "Coleridge's Health," MLN, XLV, 12; 1930. — First gathering of reliable information on the chronic sepsis which, rather than the use of opium, was a chief cause of his "Misdoings and Not-Doings."

Maclean, Catherine M.; *Dorothy Wordsworth,* 1932. — Sensitive account of the personal relationship to the Wordsworths.

Blunden, Edmund, and Griggs, E. L.; *Coleridge: Studies by Several Hands on the Hundredth Anniversary of His Death,* 1934. — Especially for (a) the fragment of E. H. Coleridge's unfinished *Life;* (b) Eaglestone's story of the spy episode of 1797, and (c) the letter from Sara Coleridge on his death.

Chambers, E. K.; "Some Dates in Coleridge's 'Annus Mirabilis,'" *Engl. Asso. Essays,* XIX; 1934.

Potter, Stephen; *Coleridge and S. T. C.,* 1935. — Overstresses the distinction between the true self and the feebler one.

Coleridge, G. H. B.; "Coleridge Discovers the Lake Country," in E. L. Griggs, ed., *Wordsworth and Coleridge,* 1939.

Armour, R. W., and Howes, R. F.; *Coleridge the Talker,* 1940. — The thesis: "The talker is the essential Coleridge, of whom [the other Coleridges] are somewhat distorted reflections." Collects the contemporary accounts of his conversation.

Griggs, E. L.; *Coleridge Fille,* 1940. — Family relationships during his last years.

Pope-Hennessy, Una; *Durham Company,* 1941. — For the Sara Hutchinson affair and the Wordsworths.

Schneider, Elisabeth; "The 'Dream' of Kubla Khan," PMLA, LX, 784; 1945. — Important clarification of how opium could, and could not, affect his work. — Cf. J. L. Lowes, *Road to Xanadu* (2nd ed., 1930); M. H. Abrams, *The Milk of Paradise* (1934); R. C. Bald in *Nineteenth Century Studies* (Cornell, 1940), and Lydia E. Wagner, "Coleridge's Use of Laudanum and Opium," *Psychoanalytic Review,* XXV, 309 (1938); also Rea, "Health," above, 1930.

Elwin, Malcolm; *The First Romantics*, 1947.—Ardent defense of Coleridge's conduct, ideas, politics, etc.; the abandonment of Pantisocracy, Southey's fault. But see TLS, Dec. 13, 1947.

The German Influence

The best introductory account is J. W. Beach's "Coleridge's Borrowings from the German," ELH, IX, 36 (1942), an exposure of his plagiarisms, which corrects A. C. Dunstan's lenient treatment in MLR, XVII, 272 (1922) and XVIII, 183 (1923).—The problem was first attacked in Alois Brandl's still valuable biography *S. T. Coleridge und die Englische Romantik*, 1886; tr. by Lady Eastlake, 1887.—A neglected early study is Anna T. Helmholtz (-Phelan)'s *The Indebtedness of Coleridge to A. W. von Schlegel* (Univ. of Wisc.), 1907.—Other noteworthy discussions (besides the Nidecker and the Snyder studies of marginalia) are the following:

Shawcross, John; Introduction and Notes to his ed. of *Biographia Literaria*, 1907.

Bradley, A. C.; "English Poetry and German Philosophy in the Age of Wordsworth," Manchester Univ. Press, 1909; rptd. in *A Miscellany*, 1929.

Morley, Edith J.; "Coleridge in Germany: 1799," 1931; rptd. in E. L. Griggs, ed., *Wordsworth and Coleridge*, 1939.

Zeydel, Edwin H.; *Tieck and England*, 1931.

Willoughby, L. A.; "Coleridge und Deutschland," GRM, XXIV, 112; 1936.

Bonjour, Adrien; *Coleridge's "Hymn Before Sunrise,"* Lausanne, 1942.

Philosophy, Political Theory, and Religion

For introductory purposes, use, among the works listed below, (a) for philosophy, Howard (1924), Snyder (1918), and especially Muirhead (1930); for political theory, TLS (1938); and for religion, Sanders (1942).—The items of earlier date than 1918 are primarily of historical interest.

Porter, Noah; "Coleridge and His American Disciples," *Bibliotheca Sacra*, IV, 117; 1847.—Cf. O. B. Frothingham, *Transcendentalism in New England* (Amer. Unitarian Asso.), 1886; and John Dewey, "James Marsh and American Philosophy," JHI, II, 131 (1941), first delivered in 1929, centenary of introduction of *Aids to Reflection* in Vermont.

Maurice, J. F. D.; *Moral and Metaphysical Philosophy* (originally an article in *Encyclopaedia Metropolitana*, 1848), 4 vols., 1850–57.—Maurice was important in the Broad Church movement.

Green, Joseph Henry; *Spiritual Philosophy, Founded on the Teaching of the Late S. T. Coleridge*, 2 vols., 1865.—Another attempt at systematization by a disciple who was Coleridge's literary executor.

Snyder, Alice D.; *The Critical Principle of the Reconciliation of Opposites as Employed by Coleridge* (Univ. of Michigan), 1918.—The first scholarly modern study in this field.

Stewart, H. L.; "The Place of Coleridge in English Theology," *Harvard Theological Review*, XI, 1; 1918.

Wilde, Norman; "The Development of Coleridge's Thought," *Philosophical Review*, XXVIII, 147; 1919.

Howard, Claud; *Coleridge's Idealism, a Study of Its Relationship to Kant and to the Cambridge Platonists*, 1924.

Potter, George R.; "Coleridge and the Idea of Evolution," PMLA, XI, 370; 1925.—Coleridge not a supporter of the idea in its strictly scientific modern form.—Cf. Joseph Needham, "Coleridge as a Philosophical Biologist," *Science Progress*, XX, 692; 1926.

Cobban, Alfred; *Edmund Burke and the Revolt against the Eighteenth Century: A Study of the Political and Social Thinking of Burke, Wordsworth, Coleridge, and Southey*, 1929.

Muirhead, John H.; *Coleridge as Philosopher*, 1930. — Most important study of his thought as a system, and in its influence on English idealism. Praised by A. D. Snyder, MLN, xlvi, 264; 1931. — Cf. Muirhead, "Metaphysician or Mystic?" in Edmund Blunden and E. L. Griggs, *Coleridge Studies*, 1934; the review in TLS Aug. 9, 1934; and Muirhead's comment, Aug. 23 (on the Logos) . — Elizabeth Winkelmann, *Coleridge und die Kantische Philosophie (Palaestra*, 184) , 1933, supports Muirhead's conclusions; stresses Cambridge Platonists, and, among Germans, Jacobi.

Wellek, René; *Immanuel Kant in England*, 1931. — More critical of Coleridge's acumen than Muirhead; holds he preserved mainly the negative part of Kant, as "prophet of the end and failure of Reason."

Wünsche, W.; *Die Staatsauffassung Coleridges (Palaestra*, 190) , 1934. — His doctrine that religious, moral, and social progress is more important than the political framework. — Cf. Harold Beeley, "The Political Thought," in Blunden and Griggs, *Coleridge Studies*, 1934, on the "national clerisy"; and the good general survey, "Coleridge on Politics," TLS, July 9, 1938.

Milley, H. J. W.; "Coleridge's 'Aeolian Harp,' " MP, xxxvi, 359; 1939. — His first good poem; before he knew Wordsworth.

McKenzie, Gordon; *Organic Unity in Coleridge* (Univ. of Cal.) , 1939. — On the alleged conflict between the principles of organic unity and reconciliation of opposites. Cf. Snyder, MLN, lv, 227; 1940.

Morgan, Roberta; "The Philosophic Basis of Coleridge's Hamlet Criticism," ELH, vi, 256; 1939.

Lovejoy, A. O.; "Coleridge and Kant's Two Worlds," ELH, vii, 341; 1940. — Skeptical analysis, by a philosophical realist, of Coleridge's beliefs about freedom and moral responsibility. Involves the problem of "Dejection."

Snyder, Alice D.; "Coleridge and the Encyclopedists," MP, xxxviii, 173; 1940. — His plan for the *Encyclopaedia Metropolitana*.

Gordon, I. A.; "The Case-History of the Monody on Chatterton," RES, xviii, 49; 1942. — Important on his early style.

Sanders, Charles R.; *Coleridge and the Broad Church Movement*, 1942. — His leadership in the effort to reconcile Christianity with modern scientific and philosophical ideas. Cf. C. F. Harrold's review, JEGP, Jan., 1944. — See also Sanders, "Coleridge as a Champion of Liberty," SP, xxxii, 618; 1935.

Davis, H. Francis; "Was Newman a Disciple of Coleridge?" DR, Oct., 1945. — A yes-and-no answer.

Fairchild, H. N.; "Hartley, Pistorius, and Coleridge," PMLA, lxii, 1010; 1947. — Corrects Muirhead on Hartley. In 1797 Coleridge found Hartley more religious, and mysticism more "rational," than later.

On Aesthetics, Imagination, and Literary Criticism

Shawcross, John; Introduction to *Biographia Literaria*, 1907.

Eliot, T. S.; *The Use of Poetry and Criticism*, 1933. — Wordsworth's Preface, youthful; Coleridge's Biographia, mature.

Richards, I. A.; *Coleridge on Imagination*, 1934. — See above, under "Of First Importance."

Isaacs, J.; "Coleridge's Critical Terminology," Engl. Asso. *Essays and Studies*, xxi, 86; 1936.

Sherwood, Margaret; *Coleridge's Imaginative Conception of Imagination*, Wellesley Coll. Press, 1937. — Chief passages, with comments; Plotinus stressed.

Raysor, T. M.; "Coleridge's Criticism of Wordsworth," PMLA, LIV, 496; 1939.

Thorpe, C. D.;
"Some Notices of 'Empathy' Before Lipps," *Papers of Mich. Acad.*, XXIII, 525; 1937.
"The Imagination: Coleridge vs. Wordsworth," PQ, XVIII, 1; 1939. — On the "nicer distinctions" that Coleridge makes.
"Coleridge on the Sublime," in E. L. Griggs, ed., *Wordsworth and Coleridge*, 1939. — The sense of infinity; related to Christian tradition.
"Coleridge as Aesthetician and Critic," JHI, V, 387; 1944. — Important defense against the New Critics.

Stallknecht, N. P.; *Strange Seas of Thought*, 1945. — See the Index, and Appendix on "Imagination in *Biographia Literaria*."

Willey, Basil; *Coleridge on Imagination and Fancy* (Warton Lecture, Brit. Acad.), 1946.

Bate, W. J.; *From Classic to Romantic*, 1946. — See Bibliography of Pre-Romantic Movement, above.

Creed, H. H.; "Coleridge on Taste," ELH, XIII, 143; 1946. — The relation of just taste to moral consciousness and religious feeling.

Kennedy, Wilma L.; *The English Heritage of Coleridge of Bristol, 1798: The Basis in Eighteenth-Century English Thought for His Distinction Between Imagination and Fancy*, 1947. — Anticipations in Berkeley, Reynolds, and Blake; English influences more important than Kant's.

Shapiro, Karl; "English Prosody and Modern Poetry," ELH, XIV, 77; 1947. — Relation of the metre of *Christabel* to G. M. Hopkins' sprung rhythm.

General

Brandes, Georg; "Naturalistic Romanticism," *Main Currents of Nineteenth Century Literature*, IV; 1880. — Illustrates the unfavorable attitude of the materialistic school.

Stephen, Leslie; *Hours in a Library*, IV; 1879. — Unfavorable. Emphasizes bad effects of opium.

Swinburne, Algernon; *Essays and Studies*, 1875. — Like Lowell (below) and most of the early admirers, values the poetry for its aesthetic and dreamlike qualities only.

Lowell, J. R.; "Coleridge: Address on Unveiling the Bust at Westminster Abbey," *Democracy and Other Addresses*, 1887.

Pater, Walter; *Appreciations*, 1889. — Admirable for its sensibility.

Robertson, John M.; *New Essays Towards a Critical Method*, 1897. — Perhaps the nadir of Coleridge criticism, and thus of historical interest. Interprets his poems as opium-dreams, his character as pitiable, and his philosophy as valueless.

Cooper, Lane; "The Power of the Eye in Coleridge," *J. M. Hart Studies in Language and Literature*, 1910. — His interest in superstitions such as the Evil Eye.

Stork, C. W.; "The Influence of the Popular Ballad on Wordsworth and Coleridge," PMLA, XXIX, 299; 1914.

Graham, Walter; "Contemporary Critics of Coleridge," PMLA, XXXVIII, 278; 1923.

Harper, G. M.; "Coleridge's Conversation Poems," *Quart. Rev.*, CCXLIV, 284; 1925. — On *Æolian Harp, Lime Tree Bower, Dejection*, etc.

Fausset, H. I'A.; *Coleridge, 1926.* — Well written, but dwells on weaknesses rather than achievement, and interprets his poetry, philosophy, and religion as escapes from reality. See TLS, June 17, 1926.

Shafer, Robert; "Coleridge," *Christianity and Naturalism,* 1926. — Illustrates the attitude of the humanistic school.

Thompson, F. T.; "Emerson's Indebtedness to Coleridge," SP, xxiii, 55; 1926.

Babbitt, Irving; "Coleridge and Imagination," *On Being Creative,* 1932. — "The imagination displayed in *The Ancient Mariner* is qualitatively different from that displayed in poetry that may be rightly regarded as serious."

Raysor, T. M.; Introduction and Notes to *Coleridge's Shakespearian Criticism,* 1930. — See review, TLS, June 11, 1931.

Strout, A. L.; "Coleridge and John Wilson," PMLA, xlviii, 100; 1933. — Wilson's criticism of *Biographia Literaria.*

Bodkin, Maud; *Archetypal Patterns in Poetry,* 1934. — Jung's psychology applied to *Ancient Mariner, Kubla Khan,* etc.

"Coleridge Is Dead," TLS, July 19, 1934. — Admirable general estimate: Coleridge's great influence on religion and philosophy, and even greater importance as a poet.

Willoughby, L. A.; "Coleridge as a Philologist," MLR, xxxi, 176; 1936.

Bewley, E. M.; "Revaluations: The Poetry of Coleridge," *Scrutiny,* viii, 406; 1940. — Hostile. — "Dejection" considered most important.

Tate, Allen; *Reason in Madness,* 1941. — Attacks him (pp. 45–51) as responsible for most bad modern criticism. See Alice D. Snyder, ELH, ix, 11; 1942.

Bonjour, Adrien; *Coleridge's "Hymn Before Sunrise,"* Lausanne, 1942. — Proves it an unacknowledged adaptation of a German poem. Over 200 pages on an 85-line poem! See R. C. Bald's review, JEGP, xliii, 135; 1944.

The Ancient Mariner

The great commentary is Lowes's *Road to Xanadu* (2nd ed., 1930) ; see under "Of First Importance."

Coleridge, E. H; "The Genesis of 'The Ancient Mariner,'" *Poetry Review,* ii, 11–15, and ix, 271–277; 1913 and 1918.

McElderry, B. R.; "Coleridge's Revision of *The Ancient Mariner,*" SP, xxix, 68; 1932. — Good on the reasons for the changes.

Nitchie, Elizabeth; "The Moral of *The Ancient Mariner* Reconsidered," PMLA, xlviii. 867; 1933.

Beyer, W. W.; "Coleridge, Wieland's *Oberon,* and *The Ancient Mariner,*" RES, xv, 401; 1939.

Bald, R. C.; "Coleridge and *The Ancient Mariner:* Addenda to *The Road to Xanadu,*" in *Nineteenth-Century Studies* (Cornell) , 1940. — Corrects some of Lowes's opinions, on the basis of the Coleridge Notebooks.

Burke, Kenneth; *The Philosophy of Literary Form,* 1941. — Interprets the poem as "a lurid personal confession" (cf. Stoll, below) .

Boas, Louise S.; EXP, May, 1944. — The "sin of isolationism."

Stallknecht, N. P.; "The Moral of *The Ancient Mariner,*" *Strange Seas of Thought,* 1945. — "The creative imagination engendering the love of Nature and of Man."

Warren, Robert Penn; Introduction to ed. of *The Ancient Mariner,* 1946. — (Illustrations childish and in bad taste) . Interpretation of main theme not as new as apparently supposed. Much elaborate arbitrary reading of meanings into the poem (cf. Stoll; below). "A chimerical interpretation" (Elder Olson, MP, XLV, 275; 1948).

Whalley, George; "The Mariner and the Albatross," UTQ, XVI, 381; 1947. — Attempt to relate the poem to his personality, his "sense of doom"; the albatross is the creative imagination.

Stoll, E. E.; "Symbolism in Coleridge," PMLA, LXIII, 214; 1948. — Corrects some of the extravagant misinterpretations by the New Critics.

Christabel

Snell, Ada L. F.; "The Meter of Christabel," *F. N. Scott Anniversary Papers* (Univ. of Chicago), 1929. — "Not irregular." — Cf. Karl Shapiro, "English Prosody and Modern Poetry," ELH, XIV, 77; 1947.

McElderry, B. R.; "Coleridge's Plan for Completing *Christabel*," SP, XXXIII, 437; 1936.

Tuttle, D. R.; "*Christabel* Sources in Percy's *Reliques* and the Gothic Romance," PMLA, LIII, 445; 1938.

Nethercot, A. H.; *The Road to Tryermaine*, 1939. — The most detailed study of the sources and composition. — Cf. Roy P. Basler, "Christabel," SR, LI, 73; 1943, which supplements Nethercot by emphasizing that the psycho-emotional theme is love and preternatural enchantment, artfully using medieval traditions.

Starr, N. C.; "Coleridge's 'Sir Leoline,' " PMLA, LXI, 157; 1946.

Kubla Khan

Chambers, E. K.; "The Date of Kubla Khan," RES, XI, 78; 1935.

Snyder, Alice D.; "The Manuscript of *Kubla Khan*," TLS, Aug. 2, 1934.

Meyerstein, E. H. W.; "Chatterton, Coleridge, and Bristol," TLS, Aug. 21, 1937; cf. Wylie Sypher, Aug. 28, and Meyerstein, Oct. 30, Dec. 4, Dec. 18, 1937. — See Wylie Sypher, "Coleridge's Somerset; A Byway to Xanadu," PQ, XVIII, 353; 1939.

[Morgan, Charles]; "Menander's Mirror: The Pork Butcher's Story," TLS, Dec. 16, 1944. — On the quality of the imagination.

Schneider, Elisabeth; "The 'Dream' of Kubla Khan," PMLA, LX, 784; 1945. — Correcting Lowes, presents strong reasons for doubting the assertion that the poem was wholly an automatic dream-composition.

Grigson, Geoffrey, et al.; correspondence about possible indebtedness to contemporary romantic landscapes, TLS, June 21 and Aug. 16, 1947.

Dejection: An Ode

De Selincourt, Ernest; in Engl. Asso., *Essays and Studies*, 1936; rptd. in *Wordsworthian and Other Studies*, 1947. — Gives the earlier version, and an authoritative account of the circumstances.

Smith, Fred. M.; "The Relation of the 'Ode on Dejection' to Wordsworth's 'Ode on Intimations of Immortality,' " PMLA, I, 224; 1935.

Stallknecht, N. P.; *Strange Seas of Thought*, 1945; pp. 159–171. — The relation to The Ancient Mariner theme.

Biographia Literaria

Murry, J. Middleton; "Coleridge's Criticism," *Aspects of Literature*, 1920. — Condemns its verbosity; praises the sections on Wordsworth.

Shawcross, John; Introduction and Notes to ed. of *Biographia*, 1907.

Brede, Alexander; *Theories of Poetic Diction* (Papers of the Mich. Acad., xiv, 537) , 1931.

Stallknecht, N. P.; "Imagination in *Biographia Literaria*," *Strange Seas of Thought,* 1945.

Lectures on Shakspeare

Raysor, T. M.; Introduction and Notes, *Coleridge's Shakespearian Criticism,* 1930.

Morgan, Roberta; "The Philosophic Basis of Coleridge's *Hamlet* Criticism," ELH, vi, 256; 1939.

Hudson, Arthur P.; "Romantic Apologiae for Hamlet's Treatment of Ophelia," EHL, ix, 59; 1942. — Coleridge's understanding of the paradoxical logic of passion.

Creed, H. H.; "Coleridge on Taste," ELH, xiii, 143; 1946. — Imagination, which discerns spiritual power, at its highest in Shakspeare.

Bibliographies

Boas, F. S., et al.; *Short Bibliographies of Wordsworth, Coleridge, Byron, Shelley, Keats* (Engl. Asso. Leaflet No. 23) , 1912. — Useful comments.

Haney, J. L.; *A Bibliography of S. T. Coleridge,* 1903.

Kennedy, Virginia M., and Barton, Mary N.; *S. T. Coleridge: A Selected Bibliography,* 1935. — Covers editions and criticisms; good comments.

Raysor, T. M.; "Coleridge," in *Cambr. Bibl. of Engl. Lit.,* iii, 172; 1941.

British Museum; *Excerpt from the General Catalogue: Coleridge,* 1947.

Concordance

Logan, (Sister) Eugenia; *A Concordance to the Poetry of S. T. Coleridge,* 1940. — Praised by Alice D. Snyder, ELH, viii, 12; 1941.

CHAPTER 5

WILLIAM WORDSWORTH

(April 7, 1770–April 23, 1850)

His Early Life.—During most of his life, Wordsworth dwelt in that part of northwestern England called the Lake District, a sparsely settled region of beautiful hills, lakes, and streams, then rarely visited by travelers. He was born in the small town of Cockermouth, situated on the river Derwent. His father was a lawyer in the service of the Earl of Lonsdale. He had three brothers and a sister, Dorothy, who was one year younger than himself. The death of his mother when he was eight years old scattered the family, William being sent to a school at Hawkshead, about fifteen miles south of his birthplace, and not far from the center of the Lake District.

By native disposition (and perhaps because of a strain of Yorkshire blood in his ancestry) William was a lad of unusual independence, with a stiff, moody, and violent temper; and it was fortunate that he was reared in Hawkshead School, the masters of which were exceptionally kind and wise in their treatment of headstrong adolescence. Fortunate, too, it was that the tone of the school was free from snobbishness, his fellow pupils being sons of businessmen, professional men, or proprietors of farms— substantial and self-respecting folk, but friendly and democratic in spirit. William, often in companionship with his schoolmates, took keen delight in vigorous country sports and pastimes. At times, however, and in solitude, he felt with quite unusual, not to say abnormal, intensity the effect upon his soul of the grandeur and mystery of nature.

He was allowed by the headmaster, William Taylor (affectionately immortalized in the Matthew poems; *Anth.*, 189), much freedom in the choice of his reading. Adventurous and emotional, he found special delight in narratives of warfare and in romances of love; but he also read, before leaving school, more realistic masterpieces by Cervantes, Fielding, Le Sage, and Swift.

Wordsworth entered St. John's College, Cambridge, at the age of seventeen, and was graduated four years later, in 1791. He was not quite as happy here as at Hawkshead, finding no one to give him the guidance he needed, and disliking the curriculum, the methods of examination, and the compulsory attendance upon chapel. During a vacation, while at Hawkshead, he experienced a decisive moment. He was on his way homeward after a dance which had lasted all night. As the sun rose in all the sweetness of dawn, the lovely sights and sounds of the countryside seemed to him to reproach the noisy gaudiness and empty prattle upon which he had been wasting his time—he who felt within him the power to serve higher purposes. He never forgot that moment of illumination, that pang of conscience. At the time he made no vow; but he felt that somehow an assurance had been given

> that [he] should be, else sinning greatly,
> A dedicated Spirit.—*Prelude;* IV, 336; *Anth.,* 253

Henceforth his life was consecrated to poetry.

When he was graduated from college, aged twenty-one, Wordsworth was a well-intentioned enthusiast, instinctively fond of nature without as yet comprehending her, religious, and devoted to ideals, especially to those cultivated by the School of Sensibility. His life had on the whole been pleasant, and he faced the future with the characteristically youthful confidence that his ideals would be smoothly and rapidly realized. Like scores of others of his age and type, he rejoiced in the outbreak of the French Revolution and expected the speedy reformation of the world. He had already begun to write verse, but none of any value. Before his soul was to be capable of genuine poetry, he had now to pass through agonizing trials.

His Period of Storm and Stress (1791—c. 1794–95).—The life of Wordsworth from his twenty-first to twenty-fifth year is difficult to perceive clearly, for, as is often the case in those years, it was the life of a disorganized and unstable personality, full of contradictions, and temporarily incapable of adjustment to its environment and problems. There was a sharp conflict between his altruistic enthusiasms and his financial means. His father had died when William was thirteen, and the estate which he left to his five children consisted of a claim of c. £4600 against the Earl of Lonsdale—a claim which was not settled until nineteen years later, in 1802. In his childhood and during the period with which we are now concerned, Wordsworth was therefore financially dependent upon relatives. They were generous enough in giving him unusually good educational opportunities; but, naturally, they expected him to enter in due course a remunerative occupation, and he could hardly rely upon them to continue giving him an allowance unless he seemed to be making progress toward self-support. To his "dedicated spirit," most professions and businesses seemed distasteful. In this predicament, and perhaps unconsciously influenced by his deep-rooted love of travel, he hit upon the plan of preparing himself for the occupation of a traveling tutor by sojourning in France and mastering the French language.

Wordsworth was in France during more than a year (30 Nov., 1791–Dec., 1792), mostly at Orleans and Blois. It was a time of intense political excitement, and he attached himself ardently to the Girondist party which seemed to him to represent the noblest revolutionary and republican ideals. One of its local leaders, Captain Michel Beaupuy, became his friend and his mentor in the doctrines of the Revolution. To Wordsworth's rebellious and aspiring temper, the old and established order of society seemed more and more a system of terror and evil; and he eagerly sought truth, liberty, and reform in radical doctrine and radical action.

In the midst of this intellectual excitement, he fell in love with Annette Vallon, a young Frenchwoman who was more than four years older than himself and who, pitying the English youth's difficulties with her native language, had volunteered to be his tutor. She was vivacious, kind-hearted, and emotional—just the type which the School of Sensibility had been encouraging. Soon Wordsworth was enraptured by her. It seemed to him that

> Arabian fiction never filled the world
> With half the wonders that were wrought for him . . .
> The house she dwelt in was a sainted shrine;
> Her chamber-window did surpass in glory
> The portals of the dawn; all Paradise
> Could, by the simple opening of a door,
> Let itself in upon him.
>
> *Vaudracour and Julia*

So great was his passion that it swept aside all considerations of foresight and prudence. For various reasons, including the political chaos of the times and Wordsworth's financial dependence, marriage was impossible; but nevertheless Annette yielded to her lover's importunities. In December, 1792, she gave birth to a daughter, whose paternity he acknowledged, and who was baptised as Anne Caroline Wordsworth. He intended to marry Annette as soon as his circumstances would permit, but now unforseen difficulties arose.

Wordsworth had returned to England in December, 1792, in order to persuade his guardians to continue his allowance, and in order to find a publisher for his first volumes of verse. He informed his sister Dorothy of his *liaison* with Annette; and both of them corresponded affectionately with her. Meanwhile the course of the French Revolution had grown more violent, and led to conflict with other nations. To Wordsworth's horror, Great Britain, in February, 1793, declared war against France. This meant that his letters to Annette, and hers to him, would be intercepted; and that if he tried to enter France, he would be in danger of arrest. There is evidence, not conclusive, that he may have taken this risk, and have been in Paris in October, 1793. By this time, however, his friends the Girondists, had been thrown out of power by extremists

and were in peril of their lives. If Wordsworth attempted to rejoin
Annette the attempt was frustrated, and he was forced to flee back to
England. The war kept them apart for nine years; and by the end of
that time their feelings had so changed that, although they met on
friendly terms, they no longer thought of reuniting their lives. This
separation was probably for the best for both Wordsworth and Annette; for fundamentally they were not suited to make each other
permanently happy. She was as typically French as he was English;
she loved the city and he the country; she had no interest in those poetical and meditative activities which were to become the absorbing aim of
his life; and she had become an ardent political intriguer for the Royalist
party, championing principles which even in his conservative old age he
regarded as wrong. The separation did not indicate on Wordsworth's
part callous neglect nor shamefaced concealment. He never kept the
matter a secret from those who had a moral right to know about it, and
during the rest of his life he did whatever his modest means permitted
for Annette and their daughter.

In the Victorian period, biographers ignored this episode, and thereby
misrepresented him as an anemic innocent who had never undergone
strong temptations nor fallen before them. In the 1930's amateur psycho-
analysts went to the opposite extreme, sensationalized the affair, and
misrepresented him as one who had vainly tried to suppress his wrongdoing and to evade his responsibilities, and thereby fatally impaired the
sincerity and the value of his poetry. Broad-minded judges have rejected
that opinion. Critics whose judgments are not narrowly secular recognize that for the poet to have passed through these phases of guilt,
repentance, and regeneration, was to have undergone a painful experience which for the rest of his life would give him a deeper sympathy
with, and insight into, our common human frailties, sufferings, and
means of transcending them. It remains nevertheless mysterious why
he did not allude to the Annette affair in *The Prelude,* and apparently
did not look upon it as one of the chief incidents that formed his mind
as a poet; but that is a psychological and aesthetic problem rather than
a moral one.

To return to 1793. In that year and the following, while he was still
tortured by the yearning, the anxiety, the disappointment, and the remorse aroused by his love affair, his political faith and hopes were pain-
fully agitated by the violent developments of the French Revolution.
He tried to remain loyal to it. In his volume of verse entitled *Descriptive
Sketches,* published in 1793, there are indications of his sympathy with
it; and he wrote (but did not publish) a *Letter to the Bishop of Llandaff,
by a Republican,* which indignantly defended it against Bishop Richard
Watson's attacks. Presently, however, the Reign of Terror and the imperialistic aggressions of the nation that purported to be devoted to
Liberty, Equality, and Fraternity, forced him to despair. To a mind like
his, this loss of hope in the immediate betterment of human society was
almost as painful as the loss of his beloved.

His agitated spirit now sought relief in something as opposite from his recent sentimental enthusiasms as possible. Feeling had betrayed him in both his personal and his political attachments, and in his despairing reaction the ultra-rationalistic philosophy of William Godwin and the anti-sentimental psychology of David Hartley seemed to him a solution of the problems of human life. Thus he says,

> I fared
> Dragging all passions, notions, shapes of faith,
> Like culprits to the bar; . . . demanding *proof,*
> And seeking it in everything, I lost
> All feeling of conviction, and, in fine,
> Sick, wearied out with contrarities,
> Yielded up moral questions in despair.
>
> *Prelude;* xi, 293

He became a necessitarian, disbelieving in free will, and hostile to the church and other institutions based upon orthodox ethics and psychology. Since this intellectual system was really out of harmony with his deeper self, he sank into perplexity and gloom.

The skies brightened for him toward the close of 1794 and the beginning of 1795. He went to live with his beloved sister Dorothy; and he was bequeathed a legacy of c. £900, which enabled them to establish a home in the country, first at Racedown in the southern part of England and two years later at Alfoxden in southwestern England. Little by little, Dorothy's sincere and unusually percipient delight in nature reawakened Wordsworth's own. Another potent influence soon followed—that of Coleridge, his friendship with whom began in the fall of 1795. During the next two or three years especially, their intercourse was profoundly beneficial. Each of them had been passing through devious personal, political, and literary experiences; and each helped the other to find himself. Probably Coleridge, with his metaphysical knowledge, was of the greatest assistance to Wordsworth in excogitating his way out of the Godwinian system. The Godwinian influence had begun about 1793; it was at its height in 1795–96. But even after it waned in 1797, so far as its rationalism and psychology were concerned, it left one permanent effect, viz., an intensification of Wordsworth's enthusiasm for the social betterment of mankind.

It was in *The Borderers* (written in 1795–96), a tragedy in verse, that Wordsworth showed his abandonment of the principles of Godwin—the plot being designed to illustrate the truth that nothing but evil and suffering can come from a rationalistic attempt to ignore or crush the natural feelings, affections, and sympathies. Commingled with that theme, one may perceive in the tragedy the effects of the author's grief over his forced desertion of Annette. Such effects are also apparent in the earlier tale in verse, *Guilt and Sorrow* (written in 1794); and indeed the theme of desertion recurs throughout his poems.

Biographically and historically interesting as are the poems of Wordsworth's period of storm and stress, they are not characteristic of the real and great Wordsworth, and they have next to no literary value. Modern materialists would like to think that Wordsworth was at his best when he was a Jacobin and a rationalist. Thus Bertrand Russell writes:

> In his youth he sympathized with the French Revolution, went to France, wrote good poetry, and had a natural daughter. At this time he was a "bad" man. Then he became "good," abandoned his daughter, adopted correct principles, and wrote bad poetry.[1]

That is the height of pert falsehood. In sober truth, it was during the time when he was what Mr. Russell ironically calls a "bad" man that Wordsworth wrote his feeblest verse—such as the *Descriptive Sketches,* the style of which was conventional and stilted. And it was in his last period, when he had become the "good" man that Mr. Russell sarcastically belittles, that he wrote the poetry which is characteristically Wordsworthian and supremely important. The great Wordsworth was he of 1797–98 to 1807 and beyond—the Wordsworth who had passed through, overcome, and left behind him the inner conflicts between extremes.

His Maturity.—In the fall of 1797, Wordsworth, Dorothy, and Coleridge, made a walking tour of several days which resulted in the composition of Coleridge's *Ancient Mariner* and ultimately in the publication of the *Lyrical Ballads.* (See Coleridge's and Wordsworth's own accounts; *Anth.,* 1095.)   In the same year, 1798, in which that epoch-making volume appeared, Hazlitt came to know Coleridge and Wordsworth (see his *First Acquaintance with Poets; Anth.,* 395). The winter of 1798–99 Wordsworth and Dorothy spent in Germany. Like so many Romantics, he was fascinated by the new intellectual and literary movements of that country; but the German influence upon his work was to be comparatively slight, hardly a trace of it being discernible in the poems written during his sojourn there. Upon returning to England, he and his sister settled in Dove Cottage, Grasmere, in the Lake District. He steadily resisted the temptation to enter upon a remunerative profession or business, although his means were narrow and although the sale of his poems was very small. His existence during the last fifty years of his long life was outwardly quiet, and withdrawn from the bustle of city life; but he loved to travel; and, on the too rare occasions when he could afford to, he made journeys to Scotland, Ireland, the Isle of Man, France, Switzerland, and Italy. Moreover, he maintained throughout his life his habit of taking walking tours into isolated and romantic regions—animated by a never failing delight in lonely mountain passes, cloud-topped eminences, forest glades, mysterious caves, and majestic ruins.

In 1802, the war against France having been suspended by a few months' peace, he and Dorothy journeyed to Calais, France, to see Annette and his daughter—the child alluded to in his famous sonnet, "It Is a Beauteous Evening" (*Anth.,* 223). This visit to France increased

---

[1] Russell, Bertrand; "The Harm That Good Men Do," *Harper's Magazine,* October, 1926.

his dislike for the tendencies of the Revolution; and when two years later Napoleon was crowned hereditary emperor, he felt surer than ever that the French had become a menace to liberty and national independence. Upon his return he married Mary Hutchinson, whom he had known from his boyhood, and who was perfectly qualified for the difficult enterprise of being a poet's wife. "She furnished," De Quincey testifies,

> a remarkable proof how possible it is for a woman neither handsome, nor comely, according to the rigor of criticism . . . to exercise all the practical fascination of beauty through the mere compensatory charms of sweetness all but angelic, of simplicity the most entire, of womanly self-respect and purity of heart speaking through all her looks, acts, and movements.
>
> *Essay on Wordsworth,* 1839

Five children were born to them during the next eight years; hence their removal from Dove Cottage to the larger houses Allan Bank and Rydal Mount, the latter place being their home for the last thirty-six years of Wordsworth's life.

Dorothy Wordsworth continued a member of the household. Coleridge was a frequent visitor, as was Southey; owing to their propinquity, the three were termed the Lake Poets or the Lake School—at first derisively. In 1809, De Quincey, who was fifteen years younger than Wordsworth, settled in the neighborhood. In the previous year had begun the visits of one who, from a practical point of view, was perhaps Wordsworth's most valuable friend, Henry Crabb Robinson (1777–1867), not himself an author, but eagerly interested in German and in English romantic writers, and particularly enthusiastic over Wordsworth's poetry. Robinson was glad to help the poet in matters of business, to negotiate with his publishers, to procure books which would be useful to him, and even to do shopping in London for Mrs. Wordsworth. He often visited the Wordsworths at Christmas; hence their household word, "No Crabb, no Christmas." He discerned the peculiar qualities and merits of Wordsworth's poetry, and extolled them far and wide among his numerous literary acquaintances, in conversation and in letters, during the many years when that poetry was neglected by the public and despised by the professional critics.

In 1800 Wordsworth published a second edition of the *Lyrical Ballads,* enlarged to two volumes, with his famous critical preface (*Anth.,* 300). In 1807, while England was still doggedly holding her own against Napoleon, he published a new volume of poems, in which appeared, among other great lyrics, his patriotic sonnets. Two years later he appeared as a champion of nationalism, in his prose tract *On the Convention of Cintra.*

From 1799 onwards his chief intention had been the composition, not of such short and occasional writings as these, but of an extensive philosophical poem in which his matured views of Man, Nature, and Society, were to find comprehensive expression. This plan he never carried out fully; but for many years the writing of two large sections of the projected poem constituted his most ambitious task. One of these was *The Prelude; or Growth of a Poet's Mind,* a poetical autobiography, addressed to Coleridge, in which he recounted and interpreted those incidents and circumstances in his childhood and in his period of storm and stress which he believed to have contributed weightily to his maturer attitude of mind. He began *The Prelude* in the spring of 1798, but frequently laid it aside and probably did not finish the first draft of it until 1805. This was not published at the time (though it was read to Coleridge), but it was repeatedly revised. The version published in 1850 after Wordsworth's death was more conservative in political opinions and more Christian in theological phraseology than were the earlier ones; and, contrary to the usual supposition, it was sometimes superior to them in style.

Wordsworth's other major undertaking was the writing of *The Excursion,* a long narrative poem intending to convey and illustrate "the sensations and opinions of a poet living in retirement," and designed as one part of a philosophical poem, *The Recluse,* only a fragment of which (*Anth.,* 277) was ever written. Begun in 1802, *The Excursion* was published in 1814. The reviewers met it with contempt and derision. When a year later he published his *White Doe of Rylstone,* the critic Jeffrey pronounced it the worst poem ever written. Wordsworth, however, manifested the fortitude which in his poems he had praised as the greatest of virtues. Never did he lose his temper, nor explode in angry retorts against his critics. Knowing that his poems were an utterly sincere expression of his convictions, and firmly believing that they were in harmony with eternal values, he bided his time.

Many difficulties and sorrows burdened Wordsworth's later years— serious trouble with his eyes, overcrowded living conditions which made it impossible for him to work uninterruptedly, the deaths of his brother John in 1805, and of two of his children in 1812, estrangements with Coleridge and De Quincey, and serious mental disturbances in his beloved sister Dorothy. His financial circumstances were rendered somewhat easier by his appointment in 1813 to a government position, a "distributorship of stamps." But his literary fame remained obscure. The theories in the *Preface to the Lyrical Ballads* (1800), even more than the poems themselves, had been attacked by Jeffrey because that influential critic discerned their liberal democratic implications. The *Poems* of 1807 were abused for their allegedly farfetched diction and "low" or trivial subjects. Apropos of a defense of Burns which Wordsworth wrote in 1816, Hazlitt drew a scornful contrast between Wordsworth's asceticism and Burns's addiction to sensual joys. Wordsworth's defiant publication of *Peter Bell* (wr. 1798, publ. 1819), with its extreme simplicities, gave his political enemies an additional opportunity for ridicule and parodies. Not until 1817 when Coleridge published his eulogy of him in the *Biographia Literaria* (*Anth.,* 331), Wordsworth being then forty-seven years old, were there any indications that his genius might be publicly recognized as of the highest order. And although John Wilson of *Blackwood's Magazine* championed his cause in the early 1820's, it still remained during that decade, as De Quincey says, a debatable issue.[2] Not before the 1830's was Wordsworth's greatness generally acknowledged, and even then its foundations were not understood. In 1843, he was appointed Poet Laureate—a post which he accepted only on the condition that he be not expected to produce poetry unless he felt sincerely moved by some occasion of national importance. At the age of eighty, he died; and, by his own desire, his remains were buried in the little churchyard at Grasmere, beneath a gravestone of characteristic unpretentiousness.

His Character.—In temperament Wordsworth was typically English, apparently inconsistent in combining outward quietude or dullness with inward moodiness or even violence of emotion—"a granite-covered volcano." He could be gracious in manner, but was often harsh toward others as well as toward himself. With a yeoman's matter-of-factness he united habits of bold imagination, profound meditation, unworldliness, and impassioned aspirations for human welfare. He was scrupulously sincere and truthful, conscious of his errors, devoted to his family and friends, and humbly grateful for the beautiful in Nature and the good in Man. In his religious life he was loyal to the Church, but characteristically distrustful of some of its ministers, and worried about his own lack of spirituality, though others felt him to be "a man living in the presence of God."

He did not overestimate the worth of his own character. He conscientiously regretted the vagaries of his earlier years

> of lapse and hesitating choice,
> And backward wanderings along thorny ways.
> *Prelude;* XIV, 137

Nevertheless he felt that in the general tenor of his life he had been true to his better self. Lacking a sense of humor, he took the world and his own mission therein with portentous solemnity. His personality is not ingratiating to those who judge by first appearances or to those who will not make allowances for the unconscious egotism of dedicated spirits. As Crabb Robinson witnesses:

> He is a sloven, and his manners are not prepossessing; his features are large and coarse; his voice is not attractive; his manners, though not arrogant, indicate a sense of his own worth; he is not attentive to others, and speaks with decision his own opinion. . . . He quotes his own verse with pleasure. . . . He also speaks with a contempt of others which I think very censurable.

"Yet with all this," Crabb Robinson admits,

> I should have a bad opinion of that person's discernment who should be long in his company without contracting an high respect, if not a love, for him. Moral purity and dignity and elevation of sentiment are characteristic of his mind and muse.

[2] "Up to 1820 the name of Wordsworth was trampled under foot; from 1820 to 1830 it was militant; from 1830 to 1835 it has been triumphant" (De Quincey).

Southey, whose intercourse with Coleridge and the other geniuses of a great age was extensive, declares that Wordsworth's conversation was "powerful beyond any of his contemporaries."

Wrong Interpretations of Wordsworth.—Several misconceptions have prevented a true understanding of Wordsworth and his poetry. It used to be assumed that he was a passionless prig, who, unlike Byron, knew too little of the temptations and agitations of ordinary mortals to be concerned about them. The recent disclosure of his affair with Annette should help to destroy that error. A second misconception, which Matthew Arnold inclined to, was that Wordsworth was purely a lyric poet, that his philosophy was unimportant, and that a knowledge of it was unnecessary to an appreciation of his work. Certainly Wordsworth was a poet rather than a systematic philosopher, i.e., he thought in concrete pictures rather than in abstract concepts; nevertheless he was in fact and in intention, as Coleridge declared, a philosophical poet—the greatest philosophical poet in our language—and in his maturity a particular system of ideas underlay his poetical works, which cannot be fully valued without a knowledge of that system. The third misconception proceeds from those who, granting that Wordsworth had a philosophy, describe it falsely. They misrepresent him as a devotee of naturalism, primitivism, naïveté, and idle reverie, in short, as a member of the School of Sensibility. Their error is to read into the poems which he wrote in his maturity those ideas which temporarily interested him in his period of storm and stress, and not to perceive the difference between such crude ideas and that fully developed and complex philosophy which he finally evolved.

The Real Wordsworthian Faith.—It is true of Wordsworth's philosophy, as of all other philosophies which are valuable, that it is not instantly clear and distinct to the hasty reader, that at first glance its complexities may seem like contradictions, and that one must read, reread, and ponder his works before one perceives their profundity. His ideas in his first period, and in his second, were much simpler than in his maturity. Some of his earlier ideas he rejected—especially the materialistic implications of Godwin and Hartley; but others he retained, ridding them however, of their former extremism by incorporating them into a system which attempted to do justice to the variety and intricacy of our universe. From his youthful period, he retained his religious (not ecclesiastical) feelings, and his sympathy for human suffering. From his period of storm and stress, he retained his belief that too little attention had been bestowed upon Man's relations with nature, upon sense-impressions, upon actual experience, and upon human life as a development rather than a status. The system within which he subsumed these ideas, it now becomes our difficult task to trace.

The Value of Nature to Man.—The most obvious point in Wordsworth's doctrines concerning nature is his testimony that he had found contact with it most beneficent in its effect upon his mind, conducive to a better temper of soul, and inspiring the feelings of love and kindliness. In that way, contact with Nature may occasionally

> give us more
> Than years of toiling reason.
> *To My Sister*

This belief, however, does not imply an agreement with the School of Sensibility. Not all natural phenomena are uplifting, nor will they exercise their healing power without the cooperation of the beholder: the libertine youth in *Ruth*, "the slave of low desires," is not reformed by contact with nature, but affected for the worse by the beautiful tropical wilderness:

> Whatever in those climes he found
> Irregular in sight or sound
> Did to his mind impart
> A kindred impulse.
>
> *Ruth,* 127

Nor will genuine poetry or art depict Nature in a false, idyllic, Arcadian manner, shedding upon it

> The light that never was, on sea or land,

but will paint with fidelity and face with fortitude

> The sea in anger, and the dismal shore.
> *Elegiac Stanzas; Anth.,* 231

He often depicts the sterner, awe-inspiring features of nature, such as night and winter. It is not in a fanciful Utopia that we are to live,

> But in the very world, which is the world
> Of all of us,—the place where, in the end,
> We find our happiness, or not at all!
> *Prelude;* XI, 140; *Anth.,* 268

Although nature is not by man's inner standards in all respects a manifestation of the perfect, it is nevertheless highly necessary for him, since in his present state he dwells in the natural world and is bodily a portion thereof, to try to understand its meaning. The obviously beautiful aspects of nature are not merely pleasing to our senses, they are at times profoundly significant as to the character of our entire Universe; [3] in other words, that portion of the Universe which we call Nature may reveal certain traits of the whole. Wordsworth had a greater respect for the phenomenal world than had Plato or the ascetic kind of Christian. To him phenomena were not mere shadows of true realities, or distorted similitudes, things to turn away from contemptuously, on the assumption that the ideal is manifested only in another world (*abstract* idealism).

---

[3] Here, and throughout, I use the term Universe in the widest possible sense, including all realities—material, human, and divine; past, present, and future.

To him these actualities were creations of the divine partly expressing their Maker; even as the God of Job declared that at the dawn of creation "the morning stars sang together, and all the sons of God (angels) shouted for joy." The phenomena of nature were accordingly authentic carriers of ideals, and might become conveyers to us of such ideals (_concrete_ idealism). It was their divine or ideal origin that made

> Beauty—a living Presence of the earth,
> Surpassing the most fair ideal forms
> _Recluse_, 42; _Anth._, 277

To man alone is given the power to discern the hidden sense of things, the deeper truths about the life of Nature. But the power operates only if he approaches Nature, not in a spirit of arid intellectualism, but with an attitude combining childlike love and humbleness with confident imaginative scrutiny. If, thus attuned, he frequently and closely observed mountains, oceans, stars, streams, trees, flowers, animal life, the succession of the seasons, etc., man would be impressed increasingly with certain qualities of his world—deriving

> authentic tidings of invisible things.
> _Excursion_, IV, 1144; _Anth._, 287

He would feel by personal experience (not as through a scientific treatise) the grandeur and sublimity of it, the enduring permanence of its relations, and the majestic regularity of its laws. The more he sensed such qualities in his universe, the less he would be interested in the petty and the worldly, the more he would turn away from the fleeting Many to the eternal One. By happy and unforced communion with nature, we would obtain a stronger faith in the consonance between the essential qualities of the Universe and the nobler traits of our own human character; we would increase our creative power; and from the great emblem of unity amid variety we would obtain suggestions and impulses for a better readjustment of the relationships between man and man (see the important passage in _The Prelude;_ XIII, 1–63; _Anth._, 271). Social ideals are in danger of remaining abstract theories until our appreciation of nature has borne in upon us the conviction that they harmonize with the Universe as it fundamentally is. In these various ways, habitual and loving contact with nature is an indispensable element in human culture.

His Mysticism.—Important as Nature is to Wordsworth, Man—because of his inner life—is even more important. To Hartley, the materialist, from whom Wordsworth learned much, man's inner life seemed _wholly_ the product of sense-impressions. To Wordsworth, however—and again he was testifying to his own experience—there were peculiar moments of consciousness ("spots of time"; _Prelude_, XII, 208; _Anth._, 270) which authentically made us feel that that inner life was not wholly derived from the environment nor dependent upon it, and that therefore mind was superior to matter, and Man to Nature. To the poet these moments often came when, having observed some object, and having perceived its beauty, he lost the consciousness both of his own finite ego and of the finite object, and passed into a state of mystical apprehension of the infinite universal One. Many mystics, and indirectly many poets,[4] have borne witness to such ineffable moments—

> when the light of sense
> Goes out, but with a flash that has revealed
> The invisible world,—

moments which give assurance that

> whether we be young or old,
> Our destiny, our being's heart and home,
> Is with infinitude and only there.
> *Prelude;* VI, 603; *Anth.,* 256

Sometimes Wordsworth's sense of the extraordinary value of mystical insight led him to belittle in comparison therewith those sense-experiences which he normally thought should not be despised; in an early draft of a passage of *The Prelude* (II, 210–232), for example, he goes so far as to say that what comes to us through ordinary experience and perception is not worthy to be deemed humanly important,

> But is the very littleness of life.

This was too extreme a statement, and was subsequently withdrawn; but he continued to feel certain that if Man was really to know the character of the Universe he must call upon a witness superior even to natural experience or to science—namely that mystical power of intuition, which he identified with genuine imagination or a higher kind of reason. (Hence the appropriateness of addressing *The Prelude* to Coleridge.)

His Transcendentalism.—Reliance upon the authenticity of intuition was the basis of Wordsworth's religion. The mystical experience assured him of the reality of a transcendent and infinite Being, to which finite Man is bound by ties of mutual love. The Universe as a whole, and Man as an existence in this world, are thus partly spiritual and partly material. Circumscribed as Man temporarily is, he, in a greater degree than merely natural creatures, has freedom of will. Good men are Powers (*Prelude;* XIV, 113; *Anth.,* 274) in the service of the spiritual. The soul of man is immortal, as from his very childhood he intuitively feels. The notion of pre-existence, though not to be taken literally, may poetically serve to suggest that Man is related to that Infinite Being which knows neither beginning nor end. His sense of our transcendental union with the eternal and divine was the true source of his poetic power in its sublimer and profounder manifestations, with their "dim and undetermined sense of unknown modes of being," their human figures beyond earthly passion

---

[4] Underhill, Evelyn; *Mysticism* (1911).—Landis. Paul, and Entwistle, A. R.; "Mysticism in English Poetry," in *The Study of Poetry* (1929).

and grief, and their "types and symbols of Eternity." These beliefs Wordsworth, in the latter half of his life, tended more and more to identify with Christianity and to express in Christian terms, although they originated not so much in the teachings of the Church as in his personal experience. Even if they were old truths, he was a new and independent witness to them. His empirical habit of mind inspired important religious leaders of the Victorian age to bring traditional doctrines to the test of their individual experience of life.

The Twofold Aim of Life.—What, in Wordsworth's judgment, is characteristic of the highest type of human being is not a regard for nature alone, nor a regard for the spiritual alone, but a perception of their intimate interrelationship and a harmonizing of one with the other. This is the conclusion at which he arrives in the last book of *The Prelude* (xiv, 100; *Anth.*, 274), where he writes of "higher minds":

> Them the enduring and the transient both
> Serve to exalt; they build up greatest things
> From least suggestions; ever on the watch,
> Willing to work and to be wrought upon,
> They need not extraordinary calls
> To rouse them; in a world of life they live,
> By sensible impressions not enthralled,
> But by their quickening impulse made more prompt
> To hold fit converse with the spiritual world,
> And with the generations of mankind
> Spread over time, past, present, and to come,
> Age after age, till time shall be no more.
> Such minds are truly from the Deity,
> For they are Powers; and hence the highest bliss
> That flesh can know is theirs,—the consciousness
> Of Whom they are, habitually infused
> Through every image and through every thought,
> And all affections by communion raised
> From earth to heaven, from human to divine;
> Hence endless occupation for the soul,
> Whether discursive or intuitive;
> Hence cheerfulness for acts of daily life,
> Emotions which best foresight need not fear,
> Most worthy then of trust when most intense.
> Hence, amid ills that vex and wrongs that crush
> Our hearts—if here the words of Holy Writ
> May with fit reverence be applied—that peace
> Which passeth understanding, that repose
> In moral judgments which from this pure source
> Must come, or will by man be sought in vain.

Students and critics of Wordsworth are prone to see only one of the two parts of his philosophy; either his doctrine about Nature or his doctrine about the human spirit. But what was to him most important was the beneficent interrelationship possible between the two, and man's deep need of steadily cultivating that interrelationship. On the one hand, if you do not habitually participate in the wholesome life of nature and the senses, your inner life will be vague or feeble; you will become fantastically theoretic and bigoted—some sort of doctrinaire with no further capacity for growth—for example, a neo-classic critic frightened by the Many and clinging to a One which is an oversimplified and pallid substitute for the terrifyingly complex real One. If, on the other hand, you rest content with nature or mere experience, and do not refer them to your inner standards, you may go astray, becoming a slave to your senses or to worldly conventions, and you will not apprehend the real meaning of life. What conduces to happiness, virtue, and wisdom is the establishing and habitual maintenance of a mutually enriching interchange between the natural and the human.

The Three Ages.—How may one participate in that joyous relationship which ought to exist between Man and Nature? How may one's soul happily orientate itself in its temporal world? No true answer to such questions, Wordsworth felt, would be found if one assumed that man's relationship to nature remained the same throughout life. To him it was not a static, but a *developing* relationship—different in childhood, adolescence, and maturity—this conception being one of the most important points of his doctrine. Under normal conditions, childhood might occasionally have intuitive perceptions of immortality (and in that respect it seemed sacred); but predominantly the child's life was a life of physical sensations, of vivid awareness, of glad animal movements, of unreflecting absorption in natural phenomena. In adolescence one became conscious of one's individual existence, and of the environment as something distinct from oneself. It was thus a period of agitation, of extraordinary bodily and mental activity, and of highly emotional response to life—feverish, rebellious, passionate, and fanciful. With maturity, the pleasure of the senses grew less keen, but the partial loss was more than compensated for. One retained not only the vivid recollection of the intenser experiences of one's childhood and youth, but one now at last came to understand their significance and value. The matrix of deep thinking was deep feeling (Preface, *Lyrical Ballads*). Maturity brought a perception of the character of the Universe and of one's place and mission therein—a feeling of being at home in one's world. Adolescent self-consciousness and egotism were superseded in maturity by love, sympathy, and serene hope. Youthful fancy gave way to sound imagination or insight.

In thus conceiving the development of human life and personality, Wordsworth was thinking of life as it ought to be and as, he believed, it individually might be. What of those lives and personalities which were failures? In his opinion the failure was often due to the fact that home and school had ignored the distinctions between the three ages. Often, as in his *Anecdote for Fathers,* or *We Are Seven (Anth.,* 190, 195) , he was indirectly pleading for a better understanding of the psychology of children and adolescents. The mistakenly trained child was, metaphorically speaking, "the father" of the man with a disorganized or perverted character. A false system of education had forced upon him in his earlier years activities and conditions not appropriate thereto. That admirable maturity which every human being could potentially attain to was hardly attainable unless he had had the opportunity of passing through the first two ages in a wholesome and natural way. It was not only futile but harmful to attempt to make children act and think like little old men and women, or to compel adolescents to behave exactly like the middle-aged. Not that youth was wiser and better than age (quite the contrary was true), but that the hollowness of the follies and illusions of youth must be personally discovered if one was ever to become a confirmed and passionate lover of truth and virtue.

> Dust as we are, the immortal spirit grows
> Like harmony [5] in music; there is a dark
> Inscrutable workmanship that reconciles
> Discordant elements, makes them cling together
> In one society. How strange that all
> The terrors, pains, and early miseries,
> Regrets, vexations, lassitudes interfused
> Within my mind, should e'er have borne a part,
> And that a needful part, in making up
> The calm existence that is mine when I
> Am worthy of myself!
>
> *Prelude;* 1, 340; *Anth.,* 243

The Pursuit of Happiness.—One of Wordsworth's chief purposes was to communicate to others his own sense of happiness—that "deep power of joy" in the Universe which helps us to "see into the life of things." He was quite aware, as his sonnet "Weak Is the Will of Man" (*Anth.,* 290) shows, that to acquire such serenity, circumstanced as we are, is very difficult. If the happiness were not to be blind or shallow, it must rest upon a profound faith in the essential rightness of the Universe. This faith could not be achieved without patience nor without a heavy price. First of all, one must cease to addict oneself to any form of worldliness,—voluptuous sloth, vain gayeties that recreate neither body nor soul, pride, envy, ostentation, personal hatred, selfish ambition, "madding passions mutually inflamed," and whatever distracts us from "plain living and high thinking."

The aim should be the closer and closer approximation to equipoise between (a) the freedom of the wholesome natural feelings, and (b) the governance and direction of those feelings by ideals revealed through the inner life of the spirit. As to (a), the natural feelings, Godwin's doctrine that they were to be scorned and suppressed, was false. To experience and to respect the primal human affections—such as the love of kindred and of home, or compassion for the undeserved distress of others

---

[5] i.e., the combination of sounds of *different* pitch.

—is fundamentally necessary to our moral growth. Hence there is much value in observing the lives and characters of simple, unsophisticated, and unselfconscious people in whom "our elementary feelings coexist in a state of greater simplicity." (*Preface to The Lyrical Ballads; Anth.,* 300.) It is not that such persons represent the highest possibilities of human nature, but that those possibilities cannot be successfully attained without a sympathetic understanding of the foundations upon which we must build. On the same principle, such ordinary events or aspects of life as the *blasé* may deem uninteresting, may really be precious means of disclosing the primary laws of our nature, and may be revelatory of our spiritual life. Hence, says Wordsworth

> I sought
> For *present* good in life's *familiar* face
> And built thereon my hopes of good to come.
> *Prelude,* XIII, 61; *Anth.,* 272

His insistence upon the worth of the natural feelings does not, however, lead to unchecked emotional indulgence, to unchartered freedom for every chance desire, or to an anarchy of individualism. Concerning (b), the inner life, the conscience, admonishes us that indulgence in feeling for its own sake is evil, as are the rebellious and anti-social passions.

> Control
> Rebellious passion: for the Gods approve
> The depth, and not the tumult, of the soul;
> A fervent, not ungovernable, love.
> *Laodamia,* 73; *Anth.,* 289

The *Ode to Duty (Anth.,* 230) expresses the conviction that a self-indulgent or detached life is unsatisfying to the soul of man, whose happiness will be secure only if he fulfills his duty to mankind, of love and self-sacrifice. In other words, the only kind of liberty that man can permanently enjoy is willing fidelity to the just laws of the Universe.

Influences Upon His Philosophy.—Wordsworth's philosophy is one variety of concrete idealism, but shows the marks of his having passed through a period of devotion to materialism. From Hartley he took over the doctrine of the three ages of man; and he attributed to education through the senses and through experience an importance greater than, without Hartley's influence, he would have been likely to assign thereto; but he differed radically from Hartley in his mysticism and transcendentalism. In what particulars Wordsworth's idealism was nourished by Coleridge is not yet fully known, although it was evident that Coleridge acted as an intermediary in the case of some idealistic authors. Either through Coleridge or through his own reading, Wordsworth absorbed various ideas of the neo-Platonists, Bruno, Boehme, the Cambridge Platonists, Isaac Newton, Spinoza, Berkeley, and Kant. Although Kant's influence was significant, Wordsworth differed from him in his views on religion; the philosopher, restricting himself to whatever the rationalizing intelligence could prove, was forced to take a comparatively skeptical attitude toward the reality of God and immortality, whereas Wordsworth, because of his entire confidence in mystical intuition, was a firm believer in them.

His Political and Social Ideals.—To Wordsworth, the determination of whether an individual's life should be virtuous and happy lay more in his own will power than in those political and social conditions in which he might be placed. Nevertheless the improvement of such conditions was to Wordsworth an important concern. His political and social principles, chiefly based upon those of Milton and Burke, began with the assumption that the self-restraint of the citizen rather than his restraint by force was the ideal to be sought. That government was the best which gave men as large a degree of freedom as was consistent with the particular stage of mental and moral development which they had reached. England, though sorrowfully reproached by the poet for its backslidings, was on the whole an admirable representative of just balance between freedom and order. To impose any law or constitution upon an unwilling people was tyranny. Not even liberty could be effectively obtained by a people through the grant thereof by a foreign ruler; it must spring out of their own vital will (*On a Celebrated Event in Ancient History*). The strength of a nation lay not in its military power so much as in its moral character:

> By the soul
> Only, the Nations shall be great and free.
> *Near Dover; Anth.,* 222

National independence was essential to the humblest citizen's dignity of soul, and no consideration of political or economic expediency could justify its destruction (*Convention of Cintra; Anth.,* 240).

Like Milton, Wordsworth lost faith in progress through political revolutions, and turned to cultural and religious means of betterment for mankind; but his politics and religion are more deeply related than Milton's to a love of ordinary humanity. Although in his old age he opposed some liberal reforms, the general tendency of his work is democratic. He sets no value upon distinctions of birth or rank or wealth; and he has a deep, affectionate respect for the plain people. He advanced the cause of democracy by his highly original presentation of such characters as the Leech Gatherer, the Old Cumberland Beggar, Michael, Margaret, Lucy, Poor Susan, and the Highland Reaper, revealing the depth and the worth of the emotional nature of common humanity. His interest in the psychology of odd and eccentric individuals, young and old, showed the same tendency. The ideals and ways of life which he advocates can be followed by men and women in the humblest circumstances. His influence was hostile to aristocracy or bourgeois plutocracy. Like Thomas Jefferson, he opposed whatever seemed to him to encourage a commercial and urban civilization rather than an agrarian one. He held that a nation should endeavor to prevent such social or economic conditions as would reduce men—divinely intended to develop in freedom their individual personalities—to standardized cogs in an industrial machine.

> Our life is turned
> Out of her course, wherever man is made
> An offering, or a sacrifice, a tool
> Or implement, a passive thing employed
> As a brute mean, without acknowledgment
> Of common right or interest in the end;
> *Excursion;* IX, 113; *Anth.,* 288

The State should support a system of popular schools in order that every citizen should have the opportunity to attain that genuine kind of freedom which only the educated man can understand and safely exercise (*Excursion;* IX, 293, *Anth.,* 288) .

The Ideal Man and Ideal Woman.—Wordsworth's ideal woman (*She Was a Phantom of Delight; Anth.,* 228; *To a Highland Girl; Anth.,* 226) was not a social butterfly, or a social leader, or a masterful clubwoman, or a political campaigner, or a clinging vine, or a useless angel; but an incarnation of spirituality, benignity, sympathy, home-bred sense, foresight, and patience—womanly rather than feminine. His ideal man (*Character of the Happy Warrior; Anth.,* 234) was not a dull-witted sportsman, or a hustling businessman, or a roystering adventurer, or an ambitious seeker after fame, or a *blasé* worldling, or a milksop, or a self-righteous reformer of others; but a generous spirit, devout, gentle and compassionate, studious and thoughtful, firm in character and of high purpose, self-forgetful, and ambitious only to help good prevail—a gentleman rather than a shrewd man-of-the-world. Emotional and spiritual apathy was one of the worst of evils. Grief was unavoidable (*why* human life should be thus conditioned, he does not pretend to explain) ; but it could be educative. It was possible "an agonizing sorrow to transmute" into serenity. In both men and women, Wordsworth thought, a virtue even nobler than compassion was fortitude, i.e., the courageous and uncomplaining endurance of the toil, trials, and adversities inevitable in human existence (*Resolution and Independence, Anth.,* 219) .

His Literary Principles.—Wordsworth stated his literary principles in the preface to the second edition of the *Lyrical Ballads* (1800) , in an *Essay, Supplementary to the Preface* (1815) , and in the preface to his *Poems* (1815) . The first of these statements (*Anth.,* 300) has long been regarded as marking a new epoch in the history of criticism. Much that it says concerning the nature of poetry and imagination is of permanent value. Some passages in it (and upon these the chief attention has sometimes been bestowed) were attacks upon bad literary fashions of the period. Wordsworth denounced neo-classicism—its excessive use of personification and allegory, its conventional figures of speech, its poetic diction, such as "reddening Phoebus" (the rising sun), "plumy people" or "busy race" (birds), "amorous descant" (love songs), and "blue expanses" (skies). He also protested against the opposite extreme—pre-romantic works such as "frantic novels, sickly and stupid German tragedies," ebullitions of crude fancy, false to truth, incoherent, morbid, and sensational. To counteract such contemporaneous extremists, it would be salutary, he asserted, to turn occasionally to very simple and familiar aspects of life, to observe them accurately, and to treat them in a style as unadorned as the diction of a peasant or the manner of an ancient ballad. This injunction, which was a plea for realism, did not constitute Wordsworth's entire literary code, although at the time it seemed to his critics the most conspicuous and objectionable part thereof. From the first, Wordsworth meant it to justify only the ballads in his volumes of 1798 and 1800, and not to apply to such "other poems" as *Tintern Abbey*. In subsequent editions of the preface he toned down some of the more extravagant of the recommendations to adopt a realistic style.[6]

The other half of Wordsworth's theory was in harmony with his idealistic philosophy. After the object has been accurately perceived, after the feelings aroused by it have been experienced, it is recollected in tranquillity. The imagination broods over it, and discerns its essential nature and deepest significance (which is another way of saying that the imagination discerns its beauty). In the first place, therefore, a poet is to make quite certain that the experience he is to write about has actually been felt by himself or another, that there is nothing unauthentic or fantastic about it; but he is not to try to reproduce it until his soul has divined its universal values, i.e., its relations to the infinite and eternal. The poet's problem is how the visible, audible, tangible, and temporal actualities of the outer world can best be used to express his inner life. Thus, as a whole, Wordsworth's poetics are not out of harmony with Coleridge's.

Whether the theme be Nature or Human Life, its poetical treatment will involve the assumption that, common-sense appearances to the contrary notwithstanding, Man is essentially in harmony with his Universe. It is by vitalizing that faith that poetry confers pleasure of the deepest and noblest kind.[7] The true poet or man-of-letters is thus the harmonizer of all relationships—including the social, national, and international.

> In spite of difference of soil and climate, of language and manners, of laws and customs, in spite of things silently gone out of mind, and things violently destroyed, the poet binds together by passion and knowledge the vast empire of human society, as it is spread over the whole earth, and over all time.
>
> *Preface, Lyrical Ballads; Anth.,* 306

[6] H. W. L. Dana, cited in Richard Rice's "Wordsworth's Mind," *Indiana University Studies,* XI, July 1, 1913.

[7] It follows, therefore, that if the Universe (as the materialists believe) is hostile or indifferent to Man's aspirations, then Wordsworth's poetics and poetry are vain imaginings, and the only true literature would be a frank depiction of the futility or hopeless horror of human existence.

His Poems.—When Wordsworth decided upon the arrangement of his poems in his collected works, he classified them under headings which are significant. Early poems, like the *Descriptive Sketches* he placed apart from his really representative work, entitling them *Poems Written in Youth*. Even his admirer Crabb Robinson privately advised an inquirer: "Pass them over, unread." Many of the headings indicated the importance of travel in Wordsworth's life, for example:

> *Memorials of a Tour in Scotland, 1803*
> *Memorials of a Tour in Scotland, 1814*
> *The River Duddon, 1806–20*
> *Memorials of a Tour on the Continent, 1820*
> *Memorials of a Tour in Italy, 1837*
> *Yarrow Revisited, and Other Poems, 1831*
> *Poems Composed or Suggested During a Tour, 1833*

A characteristic distinction is shown in his two groups: *Poems of the Fancy*, thirty-three pieces, only one of which, "The Green Linnet," is well remembered; and *Poems of the Imagination*, fifty-two, at least ten of which are now famous, including the "Lines Composed Above Tintern Abbey," "There Was a Boy," "Three Years She Grew in Sun and Shower," "A Slumber Did My Spirit Seal," "To the Cuckoo," and "To a Skylark."

One group was entitled *Ecclesiastical Sonnets*, in which he dealt with such principles and such personalities of the Church of England as he admired. A more important group was *Poems Dedicated to National Independence and Liberty*. This included those superb sonnets (*Anth.*, 216 ff.) written when England was struggling against Napoleon, of which the late Professor Dicey said:

> They are the finest war songs ever composed by a patriot to stir up the valor and the nobility of his country; they might be termed the Psalms of England, and like the psalter they combine penitence for past errors with confidence in final victory based on the belief in the final triumph of righteousness. They contain not a word which is mean, ignoble, or savage.

The following three groups likewise indicate what kinds of subjects seemed important to him: *Poems Referring to the Period of Childhood* (e.g., "We Are Seven"); *Poems Founded on the Affections* (e.g., the Lucy poems, and "Michael"), and *Poems of Sentiment and Reflection* (e.g., "Ode to Duty" and "Character of the Happy Warrior"). Add the philosophical and narrative poems, *The Prelude* and *The Excursion*, which owing to their length he did not include in any of the groups, and you have a fair survey of the chief divisions of the poet's work.

Two of the *Odes* have given rise to much misunderstanding and controversy. The *Ode to Duty* (*Anth.*, 230) supplements, but does not, as has been alleged, contradict the liberal ethics of *The Prelude;* the sense of duty which it praises finds its freedom in willing obedience to the good and the true (see Wordsworth's *Reply to Mathetes*). The *Ode:*

Intimations of Immortality (*Anth.*, 232) should not be misread as if it were an Ode to Dejection. In the fading away of childhood's sense of harmony with the Universe there is a poignant loss; but the compensations are sufficient which maturity brings to the reflective and imaginative mind, with its moments of insight and its recurrent sense of the eternal presences.

The Prelude, or Growth of a Poet's Mind (*Anth.*, 242), the best autobiography in English verse, consists of fourteen books, averaging c. 600–700 lines each. The first two books describe the poet's childhood; the third, fourth, and fifth, his college days; the sixth, his first visit to the continent and the Alps (the same theme as the *Descriptive Sketches,* the contrast between the cruder style and the mature being striking) ; and the remaining eight books are given to his period of Storm and Stress. It is not chiefly concerned with external incidents, but with the inner experiences of an intensely poetical being in his progress through the generous impulses and raptures of youth toward the idealistic convictions of manhood, in which development the symbols offered by Nature proved more enlightening than the systems excogitated by thinkers (including perhaps Wordsworth himself). Although *The Prelude* deals with one individual experience, that experience is so deeply interpreted that it becomes of broad general value, especially as to the transition from growth to maturity.

The Excursion (*Anth.*, 277), slightly longer than *The Prelude,* is divided into nine books. Here an overoptimistic idealist, called the Solitary, is described as having fallen into despondency upon the failure of the French Revolution, which made him feel that any hopes for mankind must be vain. The Solitary's melancholy (not unlike Byron's in essence, although wholly dissimilar in expression) Wordsworth conceives to be of general importance, because characteristic of youth. The Solitary meets the Wanderer, who in long discourses tries to cure his despondency. With that end in mind, the Wanderer relates many stories intended to evoke the right attitude and to illustrate wise or unwise modes of life. The manifold ways by which the Solitary may be slowly but surely restored to mental health are suggested to him, that in the end he may become wise and cheerful and no longer

read

The forms of things with an unworldly eye

Excursion; i, 940; *Anth.,* 284

The theme could hardly be dwelt upon without uttering some truisms, but, as both Coleridge and Hazlitt said, they were not dull, because they arose out of his own "experience, feelings, and reason."

His Style.—The faults which mar passages in Wordsworth's longer poems, and which have caused not a few of his shorter ones to be forgotten, largely arose out of his determination to have nothing to do with the merely decorative or fantastic or sensational but to keep faithfully to actual and often to ordinary experience. It is the blind courage of his realism that permits him to write such a prosaic line as this:

> And at the Hoop alighted, famous inn.
> *Prelude;* III, 17

The failures among the shorter poems, e.g., *The Idiot Boy* and *Peter Bell,* often are due to that zeal for stark honesty. To his best work (and what else matters?) his dedicated truthfulness gives a tone, lucid and austere, of impressive authenticity, persuasive upon us not only when he sings of simple natural scenes and incidents but also when he witnesses to his spiritual experiences, as in the *Ode on Intimations of Immortality,* when he is the prophet that John Keats describes:

> He of the cloud, the cataract, the lake,
> Who on Helvellyn's summit, wide awake,
> Catches his freshness from Archangel's wing.
> *Addressed to Haydon; Anth.,* 757

He is apt to begin on the level of impassioned simplicity, and may end there; but he may suddenly be carried aloft into impassioned sublimity. That is the systole and diastole, the vitality, of his whole being. As Tennyson remarks, Wordsworth's poetry gives us a sense of the permanent amid the transitory. "I declare my full conviction," Southey presciently said, "that posterity will rank him with Milton." He has the gravity and dignity of Milton; and, although he is not Milton's equal in awe-inspiring sublimity, he is one of the companions whom we seek when we desert that too austere master.

Wordsworth's vocabulary is extensive, and exceptionally accurate and pure. "The expression may often be called bald," says Matthew Arnold, "but it is bald as the bare mountain-tops are bald, with a baldness which is full of grandeur." He commands the metrical and rhythmical resources of the sonnet, the ode, the ballad measure, and blank verse. He has no dramatic power, and is too rarely a successful creator of imaginary characters. But in philosophic and meditative poetry, he is supreme. The emotional appropriateness of his symbolism is remarkable. "Where," asks a critic who on the whole disagrees with his philosophical opinions, "for variety and vitality of pure poetic expression can you match the wealth of Shakspeare except in Wordsworth?" (Herbert Read). He has, says Saintsbury, "the inexplicable, the ultimate, felicity of phrase which all great poets must have, and only great poets have."

His Relation to Other Romantics.—Wordsworth was more realistic than Coleridge, and far more so than Blake. With the latter he shared an interest in children, but whereas Blake loved and pitied children for their grace and helplessness, Wordsworth fathomed their inward nature more deeply. Neither Blake nor Coleridge succeeded in poetically interpreting so many and varied incidents of personal experience as Wordsworth did, nor did either of them point so clearly to a better way of life which normal human beings could follow. The one very important aspect of life which Wordsworth tended to neglect is mentioned in his own admission (to Crabb Robinson, Jan. 3, 1839): "I want flesh and blood." He admired Chaucer and Burns for the frank naturalism in which he acknowledged himself deficient, and which other Romantics, especially Keats, elaborated abundantly. Among his successors, Shelley was more melodious than Wordsworth, and Keats more colorful; but he appeals more to the heart and is ethically more fortifying than they. His influence upon nineteenth-century literature is incalculably widespread: he revealed and exemplified new ways of observing nature and human life, making both much more fascinating; and scores of authors followed his lead—e.g., Tennyson, Ruskin, Arnold, Edward Fitzgerald, Meredith, John Stuart Mill, and Robert Bridges.

His Special Value to the Anglo-American World.—Foreign readers of our literature find it difficult to understand why we rank Wordsworth next to Shakspeare and Milton. They do not admire Wordsworth as much as we do, his message and his manner being peculiarly English. He manifests that Anglo-American devotion to both the natural and the mystical, to both the commonplace and the sublime, which to the metaphysical German and the logical Frenchman, Spaniard, and Italian, seems paradoxical and puzzling.[8] He represents our peculiar conception of liberty, national welfare, morality, duty, the ideal woman, the ideal man, and the true pursuit of happiness. Not to know and to love Wordsworth is therefore to be out of harmony with the soul of our Anglo-American world. He militates against two of our most dangerous modern tendencies—the engrossing pursuit of wealth, and the ostentatious squandering thereof—by revealing the beauty and joy of plain living and high thinking.

The remarkably representative and influential place of Wordsworth was unintentionally shown in certain passages of the famous *Memorandum* written by Prince Lichnowsky, German ambassador in England just before World War I. At that time, Sir Edward Grey was Secretary of State. To Prince Lichnowsky, Grey seemed a wonderfully typical exponent of the English character and of English ways and manners. To the German diplomat, used to the pomp and artificiality of continental courts, those ways were astonishingly strange, as may be read between the lines of the following remarks in his *Memorandum:*

> Sprung from an old family, possessing estates in the north of England, . . . he attached himself to the left wing of his party and sympathized with socialists and pacifists. He may be described as a socialist in the most ideal sense of the term; for he carries the theory of socialism even into his private life, which is marked by the greatest simplicity and absence of all preten-

---

[8] See especially Salvador Madariaga, *Shelley and Calderon*, 1920; and his *Englishmen, Frenchmen, Spaniards*, 1928. — Also Wilhelm Dibelius, *England*, 1923; André Siegfried, *L'Angleterre d'Aujourdhui*, 1924; and Louis Cazamian, *Ce Qu'il Faut Connaître de L'Ame Anglaise*, 1927; and the delightful essay, "The English," TLS, Aug. 7, 1948.

sion, although he is possessed of ample means. Display of any sort is foreign to him. He had in London modest quarters only, and gave no dinners except the one official dinner in the Foreign Office on the king's birthday. If, exceptionally, he asked a few people to his house, it was to a simple meal or to a small luncheon served by a maid. He shunned large gatherings and celebrations. Like his colleagues, he regularly spends his week-ends in the country, but not at large, fashionable house parties. For the most part he lives alone, in his cottage in the New Forest, where he takes long walks to watch the ways of birds, being a devoted lover of nature and an ornithologist. Or, on the other hand, he goes north, to his property, where he feeds squirrels that make their way in through the window and breeds different kinds of water-fowl. He was specially fond of occasional excursions to the Norfolk marshes, to watch during the breeding season some rare varieties of heron that nest only in that region. In his youth he was a noted cricketer and tennis player. Now his chief sport is salmon and trout fishing, in Scotch waters, in the company of his friend Lord Glenconner, Mr. Asquith's brother-in-law. "All the rest of the year I am looking forward to it." He has published a book on fishing. When on one occasion we spent a week-end with him alone, at Lord Glenconner's, near Salisbury, he arrived on a bicycle and returned in the same way to his cottage, some thirty miles distant.

The simplicity and sincerity of his character won for him the esteem of his opponents, who were to be found rather in the field of domestic politics than in that of foreign affairs. Falsehood and intrigue are equally foreign to him.

Finally, Prince Lichnowsky almost casually added:

Wordsworth is his favorite poet, and he is able to recite passages from him by memory.

He apparently did not see the intimate connection between that discipleship and Earl Grey's life, but to us it should be obvious.

SELECTED BIBLIOGRAPHY

OF FIRST IMPORTANCE

Selections

Arnold, Matthew, ed.; Macmillan, 1879.
Dowden, Edward, ed.; Ginn, 1897.
Grey (Viscount), ed.; Nelson, 1910.
Hall, Howard J., ed.; Scott Foresman, 1918.
Harper, G. McL., ed.; Scribner's, 1923.

Texts

Complete Poetical Works of William Wordsworth, ed. Thomas Hutchinson (Oxford Poets), 1895. — Admirable, inexpensive edition in one volume. — With introduction and notes by G. McL. Harper, 1933. — Revised by E. De Selincourt, 1942.

The Prelude, edited from the manuscripts, with introduction, textual and critical notes, by E. De Selincourt, Oxford Univ. Press, 1926; second impr., 1928. — On the right-hand page, the text which Wordsworth authorized and which was published in 1850. On the left-hand, printed for the first time, the text which he read to Coleridge in 1806–07. Variant readings from all other extant ms. drafts of the poem. Introduction discusses the general significance of the changes. A monument of scholarship.

Standard Biography

George McL. Harper's *William Wordsworth: His Life, Works, and Influence*, 2 vols., 1916; revised and abridged, 1929. — The best full-length account, although impaired by "one-sided political and literary criticism" (TLS, Aug. 29, 1935).

Best Introductory Critical Discussions

Stephen, Leslie; "Wordsworth's Ethics," 1876; rptd. in *Hours in a Library*, III, 1879. — See comment on next item.

Arnold, Matthew; "Wordsworth," 1879; rptd. in *Essays in Criticism*, 1888. — Stephen had stressed Wordsworth's teachings; Arnold protested that he was primarily a poet. — Cf., Lane Cooper, *Evolution and Repentance*, 1935.

Bradley, A. C.; two lectures on Wordsworth, 1903; rptd. in *Oxford Lectures on Poetry*, 1909.

Dicey, A. V.; *The Statesmanship of Wordsworth*, 1917. — On his democratic faith, and on the originality of his ideas about patriotism.

Beatty, Arthur; *William Wordsworth: His Doctrine and Art in Their Historical Relations*, 1922; rev. ed., 1927. — Fundamentally important in disclosing the influence of Hartley. As to the ways Wordsworth modified Hartley, see the studies of Wordsworth's philosophy below, including Rader, Rea, and especially Stallknecht.

Garrod, H. W.; *Wordsworth*, 1923. — "The real man seen not in the conflict, but in the issue of the conflict."

Gingerich, S. F.; *Essays in the Romantic Poets*, 1924. — Elementary; but a sound introduction, especially on Wordsworth's religion.

Whitehead, A. N.; *Science and the Modern World*, 1925; ch. 5, "The Romantic Reaction." — How Wordsworth goes beyond the truths of science.

Powell, Annie E. (Mrs. E. R. Dodds) ; *The Romantic Theory of Poetry*, 1926.

Herford, C. H.; *Wordsworth*, 1930. — A good brief survey of the life and works; appreciative, but judicious. On the weakness, see TLS, Dec. 18, 1930.

Patton, Cornelius H.; *The Rediscovery of Wordsworth*, 1935. — A good general introduction. Stresses his "unique significance for our own time," and sensibly discusses the main views of recent critics.

Havens, R. D.; *The Mind of a Poet: A Study of Wordsworth's Thought with Particular Reference to "The Prelude,"* 1941. — Thorough commentary on Wordsworth's masterpiece, and basic for the interpretation of *all* his work. Helpful index.

Knight, G. Wilson; *The Starlit Dome: Studies in the Poetry of Vision*, 1941; ch. 1, "The Wordsworthian Profundity." — Some overbold speculation; but valuable appreciation of some of the higher, spiritual qualities of the poems.

FOR ADVANCED STUDENTS

The bibliography of Wordsworth is larger than that of any other Romantic, and selection from it unusually difficult. To pursue any investigation further than indicated by the data here given, consult James V. Logan's *Wordsworthian Criticism: A Guide and Bibliography* (1947) , which lists and describes 661 editions and criticisms published from 1849 to 1944. To pursue any special topic (e.g., an episode in Wordsworth's life, or the influence of a particular author upon him, or the interpretations of one of the poems) use Logan's Index, supplemented by the Index of Havens' *Mind of a Poet*.

Important Additional Texts

The Poetical Works of William Wordsworth, ed. from the MSS., with textual and critical Notes, by Ernest De Selincourt and Helen Darbishire, vols. I–IV, 1941–48; to be completed in five or six volumes.

Lyrical Ballads, ed. George Sampson, 1903. — Noel Douglas Replica, 1926. — On the bibliographical problems, articles by J. E. Wells and others, listed in Logan, Nos. 422 ff.; also M. Peacock, Jr., MLN, LXI, 175 (1946).

Poems of 1807, ed. Helen Darbishire, 1914.

The Prelude, ed. E. E. Reynolds, 1932. — *The Excursion,* ed. E. E. Reynolds, 1935. — Handy, well-edited Golden Treasury eds., small format.

The White Doe of Rylstone, ed. Alice P. Comparetti, 1940.

Ecclesiastical Sonnets, ed. Abbie F. Potts, 1922.

Prose Works, ed. A. B. Grosart, 3 vols., 1876. — Ed. W. A. Knight, 2 vols., 1896.

Literary Criticism, ed. Nowell C. Smith, 1905.

Preface to "The Borderers," ed. E. De Selincourt, in his *Oxford Lectures on Poetry,* 1934 (first published in 1926).

Tract on the Convention of Cintra, ed. A. V. Dicey, 1915.

Wordsworth and Coleridge Marginalia in Knight's "Principles of Taste" [c. 1808], ed. Edna T. Shearer and J. T. Lindsay; *Huntington Libr. Quart.,* I, 63; 1937.

Guide to the Lakes, ed. E. De Selincourt, 1926. — Facsimile of 1835 ed., Tantivy Press, Malvern, 1948.

The Letters of William and Dorothy Wordsworth, ed. E. De Selincourt, 6 vols., 1935–39.

The Journals of Dorothy Wordsworth, ed. E. De Selincourt, 2 vols., 1941.

The *Correspondence of Crabb Robinson with the Wordsworth Circle,* ed. Edith J. Morley, 2 vols., 1927.

Wordsworth and Reed: The Poet's Correspondence with His American Editor, 1836–1850, ed. L. N. Broughton, 1933. — This item, and the preceding one, contain letters not in the six-vol. De Selincourt ed.

Chiefly Biographical

Wordsworth, Christopher; *Memoirs of Wordsworth,* 2 vols.; 1851. — By his nephew, a bishop; the "official" biography. Discreet (no mention of Annette). Of historical interest.

Legouis, Emile H.; *La Jeunesse de Wordsworth: 1770–1798,* 1896. Eng. transl., *The Early Life of Wordsworth,* 1897; 3rd ed., 1932. — Focused on *The Prelude.* Brilliantly opens the modern study of the poet's life and work. Supplementary is Legouis' account of the *Lyrical Ballads* in E. L. Griggs, ed., *Wordsworth and Coleridge,* 1939.

Cooper, Lane; "Wordsworth's Reading," MLN, XXII, 83, 110 (1907); revised in *Cornell Studies,* XXXI (1940). — Shows him more bookish than usually supposed. — Cf. the *Rydal Mount Catalogue* of his books, *Wordsworth Society Transactions,* No. 6; Kurt Lienemann, *Die Belesenheit,* 1908; and H. G. Wright, MLR, XLII, 31; 1947.

On Harper's *Wordsworth* (1916) and its theory that his poetry was at its best only as long as he was politically an extreme liberal, see the following reviews: John Bailey's, *Quart. Rev.,* July, 1916 (hostile); G. H. Palmer's, *Harv. Theol. Rev.,* Jan., 1917 (favorable); and C. Vaughan's MLN, Oct., 1916 (dispassionate); also Garrod's attack, *Wordsworth,* 1923; and De Selincourt's, *The Early Wordsworth,* 1936.

On the Annette Vallon Episode

The basic accounts of the main facts in G. McL. Harper, *Wordsworth's French Daughter*, 1921 (also in 2nd ed. of *Life*, 1929) ; and in Emile H. Legouis, *Wordsworth and Annette Vallon*, 1922 (more detailed). — Secondary matters in (1) G. McL. Harper, "Did Wordsworth Defy the Guillotine?" rptd. in *Spirit of Delight*, 1928, on whether he attempted in 1793 to rejoin Annette (cf. J. V. Logan, TLS, Nov. 20, 1937) ; and (2) Kenneth Curry, "Southey's Visit to Caroline Wordsworth Baudouin," PMLA, LIX, 599, 1944; on his support of his daughter by Annette (cf. MacGillivray, Batho, et al., TLS, Sept. 5, 1929; Apr. 3, Apr. 17, May 8, May 17, 1931) .

Two brilliantly written interpretations, carrying to extremes the theory that the episode made Wordsworth's life a moral failure and his poetry sentimental hypocrisy, are:

Read, Herbert; *Wordsworth*, 1930. — Cf. TLS, Dec. 18, 1930.

Fausset, H. I'A.; *The Lost Leader*, 1933.

Similar attitudes toward his career as frustrated or inharmonious, in Bertrand Russell, "The Harm That Good Men Do," *Harper's*, Oct., 1926; and K. G. Pfeiffer, "The Theme of Desertion," *State Coll. Wash. Research Studies*, XII, 122; 1944.

Broad-minded and just interpretations are given by Patton, *Rediscovery of Wordsworth*, pp. 202–216; and by Havens, *Mind of a Poet*, pp. 508–513. In essential agreement with them, and rejecting extreme charges of neglect, remorse, and consequent paralysis of poetic powers, are Sperry (1935) , De Selincourt (1936) and A. L. Strout (1940) ; see below.

Chiefly Biographical (Continued)

Knaplund, Paul; "The Grant of a Civil List Pension in 1842," MLN, XLII, 385; 1927. — Evidence on his narrow means.

Harper, G. McL.; "The Crisis in Wordsworth's Life and Art," *Queen's Quart.*, XL, 1; 1933. — Death of his brother.

Potts, Abbie F.; "First Meeting with Hazlitt," MLN, XLIV, 296; 1929. — On the estrangement, see E. L. Griggs, MLN, XLVIII, 173; 1933.

Magnus, Laurie; "Wordsworth and His Biographers," *Nineteenth Cent. and After*, CXIII, 629; 1933. — Victorians slighted his youth; Legouis and Harper overstressed it; Fausset misinterprets it.

De Selincourt, Ernest; *Dorothy Wordsworth*, 1933. — Authoritative and masterful. — Catherine M. Maclean's *Dorothy Wordsworth: The Early Years*, 1932, is an excellent popular biography, well interpreting the emotional and spiritual aspects.

Bishop, D. H., "The Origin of 'The Prelude,'" SP, XXXVIII, 494; 1941. — Cf. his earlier article, SP, XXXII, 483; 1935; and R. D. Havens' objections, SP, XXXIII, 55; 1936. Bishop maintains that *The Prelude* was not planned until 1799.

Hartsell, E. H.; "The Date of the 'Ode to Duty,'" TLS, May 30, 1935. — Composed probably not later than Sept., 1804, several months earlier than his brother's death. Cf. Nowell Smith, TLS, June 20, 1935.

De Selincourt, Ernest; *The Early Wordsworth*, 1936 (as "The Young Wordsworth") in *Wordsworthian and Other Studies* (ed. Helen Darbishire, 1947) . — Unpublished verse, helpful in modifying views of Harper and others about Annette, the relatively greater importance of Mary, etc. — See TLS, Jan. 9, 1937, and Apr. 19, 1947.

Beatty, Frederika; *William Wordsworth of Rydal Mount*, 1939. — Friendly interpretation of his personality in his old age; attacks some of De Quincey's gossip.

De Selincourt, Ernest; "Wordsworth and His Daughter's Marriage," in E. L. Griggs, ed., *Wordsworth and Coleridge*, 1939; rptd., *Wordsworthian Studies*, 1947. — His objections to Dora's marriage to Quillinan.

Strout, A. L.; "Wordsworth's Desiccation," MLR, xxxv, 162; 1940. — Judicious; recognizes that many different causes affected the decline of his powers.

Weaver, Bennett; "The Property of Fortitude," SP, xxxvii, 610; 1940. — Wordsworth never evaded the painful or tragic side of life (corrects Fausset, Read, B. P. Kurtz's *Pursuit of Death,* et al.) .

Meyer, G. W.; *Wordsworth's Formative Years* [to 1798], 1943. — Bold and frank attempt to rewrite the life on the basis of factual evidence. *The Prelude* regarded as of no autobiographical value. Helpful as a corrective and irritant, but too prosaic to interpret fully the growth of a poet's personality. See reviews: TLS, Jan. 22, 1944; Bennett Weaver, ELH, xi, 20, 1944; Helen Darbishire, RES, xxi, 71, 1945.

McNulty, J. B.; "Wordsworth's Tour of the Wye, 1798," MLN, lx, 291; 1945.

Wells, J. E.; "Wordsworth and the Railways, 1844–45," MLQ, vi, 34; 1945.

Chiefly on His Philosophy, Political Theory, or Religion

See above, under "Of First Importance," Leslie Stephen (1876) , Whitehead (1925) , Dicey (1917) , and Beatty (1922) .

Inge, W. R.; *Studies of English Mystics,* 1906.

Campbell, O. J.; "Sentimental Morality in Wordsworth's Narrative Poetry," *Univ. of Wisc. Studies,* 1920. — Campbell, O. J., and Mueschke, Paul; "Guilt and Sorrow," MP, xxiii, 293; 1926; "The Borderers," MP, xxiii, 465; 1926; and "Wordsworth's Aesthetic Development, 1795–1802," *Univ. of Mich. Essays and Studies,* 1933. — Campbell, O. J.; "Wordsworth's Conception of the Esthetic Experience," in E. L. Griggs, *Wordsworth and Coleridge,* 1939. — These articles stress the influence of the School of Sensibility and its cult of "virtue in distress," and also Wordsworth's alleged remorse for the Annette episode. The overemphasis on "furtive expression" of remorse is pointed out in R. D. Havens' review, MLN, li, 389; 1936; and in G. W. Meyer's *Wordsworth's Formative Years,* 1943, pp. 111, 223, 227, etc.

Cerf, Barry; "Wordsworth's Gospel of Nature," PMLA, xxxvii, 615; 1922. — Typical attack by a member of the More and Babbitt "humanistic" school. Rebuttal by J. W. Beach, PMLA, xl, 346; 1925. — Cf. J. P. Lilley, *Hibbert Journal,* xix, 532; 1921; and Walter Garstang, *Nature,* Jan. 16, 1926, a defense from a naturalist's standpoint.

Cobban, Alfred; *Edmund Burke and the Revolt against the Eighteenth Century: A Study of the Political Thinking of Burke, Wordsworth, Coleridge, and Southey,* 1929. — Cf. E. H. Hartsell, "Wordsworth's 1835 Postscript: An Advanced Program for Labor," SP, xlii, 617; 1945; rptd. in *No. Car. Studies in Lang. and Lit.,* 1945.

Potts, Abbie F.; "Wordsworth and Fleetwood's Sermons," SP, xxvi, 444; 1929. — On the pervasive Christian beliefs and assumptions, often ignored. — Cf. W. A. Claydon, "The Numinous," *Hibbert Journal,* xxviii, 601; 1930.

Babbitt, Irving; "The Primitivism of Wordsworth," Bookman, 1931; rptd. in *On Being Creative,* 1932. — The chief attack by the "humanists."

Rader, M. M.; *Presiding Ideas in Wordsworth's Poetry,* Univ. of Wash., 1931. — Review: JEGP, xxxii, 422; 1933. Corrects Beatty's overemphasis on Hartley, by stressing the transcendental; see Rader's earlier study, MP, xxvi, 169; 1928.

Dunn, S. G.; "Wordsworth's Metaphysical System," Engl. Asso. *Essays and Studies,* 1933. — Its relation to Newton and Christianity. — Cf. John D. Rea, "Coleridge's Intimations of Immortality from Proclus," MP, xxvi, 201; 1928; and Stallknecht, below.

Sherwood, Margaret; *Undercurrents of Influence in English Romantic Poetry,* 1934. — Influence of the philosophic-religious tradition from the seventeenth century. Cf. J. Crofts, *Wordsworth and the Seventeenth Century,* 1940, which exaggerates that influence.

Beach, J. W.; *The Concept of Nature in Nineteenth-Century English Poetry*, 1936. — Cf. his "Reason and Nature in Wordsworth," JHI, I, 335; 1940.

Willey, Basil; *The Eighteenth Century Background*, 1940. — In Beach and Willey, the Babbittian misinterpretation of Wordsworth's nature philosophy is corrected; but Wordsworth's philosophy is nevertheless assumed to be erroneous. That assumption is attacked in Bernbaum's "Is Wordsworth's Nature-Poetry Antiquated?" ELH, VII, 333; 1940.

Martin, A. D.; *The Religion of Wordsworth*, 1936. — A religion of gratitude for Nature, for humanity at its best, and for the Scriptures.

Geen, Elizabeth; "The Concept of Grace in Wordsworth's Poetry," PMLA, LVIII, 689; 1943. — The persistence of Christian beliefs in him. Errs by assuming panentheism to be pantheism.

Stallknecht, Newton P.; *Strange Seas of Thought*, 1945. — Important testimony, from a professor of philosophy, that (1) Wordsworth's philosophy is not a shallow one (as has been alleged by the "humanists," the "New Critics," and even by some Wordsworthians); and that (2) his theory of Creative Imagination is in harmony with certain points of Christian faith. — H. I'A. Fausset's "Wordsworth's Mysticism," *Aryan Path*, XVIII, 23; 1947; an appreciative criticism of Stallknecht, is also notable as showing the critic's change from his earlier (*Lost Leader*, 1933) unsympathetic opinions about Wordsworth.

Worthington, Jane; *Wordsworth's Reading of Roman Prose*, 1946. — The influence of Latin literature, especially Stoicism, on his ethical and political principles. — Rev. JEGP, XLV, 355; 1946.

Lacey, Norman; *Wordsworth's View of Nature*, 1948. — "Certain events in his experience bear a significance other than that which he assigned to them."

General

Bagehot, Walter; "Wordsworth, Tennyson, and Browning," 1864; in *Literary Studies*, 1879. — Contrast between "Pure, Ornate, and Grotesque Art," Wordsworth exemplifying the pure.

Hutton, R. H.; *Literary Essays*, 1871. — Wordsworth's sincere faith in the spiritual values of the common or ordinary. — See G. C. Le Roy, "Hutton," PMLA, LVI, 834; 1941.

Brooke, Stopford; *Theology in the English Poets*, 1874, and *Naturalism in English Poetry*, 1902. — Wordsworth's ideas important, but it is his intense feelings (joy, awe, etc.) that make him a poet.

Brandes, Georg; *Main Currents in Nineteenth Century Literature*, orig. Danish, 1871 ff. — Vol. IV, "Naturalism in England," illustrates the continental materialistic interpretation of the Romantics as rebels.

Pater, Walter; "Wordsworth," 1874; in *Appreciations*, 1889. — Delicate appreciation of Wordsworth's susceptibility to deeper realities, impassioned contemplation, and pregnant style.

Caird, Edward; "Wordsworth," 1880; in *Essays on Literature and Philosophy*, 1892. — By an Hegelian idealist; contrasts him with Rousseau.

Swinburne, A. C.; "Wordsworth and Byron," 1884; in *Miscellanies*, 1886. "It is better to be a Wordsworthian than a Byronite" (vs. Arnold).

Morley, John; Introduction to *Complete Poetical Works* (Globe ed.), 1888. — "To assuage, to reconcile, to fortify . . . whether to do or to endure."

Raleigh, Walter; *Wordsworth*, 1903.

Bradley, A. C.; *English Poetry and German Philosophy*, 1909. — On Hegel and Wordsworth. See M. J. Herzberg, "Wordsworth and German Literature," PMLA,

XL, 302; 1925, on Friederike Brun, Bürger, and Schiller; and L. A. Willoughby in *German Studies Presented to H. G. Fiedler*, 1938, which stresses his insularity. His relations to Herder are studied in a Univ. of Illinois dissertation by Stephen F. Fogle, 1945, not yet published.

Stork, C. W.; "The Influence of the Popular Ballad on Wordsworth and Coleridge," PMLA, XXIX, 299; 1914. — Fuller treatment by Paul G. Brewster, SP, XXXV, 588; 1938.

Barstow, Marjorie L.; *Wordsworth's Theory of Poetic Diction: A Study of the Historical and Personal Background of the Lyrical Ballads*, 1917. — Cf. Alexander Brede, "Theories of Poetic Diction," *Papers of the Michigan Academy of Science, Arts and Letters*, XIV, 537; 1931; T. S. Eliot, "Wordsworth and Coleridge," in *The Use of Poetry*, 1933; G. McL. Harper, "Wordsworth's Poetical Technique," in *Literary Appreciations*, 1937; T. M. Raysor, "Coleridge's Criticism of Wordsworth," PMLA, LIV, 496; 1939; and E. B. Burgum, "Wordsworth's Reform in Poetic Diction," *Coll. Engl.*, II, 207; 1940. — The question of the validity of Wordsworth's theory should not be confused with that of the value of his poems.

Broughton, L. N.; *The Theocritean Element in Wordsworth*, 1920.

Knowlton, E. C.; "The Novelty of 'Michael' as a Pastoral," PMLA, XXV, 432; 1920. — No amorous theme. Cf. MLN, XXXII, 471; 1917. — See Knowlton on Hugh Blair, PQ, VI, 277; 1927.

Madariaga, Salvador; *Shelley and Calderon, etc.*, 1920. — The Latin point of view: Wordsworth too provincial and moralizing.

Babenroth, A. C.; *English Childhood; Wordsworth's Treatment*, 1922. — Compared with eighteenth-century treatments. See C. T. Ryan, SAQ, XLI, 192; 1942, and W. R. Niblett, *London Quarterly*, Jan., 1944.

Grey, (Sir) Edward; "Wordsworth's 'Prelude,'" 1923; in *Fallodon Papers*; 1926. — Appreciation by a famous statesman and naturalist. Cf. "Lord Grey and 'The Prelude,'" TLS, June 7, 1923.

Thompson, Frank T.; "Emerson's Theory and Practice of Poetry," PMLA, XLIII, 1170; 1928. — Wordsworth's influence on him.

Huxley, Aldous; "Wordsworth in the Tropics," in *Do What You Will*, 1929. — Alleges that he misrepresented Nature by "pumping the dangerous Unknown out of Nature." — An influential falsehood. See Havens, *Mind of a Poet*, ch. 6.

Mead, Marian; *Four Studies in Wordsworth*, 1929. — Especially on his use of light and color.

Harrington, Janette; "Wordsworth's 'Descriptive Sketches' and 'The Prelude,'" PMLA, XLIV, 1144; 1929. — See E. N. Hooker's criticism, PMLA, XLV, 619; 1930. — The issue between them is whether Wordsworth interpreted the same experience differently.

Empson, William; *Seven Types of Ambiguity*, 1930. — The elaborate misinterpretation of *Tintern Abbey* (pp. 191–194) is a typical illustration of the hostility of the "New Critics." — Cf. Empson's ludicrous affectation of a liking for a Basic English version of Wordsworth; *Kenyon Review*, II, 449; 1940.

Batho, Edith C.; *The Later Wordsworth*, 1933. — The earlier Wordsworth not as much superior poetically as usually maintained (e.g., by Helen Darbishire, "Wordsworth's Prelude," *Nineteenth Century*, XCIX, 718; 1926). A thesis similar to Miss Batho's is upheld in Mary E. Burton's *The One Wordsworth*, 1942. In emphasizing the oneness and extending the period of creative power, they sometimes go too far and confuse the power to make improvements in style with the power to achieve new creation.

Weaver, Bennett; "Wordsworth's Prelude: An Intimation of Certain Problems," SP, XXXI, 534; 1934; "The Poetic Function of Memory," SP, XXXIV, 552; 1937; "Forms and Images," SP, xxxv, 433; 1938; "The Growth of a Poet's Mind," *Papers of Mich. Acad. of Science, Arts, and Letters,* 1939; "The Aesthetic Intimation," PQ, xix, 20; 1940; "The Shaping Spirit," SP, xxxvii, 75; 1940.—Should be collected into a book. A psychological approach, poetically sensitive. Traces the changing functions of sense experience, affections, memory, reflection, and imagination, in Wordsworth's aesthetic-religious experience. Against the strict systematizers.—Perhaps Weaver overstates the antagonism between sense experience and imagination, as Francis Christensen asserts in "Creative Sensibility in Wordsworth," JEGP, xlv, 361; 1946.

Sperry, W. L.; *Wordsworth's Anti-Climax,* 1935.—Rejects Fausset's and Read's emphasis on the Annette episode, but advances another over-simple explanation, viz., that Wordsworth's aesthetic theory impaired his work. See Havens' review, MLN, li, 389; 1936; and Strout, MLR, xxxv, 162; 1940. Sperry is sound on Wordsworth's personality and religion.

Leavis, F. R.; "Wordsworth," in *Revaluation,* 1936.—Appreciates his "critical intelligence," and his transmitting what was best in the eighteenth-century tradition.

Bush, Douglas; *Mythology and the Romantic Tradition,* 1937.—Wordsworth original and influential in adapting ancient myths to express modern ideals. Cf. Bush's "Wordsworth and the Classics," *Univ. Toronto Quart.,* ii, 359; 1933.

Grierson, Herbert J. C.; *Milton and Wordsworth,* 1937.—Both prophets, and disappointed in political revolutions; but Wordsworth has more faith in culture, humanity, and happiness.

Murry, J. Middleton; *Heroes of Thought,* 1938.—Wordsworth "one of the creators of the modern world"; within his limitations, democratic; his patriotism critical and ethical.

Comparetti, Alice P.; Introduction to *White Doe of Rylstone,* 1940.—His understanding of more than one kind of religious experience; excellent on the inwardness, p. 124.—Cf. C. B. Bradford, MP, xxxvi, 59; 1938.

Miles, Josephine; *Wordsworth and the Vocabulary of Emotion,* Univ. of California, 1942.—On the basis of statistical facts draws inferences about changes in style, mood, and intent.—Cf. her "Wordsworth and Glitter," SP, xl, 552; 1943; on his theory.

Trilling, Lionel; "Wordsworth's Ode: Intimations of Immortality," *Engl. Inst. Annual,* 1942.—Not a farewell to his art; in maturity there may flourish imagination, the philosophic mind, and the percipience of true reality.

Tillett, Nettie S.; "The Poet of the Present Crisis," SR, lii, 367; 1944.—Cf. the turning to Wordsworth in World War I, above, A. C. Dicey, *Statesmanship,* 1917.

Sutherland, J. R.; *Wordsworth and Pope,* 1944.—Not to be judged by the same standards; each great in his way.

Shackford, Martha H.; *Wordsworth's Interest in Painters and Pictures* (Wellesley, Mass.), 1945.—His insistence that art should express significance.

Van Doren, Mark; *The Noble Voice,* 1946.—Considers ten great poems of world literature; disparages *The Prelude;* poems should have "other subjects than their authors."

Sackville-West, Victoria; "Wordsworth and Modern Poetry," *Trans. Royal Soc. of Lit.,* 1946.—The moderns who accept his theory have pushed it too far.

Reynolds, Lorna; "In Defence of Romanticism," *Dublin Mag.,* xxi, 24; 1946.—Against T. S. Eliot et al.; Wordsworth made chief defender.

McNulty, J. B.; "Milton's Influence on Wordsworth's Early Sonnets," PMLA, lxii, 745; 1947.—Wordsworth "contributed quite as much as he borrowed."—Cf. Havens, PMLA, lxiii, 751; 1948.—On the influence of Wordsworth's sonnets on the Victorians, see G. B. Sanderlin, ELH, v, 225; 1938.

Fairchild, H. N.; "Wordsworth's Doctrine of Creative Delusion," SAQ, XLVI, 545; 1947. — Maintains that he supposed "beliefs repugnant to reason justifiable if they foster the sense of imaginative power." Questionable.

Elwin, Malcolm; *The First Romantics*, 1947. — Good on Coleridge; a "grotesque caricature" of Wordsworth (TLS, Dec. 13, 1947).

Fink, Z. S.; "Wordsworth and the English Republican Tradition," JEGP, XLVII, 107; 1948. — Well-documented study of his place in English political and moral philosophy.

Additional References on Individual Poems

On *Tintern Abbey:* Charles H. Gray, "Wordsworth's First Visit," PMLA, XLIX, 123; 1934; John C. Ransom, *The New Criticism*, pp. 115–119; 1941; John B. McNulty, "Autobiographical Vagaries," SP, XLII, 81; 1945; and "Wordsworth's Tour," MLN, LX, 291; 1945.

On the *Lucy Poems:* "Wordsworth's First Love," TLS, July 15, July 22, Nov. 11, Dec. 9, 1926; Jan. 30, Feb. 13, March 6, April 3, April 17, May 8, 1930; J. D. Rea, "Hartley Coleridge and Wordsworth's Lucy," SP, XXVIII, 118; 1931; Herbert Hartman, "Lucy Poems," PMLA, XLIX, 134; 1934; J. R. Harris, *Wordsworth's Lucy* (After-glow Essays), 1935; and review of *Early Letters*, TLS, Aug. 29, 1935.

On the *Ode: Intimations of Immortality:* Begin with Lionel Trilling, *Engl. Inst. Annual for 1941*, 1942; and N. P. Stallknecht, *Strange Seas*, Appendix to ch. 5. — Add H. I'A. Fausset, *Proving of Psyche*, p. 178, 1929; G. Wilson Knight, *Christian Renaissance*, pp. 69 and 265; 1933; Herbert Hartman, RES, VI, 129; 1930; J. D. Rea, "Palingenesia," RES, VIII, 82; 1932; D. A. Stauffer, "Cooperative Criticism," *Kenyon Review*, IV, 133; 1942; Cleanth Brooks, *The Well Wrought Urn*, 1947. — On textual variants, E. H. W. Meyerstein, TLS, Oct. 12, 1946. — Horace Gregory's essay in *The Shield of Achilles*, 1944, is fantastic.

On *The Prelude;* Supplement De Selincourt's edition, and Havens' *Mind of a Poet*, with: Bennett Weaver, SP, XXXVII, 75; 1940; D. H. Bishop, "The Origin," SP, XXXVIII, 494; 1941; Mary E. Burton, "How Wordsworth Changed the Diction," CE, Oct., 1941; Francis Christensen, "Creative Sensibility," JEGP, XLV, 361; 1946; and C. Clarke, "Nature's Education of Man," *Philosophy*, XXIII, 302; 1948.

On *The Excursion:* M. Ray Adams, "Joseph Fawcett and Wordsworth's Solitary," PMLA, XLVIII, 508; 1933.

On the History of the Interpretations of Wordsworth

For a general survey: Part I ("Trends in Criticism") in J. V. Logan, *Wordsworthian Criticism*, 1947. Supplement this as follows:

On the early, and on the Victorian, biographical and critical writings, see especially Katherine M. Peek, *Wordsworth in England*, 1943. Also R. C. Bald, *Literary Friendships in the Age of Wordsworth*, 1932; Elsie Smith, *An Estimate of Wordsworth by His Contemporaries*, 1932 [on its "glaring faults," see TLS, May 26, 1932]; W. S. Ward, "Wordsworth, the 'Lake' Poets, and Contemporary Magazine Critics," SP, XLII, 87; 1945; Russell Noyes, *Wordsworth and Jeffrey*, 1941, do. on Burns, PMLA, LIX, 813; 1944; J. R. Derby, "The Paradox of Jeffrey," MLQ, VII, 489; 1946; and J. Dover Wilson, *Leslie Stephen and Matthew Arnold as Critics of Wordsworth*, 1939; on which subject see also A. C. Bradley, *Oxford Lectures*, 1909, and TLS, "Wordsworth's Experience," July 22, 1939.

Annabel Newton, *Wordsworth in Early American Criticism*, 1928, is severely criticized by Norman Foerster, SP, XXVI, 85; 1929.

On the later history, supplement Logan with: Lane Cooper, PMLA, XXIII, 119; 1908; Richard A. Rice, *Wordsworth Since 1916*, 1924; Emile Legouis, *Revue Anglo-Américaine*, III, 531; 1926; Laurie Magnus, "Wordsworth and His Biographers," *Nineteenth Century*, CXIII, 629; 1933; and C. H. Patton, *The Rediscovery of Wordsworth*, 1935.

Bibliographies

Logan, James V.; *Wordsworthian Criticism: A Guide and Bibliography*, 1947.

Broughton, L. N., ed.; *The Wordsworth Collection* (Cornell), 1931, and Supplement, 1942.

Patton, C. H., ed.; *The Amherst Wordsworth Collection*, 1936.

Concordance

Cooper, Lane; *A Concordance to the Poems of William Wordsworth*, 1911.

CHAPTER 6

CHARLES LAMB

(February 10, 1775–December 29, 1834)

His Life.—Charles Lamb, whose father was clerk to a wealthy lawyer, Mr. Salt, was born in London. His father's means were small; but Charles obtained a thorough schooling at Christ's Hospital, to which he was admitted through Mr. Salt's influence, and where Coleridge, three years older than himself, was likewise a pupil. Here he remained from his eighth to his fifteenth year, some of his holidays being happily spent with his grandmother in the county of Hertfordshire. His means did not permit him to gratify his studious cravings by going to college, and perhaps his stammering also prevented it. On leaving school, he went to work in an office; and two years later he became a bookkeeper in the India House, where he was employed for thirty-three years. Thus Lamb was not a professional man-of-letters, but a man of business, toiling in his office with daily regularity, and able to devote only his leisure to literature.

At the age of twenty he fell in love with Anne Simmons, whom he had met in Hertfordshire. His earliest verses were inspired by this attachment; and many years later he made veiled allusions to her as "Alice W." in his essays. His hopes of marrying her were disappointed. The dark cloud of hereditary madness hung over his family. Lamb himself was once temporarily insane; and his beloved sister Mary, upon a frightful day in 1796, became violently mad and stabbed their invalid mother to death. Their elder brother, John, a bachelor with a sufficient salary, ought to have been the mainstay of the family; but it was Charles who assumed the burden. It would have been the usual thing to let the law take its course, and have poor Mary Lamb committed to an asylum for life. Charles, however, declared that he would protect her and take full responsibility for her. He gave up his dream of marriage, and for the rest of his life devoted himself to his sister. Her insanity was of the recurrent type; and she suffered several other attacks, during which she had to be confined. Normally she was a woman of great charm and intelligence. She took an eager interest in her brother's studies and writings, and became his collaborator in several books for children. That Lamb lived in a state of constant anxiety over the mental health of her who was dearest to him should be borne in mind by anyone wishing to comprehend his life and character. Most men in his position—burdened with business drudgery, harassed by domestic worries, and hampered by narrow means and lack of a college education—would have found sufficient excuses for stagnating intellectually. Not so Charles Lamb; despite all his disadvantages, he achieved in the course of time a rare degree of culture and a mastery of style.

In 1796, four of Lamb's sonnets were published with Coleridge's *Poems*. Two years later Lamb and Charles Lloyd issued a volume, *Blank Verse*, in which Lamb's *Old Familiar Faces* (*Anth.*, 375) appeared; and in the same year he published his prose tale, *Rosamund Gray*. In 1802, he attempted a tragedy in the Elizabethan manner, *John Woodvil;* and in 1806, hoping to fill his scanty purse, he produced a farce at Drury Lane—*Mr. H.* None of these efforts was successful; the farce, indeed, was such a wretched failure that it was hissed—Lamb characteristically joining in the hisses.

A slight turn for the better came, in a curious manner in 1807. William Godwin,[1] the former rationalistic radical, who since the days of his *Political Justice* had grown mellow and almost sentimental, and who was issuing a "Juvenile Library," asked Lamb to contribute to this series. Thus originated *Tales from Shakspeare: Designed for the Use of Young Persons*, being prose versions of twenty of the plays, Charles writing the six tragedies, and Mary the fourteen comedies. This venture was a success in its field, and was followed by several other books for children.

Lamb had been assiduously collecting and reading the Elizabethan dramatists, sometimes purchasing a folio when to common sense a new suit of clothes seemed more needful (*Anth.*, 388). Luckily he obtained a commission to edit *Specimens of English Poets Who Lived About the Time of Shakspeare* (1809). This proved the second step toward a recognition of his real powers—the felicity of his selections, and particularly the excellence and charm of his annotations, attracting attention. By 1811 he was anonymously contributing essays to Leigh Hunt's *Reflector* and in 1813 to *The Examiner*. By 1818 he was so well known that a publisher encouraged him to collect his poems and essays and issued them as *The Works of Charles Lamb: in Two Volumes*, the title seeming rather grandiloquent to the modest author. It was not until 1820, when Lamb was forty-five years old, that he began that series of essays for the *London Magazine*, the *Essays of Elia* (a foreigner named Elia had been a fellow clerk in his office) which constituted his most brilliant and celebrated work. The first series was collected in 1823, and *The Last Essays of Elia* ten years later.

The friendships of Lamb played a great part in his life and in the development of his genius. Among those whom he cherished were Coleridge, Wordsworth, Southey, Henry Crabb Robinson, and Hazlitt—the latter being the most difficult to avoid quarrels with. His Wednesday evenings at home usually sparkled with wit and hilarity. In his middle years his increased salary enabled him and Mary to live more comfortably.

---

[1] See, above, p. 29.

In 1825, when he was fifty, he was retired on a pension of two-thirds his salary. He and Mary had adopted into their household a young lady, Emma Isola, the orphaned daughter of a teacher of Italian; and her youthful presence cheered their home until 1833, when she was married. Mary's attacks and enforced confinements became unfortunately more frequent and protracted in Lamb's last years. The death of Coleridge whom he so loved and revered, in 1834, was a great blow to him; and, in his loneliness, his own death in the same year came as a relief. His sister outlived him twelve years, and was buried beside him.

His Character.—In some ways the best characterization of Lamb is the following, which he amused himself by drawing up in 1827:

> Charles Lamb, born in the Inner Temple, 10th February, 1775; educated in Christ's Hospital; afterwards a clerk in the Accountant's Office, East India House; pensioned off from that service, 1825, after thirty-three years' service; is now a gentleman at large; can remember few specialities in his life worth noting, except that he once caught a swallow flying (*teste sua manu* [2]). Below the middle stature; cast of face slightly Jewish, with no Judaic tinge in his complexional religion; stammers abominably, and is therefore more apt to discharge his occasional conversation in a quaint aphorism, or a poor quibble, than in set and edifying speeches; has consequently been libelled as a person always aiming at wit; which, as he told a dull fellow who charged him with it, is at least as good as aiming at dullness. A small eater, but not drinker; confesses a partiality for the production of the juniper berry,[3] was a fierce smoker of tobacco, but may be resembled to a volcano burnt out, emitting only now and then an occasional puff. Has been guilty of obtruding upon the public a tale in prose, called *Rosamund Gray,* a dramatic sketch named *John Woodvil,* a *Farewell Ode to Tobacco,* with sundry other poems and light prose matter, collected in two slight crown octavos, and pompously christened his *Works,* though in fact, they were his recreations; and his true works may be found on the shelves of Leadenhall Street,[4] filling some hundred folios. He is also true Elia, whose essays are extant in a little volume. He died 18—, much lamented. Witness his hand,—
>
> *Charles Lamb*

Strange as it may seem to the modern reader who enjoys Lamb's essays, some of his contemporaries disliked him, especially on first acquaintance. When heated with alcohol, or when irritated by prosaic and smug conversation, he would sometimes appear perversely contradictory, peevish, shocking, or frivolous. Keats thought him lacking in sensibility. Carlyle disliked him—perhaps because he felt that Lamb detested the hortatory, which was the breath of Carlyle's life. But those who knew him best, like Coleridge, Southey, and Wordsworth, understood and forgave some of the peculiarities of manner, and revered the man, with his quiet heroism that never wore an air of conscious martyrdom, his self-deprecia-

[2] Witness his hand.
[3] gin
[4] i.e., in the office where he worked.

tion, his utter lack of jealousy of fellow authors, his candor, and his loyalty toward his friends. He showed more patience with Hazlitt than did any other friend of that exasperating son of discord. It was at the time when Hazlitt's repute was at its worst that Lamb made public profession of his unalterable regard for him, saying, "I think William Hazlitt, in his natural and healthy state, one of the wisest and finest spirits breathing"; and he remained faithful to him unto death. De Quincey, with his acute understanding of the problems of morbid psychology and appreciative of all that Lamb had to live through in his long vigilance over Mary, wrote: "Considering the quality of the resistance and the humble resources in money and friends, we have come to the deliberate judgement that the whole range of history scarcely presents a more affecting spectacle of perpetual sorrow, humiliation, or conflict, and that was supported to the end (that is, through forty years) with more resignation, or with more absolute victory." It was Coleridge that Wordsworth praised as "the most wonderful man he had ever known"; but it was to Lamb that he paid the tribute:

O, he was *good,* if e'er a good man lived!

And Coleridge said of him: "He has more totality and individuality of character than any other man I know."

His Views.—Many readers of Lamb do not think of him as a sage or philosopher, because instead of expounding his wisdom in treatises or sermons he insinuated it in familiar essays, often humorous in tone and sometimes indulging in palpable exaggerations or sallies of mere fooling. He was indeed a laughing philosopher—but a philosopher nevertheless; and his chief thoughts constitute a system having something of that "totality and individuality" which Coleridge discerned in his personality.

Like Wordsworth and Coleridge, he was in his youth a sentimentalist; and a devotee of Bowles and Cowper. His *Rosamund Gray,* the story of a young girl ruined by a villain, was merely the old theme of virtue-in-distress treated with unusual delicacy; and in his early verses plaintiveness was the keynote. The stern actualities of his life, however, presently taught him to overcome this softness. In his mature works there is much grace but little weakness. He recognized that existence involves evils and burdens: *"sunt lachrimae rerum* [life is full of tears]," he writes to Wordsworth, "and you and I must bear it." How the burden of existence might best be borne, he had pondered deeply. Many of the ways to happiness usually recommended did not appeal to him. He rejected the various recipes of the School of Sensibility; its idyllic misrepresentations of life, and its dreams of utopian perfection only resulted in dissatisfaction with reality, in a fatal "disgust with common life." "It is better," he said, "not to think too much of pleasant possibles, that one may not be out of humor with present insipids." As for the state of nature and noble savages, he had no faith in them. "I can just endure Moors," he tells Southey, "because of their connection as foes with Christians; but Abyssinians, Ethiops, Esquimaux, Dervises, and all that tribe, I hate. . . . I am a Christian, Englishman, Londoner, Templar." When his friend Manning became enthusiastic about the free-born Tartars, and took a notion to become a missionary among them, Lamb implored him to take a look at a Tartar who was on exhibition in the city and was "no very favorable specimen of his countrymen," and protested that such abilities as Manning's ought not to be "buried in heathen countries among nasty, unconversible, horse-belching Tartar-people!"

The political way of obtaining happiness, Lamb likewise scorned, whether by a revolution like the French, or by constitutional changes such as were advocated in England, or by pantisocratic schemes of trans-atlantic freedom. Godwin's way—the attainment of serenity by the suppression of the feelings—was humanly impossible. He liked the aged Godwin personally; but rationalistic metaphysics he rejected. The ecclesiastical and theological ways were just as uncongenial to him. He sincerely believed in the loving God of the New Testament, but he was skeptical of church dogma. He thought it professed to know too much about the unknowable:

> The economy of Heaven is dark,
> And wisest clerks have missed the mark.

Trying to make one's religion too clear and distinct, as the Deists attempted, was not necessarily making it sounder: "I am determined," he playfully pretended, "my children shall be brought up in their father's religion, *if they can find out what it is!*" (To John Chambers, 1818.) He also saw the limitations of scientific knowledge: "There is a march of science," he remarked; "but who shall beat the drum for its retreat?"

The most significant of Lamb's antipathies, however, was against dogmatic moralists and reformers who assumed that virtue was attainable by dragooning others, young and old, into obeying certain positive rules of conduct. This program was odious to him in every particular—in the type of persons who believed in it, in the character of their rules, and in the method by which they would apply them. Not all these reformers were canting hypocrites like Burns's "unco' guid," though some of them were; but even the sincere and well meaning among them had too little experience and imagination to realize what a complicated and difficult undertaking it was to set themselves up as judges of all their fellow men. The formal rules they had laid down for conduct were altogether too narrow to result in justice when applied to actual cases widely differing in circumstances; they were like popular proverbs or copybook maxims, at best half-truths. And, even if such moral rules were sound, to impose them by compulsion or solemn exhortation or command instead of genial persuasion was only to defeat their purpose. "Damn virtue that's thrust upon us," he exclaimed, "it behaves itself with such constraint, till conscience opens the window and lets out the goose."

Lamb assailed our human propensity to simplify the art of living by reducing its broad principles to narrow formulae. Even a noble principle thus converted into a conventional code lost its efficacy. In its origin the chivalrous respect for womanhood was admirable; but whenever in modern times it became merely social etiquette, and while vaunting itself upon its regard for woman ignored the ugly truth that in many ways women who did not happen to be rich and beautiful were treated unjustly and even brutally, our boasted politeness was a mockery (*Modern Gallantry; Anth.*, 381). All this was formalism, the petrifaction of what should be a vital ideal; and formalism was to Lamb the archenemy of truth, virtue, and beauty.

If one was to approach a solution of the problem of securing a reasonable degree of happiness in life as it is, one must first of all not expect too much of human nature, and not forget that even the best of men and women had their weaknesses (like oneself). He said:

> I am determined to lead a merry life in the midst of sinners. I try to consider all men as such, and to pitch my expectations from human nature as low as possible. In this view, all unexpected virtues are Godsends and beautiful exceptions.

This did not imply cynicism. The Godsends were to be met with more frequently than might be expected; but one must not frustrate one's search by being snobbish or exclusive in one's companionships:

> The odds are, that under every green hill, and in every crowded street, people of equal worth [with those of one's narrow circle] are to be found, who do more good in their generation, and make less noise in the doing of it.

Such discovery of moral beauty and strength in our fellow sinners was one of the purest of joys, and not marred, like fault finding, by pharisaical pride.

He loved to fall into reveries about the mysterious margins of ordinary human life—for instance, about dreams (*Dream Children; Anth.*, 383). There was, too, the pleasure, both aesthetic and philosophical, of perceiving the strange and infinite variety of human character. Here also, the narrow minded lost much, who expected or desired individuals to conform to one dull pattern, and were frightened by "queerness," or angered by it, or (worst of all) not interested in it. "I have never made an acquaintance that lasted," he wrote, "or a friendship that answered, with any that had not some tincture of the absurd in their characters" (*All Fools' Day*). Life was the prince of entertainers, never repeating his jests or his magical experiments; and the fault lay in us if we remained stolidly unappreciative of his inexhaustible genius. Landscapes and gardens were well enough in their way, but city dwellers had their rich compensation in the fascinating spectacle of human life. To him who sought, the universe disclosed its nature in Fleet Street as well as upon the summit of Helvellyn. Thus the message of Charles Lamb complemented that of Wordsworth.

His Literary Principles.—In books, as in people, Lamb detested the wishy-washy, the namby-pamby, the pretentious, the conventional, the pharisaical; and he loved the strongly individual, the positive, the impassioned, the intense, the outspoken, even when accompanied by grave or absurd faults. His playful manner hid his deeper seriousness. Books, pictures, and dramatic performances—provided they be of the best—were to him sources of unfading pleasure. He delighted in romances which had a strong infusion of common sense, such as those of Scott, and in novels which would cure any finical distaste for ordinary life, such as those of Defoe and Fielding. The latter's courageous autobiographical *Voyage to Lisbon* was one of his favorite books. He liked Keats's *Isabella, or The Pot of Basil* better than *Hyperion* (Review of Keats's *Lamia* volume), for he preferred poetry that did not get too far away from mundane life. He was unable to appreciate Shelley, whose poetry he found "thin sown with profit or delight." For Byron's character and genius he felt positive aversion, not because of his boldness but because of his cynicism:

> I never much relished his lordship's mind. . . . He was to me offensive, and I can never make out his power, which his admirers talk of. Why, a line of Wordsworth's is a lever to lift the immortal spirit. Byron can only move the spleen. He was at best a satirist,—in any other way he was mean enough. I dare say I do him an injustice, but I cannot love him nor squeeze a tear to his memory.

Wordsworth, on the other hand, who had overcome despondency, he admired. *The Excursion* he praised as follows:

> The general tendency of the argument (which we might almost affirm to be the leading moral of the poem) is to abate the pride of the calculating understanding, and to reinstate the imagination and the affections in those seats from which modern philosophy has labored but too successfully to expel them.

His opposition to materialism and rationalism is shown also in his dislike of histories written in the manner of Hume, having "that damned philosophical Humeian indifference, so cold and unnatural and inhuman"; whereas history should be

> full of scandal, which all true history is. No palliatives, but all the stark wickedness that actually gives the momentum to national actors; truth and sincerity staring out upon you perpetually in *alto relievo* [high relief].

Books, like men, were uninteresting if without idiosyncrasies; hence, in part, his joy in writers like Robert Burton, Thomas Fuller, and Sir Thomas Browne. The greatness of masters like Hogarth, or the Elizabethan dramatists, or the supreme genius, Shakspeare, lay in their undistorted rendering of the richness of life,

> where there is no such thing as pure tragedy to be found, but merriment and light-weight infelicity, ponderous crime and feather-light vanity, like twin-formed births, disagreeing complexions of one intermixture, perpetually uniting to show forth a motley spectacle.

Shakspeare saw life imaginatively, namely "his subject has so acted that it has seemed to direct *him*,—not to be *arranged* by him."

Lamb applied these romantic principles of literature to the field of children's books. Here he found what seemed to him a sad state of affairs. Earnest but misguided souls like Mrs. Barbauld,[5] scorning what they deemed silly nursery tales, were trying to improve the young by providing them with heavily moralized stories and with matter-of-fact information concerning geography and the various -ologies. Lamb had evolved no theory like Wordsworth's about the three ages of man; but he sympathetically understood the minds of children, and in a letter to Coleridge he protested against the methods of Mrs. Barbauld as follows:

> Knowledge insignificant and vapid as Mrs. B's books convey, it seems, must come to a child in the *shape of knowledge*, and his empty noddle must be turned with conceit of his own powers when he has learnt that a horse is an animal, and Billy is better than a horse, and such like; instead of that beautiful interest in wild tales which made the child a man, while all the time he suspected himself to be no bigger than a child. Science has succeeded to poetry no less in the little walks of children than with men. Is there no possibility of averting this sore evil? Think what you would have been now, if instead of being fed with tales and old wives' fables in childhood, you had been crammed with geography and natural history! . . .
> Damn them!—I mean the cursed Barbauld crew, those blights and blasts of all that is human in man and child.

His Works.—Among the Lambs' books for children, besides the *Tales from Shakspeare,* were *The Adventures of Ulysses* (1808), based upon the *Odyssey, Mrs. Leicester's School* (1809), and *Poetry for Children* (1809).

His essays may be loosely classified as personal reminiscences, character sketches, literary criticisms, and hints on the art of living; although these types are usually intermingled. Famous among the personal essays are *Blakesmoor, Mackery End, My First Play, Christ's Hospital, Old China (Anth.,* 388), *The Superannuated Man,* and *Dream Children: a Reverie (Anth.,* 383). His skill in characterization is shown in *Mrs. Battle, Captain Jackson, Old Benchers, South Sea House,* and *Poor Relations.* His general critical principles appear in *The Genius of Hogarth, The Barrenness of the Imaginative Faculty in Modern Art, The Sanity of Genius (Anth.,* 390), and *The Genteel Style;* and his application of them to special authors or topics is shown in *Wordsworth's Excursion, Keats's Lamia, Sidney's Sonnets, Defoe's Secondary Novels,* and *The Artificial Comedy of the Last Century.* His criticism of life is often disguised as humorous confession of his likes and dislikes, as in *Imperfect Sympathies* or *All Fools' Day.* Sometimes he is more directly combative, as in *Modern Gallantry (Anth.,* 381), and in the series entitled *Popular Fallacies (Anth.,* 390). In the latter, he fought against proverbs and platitudes

[5] On her conflict with Coleridge, see above, p. 61.—Such compensating merits as she had are sketched in TLS, June 19, 1943.

which, he said, at best were of service only to teach the first rudiments of humanity, and at worst, when quoted by the unobservant and the unthinking, were hypocritical and false. Such commonplace scraps of pseudo-wisdom were "Enough is as good as a feast" (" a vile cold-scrag-of-mutton sophism!"), "We must not look a gift-horse in the mouth," and "Handsome is that handsome does."

Form and Style.—Lamb's conviction that truth was stifled when rendered formal and dogmatic, made the familiar essay the perfect means of expression for him. He has no superior in that type of literature, which probably demands more than any other the art that conceals art. Instead of assuming the magisterial air of one wiser and better than yourself, he wins your confidence by the absence of any pretense at superiority. He confesses as to a fellow mortal his weaknesses of the flesh and of the spirit, and his admittedly unreasonable prejudices. Ingratiating but never obsequious, he seems to assume that you, like himself, are a lover not of sensational and garish things but rather of the unobtrusive and precious realities of human life, whether old or new; and his assumption that you appreciate such things, magically creates that appreciation within you. Informally he traverses now this, now that, aspect of existence. At first sight his topics seem insignificant, though they are always curiously real, and presently, as he discloses the intermingled humor and pathos of them, you feel with Landor:

> What wisdom in thy levity, what truth
> In every utterance of that purest soul!

His style was charged with sometimes being unnecessarily antiquated and imitative, and it is true that now and then the archaic became a mannerism with him; but as a rule when he employs the old-fashioned utterance it is because it conveys his own sincere feelings more delicately and precisely than would the modern style. Both his *Essays* and his *Letters* are sincere expressions of his personality as disciplined and deepened by affliction, elevated by fortitude, and brightened by a sense of humor.

His Relation to Other Romantics.—There are authors for whom we feel a strong personal affection, not wholly dependent upon our esteem for their works. One of them is Dr. Johnson, the most beloved of eighteenth-century authors. Another is Lamb, the most beloved of the Romantics. They had not a few traits in common, but the contrasts between the views and the manner of Dr. Johnson and those of Lamb typify the differences between the two periods.

Lamb looked up to Coleridge deferentially as a superior intellect, as his teacher, and as one who had "rescued him from the polluting spirit of the world." "I cannot think a thought," he avowed, "I cannot make a criticism on men or books without an ineffectual turning and reference to him; he was the proof and touchstone of all my cogitations." But the temper of his mind was more nearly similar to Wordsworth's. He was, to be sure, not as philosophical and as mystical as Wordsworth, nor was he solemn. But he approached the problems of life in a similar way, keeping close to his own experience, and seeking the ideal in the actual. He, too, counselled cheerful courage, faith in the affections, plain living, and, if not high thinking, at least kindly thoughtfulness. He supplemented Wordsworth's message by disclosing how one's life could come into contact with ideal values in the city as well as in the country; how urban life might mean something finer than an alternation of toil and frivolity; and how, even to the poor in purse, there were open sources of abiding satisfaction in the human scene, in friendships, and in the pleasures of literature, drama, and the fine arts. It was Lamb's enthusiasm for the Elizabethans that sowed in Hazlitt the seeds of his Shakspearian criticism. Lamb's chief general contribution, however, was his persuasive warning against narrow formalization of one's conceptions of human life and character. All the Romantics were in principle opposed to the petrification of ideals into codes, but none was as skillful as Lamb in creating a distaste for the state of mind of a formalist and dogmatist who at best was a bore and at worst a purblind reformer, and, on the other hand, a love for those who try to make of living an art rather than a system or regimen.

SELECTED BIBLIOGRAPHY

OF FIRST IMPORTANCE

Selections

> The Portable Charles Lamb, ed. John Mason Brown, 1948. — Vivid Introduction.
> Everybody's Lamb, ed. A. C. Ward, 1933.
> A Shorter Lamb, ed. E. E. Reynolds, 1930. — Essays and Letters arranged as a kind of autobiography.
> Lamb's Criticism, ed. E. M. W. Tillyard, 1923.

Texts

> Works in Prose and Verse of Charles and Mary Lamb, ed. Thomas Hutchinson, 2 vols. in 1, 1924. The first volume contains all the Essays of Elia, and the most important other prose, and is obtainable separately. — Does not include the letters, but otherwise preferable to Complete Works and Letters (Modern Libr. Giant), 1935.

Good Introductory Studies

> Howe, Will D.; Charles Lamb and His Friends, 1944. — Sympathetic insights into personal traits and relationships, but superficial on Lamb's convictions about life and literature; see rev. JEGP, XLIII, 482; 1944.

> Pater, Walter; in Appreciations, 1889. — A celebrated essay.

> Winchester, C. T.; in A Group of English Essayists, 1910.

> Blunden, Edmund; Charles Lamb and His Contemporaries, 1933. — Sensitive and scholarly.

FOR ADVANCED STUDENTS

Important Additional Texts

> Works of Charles and Mary Lamb, ed. E. V. Lucas, 7 vols., 1903–05; rev. ed., 6 vols., 1912 (omits Dramatic Specimens).

The Letters of Charles Lamb, to Which Are Added Those of His Sister Mary Lamb, ed. E. V. Lucas, 3 vols., 1935. — Standard edition of the correspondence, with valuable annotations; abbreviated in the Everyman ed. below.

The Letters of Charles Lamb, ed. Guy Pocock, 2 vols. (Everyman's Libr.) , 1946. — Revised from Lucas' ed., with additional letters.

J. M. Turnbull publishes what may be an additional essay in RES, III, 68; 1927.

Chiefly Biographical

Lucas, E. V.; *Life of Charles Lamb,* 2 vols., 1905; rev. 5th ed., 1921. — The standard Life.

Blunden, Edmund; *Charles Lamb: His Life Recorded by His Contemporaries,* 1934.

Johnson, Edith C.; *Lamb Always Elia,* 1935. — Elia not an "escape-personality." Important on his friends, including Manning. Cf. TLS, Aug. 31, 1946.

Finch, Jeremiah S.; "Companionship in Almost Solitude," *Princeton Univ. Libr. Chronicle,* VI, 179; 1945. — Emma Isola, Lamb MSS., etc.

McKechnie, Samuel; "Charles Lamb of the India House," N&Q, CXCI and CXCII, 1946–47. — Ten valuable studies of his workaday life and business associates, based on official records. Cf. William Foster, *The East India House,* 1924.

Anon.; "Charles Lamb's Best Friend," TLS, May 24, 1947. — Best brief characterization of his sister.

Biographical and Critical

There are noteworthy contemporary comments on Lamb by De Quincey (*Works,* V, 455) , Henry Crabb Robinson, Hazlitt, Leigh Hunt (*Autobiography*) , P. G. Patmore (*My Friends and Acquaintances*) , George Daniel (*Love's Last Labour Not Lost*) , T. N. Talfourd (Sketch, introducing *Letters,* 1837) , and Carlyle (*Reminiscences; dourly* contemptuous) .

Ainger, Alfred: *Charles Lamb* (Engl. Men of Letters) , 1882. — Good appreciations.

Birrell, Augustine; *Obiter Dicta,* Second Series, 1885. — Protest against calling Lamb "poor" or "gentle."

Lake, Bernard; *A General Introduction to Charles Lamb,* Leipzig, 1903. — Emphasizes relationship to Burton's *Anatomy of Melancholy.*

Derocquigny, Jules; *Charles Lamb: Sa Vie et Ses Oeuvres,* 1904. — Thorough, and sometimes subtle. See More's comments, below, IV.

More, Paul Elmer; *Shelburne Essays,* II and IV, 1905–06.

Macdonald, Wilbert L.; "Charles Lamb, the Greatest of the Essayists," PMLA, XXII, 547; 1917. Comparison with Montaigne, Addison, Stevenson, etc. — On Lamb and Montaigne see Charles Dédéyan, *Montaigne Chez Ses Amis Anglo-Saxons,* 1947. which, however, underestimates Lamb's philosophy.

Bradford, Gamaliel; *Bare Souls,* 1924.

Morley, F. V.; *Lamb Before Elia,* 1932. — Cf. Edith C. Johnson, *Lamb Always Elia,* 1935.

Lucas, E. V.; *Lemon Verbena and Other Essays,* 1932.

French, J. Milton; "Lamb and Spenser," SP, XXX, 205; 1933.

Law, Marie Hamilton; *The English Familiar Essay in the Early Nineteenth Century,* 1934. — Relationship of his essays and letters.

Plesner, K. F.; *Elia Og Hans Venner,* Copenhagen, 1934. — A neglected piece of sensitive criticism; contrasts Lamb with Hazlitt and De Quincey.

Boyce, Benjamin; "Tom Brown and Elia," ELH, IV, 147; 1937.

Cook, E. Thornton; *Justly Dear: Charles and Mary Lamb,* 1939. — An historical novel, introducing other Romantics also.

Ross, Ernest C.; *The Ordeal of Bridget Elia,* 1940. — Brings out Mary Lamb's own contributions to the movement.

Daggett, G. Harris; "Lamb's Interest in Dreams," CE, Dec., 1942.

Houghton, Walter E., Jr.; "Lamb's Criticism of Restoration Comedy," ELH, X, 61; 1943. — Maintains it is not as fantastic as it has usually been thought.

Boas, F. S.; "Lamb's Specimens," Engl. Asso. *Essays and Studies, 1943,* 1944. — Cf. R. C. Bald, below, 1946.

Anthony, Katherine; *The Lambs,* 1945. — Fantastic misinterpretations, based on "shop-soiled psychiatry." See reviews by Carlos Baker (*N. Y. Times Book Rev.,* March 18) and R. Ellis Roberts (*Sat. Rev. Lit.,* May 26).

Barnett, G. L.; "First American Review of Lamb," PMLA, LXI, 597; 1946. — In *N. Y. Mirror* of 1832.

Anon.; "The Letters of Charles Lamb," TLS, June 15, 1946.

Bald, R. C.; "Lamb and the Elizabethans," *Studies in Honor of A. H. R. Fairchild,* Columbia, Mo., 1946. — His limitations.

———

There is a Charles Lamb Society, of which particulars are obtainable from the secretary, Ernest G. Crowsley, 37–40 Tavistock Sq., London, W. C. 1.

CHAPTER 7

WILLIAM HAZLITT

(April 10, 1778–September 18, 1830)

1805 Principles of Human Action	1820 Lectures on the Dramatic Literature
1817 The Round Table	of the Age of Elizabeth
1817 Characters of Shakspeare's Plays	1823 Liber Amoris
1818 Lectures on the English Poets	1825 Spirit of the Age
1819 Lectures on the English Comic	1826 The Plain Speaker
Writers	1828–30 Life of Napoleon

His Life.—It was partly the good fortune and partly the misfortune of William Hazlitt that, although naturally of an emotional and sentimental temperament, he was born and reared in an environment where the intellectual and rationalistic was emphasized. His father, a clergyman who valued those aspects of Christianity which appealed to the reason, was an admirer of Price and Priestley,[1] and so confident that the American Revolution had created an Utopia of freedom that he emigrated to the United States with his family in 1783. Three years later, however, they returned. William's childhood was passed in an atmosphere of radical argumentation concerning the glorious French Revolution and the iniquities of the enemies of liberty and enlightenment. Unlike Wordsworth, Coleridge, and Lamb, he did not come in touch with the cultural traditions of an ancient school or university. His father, desiring to shape him after his own image, sent him, when fifteen years old, to a dissenting theological school; and here, too, his environment was predominantly rationalistic. He soon proved unwilling to become a clergyman, and his reading suggested that he was ambitious to become a metaphysician or a political philosopher. He believed he had hit upon an original conception of human nature, and planned an essay on the subject; and he formed the acquaintance of radicals like Godwin, Holcroft, and Fawcett.[2] At the age of eighteen, he returned home, where he spent two happy years of self-directed study and meditation over "some knotty point" or "abstruse author." Not until this period did he become interested in *belles lettres* and take eagerly to the reading of poets and novelists. This interest was intensified by his meeting in January, 1798, the golden-tongued Coleridge (see *My First Acquaintance with Poets; Anth.,* 395). He was also stirred by reading Rousseau's *Nouvelle Héloïse*—just the right nourishment for the half-starved emotional side of his nature. Later he said, probably with some exaggeration, that he had spent two

[1] See, above, p. 27.
[2] See, above, p. 29.

whole years in reading that novel and Rousseau's *Confessions,* and in shedding tears over them.

For the time being, he was to be neither a philosopher nor a poet. His brother John was a successful painter of miniatures, and William at the age of twenty began under his guidance to study painting. His enthusiasm for art was aroused by a visit to a gallery, where, he says, "A mist passed away from my sight, the scales fell off: a new sense came upon me, a new heaven and a new earth stood before me"—an experience which reminds one of Blake's.[3] For some fourteen years, i.e., until he was thirty-four, he was a portrait painter of only mediocre ability, and not an author; and indeed it was not until he was nearly forty that he learned what his real powers were. During his period as an artist he spent some time in Paris where he beheld Napoleon, whom he idolized as the destroyer of kings. By this time his friends Coleridge and Wordsworth had come to look upon Napoleon as a military tyrant and imperialist, which seemed to Hazlitt apostasy to the cause of liberty, and aroused his wrath. He gained new friends, however, in Leigh Hunt and in Charles Lamb, the latter enduring his irritating outbursts most tolerantly. In 1808 he married an acquaintance of the Lambs, Sarah Stoddart, whose best qualifications as a wife to such a man were the ownership of a house (at Winterslow) and a small income. Although she had too little sensitiveness and no intellectual interests, no serious domestic troubles arose between them for some years.

In 1804 Hazlitt had at last found himself able to compose an essay on that philosophical problem which had puzzled him in his youth, and it was published with the title *Principles of Human Action.* Seven years later the need of money led him to give a series of public lectures on the English philosophers, which attracted attention less because of their substance than because of their vigorous style. In 1813 he began to contribute to the *Morning Chronicle* criticisms of dramatic performances, and was fairly launched upon his true vocation. Fortune favored him in this case, for Edmund Kean was just about to begin his glorious career (Drury Lane; January 26, 1814) as a Shakspearian actor; and thus Hazlitt found a subject worthy of his brilliant pen. He fell into a disagreement with his associates and lost his position; but his reputation was now such that it was easy for him to find new outlets for his writings, including Leigh Hunt's *Examiner,* to which he contributed familiar essays. The bold and sometimes tactless utterance of his opinions drew upon him bitter and often unfair attacks from critics like Gifford of the *Quarterly,* who judged everything by their political prejudices. Unhappily Hazlitt also fell at odds with those who were disposed to be his friends—with Wordsworth, with Coleridge, with Southey, and even with Lamb. He repeatedly denounced the three Lake poets, who had once admired the French Revolution and now were "bigots of war against the French." He called them deserters from the cause of liberalism, "following the train of the Pope

[3] See, above, p. 44.

and the Inquisition and the Bourbons, . . . with the emblem of the human heart thrown beneath their feet, which they trampled and spit upon!" (*Works;* VII, 152). The resentment which such outbursts provoked may be seen by comparing Wordsworth's friendly letter of March 5, 1804, to Hazlitt with the one of June 11, 1816, to John Scott, in which Hazlitt is absurdly called "a man of low propensities, . . . too corrupt to understand my poetry."—The defeat of Napoleon at Waterloo in 1815 seemed to Hazlitt the triumph of evil, and it helped to embitter his temper.

He reached the height of his critical power in the lectures—delivered in a very passionate and dramatic manner—on the *English Poets, English Comic Writers,* and *Elizabethan Dramatists,* which he gave in 1818–20. Despite violent attacks upon him by the *Quarterly* and *Blackwood's,* the general admiration for his genius as a critic grew greater and greater. But his private life continued to be vexed with discord. He was accused of having tactlessly helped to bring about the duel in which John Scott, editor of the *London Magazine,* was killed; and by equally tactless remarks about "people with one idea," he offended his closest ally, Leigh Hunt. He seems to have been unable to understand why his bluntness was found annoying: in a bewildered manner, he wrote to Hunt, "I want to know why everybody has such a dislike to me."

In 1819, Hazlitt and his wife had agreed to live apart. It was a year later that he met Sarah Walker, whose mother kept a lodging house in which Hazlitt had taken rooms. Sarah was a handsome creature, and Hazlitt, who had heretofore never known what real passion was, fell violently in love with her:

> In her sight [he wrote] there was Elysium; her smile was heaven; her voice was enchantment; the air of love waved round her, breathing balm into my heart: for a little while I had sat with the gods at their golden tables, I had tasted of all earth's bliss.

All his extraordinary emotional force, which heretofore had too often discharged itself only in anger and hatred, now burst forth in the very extravagance of love. Completely infatuated, he did not perceive that Sarah was vulgar, wanton, and fickle. He begged his wife to divorce him, and she calmly consented; but when this was accomplished, Sarah refused to marry him.

He had records of this affair, in which he had set down the mad course of his feelings—his enchantment, his rapture in her supposed consent, his golden hopes, his awakened jealousy, and his frenzy of disappointment. If that had been the end of the story, if Hazlitt had suppressed the records of his folly and anguish, only the "unco' guid," secure in the insusceptibility of their withered hearts, would severely condemn him. But Hazlitt published an account of it as *Liber Amoris;* and many who would say nothing harsh about his frailty, deplored its publication. The *Quarterly,* soon penetrating behind the anonymity of the book, exulted; and many denounced the author.

The agony of this episode had curiously little effect upon the quality of Hazlitt's writing. He showed no wavering of his powers in his *Table Talks, Spirit of the Age,* or *Plain Speaker.* Lamb not only remained loyal to him, but tried to patch up the quarrel between him and Southey. In 1824, Hazlitt was married again—to a widow, Mrs. Isabella Bridgwater, the exact opposite of his first wife, being a gracious, ladylike person with a genuine interest in his literary work. Her son by a previous marriage, however, caused trouble between them, and she left Hazlitt in 1827. Going abroad, he foregathered at Florence with Landor, whom he greatly admired; and in the region associated with *La Nouvelle Héloïse* he wrote a defense of Rousseau. His chief occupation in his last years was the writing of his *Life of Napoleon,* which he supposed would be regarded as his greatest work. His health now failed him, and at the age of fifty-two he died, in the presence of Charles Lamb, and with the words "Well, I have had a happy life!"

His Character.—"I should belie my own conscience," wrote Lamb, "if I said less than that I think William Hazlitt to be, in his natural and healthy state, one of the wisest and finest spirits breathing." The deplorable fact, however, was that Hazlitt so frequently fell short of that natural and better self. He was a lonely spirit. Partly owing to poor health, he was irritable, and occasionally broke out into hysterical rages. In his youth he had fancied that he would find the world full of virtue and happiness, and his *Essay on the Principles of Human Action* had denounced "the metaphysical doctrine of the innate and necessary selfishness of the human mind." But this, his subsequent experiences taught him, was "to be wrapped in lamb's wool, lulled in Elysium" (*Anth.,* 400). Disappointed with life as it was, but remaining an impassioned lover of high ideals, and certain that his principles were the only just ones, he intolerantly despised anyone whose opinion disagreed with his. He was unwilling to make the concessions necessary to secure friendship and peaceful social intercourse, and his outbreaks of intolerance and peevishness aroused strong prejudice against him. Yet what "an old and attached friend" inscribed on his gravestone is also true, and more important than his weaknesses, viz.: "He lived to see his deepest wishes gratified—the downfall of the Bourbons, some prospect of good to mankind, and his leaving some sterling work to the world; he was a man of true moral courage, who sacrificed profit and present fame to principle; he lived and died the unconquered champion of Truth, Liberty, and Humanity."

His Views.—Hazlitt had much wider interests than may be supposed by those who read only his famous literary and dramatic criticism. All his views were rooted in a comprehensive philosophy, originally influenced by Coleridge's, but developed through independent cogitations about metaphysics, ethics, economics (*A Reply to Malthus' Essay on Population,* 1807), linguistics (*A New and Improved Grammar,* 1810), psychology (e.g., the *Essay on Dreams,* foreshadowing Freud), etc. Though his treatises on those subjects are now little read, they contain passages as brilliant as any in his other works; his style, like Swift's, could make even a broomstick fascinating. One of the bad effects of Hazlitt's early environment was that it fixed in him the notion that politics are a more important matter than *sub specie æternitatis* they are. There are a few broad political principles that are permanently important; but politics—the disputatious struggle as to just how those principles shall be applied to the fleeting problems of any single generation—are largely a practical and ephemeral activity, generating more heat than light. It was not in his general political ideals that Hazlitt was wholly at odds with Wordsworth, Coleridge, Southey, and the other Romantics; they too were opposed to the evils of the old régime, and desired a more just, free, and democratic state. But when Hazlitt applied such ideals to contemporaneous questions, such as the relation of Napoleon to liberty, they were unable to agree with him. He reviewed Wordsworth's *Excursion* favorably, and called its author "decidedly at the head of the poets of the present day"; but he was always likely to qualify his appreciation of the literary merits of Wordsworth, Coleridge, and Southey with slurs against their alleged political apostasy, and to rail at Scott and Byron for their aristocratic tendencies.

Hazlitt looked upon the English people between 1795 and 1830 as one which had proved false to a great opportunity. Under the inspiration of the French Revolution, it might have been a generation of "patriots and friends of freedom," instead of which it had "linked with kings to rivet on the chains of despotism and superstition." The tide of conservatism had carried with it even the poets, and in every direction the standards of life had been degraded. Said Hazlitt in an essay significantly called *On the Pleasure of Hating:*

> In private life do we not see hypocrisy, servility, selfishness, folly and impudence succeed, while modesty shrinks from the encounter, and merit is trodden under foot? How often is "the rose plucked from the forehead of a virtuous love to plant a blister there!" What chance is there of the success of a real passion? What certainty of its continuance? Seeing all this as I do, and unraveling the web of human life into its various threads of meanness, spite, cowardice, want of feeling, and want of understanding, of indifference towards others and ignorance of ourselves—seeing custom prevail over all excellence, itself giving way to infamy—mistaken as I have been in my public and private hopes, calculating others from myself, and calculating wrong; always disappointed where I placed most reliance; the dupe of friendship, and the fool of love; have I not reason to hate and to despise myself? Indeed I do; and chiefly for not having hated and despised the world enough.

In such moods, Hazlitt seems a kind of prose Byron.

Unlike Byron, however, he found many things which he could love and admire. He found them for the most part not among the actualities of life—although he occasionally took pleasure in a journey or a prize fight

—but in art and literature. "All that is worth remembering in life is the poetry of it. Fear is poetry, hope is poetry, love is poetry, hatred is poetry; contempt, jealousy, remorse, admiration, wonder, pity, despair, or madness, are all poetry!" Men had not always been as perverse and unintelligent as his own generation, and in the existence of the masterpieces of our literature we had the evidence that virtue and genius were not empty names or vain aspirations. The fact that a Titian, a Milton, and a Shakspeare had lived was a warrant that human nature would not always be misconceived or misguided.

Hazlitt as a Critic.—If Coleridge was the profoundest theorist among our critics, Hazlitt was the greatest practitioner. In essays filling many volumes, he applied the principles of romanticism to innumerable authors and books, covering more ground than Coleridge, Lamb, or even De Quincey. He wrote upon almost every important author from Elizabethan times to his own age, and there are few, if any, surveys of English literature that give us a more valuable series of critical judgments than Hazlitt provides. Here was a field in which there collaborated harmoniously the sensitiveness of his feelings and the analytical powers of his mind.

Hazlitt occasionally overstated some one principle of beauty, such as the need of emotion in poetry or the need of objectivity in all kinds of art; and it would be easy to quote sentences of his which, detached from their context, would seem false or exaggerated. As a whole, however, his philosophy of art and literature is sound. He attacked the *Discourses on Painting* of Sir Joshua Reynolds because they seemed to him to emphasize too much, after the eighteenth-century manner, the desirability of avoiding realism and of portraying the general rather than the individual, especially when the general was conceived of as a "medium or a center" of the various forms of an object. The true ideal, said Hazlitt, was not an average or compromise of that unimaginative sort. Nor was it something existing only in one's mind, something abstract or idyllic, "but the preference of that which is fine in nature to that which is less so." The neoclassic tendency to set up a sharp distinction between the general and the particular was not helpful to art, "the highest perfection of which depends, not on separating but on uniting general truth and effect with individual distinctness and accuracy."

Neither the artist nor the poet must confuse his personal notions about any object or about life as a whole with its true significance, which could be perceived only by those who unegotistically tried to behold things as they really were. On that ground he set Scott higher than Byron:

> We confess, however much we may admire independence of feeling and erectness of spirit in general or practical questions, yet in works of genius we prefer him who bows to the authority of nature, who appeals to actual objects, to mouldering superstitions, to history, observation, and tradition, before him who consults the pragmatical and restless workings of his own breast, and gives them out as oracles to the world.

One of the reasons why he delighted in Defoe and Fielding was that in
such novels as theirs we find

> . . . a close imitation of men and manners; we see the very web and
> texture of society as it really exists.

In Hazlitt, as in Byron, the devotion to realism is very strong. But
what he favors and practises is not a realistic copying of the superficial
surface-appearances of actuality. The factual and particularly the emotional features of life must not be neglected in literature; but life can
never be seen truly nor presented artistically by means only of common-
sense perception of them. Reason only analyzes and abstracts; what the
artist needs is Imagination, which *identifies* the observer with the object
in sympathy and therefore in discernment. This doctrine is the center
of Hazlitt's ethics, as well as of his aesthetics. Literature should focus
upon the particular, individual, and concrete; but only imaginative vision
can make the picture both true to inward reality and delightful to mind
and feelings of the reader.

The greatest authors, because prolonged imaginative habit had developed in them unusual sagacity of perception, were Milton, and, above
all, Shakspeare. Shakspeare had the power which eighteenth-century
authors, even the great Dr. Johnson, lacked, namely, to "show how the
nature of man was modified by the workings of passion, or the infinite
fluctuations of thought and accident." Hazlitt's bitter disappointment
with life had one good fruit: it disgusted him with literature that represented life as free from trouble or evil; and in Shakspeare's world there
was villainy enough to manifest its authenticity. Yet Shakspeare did not
wax moralistic:

> The object of the pedantic moralist is to find out the bad in everything:
> his was to show that "there is some soul of goodness in things evil" . . .
> In one sense, Shakspeare was no moralist at all: in another, he was the
> greatest of all moralists. He was a moralist in the same sense as which
> nature is one. He taught what he had learned from her. He showed the
> greatest knowledge of humanity with the greatest fellow-feeling for it.

Some of Hazlitt's ideas about Shakspeare were similar to those of Coleridge and Lamb, but he applied their romantic views and methods in new
directions. To the analyses of Shakspearian characters, he added many
brilliant pieces, such as his study of Iago. He was original in emphasizing the truths that Shakspeare's power in delineating women was unrivalled, and that his political wisdom was profound.

In his *Characters of Shakspeare's Plays* (1817), he hoped to improve
on Schlegel's famous *Lectures on the Drama* (1809–11), which he admired
more than the Shakspeare-criticism of Dr. Johnson, by "avoiding mysticism
in style, and in bringing illustrations from particular passages of the plays
themselves"—in short, by keeping the eye on the object.

Method and Style.—Although Hazlitt was not widely read in the
world's literature, his range was sufficiently extensive to enable him to

employ the comparative method with striking effect; and his contrasts between the values of epic poetry and those of dramatic, or between French tragedy and English, are famous. "We need," he said, "a more catholic spirit in literature." He thought Lamb's literary preferences too exclusive and eccentric. In his literary judgments he was more conservative than in his political.

Some critics excel in perceiving the intellectual content and significance of a work; others excel in responding to its emotional or aesthetic appeal; still others excel in expressing whatever, intellectually or emotionally, the work has meant to them. Hazlitt combined in an unusual degree these three powers—subtlety, gusto, and lucidity. Hence few critics can describe a work *in its entirety,* and in its *total* effect upon us, so well as Hazlitt can. As he said, "a genuine criticism should reflect the colors, the light and shade, the soul and body of a work"—not the body only, as mere matter-of-fact scholars do.

He practised that "unaffected" familiar style which he recommended. Lamb indulged in playful sallies and in archaic diction. Hazlitt kept closer to the norm of style, and was on that account more widely influential upon later prose writers. In his choice of words he avoided both the pedantic and the trite. He was as lucid as the eighteenth-century masters, but had more grace and ease than most of them. "We are fine fellows," said Robert Louis Stevenson, "but we can't write like William Hazlitt."

His Relation to Other Romantics.—Hazlitt was more deeply interested in philosophical problems than Wordsworth, and he discussed them less obscurely than Coleridge and less vaguely than Shelley. Like Wordsworth, however, he had great confidence in the value of personal experience and feelings. Like Byron, and all the more so because his medium was prose, he cultivated realism; and he is an important illustration of the possibilities of Romanticism in that direction (cf. Stendhal in continental literature). Yet he greeted Keats's poetry enthusiastically; and Keats said he felt reconciled to the defects of his times whenever he thought of Hazlitt's "depth of taste" and fearless frankness in political and critical controversies ("he is your only good damner," said Keats).

Hazlitt's manner toward his readers was not so friendly and informal as that of Lamb, but in his manner toward his author there was nothing neo-classically magisterial. He sought merits rather than faults; and it had not occurred to him that the art of criticism lay in telling his readers about books which were so wretched that they ought not to be read.

Lamb is superior to Hazlitt as a guide through life, but of the two, Hazlitt is the greater critic of literature. If he had not so often allowed politics to affect his discussions of his contemporaries, he might have become the best critic and advocate of the Romantics, even as Coleridge was their best philosopher. As it was he surpassed the others in the extent and the brilliance of his criticisms of the poets, dramatists, essayists, and novelists of earlier times. He disclosed in the older authors innumerable qualities that had been ignored; and repeatedly he was the first to state successfully their significance from the romantic point of view.—In our own age, Somerset Maugham has recommended the reading of Hazlitt as a needed counter-influence to our commonplace journalistic prose, because Hazlitt is so "vivid, bracing, and energetic."

SELECTED BIBLIOGRAPHY

OF FIRST IMPORTANCE

Selections

Selections from Hazlitt, ed. Will D. Howe, 1913. — Good annotations.
Selected Essays, ed. Geoffrey Keynes (Nonesuch), 1930. — Comprehensive.
Hazlitt on English Literature, ed. Jacob Zeitlin, 1913. — The chief literary essays arranged so as to constitute a survey from the age of Elizabeth to Hazlitt's own times, with valuable Introduction.

Texts

The Complete Works, ed. P. P. Howe, 21 vols. (the last, the Index), 1930–34. — Supersedes The Collected Works, ed. A. R. Waller and A. Glover, 13 vols., 1902–06.

Best Biography

Howe, P. P.; The Life of William Hazlitt, 1922 (new eds., 1928, 1947). — Had no serious competitor until the appearance of Catherine M. Maclean's Born Under Saturn, 1943, which is especially good on Hazlitt's problematic personality and his battles for liberalism.

Good Introductory Studies

Zeitlin and Maclean, above.

Saintsbury, George; in Essays in English Literature, 1890. — Despite Saintsbury's Toryism, keenly appreciative of Hazlitt's powers as a critic.

Birrell, Augustine; William Hazlitt (English Men of Letters Series). — Almost too lenient in its judgments.

FOR ADVANCED STUDENTS

Important Additional Texts

Other good selections are numerous; among the following, some are especially valuable for annotations:

Selected Essays, ed. George Sampson, 1917.
The Best of Hazlitt, ed. P. P. Howe, 1923.
Essays, ed. P. van D. Shelly, 1924.
Essays, ed. C. H. Gray, 1926.

Some of the chief separate works — Characters of Shakspeare's Plays, Lectures, Spirit of the Age, etc. — are available in The World's Classics and in Everyman's Library.

Memoirs of the Late Thomas Holcroft, ed. Elbridge Colby, 1925 (World's Classics, 1926).

Liber Amoris, ed. Richard Le Gallienne, 1893. — The text as Hazlitt published it in 1823, with what the editor inaccurately calls the "original manuscript," consisting of letters and records of the episode.

Hazlitt in the Workshop: The Manuscript of 'The Fight,' ed. S. C. Wilcox, Johns Hopkins Press, 1943.

Biographical and Critical

Patmore, P. G.; *My Friends and Acquaintances,* 3 vols., 1854. — By one who knew Hazlitt personally.

Hazlitt, W. C.; *Memoirs of William Hazlitt,* 2 vols., 1867. — By his grandson. Valuable materials, but ill-arranged and uncritical. The same is true of his *Four Generations of a Literary Family,* 2 vols., 1897; *Lamb and Hazlitt,* 1899; and *The Hazlitts,* 2 vols., 1911–12.

Stephen, Leslie; *Hours in a Library,* Second Series, 1876. — Tends to overemphasize Hazlitt's egotism.

Saintsbury, George; *A History of Criticism,* III, 251; 1904. — Best account of Hazlitt's place among great critics. Cf. H. W. Garrod, *The Profession of Poetry,* 1929.

More, P. E.; *Shelburne Essays,* II; 1905. — The "humanistic" attitude: gusto or passion the mainspring of Hazlitt's criticism, and his judgment weak.

Douady, Jules; *Vie de William Hazlitt, l'Essayiste,* 1907. — Sympathetic and rather uncritical.

Sichel, Walter; "Romantic and Amorist," *Fortnightly Review,* CI, 94; 1914. — Condemnation of his conduct in the affair with Sarah Walker. — Cf. P. P. Howe for the defense, in *Fortnightly Review,* CV, 300; 1916.

Chase, S. P.; "Hazlitt as a Critic of Art," PMLA, XXXIX, 179; 1924. — Deals also with his theory of literature; but cf. Schneider, *Aesthetics,* 1933, below; and G. M. Sergeaunt, *The Classical Spirit,* Bradford, The Cloanthus Press, 1936.

Griggs, E. L.; "Hazlitt's Estrangement from Coleridge and Wordsworth," MLN, XLVIII, 173; 1933. — Apropos of Griggs' *Wordsworth and Coleridge,* 1939, p. 173, note that it was not Hazlitt but Jeffrey who was responsible for the attack on *Christabel.*

Schneider, Elisabeth; *The Aesthetics of William Hazlitt: A Study of the Philosophical Basis of His Criticism,* 1933. — Of basic importance, not only on his literary theories but also on his philosophy, its relation to Coleridge's, and its originality.

Pearson, Hesketh; *The Fool of Love,* 1934. — Overemphasizes the Sarah Walker episode. Smart, extravagant.

Vigneron, Robert; "Stendhal et Hazlitt," MP, XXXV, 375; 1938.

Bullitt, John M.; "Hazlitt and the Romantic Conception of the Imagination," PQ, XXIV, 343; 1945. — Perspicacious. Cf. W. J. Bate, *From Classic to Romantic,* 1946.

Anon.; "The Devil's Visits," TLS, Oct. 19, 1946. — On Hazlitt's enlightening *Conversations of James Northcote.* Cf. S. C. Wilcox, ELH, VII, 325; 1940.

Thorpe, Clarence D.; "Keats and Hazlitt," PMLA, LXII, 487; 1947. — Their important reciprocal influence.

Bibliography

Keynes, Geoffrey; *Bibliography of William Hazlitt,* Nonesuch, 1931.

CHAPTER 8

SIR WALTER SCOTT

(August 13, 1771–September 21, 1832)

His Early Life.—Many Scotchmen—among them Ramsay, Thomson, Macpherson, Mackenzie, and Burns—had notably promoted the Pre-Romantic Movement; and Collins' *Ode on the Highlands of Scotland* had looked forward to that land becoming a home of romance. Finally, in fulfillment, came he whose family name signified "the Scotchman," Walter Scott. His remoter ancestors had been a wild, cattle-raiding and fighting folk; in more recent times, they had been supporters of the lost cause of the Stuart kings. The father of Scott was a lawyer, a sensible and conscientious man; his mother was more vivacious and fond of ancient lore. The two temperaments were blended in their son. He was a sickly child, paralytic, slightly lame; but out-of-door life and his dauntless energy enabled him to overcome his handicap. His schooling was irregular, and often interrupted by illnesses; but from his earliest youth he was a voracious reader, delighting in poems like *Hardyknute* and in Percy's *Reliques;* and fond of retelling to his playmates the romantic incidents that had stirred his blood.

In his youth, Scott did not expect to become an author, his chief occupation being the study of law. But several of his avocations and pleasures prepared him unconsciously for his later career. His intensely social disposition, and his readiness to make friends with all sorts and conditions of men, rapidly broadened his knowledge of the varieties of human character. He was equally fond of a steady, hard-working, intellectual youth like William Erskine, with his refined taste in literature; a harum-scarum, talkative young fellow like William Clerk; a jovial shepherd like James Hogg; and an enthusiast for antiquarianism like John Leyden. And, whether by divine grace or his own common sense, he chiefly drew from each type not the faults but the merits. Thus he caught Leyden's passion for collecting unrecorded ballads, and his willingness to trudge a score or two of miles into the hills, if need be, to recover from the lips of some old crone one such treasure.

The young Scott's interest was not confined to legends and oral traditions. A long illness at the age of fifteen gave him the opportunity to become extraordinarily familiar with certain tracts of literature that were ultimately to prove of the highest importance in his development. When, more than forty years later, he came to write the general preface to his novels, he felt this course of reading to have been so influential that he described it in some detail as follows:

> There was at this time a circulating library in Edinburgh, founded, I believe, by the celebrated Allan Ramsay, which, besides containing a most respectable collection of books of every description, was, as might have been expected, peculiarly rich in works of fiction. It exhibited specimens of every kind, from the romances of chivalry, and the ponderous folios of Cyrus and Cassandra,[1]—down to the most approved works of later times. I was plunged into this great ocean of reading without compass or pilot; and unless when some one had the charity to play at chess with me, I was allowed to do nothing save read, from morning to night. I was, in kindness and pity, which was perhaps erroneous, however natural, permitted to select my subjects of study at my own pleasure, upon the same principle that the humors of children are indulged to keep them out of mischief. As my taste and appetite were gratified in nothing else, I indemnified myself by becoming a glutton of books. Accordingly, I believe I read almost all the romances, old plays, and epic poetry, in that formidable collection, and no doubt was unconsciously amassing materials for the task in which it has been my lot to be so much employed.
>
> At the same time I did not in all respects abuse the license permitted me. Familiar acquaintance with the specious miracles of fiction brought with it some degree of satiety, and I began, by degrees, to seek in histories, memoirs, voyages and travels, and the like, events nearly as wonderful as those which were the work of imagination, with the additional advantage that they were at least in a great measure true. The lapse of nearly two years, during which I was left to the exercise of my own free will, was followed by a temporary residence in the country, where I was again very lonely but for the amusement which I derived from a good though old-fashioned library. The vague and wild use which I made of this advantage I cannot describe better than by referring my reader to the desultory studies of Waverley[2] in a similar situation; the passages concerning whose course of reading were imitated from recollections of my own.

[1] Heroic romances of the seventeenth century—La Calprenède's *Cassandre* (1642–50), and Mlle. de Scudéry's *Le Grand Cyrus* (1650). They were historical novels of enormous length. The manners were anachronistically modern, but their tone was noble and idealistic.

[2] Waverley was the titular hero of Scott's first novel, at the beginning of which he is described as a dreamer and bookish youth who had not yet learned the true values and aims of life. "Knowing much that is known but to few, Edward Waverley might justly be considered as ignorant, since he knew little of what adds dignity to man, and qualifies him to support and adorn an elevated situation in society" (ch. 3).

When he was about twenty years of age, Scott fell in love with Wil-liamina Belches, the fifteen-year-old daughter of John Belches (latei Sir John Belches Stuart) ; and for six years his highest hopes were cen-tered upon her. She herself was not unwilling to encourage his ardor; but from the point of view of her wealthy and highly connected parents, his worldly prospects were not sufficiently promising. This was the deepest passion and disappointment of his life; for years he could not bear to allude to it; but it left traces in some of his poems—e.g., *The Violet (Anth.,* 417) —as well as in *The Antiquary, Kenilworth,* and *Redgauntlet.* It did not, however, reduce him to a state of Byronic self-pity.

A year or two afterwards he married Charlotte Carpenter (originally Charpentier) , a refugee from the French Revolution. The history of her family and of her early years is not clearly known; but there is no doubt Scott's marriage was a happy one, although his wife had little interest in literary or intellectual matters. She was sociable and pleasure-loving, and happily companionable with Scott in the very active social side of his busy life. They had five children.

His Middle Period.—From the age of twenty-six to forty-three, Scott threw himself into activities which would have taxed the energies of two or three ordinary men. In the first place, he successfully pursued the profession of law, out of which grew his appointment as a sheriff and later as a clerk of a court. In the second place, he maintained his scholarly and literary interests, and at the age of thirty-one produced a collection of ancient ballads and poems, *The Minstrelsy of the Scottish Border,* which many a man whose chief profession was not literature would re-gard as a notable achievement of a whole lifetime's leisure. Three years later, the lawyer and scholar appeared also as a poet, with *The Lay of the Last Minstrel,* which was an immediate popular success. Within eight years, he followed it with no less than five other long romances in verse. In 1813 he was offered the Poet-Laureateship, but declined it in favor of Southey.

One would assume that a man of so many legal and literary activities must spend all of his days and nights in his office and his study, but Scott was as strenuous in play as in work. He was a fearless, not to say reck-less, rider to hounds; and his devotion to his dogs, Camp, Maida, and Nimrod, was one of his most marked peculiarities. Although his profes-sion required him to live much in Edinburgh, he preferred life in a country house, and owned a succession of these, the last being the cele-brated Abbotsford. When he bought it, it was nothing but a cottage and mountain farm surrounded by unwooded hills. He replaced the cot-tage with a mansion, and the mansion with a castle. Acres upon acres of the bare hills he reforested. He loved the large and lasting effects in landscape as well as in literature; and one of the joys of a visit to Abbots-ford nowadays, a sight almost as impressive as that of his magnificent library, is to behold the great environing woods which he created.

The only step in these busy years which one may regard with disapproval was his becoming involved in a kind of partnership with a firm of printers, the Ballantynes, and especially his doing so secretly. The secrecy was owing to the fact that it was then regarded as unprofessional for a lawyer to engage in a trade like printing. His chief motives in the venture were his desire to make money and to leave his children wealthy, and his scholarly desire to be in a position where he could facilitate the publication of learned works. As it proved, he never obtained any substantial amount of money from the business, and ultimately his connection with it was disastrous.

The Summit of His Fortune.—In 1814, Scott published the first of his novels, *Waverley*. He had begun it nine years earlier but had lost confidence in its value. Happening to find the manuscript, he felt impelled to try again, and with his usual rapidity he completed the work in a few weeks. The recent furore over the narrative poems of Byron, whom Scott with characteristic modesty acknowledged to be his superior in poetry, made it wise for him to leave that field to his new rival. For various reasons Scott published *Waverley* anonymously: he was dubious about its success; he did not wish to put himself in a position where he might have to defend his views on controversial historical points; and, boyishly fond as he was of a hoax, he enjoyed the mystifying of the public and the critics. It was not until thirteen years later that he publicly acknowledged his authorship of the Waverley novels, but long before that the truth was more than half suspected.

The vastness of his reading, the retentiveness of his memory, and the ready flow of his invention enabled him within eleven years (1814–25) to produce twenty novels. Their success was indescribably sensational. Thousands of readers throughout Great Britain eagerly awaited the day of publication of each, and in the capitals of Europe writers intending to translate them struggled against one another to lay hands upon the first copy to arrive. His fortune seemed now assured. He increased the lands and treasures of Abbotsford, and made it the center of bounteous hospitality. Distinguished men in all walks of life were his visitors; and after his usual long hours of literary work from very early morning until midday, and his afternoon of outdoor sport, he engaged in the evening with tireless zest in learned and brilliant conversation with some celebrated scientist like Sir Humphrey Davy, or a poet like Wordsworth, or a man of letters from abroad like Washington Irving. In 1820, he was made a baronet. Affectionately devoted to his family as he was, probably the happiest moment of his life was that evening in January, 1825, when the entire castle blazed with lights, and a great ball was given in honor of the engagement of his oldest son to a niece of Sir Adam Ferguson. To this young couple, Abbotsford was to descend, and thus Sir Walter Scott had achieved, in the founding of a line of landed gentry, his highest worldly ambition.

His Calamity and Heroism.—In December of the same year, 1825, the London publishing firm, Constable, went bankrupt, carrying with them into ruin the Ballantynes, with whom Scott was secretly in partnership. The liabilities amounted to a sum then huge, c. £100,000, and the assets were almost nonexistent. In what way, and to what degree, Scott was morally blameworthy in his business connections has been a matter of violent and prolonged contention. Unfriendly critics, such as Donald Carswell, condemn him as unprofessional for going into business at all, and even as greedy and dishonest. The verdict of Grierson and other fair-minded judges is that he was not guilty of mean motives or unethical conduct, but that he was censurable for being much too enterprising, overconfident, and imprudent. After the crash, he did not try to escape the consequences of his rashness, as he might have done. He could legally have limited his own losses to a small fraction of the sum involved; and, at his age (fifty-five) and in the weakening state of his health and eyesight, the course which he took seemed quixotic. Rejecting the tempting persuasions of prudence and common sense, he took the idealistic position that his honor as a gentleman was involved; and he determined that, unless his strength should fail him, he would by his labors earn enough to clear the debt. Through herculean toil he actually succeeded in doing so in the remaining six years of his life. This self-imposed expiation of his error shows that he was no sentimentalist when he wrote in *Ivanhoe,*

> Chivalry alone distinguishes the noble from the base, the gentle knight from the churl and the savage; it rates our life far, far beneath the pitch of our honor; raises us victorious over pain, toil, and suffering; and teaches us to fear no evil but disgrace.

He uttered no complaints against others, and made no excuses for himself; nor did there creep into his writings any tone of disillusionment or gloom. With cheerful courage he returned to his desk, sometimes working twelve hours a day, and doggedly fighting against growing infirmities. He was grateful that the blow had not weakened his literary powers—one of the best Waverley Novels, *The Fair Maid of Perth,* being composed three years after it fell. In addition to six novels, he produced in these last years his long *Life of Napoleon,* partly based upon unpublished sources requiring laborious scrutiny, as well as a mass of other writings. The public becoming conscious that he whom they had admired as a delineator of chivalric and honorable characters was now exemplifying the virtues he had depicted, showed that he had won its deep affection; and the reports of his illness were received with widespread anxiety. When, in 1831, he was compelled to go to the Mediterranean in search of health, the government placed a frigate at his disposal. The journey was in vain. On his return to Abbotsford, when seated in his wheelchair, he begged to be moved to his desk and to be given his pen. His daughter put it into his hand, but he was too feeble to close his fingers upon it, and silently weeping, he gave up the struggle. Shortly afterwards he passed peacefully away, in the presence of his children. Many of the newspapers placed the announcement of the event within deep black borders, a sign of mourning usually reserved for the death of a royal sovereign.

His Character.—Among Americans, Theodore Roosevelt most re- sembles Scott in the abounding richness and strenuousness of his life, in combining joy in action with delight in books. The dashing and enter- prising side of his character is well expressed in the motto which he pre- fixed to one of the chapters of *Old Mortality:*

> Sound, sound the clarion, fill the fife;
> To all the sensual world proclaim
> One crowded hour of glorious life
> Is worth a world without a name!

This was indeed a merit which he pushed to an extreme: at times it be- came rashness, and involved him in schemes like that which led to the Ballantyne failure. His chief weakness was a too great admiration for wealth, rank, and the worldly success which their possession implied. He was, however, not proud or selfish, but kind and generous, and had friends in every walk of life. Northcote, who painted his portrait, praised his modesty, and remarked how unlike he was to "his friends, the Lake poets, who talk of nothing but their own poetry." He felt no jealousy toward his literary rivals, and was more likely to exaggerate their superiority over him than to underestimate their merits. Several of the great Ro- mantics surpassed him in some single element of personality—Byron in passion, Coleridge in subtlety of mind, Shelley in power of imagination, Keats in delicacy of the senses—but, with the possible exception of Words- worth, none of them showed so well balanced a nature, such an approach to harmony between strong emotion, keen understanding, and bold imagination.

His Miscellaneous Prose Works.—Scott was by far the most volu- minous of the Romantics. He wrote and edited so much that no complete edition of his writings has ever been issued. He edited and annotated the works of Dryden in eighteen volumes (1808), and those of Swift in nine- teen (1814); in each case writing substantial biographies of those authors. For Ballantyne's *Novelists' Library* he prepared biographical introduc- tions. These were subsequently collected in one volume, entitled *Lives of the Novelists* (1825), rich in generous appreciations of the various merits of his predecessors, including Cervantes, Le Sage, Richardson, Fielding, Smollett, Sterne, Mackenzie, Clara Reeve, Anne Radcliffe, and Bage. For his grandson he wrote histories of Scotland and of France, published as *Tales of a Grandfather* (1827–30). Among the writings displaying his knowledge of folklore were the *Letters on Demonology and Witchcraft* (1830). Although these works are little read today, the mere list of their titles should remind us that in the range of interests and in knowledge Scott surpassed most poets and novelists.

His Poems.—Scott was first inspired by that native poetical tradition of ballads and songs which had culminated in Burns. A second source of inspiration was the romantic literature of Germany. In 1799 he translated the storm-and-stress prose-drama, *Götz von Berlichingen* by Goethe. Three years earlier, in *William and Helen* (*Anth.*, 414), he had composed a version of Bürger's *Lenore,* which had already been rendered into English by William Taylor, and which itself was based upon the old English ballad *Sweet William's Ghost.* In 1801 Scott published a little volume of poems including such pieces as *The Eve of St. John* (*Anth.*, 417) which showed how closely his loving study of ballads had enabled him to approach the spirit of medieval times. A very substantial result of that study was his annotated collection, *The Minstrelsy of the Scottish Border* (1802–03).

The Lay of the Last Minstrel (1805) was originally intended to be another short border ballad, but developed into his first long poetical romance. Partly based upon traditions of his own ancestors, it was enthusiastically received by his fellow borderers as a spirited recovery of their heroic past. Its metre was taken from Coleridge's *Christabel;* but although it included an element of the supernatural, it did not have the atmosphere of sustained magical enchantment, being much more realistic in tone. In *Marmion* (1808; *Anth.*, 423) he daringly chose as his theme one of the greatest defeats in Scottish history, that of Flodden Field; and pseudo-patriots absurdly condemned him as unpatriotic. But Scott knew that valor in defeat may shine even more brightly than in victory, and in his battle scenes there was found abundance of glory and honor on both sides of the conflict. In *The Lady of the Lake* (1810; *Anth.*, 431) he turned to the Highland clans, their bravery, love, and religion, intending, as he said, to give "as far as I can, a real picture of what that enthusiastic race actually were before the destruction of their patriarchal government." This was the best of his narrative poems; those that followed— *Rokeby, The Bridal of Triermain, The Lord of the Isles,* and *Harold the Dauntless* (1813–17)—not equaling the vigor and beauty of his three masterpieces.

As a poet Scott did not attempt the mystical, the profound, the subtle, or the ornate. He commanded a wider range, however, than is sometimes recognized. In some of his lyrics, such as *The Sun Upon the Weird-law Hill* and *Rebecca's Hymn* (*Anth.*, 446), he was successful in the noble, reflective style of the eighteenth century. In others, like *Proud Maisie* and *County Guy* (*Anth.*, 446), he could evoke an atmosphere of remoteness and wonder. His epic poetry was a trumpet call. Much of it was composed in the saddle and avowedly addressed to "soldiers, sailors, and young people of bold and active dispositions." Its spontaneity, its impetuous stride, the swift strokes of its descriptions of nature, the animation and clarity of its battle scenes, and its appeals to patriotic sentiment, reminded readers, more than any other English narratives in verse, of *The Iliad.* It was a comparison which Scott himself would have deprecated; but despite the obvious differences, the resemblances were too many to be denied. Long after Scott's death, and at a time when his reputation as a poet was far from being as great as it had been, the learned Homeric scholar, Sir Richard Jebb, declared:

> Nowhere else, perhaps, in modern literature could any one be found who in an equal measure with Scott, has united these three conditions of a true spiritual analogy to Homer: living realisation of a past heroic age; a genius in native sympathy with the heroic; and a manner which joins the spontaneous impulse of the balladist to a higher order of art and intellect.
>
> *Introduction to the Iliad and Odyssey*

The Waverley Novels.—There is some difference of opinion as to which of the thirty-two Waverley novels are the best, but probably most readers would regard the following seventeen as in that category. To show how wide a tract of history Scott covered, they are arranged in the order of the periods in which their actions are laid.

Approximate Date of the Action	Period	Title	Date of Publication
1192–93	Third Crusade	The Talisman	1825
1194	Richard Coeur-de-Lion	Ivanhoe	1820
1390–1406	Robert III of Scotland	Fair Maid of Perth	1828
1468–69	Louis XI of France	Quentin Durward	1823
1568–69	Mary Stuart	The Abbot	1820
1575	Elizabeth	Kenilworth	1821
1620	James I	Fortunes of Nigel	1822
1645–46	Civil War	Legend of Montrose	1819
1651–52	Commonwealth	Woodstock	1826
1679–89	The Stuarts	Old Mortality	1816
1695	William and Mary	Bride of Lammermoor	1819
1715	Jacobite Rebellion	Rob Roy	1818
1745	Jacobite Rebellion	Waverley	1814
1736–51	George II and Caroline	Heart of Midlothian	1818
1763	Jacobite Plot	Redgauntlet	1824
1744–65	George II and III	Guy Mannering	1815
1795	War against France	The Antiquary	1816

If one were forced to name the three or four best of these, one might choose *Old Mortality, The Heart of Midlothian, The Fortunes of Nigel,* and *Quentin Durward;* but in so narrow a choice there would be no general agreement.

Several of the works in the above list are not historical novels in the usual sense of the term—*The Antiquary* because its period lies within the lifetime of its author. *Guy Mannering* and *The Bride of Lammermoor* are exceptional in being tragic throughout. *Redgauntlet* is noteworthy as containing *Wandering Willie's Tale (Anth.,* 460) , the best ghost story written during the Romantic Movement, and one of the best in the world's literature. A glance at the list will show that most of his best novels were laid in the seventeenth and eighteenth centuries, and were Scotch in background (this includes the *Fortunes of Nigel,* James I of England being a Scotchman). In many of them, a prominent feature was the portraiture of rulers or princes, such as Richard Coeur-de-Lion, Saladin, Louis XI, Mary Stuart, Elizabeth, James I, Cromwell, Charles I, Charles II, Queen Caroline, and the Stuart Pretenders. Usually the main action is affected by political conflict, of Christian against Saracen, clan against clan, king against nobles, Cavalier against Puritan, or Jacobite against Hanoverian.

The Historical Novel Before Scott.—Not only in the eighteenth century, but from the days of Xenophon onwards, innumerable attempts had been made to write historical novels. Some of these attempts, like the French heroic romances of the seventeenth century, had been successful in their generation; but for one reason or another, all had failed in the long run. To appreciate the differences between Scott's work and that of his predecessors, and the reasons why he succeeded where they did not, one must consider in what spirit and with what intentions those predecessors had turned to the past for the setting of their stories. In some cases they had done so not because they were especially hostile to contemporaneous life, or bored by it, but merely because they were full of antiquarian curiosity about anything that happened to be old, and because they wanted to impart their erudite information. The learned French Abbé Barthélemy's *Anacharsis in Greece* (1788) was an historical novel of this type; and so was the unfinished *Queenhoo Hall* by the antiquary Joseph Strutt, for which Scott himself had written a conclusion in 1808. Novels of this kind perished because they were dull.—Of the second kind of mistaken attempts in this genre we have seen examples in Pre-Romanticism. Many of the eighteenth-century sentimental romances of adventure [3] were historical novels. (For that matter, Macpherson's *Ossian* might also be so termed.) The purpose of their authors was to get away from the contemporary to an era presumed to be more nearly perfect, to one where men and women were admirably virtuous, even if their virtue was often in undeserved distress. But this resulted in unreality, both in the characters and the background, and likewise failed.

A third type of historical novelists turned away from the contemporaneous, not because they thought earlier ages better, but because those ages, being less peaceful and in general less dominated by rationality, would give them a greater opportunity for exhibiting in vigorous actions and characters those potentialities of human feeling and thought that were too much restricted in the more circumscribed conditions of modern life. Here indeed was a sound theory, not at odds with historic truth; and several kinds of novelists made their attempts upon that principle. Unfortunately, however, they overlooked certain other important considerations. Of this class were the writers of the eighteenth-century

[3] See, above, p. 32.

novel of terror.[4] They placed the actions of their stories in eras like that of the Inquisition, when the agitation of emotions might be extraordinary; but they made the fatal mistake of caring only for sensational effects upon their readers and consequently indulged in those incredible misrepresentations of human nature that Coleridge rightly condemned.[5] Here too belong, despite many differences, the authors of the seventeenth-century heroic romances. No one had understood the *theory* of historical fiction better than they did. They excogitated the principles that a novel, in order to create verisimilitude, must have reality, and in order to be interesting must not deal with the commonplace; wherefore, they inferred, the logical thing was to turn to past events, which had reality because they had actually occurred, and had strangeness because they differed from the modern. The enormous popularity of the heroic romances testifies to the validity of their theory. But here again there was a flaw in the method—one which did not become immediately apparent, but which presently antiquated this variety of historical fiction. They believed that civilization had reached its height in their own times, the great era of Louis XIV, and that the manners of the ladies and gentlemen of the court were complete models of ideal excellence. Hence they patterned upon them the heroes and heroines of their romances ("confusing nobility of language with the language of nobility"), regardless of the ludicrous anachronism of making a Persian noble of the days of Cyrus, or a Roman lady of those of Augustus, talk and act and think like themselves.

One reason why Scott succeeded where so many had failed is that he avoided the chief errors of his predecessors. His feeling that literature, whatever else it did in addition, must entertain, saved him from antiquarianism. His wide first-hand knowledge of history kept him from representing any period as idyllic (he had no addiction whatever to sentimental theories about noble children of nature). His scholarship made him keenly aware of the way in which different periods are distinguished by different manners and by different ways of feeling and thinking. And, his practical experience and common sense prevented him from indulging in melodramatic falsifications of human nature.

His Views of Life and History.—Carlyle and others have reproached Scott with having no philosophy. The charge is quite true in the sense that he had evolved no system of metaphysics or of theology. He felt none of the subtler spiritual or mystical promptings that characterized Wordsworth and Coleridge. He made no attempts in either his poems or his novels to interpret the higher religious experiences, though sectarian and ethical consequences of religion were within his sphere. He was a man of simple faith, and thought it vain to speculate about ultimate causes. "We are men," he said, "and have endured what men are born to bear." Why we should bear it, was not profitable for us to inquire.

[4] See, above, p. 33.
[5] See, above, p. 62.

Scott had, however, certain convictions regarding life which notably determined his interpretation of it, and in which there was a good deal more of sagacity and originality than is realized by those who dismiss him as unintellectual. He had thought much about the meaning of human history. As has been said, he rejected the notion that man's experience had in any age been perfect; but he likewise rejected the cynical commonplace that it had been nothing but a succession of follies and vanities from age to age. Satire he regarded (although he was the editor of Dryden and Swift) as the least admirable form of literature; and he saw no justification in directing it in any sweeping way against the past, for in his study of earlier times he had met with too many unmistakable manifestations of noble intent and achievement to make him feel superior or scornful. While therefore he did not go to the past as a pleasant refuge from the present, it seemed to him often to disclose the real presence of permanent values. Thus in the introduction of his *Minstrelsy of the Scottish Border,* he described the ballads as expressing the "rough chivalry" of their time. He did not gloss over the roughness, but neither was he blind to the chivalry. And so with every age or group that he turned to: medieval times had their brutalities, but knighthood was sometimes an actualized ideal; the sectarian bigotry of the Puritan was grotesque, but his sincerity, his unworldliness, and his willingness to die for his principles set before us a living example of real faith.

Likewise through his knowledge of the past and his imaginative insight, Scott developed very striking and fruitful ideas about the nature of a nation. The history of Scotland and England was not to be envisaged as that of one national type, but as that of many, some of them delightfully and humorously different from the norm. One of the reasons why his novels were superior to his poems as expressions of his full personality was that they enabled him to delineate the rich variety of those types which had made their contributions to British life. Like Burke, Scott conceived of a nation not as a constitutional and legal system but as a living organism, and of its present as therefore only most superficially intelligible without a knowledge of its past. What we were today could only be appreciated through sympathetically apprehending what our forebears had been. Toward those forebears, though he never concealed the faults and limitations that commingled with their merits, Scott felt the deepest sympathy and gratitude—in which sentiments, rather than in a sense of superiority to other nations, he considered true patriotism to consist. And thus the historical novel, in the hands of its creator, became a means of national self-consciousness, self-knowledge, and patriotism.

His Literary Methods.—In his novels Scott rarely if ever expressed his views directly. The first requisite of prose fiction, in his opinion, was that it should give the reader pleasure; and the intrusion of moral lessons in it was inartistic. It had, to be sure, moral value; but that value might be depended on to take care of itself, provided the story gave a faithful representation of human life. His general views, however, without being obtruded, controlled the choice and arrangement of his materials. When it is borne in mind that to him the entire complex of a nation's life, the correlation of its diverse social forces, and the intermingling of its classes from king to commoner, were more interesting than the personal fortunes of a pair of lovers, some of the methods and effects of his novels will become clear.

Usually he did not make the character who was historically the most prominent, for example a King Richard or a Cromwell, the central personage in the plot; for to do so would be to hamper his liberty in the conduct of the story. It was better to place purely imaginary characters, about whose personality and deeds the reader had no previous information, in the center of the events. Moreover, these central characters, usually lovers, must not be of such highly individual natures as to monopolize the reader's interest; for what was of the greatest importance in an historical novel was not what the lovers were or did, but the historical circumstances amid which they moved. Often the central characters were young persons of no marked peculiarities who found themselves involved in powerful social or political movements and surrounded by characters much more forceful than themselves. To Scott these technically secondary characters were the most significant. They might be kings or queens, warriors or lawyers, Cavaliers or Puritans, gypsies or smugglers —provided they were representative of some colorful strand in the national web, and especially if they embodied a force still influential upon the national character, they were summoned within his charmed circle.

The historical background—the general conditions of life, the manners, the prevailing ideas and feelings, the prominent types of characters —were very important. As for the plot, Scott confessed he had no skill in its construction; and he doubted whether it should be carefully planned beforehand. If the action did not spontaneously flow onward, it was likely to seem artificial. Fielding, who managed to give to a previously conceived plot the air of natural development, was, he opined, an exception to the rule. As for himself, he improvised, and often did not know, when he began his tale, how it would end.

He would not countenance "working up" one's historical materials just before writing an historical novel. If you had not steeped yourself long ago in your period merely because you were fascinated by it, and without ulterior purpose, you could not convey its spirit. He himself had been studying the political, social, and literary history of his people, out of the pure love of it, for decades before he wrote his novels; and to summon up the past in his mind vividly was to him no great effort of imagination. While composing his stories, he would occasionally turn back to his sources for verification of his memory, or to fortify with quotations those notes that he delighted to append to them; but usually this was like revisiting old friends. The more the relations of the Waverley Novels to their historical sources are investigated, the clearer it becomes that, despite errors in details, he was on the whole remarkably sound in his interpretation of the past. He used his materials with the requisite freedom of an artist, but he was never knowingly anachronistic on any point of real importance. He did not convert into saints or heroes historical personages who were actually villains; and he gave no false impressions concerning the general drift of political events, the motives of popular leaders, or the characteristic traits of any important group or class.

Faithful as he tried to be to the main features of each period, he rightly maintained that the historical novelist would defeat his purpose by trying to reproduce the past literally. Some archaisms should be cautiously introduced into the dialogues to suggest the style of the former epoch; but to go further, to make, say, the characters in *Ivanhoe* talk in Middle English, would be bad art. An historical novel, in other words, was not to be fabrication (like Chatterton's *Rowley Poems*) pretending to be a story told in former times; it was to be avowedly a story told by a modern author which, in language intelligible to his contemporaries, should attempt to evoke the life of the past in their imaginations.

The best evidence of the general soundness of Scott's theories and methods is that for more than a hundred years his chief successors have been guided by them, and that only in rare instances have any of them been departed from with good results.

Merits and Defects of the Novels.—Even the best of Scott's novels have their faults and limitations. They are apt to begin in what seems a languid manner, and their conclusions are often hurried and confused. Now and then the style is slovenly or heavy. The young heroes and heroines (if one must call the central characters by those conventional terms) are in many cases too normal to be interesting; the young ladies are particularly so, as if Sir Walter were afraid to attribute to them any of those little caprices or follies which he relished in all other classes and which would make them seem youthfully human. Scott also turns away from anything approaching the higher religious experiences of mankind. In one or another of his novels, he had opportunities to delineate such spiritual leaders as Hooker, Knox, Milton, and Wesley; but he shrank from any attempt to interpret such inner experiences as theirs. In this respect, as in many others, his historical novels resemble the chronicle histories of Shakspeare, in which likewise the religious depths of life have been left unfathomed.

Such defects detract little from the many merits of the novels. Not since Shakspeare's time had any author presented such a vivid series of historical scenes and types, such a large number of lifelike and nationally representative characters. It was a gallery in which kings and queens were depicted as men and women without losing their royalty, and in which a maiden like Jeanie Deans, by virtue of her nobility of soul was revealed as queenly. Tory though he was in politics, Scott exhibited in his works no partiality for any class; and even though he might personally sympathize with one party to the struggles he depicted rather than with the other, he was as just to the Normans as to the Saxons, to the Covenanters as to the Royalists, and to the English as to the Scottish. His actual knowledge of life was incomparably more wide and varied than that of any novelist since Fielding. Even these great merits, however, would have failed to make the novels as excellent as they are had he not joined to his scholarship, experience, sense of justice, and wisdom, a joyous delight in strongly individual characters. His sense of humor, instead of hampering his romantic imagination, combined with it to create works which were true to the complexity of existence, or, as he himself put it, to "that medley of the tragic and comic with which life presents us."

His Relation to Other Romantics.—Scott lacked the profundity of Coleridge and Wordsworth, and the critical powers of Coleridge and Hazlitt. His especial service to the Romantic Movement was to give it a new sense of the value of the past. Romantics like Wordsworth and Lamb were at their best in dealing with the present, and with one's happier adjustment thereto. Scott disclosed that a true depiction of the past was also a means of contact with the permanent and universal, and that rich sources of strength and inspiration were to be found in the historical and national experiences of mankind. He showed that it was unnecessary to misrepresent those experiences, as the sentimentalists had done, in order to find traces of the ideal among them: the actual truth about the past was an encouragement to the present and the future. Thus his labors powerfully fostered that spirit of nationalism and patriotism which in Wordsworth's work was only one element.

In the creation of characters, Scott was more prolific than the other Romantics. All of them felt that the neo-classic conception of human nature was too narrow; but Scott, with his rich array of vivid characters, serious and humorous, brilliantly illustrated and fortified the romantic belief that man had greater and more variable potentialities than Neo-Classicism had assumed.

The scope of Scott's work was wider than that of any other great Romantic. He achieved extreme popularity in *both* verse and prose. Even Byron, not given to praising others, acknowledged the sovereign sway of Scott, saying to him, "Of whom could you be jealous?—of none of the living, certainly—and of which of the dead?" Scott, moreover, was the *first* of the Romantics to gain great popularity. Blake in 1783 and 1789 had published what long afterwards were to be recognized as important poems; Coleridge and Wordsworth had done likewise in 1798 and 1800: but they were not yet appreciated when Scott's poems, beginning in 1805, and his novels, beginning in 1814, were enthusiastically welcomed. It was not until 1812, when Byron's star arose, that he had a rival in contemporaneous fame, and then it was only in the field of nar-rative verse.

Founder of the modern historical novel, Scott had not only scores of followers in England and America (Bulwer-Lytton, Cooper, Dickens, Hawthorne, Reade, Kingsley, Thackeray, George Eliot, Stevenson, etc.), but also hundreds in continental Europe (Manzoni, Hugo, Mérimée, De Vigny, Dumas, Coster, Hauff, Freytag, Ingemann, Jokai, Gogol, Tolstoi, Lagerlöf, etc.). Several nations liberated by World War I, such as Czechoslovakia and Poland, owed the preservation of their national self-consciousness during the period of their oppression largely to historical novels, written by authors like Jirasek and Sienkiewicz, that kept alive among their people the memory of their former greatness and independence. The historical novel then performed a liberating function which, alas, has not been rendered obsolete by the results of World War II.

The historical novel has an exceptionally close relation to the rise and spread of the Romantic Movement. Other types of literature that were favorite media of expression for the romantic spirit—such as the sonnet, the ode, the ballad, and the familiar essay—were neither invented nor perfected by it, but were inherited from earlier literary periods; but the form which Scott gave to the historical novel was so radically different from the previous approaches as to be essentially original; and throughout the world literature of the nineteenth century it proved a favorite means of expressing the romantic attitude. When, about the 1860's and 1870's, the reaction against romanticism set in, Scott and the other historical novelists were accordingly shining marks for the attacks of hostile critics. Anti-romantics of various kinds, such as Leslie Stephen, Georg Brandes, and Ferdinand Brunetière scorned or denounced the historical novel, usually on the ground that it was not a literal or "scientific" reproduction of the past, and for other reasons which, thoroughly weighed, would invalidate every kind of imaginative literature and leave room only for the starkest kind of realism.

Scott's own novels have never recovered as great popularity as they enjoyed in his lifetime. Many modern critics ignore and some even despise them. Yet as J. T. Hillhouse, the historian of their vicissitudes, says, there remains a group of militantly aggressive writers on Scott who feel that his great merits are neglected, who praise him in terms just as favorable as his work received in its heyday, and who have, with their nineteenth- and twentieth-century perspective, a full realization of its permanent values and abiding influence.

SELECTED BIBLIOGRAPHY

OF FIRST IMPORTANCE

Selections

The Heart of Scott's Poetry, ed. John Haynes Holmes, 1932.
The Waverley Pageant, ed. Hugh Walpole, 1932. — Passages from the novels, with explanatory links. Topically arranged.

Texts

Complete Poetical Works, ed. H. E. Scudder (Houghton Mifflin) , 1900.

Of the *Waverley Novels* there are several good editions (Macmillan, Oxford Univ. Press, Nelson, etc.) . The "Border Edition," ed. Andrew Lang, 25 vols., 1902–04 (Macmillan) has the best introductions.

Biography

The original authority remains John Gibson Lockhart's *Memoirs of the Life of Sir Walter Scott,* 2 vols., 1837–38; 10 vols., 1839; of which the best modern edition is that published by Houghton Mifflin, 1901, and of which there is an abbreviated edition in Everyman's Library. — Lockhart's *Life* was long regarded as one of the two or three greatest biographies in English; but recent discoveries that he edited Scott's correspondence arbitrarily have lessened its fame and reliability.

The best brief biography is (Sir) Herbert Grierson, *Sir Walter Scott, Bart.: A New Life Supplementary to and Corrective of Lockhart's Biography,* 1938. — Based on the new 1932–37 edition of the Letters; factual and candid.

Good Introductory Studies

Shairp, John C.; "The Homeric Spirit in Walter Scott," *Aspects of English Poetry,* 1881.

Stevenson, Robert Louis; "A Gossip on Romance," *Memories and Portraits,* 1887. — Praise by a distinguished successor.

Saintsbury, George; "The Historical Novel," in *Essays in English Literature,* ii, 1895, and *Sir Walter Scott,* 1897. — Brilliant.

Lang, Andrew; Introductions to the Border Edition of the novels, 1902–04. — The best account of Scott's use of his sources.

Young, Charles A.; *The Waverley Novels,* 1907. — Good general estimate.

Grant, Arthur J.; Introduction to selections from the novels in *Scott* (Masters of Literature Series) , 1907. — Sound discussion of the relative merits of the best Waverley Novels.

Dixon, W. Macneile; "Scott" (wr. 1931) , *An Apology for the Arts,* 1944. — Modern in its approach.

Walpole, Hugh; Introduction to *The Waverley Pageant,* 1932. — An appreciation by a well-known novelist of today.

Baker, Ernest A.; *The History of the English Novel,* vi, ch. 6–9, 1935. — Places Scott in the general history of English fiction.

FOR ADVANCED STUDENTS

Important Additional Texts

Minstrelsy of the Scottish Border, ed. T. F. Henderson, 4 vols., 1902, 1932. — One-volume editions: by Alfred Noyes, 1908; by T. F. Henderson, 1931.

Miscellaneous Prose Works, 30 vols., 1834–71.

Letters of Sir Walter Scott, ed. H. J. C. Grierson and others, 12 vols., 1932–37. — Authoritative. — Cf. *Huntington Libr. Quart.,* ii, 319; 1939; and TLS, Oct. 25, 1947; March 27, April 10, April 24, 1947, for additional letters.

The Journal of Sir Walter Scott, ed. J. G. Tait and W. M. Parker, 1947. — Important for the last, heroic years.

The Private Letter-Books, 1930; and *Sir Walter's Postbag,* 1932; ed. W. Partington — Abbotsford MSS, illustrating his wide interests.

Biographical and Critical

Adolphus, John Leycester; *Critical Remarks on the Series of Novels Beginning with 'Waverley,' and an Attempt to Ascertain Their Author,* 1821. — Ingenious, and still of value on Scott's style and manner.

Hazlitt, William; "On the English Novelists," "The Spirit of the Age," "Why the Heroes of Romance Are Insipid," etc. in *Complete Works;* see the Index for other passages on Scott. — Against his Toryism, but otherwise appreciative.

Carlyle, Thomas; "Sir Walter Scott" (1838), in *Critical and Miscellaneous Essays.* — Considers him sincere, able, and wholesome; but too worldly and superficial. — See H. J. C. Grierson, "Scott and Carlyle," Engl. Asso. *Essays and Studies,* XIII, 1927.

Ruskin, John; *Modern Painters,* 1856; *Fors Clavigera,* 1873 (*Works,* v, 317; xxviii, 188). — Unsympathetic. — See H. H. Carter in *Sewanee Review,* xxx, 130; 1922.

Stephen, Leslie; "Some Words About Walter Scott" (1874), *Hours in a Library,* I, 137. — Attack from the rationalistic point of view.

Bagehot, Walter; "The Waverley Novels" (1858), in *Literary Studies.* — One of the best essays; judicious.

Veitch, John; *The History and Poetry of the Scottish Border,* 2 vols., 1878.

Howells, W. D.; *Criticism and Fiction,* 1891, pp. 21–24. — Typical attack from the realistic school.

Maigron, Louis; *Le Roman Historique à l'Europe Romantique,* 1898. — Scott's influence on French Romantics. Cf., below, Dargan, 1934; Genévrier, 1935; and Wenger, 1947.

Hudson, W. H.; *Sir Walter Scott,* 1901. — Pays particular attention to his place in the Romantic Movement.

Crockett, W. S.; *The Scott Country,* 1902; 2nd ed., 1911; also *Footsteps of Scott,* 1914.

More, Paul Elmer; "Scotch Novels and Scotch History," *Shelburne Essays,* III, 82; 1905. — More sympathetic than most of Mr. More's interpretations of the Romantics. Stresses the value of the novels as picturing the national life as a whole.

Lang, Andrew; *Sir Walter Scott* (Literary Lives Series), 1906. — Learned and delightful.

Elliot, Fitzwilliam; *The Trustworthiness of the Border Ballads,* 1906; and *Further Essays on the Border Ballads,* 1910. — Attack on Scott's editorial methods. — Refuted by Andrew Lang in *Sir Walter Scott and His Border Minstrelsy,* 1910.

Ball, Margaret; *Sir Walter Scott as a Critic of Literature,* 1907. — Thorough and judicious.

Williams, A. M.; "Scott as a Man of Letters," *Engl. Studien,* xxxvii, 100; 1907. — Best survey of his miscellaneous works.

Verrall, Arthur W.; "The Prose of Sir Walter Scott," *Collected Literary Essays,* 1913. — Thorough study of its weaknesses and its strength.

Lieder, Paul R.; *Scott and Scandinavian Literature: the Influence of Bartholin and Others* (Smith College Studies), 1920.

Emerson, Oliver F.; "The Early Literary Life of Sir Walter Scott," JEGP, xxiii, 29, 241, 389; 1924. — Painstaking verification and correction of Lockhart's account of the years 1796–1810.

Macintosh, W.; *Scott and Goethe: German Influence on the Writings of Sir Walter Scott,* Galashiels, 1925. — Useful, though uncritical.

Graham, Walter; "Scott's Dilemma," MLN, xli, 45; 1926. — Shows that Scott, before his authorship of the novels was acknowledged, had written (at least a part of) a favorable review of his *Tales of My Landlord* in the *Quarterly* of Jan., 1817.

Koch, J.; "Scott's Beziehungen zu Deutschland," *Germ.-Rom. Monatsschrift*, xv–xvi, 1927.

White, Henry A.; *Sir Walter Scott's Novels on the Stage* (Yale Studies in English), 1927.

Baldensperger, Fernand; "La Grande Communion Romantique de 1827: Sous le Signe de Walter Scott," *Rev. Litt. Comp.*, vii, 47; 1927. — Best brief survey of Scott's influential position in European romanticism.

Boas, Louise S.; *A Great Rich Man: the Romance of Sir Walter Scott*, 1929. — Misleading emphasis on his worldliness.

Haber, T. B.; "The Chapter-Tags in the Waverley Novels," PMLA, xlv, 1140; 1930.

Carswell, Donald; *Sir Walter Scott: A Four-Part Study in Biography*, 1930, 1932. — Derogatory, almost malignant.

Wolfe, Clara S.; "Scott's Indebtedness to Spanish Literature," *Rom. Rev.*, xxiii, 301; 1932.

Buchan, John; *Sir Walter Scott*, 1932. — Appreciation by a well-known statesman.

McKillop, A. D.; *Sir Walter Scott in the Twentieth Century*, The Rice Institute, 1933.

Dargan, E. P.; "Scott and the French Romantics," PMLA, xlix, 599; 1934.

Genévrier, P.; *Walter Scott, Historien Français*, 1935. — Focusing on *Quentin Durward*, and applying thorough tests, finds Scott's treatment of history, on the whole, sound. — Cf. Max Korn, "Sir Walter Scott und die Geschichte," *Anglia*, lxi, 416; 1937.

Hillhouse, James T.; *The Waverley Novels and Their Critics*, 1936. — Best survey of the history of the criticism. See A. D. McKillop's rev., ELH, iv, 16; 1937.

Landis, P. N.; "The Waverley Novels," PMLA, lii, 461; 1937.

Munroe, David; "Sir Walter Scott and the Development of Historical Study," *Queen's Quart.*, xlv, 216; 1938. — Cf. James F. Walker, "Scott as a Popularizer of History," *Aberdeen Univ. Rev.*, xxiii, 212; 1936.

Smith, J. C.; "Scott and Shakespeare," Engl. Asso. *Essays and Studies*, xxiv, 114; 1939. — Cf. R. K. Gordon, *Trans. Royal Soc. Canada*, xxxix, 111; 1945.

Fiske, Christabel F.; *Epic Suggestion in the Imagery of the Waverley Novels*, 1940. — Applies a somewhat forced distinction between "epic" and "romantic," but richly illustrates Scott's relation to the Homeric and heroic tradition. — Cf. W. S. Knickerbocker, *Sewanee Review*, xlviii, 519; 1940.

Moore, John R.; "Defoe and Scott," PMLA, lvi, 710; 1941.

Orians, G. H.; "Walter Scott, Mark Twain, and the Civil War," SAQ, xl, 342; 1941.

Parsons, Coleman O.; "Scott's Letters on Demonology and Witchcraft," "Minor Spirits and Superstitions," and "The Interest of Scott's Public in the Supernatural," N&Q, clxxxii–clxxxv; 1942–1943. — Cf. Parsons, "Scott's Fellow Demonologists," MLQ, iv, 473; 1943; and Mody C. Boatright, "Demonology in the Novels," and "Witchcraft in the Novels," Univ. of Texas Studies, 1934 and 1935, and "The Use of the Supernatural," PMLA, i, 235; 1935.

Brightfield, Myron F.; "Scott, Hazlitt, and Napoleon," *Univ. of Cal. Essays and Studies*, xiv, 181; 1943.

Pottle, F. A.; "The Power of Memory in Boswell and Scott," *Essays Presented to David Nichol Smith*, 1945.

Wenger, Jared; "Character-Types of Scott, Balzac, Dickens, Zola," PMLA, lxii, 213; 1947. — Cf., above, Maigron, 1898; Baldensperger, 1927; Dargan, 1934; and Genévrier, 1935.

Woolf, Virginia; "Scott," *The Moment and Other Essays*, 1948.

Mayo, Robert D.; "The Chronology of the Waverley Novels: The Evidence of the Manuscripts," PMLA, LXIII, 935; 1948. — Refutes the theory of Una Pope-Hennessy and Donald Carswell that some of the novels were originally composed long before 1814.

Bibliographies and Reference Books

Corson, James C.; *A Bibliography of Sir Walter Scott*, 1943. — Lists nearly 3,000 items.

Ruff, William; *A Bibliography of the Poetical Works of Sir Walter Scott: 1796–1832*, Edinburgh Bibl. Soc. Trans., 1938. — Twenty-three facsimile title pages.

Burr, Allston; *Sir Walter Scott, an Index, Placing the Short Poems in His Novels and His Long Poems and Dramas*, 1936. — Useful so far as it goes, but defective.

Worthington, G.; *Bibliography of the Waverley Novels*, 1930. — Cf. M. L. Poston, "Addenda," TLS, May 29, 1943.

Husband, Margaret F. A.; *Dictionary of Characters in the Waverley Novels*, 1910.

CHAPTER 9

ROBERT SOUTHEY

(August 12, 1774–March 23, 1843)

His Early Life and Works.—Robert Southey was the son of a merchant in Bristol, but from the age of three was reared by his aunt, Miss Tyler of Bath, a well-to-do maiden lady of marked peculiarities and strong opinions. She brought him up without much contact with other children, and according to principles which she believed to be those of Rousseau. A devoted theater goer, she took him at an early age to see plays; and she encouraged him to read Shakspeare and other Elizabethan dramatists, Sidney, and Spenser, and translations of Tasso and Ariosto, long before the age when such authors are usually read. When he was fourteen, an uncle, the Rev. Herbert Hill, enabled him to enter Westminster School, where his lifelong interest in mythologies and folklore was first aroused, and where he showed his first signs of rebelliousness by contributing to the school magazine an article, *The Flagellant,* against flogging, for which he was expelled. He entered Balliol College, Oxford, his uncle hoping that he would become an Anglican clergyman. It soon appeared, however, that this was impossible, for his religious faith had been shaken by the reading of Gibbon. In June, 1794, he met Coleridge; and, as has already been described, they conceived their scheme of Pantisocracy,[1] and collaborated in the drama, *The Fall of Robespierre.*

Southey was keenly aware of the new possibilities, both cultural and political, that were dawning in many fields of human activity. Less meditative than Coleridge, he was aflame with zeal for carrying new ideals into practical action. He wrote a play glorifying Wat Tyler, the fourteenth-century rebel; but this was too daring to be published at the time. (Years later, in 1817, when he had become a conservative, his enemies maliciously had it published, to his embarrassment.) He composed a poem, *Joan of Arc* (first draft finished 1793; published 1796), which depicted the Maid of Orleans as inspired by the legendary and supernatural traditions of France, and as a child of nature whose in-

[1] See above, p. 31.

nocence and intuitive wisdom dumfounded the subtleties of the wicked
churchmen who tried to entrap her into heretical statements. He wrote
several sonnets against the slave trade, and other poems of humanitarian
tendencies, including some on those convicts who were regarded as the
most vicious of criminals, and who were sent to the Australian penal
colony at Botany Bay. To these poems Southey gave the startling title,
Botany Bay Eclogues, which had about the same incongruous and provocative effect upon his generation as the title *Sing Sing Pastorals* or *Leaven-
worth Idylls* would have upon ours. In one of the *Eclogues* he intimated
that the convict who was removed from civilization was happier and more
peaceful in his enforcedly simple life than the respectable citizen who
was a slave to vanity and luxury.

Rightly feeling that the usual forms of verse were not suitable means
of expressing revolutionary sentiments, Southey tried various experiments
with dactylics and sapphics. One of his sapphics was entitled *The
Widow,* and began as follows:

> Cold was the night wind, drifting fast the snows fell,
> Wide were the downs and shelterless and naked,
> When a poor Wanderer struggled on her journey
>   Weary and way-sore.

Both the crudity of versification in such productions, and the radical
sentiments, were attacked in the brilliant conservative journal, the *Anti-
Jacobin* (1797–98). In this appeared many parodies, including the following "sapphics" by George Canning:

THE FRIEND OF HUMANITY AND THE KNIFE–GRINDER

FRIEND OF HUMANITY

> "Needy Knife-grinder! whither are you going?
> Rough is the road, your Wheel is out of order—
> Bleak blows the blast;—your hat has got a hole in't,
>   So have your breeches!
>
> Weary Knife-grinder! little think the proud ones,
> Who in their coaches roll along the turnpike-
> Road, what hard work 'tis crying all day 'Knives and
>   Scissars to grind O!'
>
> Tell me, Knife-grinder, how you came to grind knives?
> Did some rich man tyrannically use you?
> Was it the 'Squire or Parson of the Parish?
>   Or the Attorney?
>
> Was it the 'Squire for killing of his game? or
> Covetous Parson for his Tythes distraining?
> Or roguish Lawyer made you lose your little
>   All in a law-suit?

(Have you not read the Rights of Man, by Tom Paine?)
Drops of compassion tremble on my eye-lids,
Ready to fall, as soon as you have told your
                                        Pitiful story."

KNIFE-GRINDER

"Story! God bless you! I have none to tell, Sir,
Only last night a-drinking at the Chequers,
This poor old hat and breeches, as you see, were
                                        Torn in the scuffle.

Constables came up for to take me into
Custody; they took me before the Justice;
Justice Oldmixon put me in the Parish-
                                        Stocks for a Vagrant.

I should be glad to drink your Honor's health in
A Pot of Beer, if you would give me Sixpence;
But for my part, I never love to meddle
                                        With Politics, Sir."

FRIEND OF HUMANITY

"*I* give thee Sixpence! I will see thee damn'd first—
Wretch! whom no sense of wrongs can rouse to vengeance—
Sordid, unfeeling, reprobate, degraded,
                                        Spiritless outcast!"

*(Kicks the Knife-grinder, overturns his Wheel, and exit in a
transport of republican enthusiasm and universal philanthropy.)*

Like Coleridge and Wordsworth, Southey was temperamentally somewhat inclined toward the School of Sensibility, but for a time was fascinated by the rationalism of Godwin. In his case, as in theirs, however,
the failure of the French Revolution caused him, not without painful
regrets, to abandon some of his extravagant hopes and schemes. In his
recovery from the revolutionary fever, he found much strength and comfort in the noble and unworldly counsel of the stoic Epictetus. By 1796
he had fairly well abandoned radicalism, sentimentalism, and primitivism.
His persevering studies in one of his favorite fields, folklore, had by that
time convinced him that civilized man, imperfect as he was, had nothing
to gain by trying to revert to savagery. "The savage and civilized states,"
he mournfully says (in 1797) "are alike unnatural, alike unworthy the
origin and end of man." When in 1799 he heard a disciple of Rousseau
lecture on the advantages of savage society over civilized, he was "amused
to find him mistaken in every fact he adduced respecting savage manners."
He was also done with emotion for emotion's sake: Goethe's *Werther*
"gives me now [1799] unmingled pain."
    Meanwhile he had married Edith Fricker (14 Nov., 1795), and had
spent the winter of 1795–96 in Lisbon, Portugal, where his uncle was
clergyman to the British residents. He became deeply interested in the

literature and history of Portugal and Spain, and soon acquired a knowledge of them quite unusual among Englishmen. On returning home he tried to fit himself for one or another means of livelihood, including the law, but was unable to find anything congenial except a literary life. Fortunately a wealthy schoolmate, C. W. Wynn, encouraged him to remain faithful thereto by assuring him of an annual income. The allowance was a small one (c. £160), but it helped to keep the wolf from the door. In 1803, Southey settled in the Lake region, at Greta Hall, Keswick, which was to be his home for the rest of his life. His wife's sister, Mrs. Lovell, whose husband had died and left her penniless, came to live with the Southeys; and his other sister-in-law, Mrs. Coleridge, was likewise a member of the Southey household. Most men would have tried to shift these burdens, but Southey bravely bore them. After 1807, his friend Wynn's allowance was superseded by an annual government pension of c. £200. The rest of his income was earned by unremitting literary toil.

The Poems of His Middle Years.—The abandonment by Southey of merely subjective and fantastic assumptions concerning life may be observed at least as early as in the poems which he published in 1799, for example, in the admirable ballad entitled *The Old Woman of Berkeley*. Its source was an anecdote in the medieval Latin chronicle of Matthew of Westminster, which he had read, standing upon a chair, in a copy chained to an upper shelf of a cathedral library. It was the story of an old witch who upon her deathbed tried to escape her doom by providing for constant masses and vigils, but who was nevertheless borne away by Satan and his crew. The subject was one which would have tempted a skeptic to treat it in such a way as to satirize the superstition and credulity of the people and the rapacity of the clergy, and which a member of the School of Terror would have seized upon as an opportunity for grotesque and blood-curdling horrors. Southey, however, who in his earlier writings had dealt with his sources, whether in books or experience, arbitrarily, now treated his materials with conscientious objectivity, and rendered the tale in such a manner that the medieval atmosphere of the original was faithfully preserved.

This new attitude he likewise adopted in interpreting savage or barbaric life, a field to which a large part of his labors were to be devoted. He was steadily enlarging his knowledge of the history and customs of primitive peoples, whether ancient or modern; and for many years he was the leading reviewer of books written by missionaries or travelers who gave reports of the tribes with which they had come in contact. In his *Songs of the American Indians* (1799), containing such poems as "The Huron's Address to the Dead" and "The Peruvian's Dirge over the Body of His Father," he showed more accurate knowledge of Indian customs than any previous poet. He had set his feet upon the middle road which avoided on the one hand the neo-classic ignorance and contempt of any forms of human experience that were not directly connected

with the Greek, Roman, or Hebraic tradition, and on the other the sentimental phantasies about the perfectly noble savage. The five poems in
this series are dramatic lyrics; they let the Indian speak for himself, and
express his vengeful and bloodthirsty feelings as well as his bravery and
loyalty.

From such preliminary studies, Southey proceeded to the composition
(c. 1799–1814) of the four long narrative poems (he disliked to give them
"the degraded title of epics") which not only he himself but also his many
friends confidently believed would win him one of the highest places
among English poets. As a rule, his mornings were devoted to their
composition, his afternoons and evenings being employed in the literary
drudgery necessary for his support. Each of the poems drew upon a large
fund of folklore and history, and some scholarly modern readers find
Southey's annotations more interesting than his text. He himself, however, was not actuated by a merely antiquarian purpose. His theme in
every case bore a relation to these problems: what were the characteristics
of a real hero and leader and what was the best type of civilization?

Thalaba the Destroyer, based upon Arabian legend and Mohammedan
mythology, relates the overthrow of a powerful band of devil worshippers
—devotees of the same evil spirit, Eblis, that Beckford had depicted in
Vathek—by a young hero who has undergone a discipline not so much
of the body as of the soul. Before he achieves his mission, he has to learn
not only to overcome the temptations of the flesh, but to rid his mind of
various illusions and prejudices, such as his trust in magic rather than in
religious faith, and in vengeance rather than forgiveness. The poem was
written in loose, unrhymed rhythms modelled upon those of the *Dramatic
Sketches of Northern Mythology* (1790) of Frank Sayers.

Madoc tells of a Welsh prince of the twelfth century, who was reputed
to have discovered America. After his first voyage, he returned to Wales,
gathered a band of followers, and settled in Florida, amid tribes of various degrees of culture. One of these, the Aztecas, given to idolatry and
human sacrifices, he finally overcame; this defeated tribe then emigrated
to Mexico where they subsequently founded the celebrated Aztec empire.
Southey made a painstaking effort to keep the representation of the manners and customs of the ancient Welsh and of the several Indian tribes
faithful to the best authorities in the various fields. He discriminated between the comparatively peaceful and attractive natives and the Aztecas
with their abhorrent rites; but he regarded the conversion of Indians to
Christianity as a noble and heroic enterprise.

The Curse of Kehama (1810), composed during the depressing years
when Napoleon domineered over Europe and seemed invincible, relates
the story of an ancient Indian potentate, Kehama, whose power it seemed
likewise futile to oppose. He had unjustly condemned the Brahmin sage
Ladurlad to be bereft of every pleasure in life and yet not to be allowed
to die. Thalaba and Madoc had been heroes in action; Ladurlad, who
had every reason for despair, illustrated the truth that one may be equally
heroic merely through patient faith in the ultimate victory of righteous-

ness. In the end his faith is justified: Kehama, lusting after Ladurlad's daughter, tries to win her by offering her immortality; but when they drink of the mystical cup which confers it, his life is extinguished, while hers is saved, for the elixir has the property of releasing the spiritual element from the material and in Kehama there is nothing of the former whatever. Thus the extravagant superstitions of Hindu mythology, which Southey regarded as "of all false religions the most monstrous in its fables," were made to serve a purpose not unlike that of Wordsworth's Wanderer. Like Byron and Moore he was interested in Oriental and Mohammedan civilizations, but he did not let their picturesqueness lull to sleep his critical judgment, and he looked upon them as inferior to western Christianity.

Some critics regard *Kehama,* because it is full of picturesque strangeness, as the most interesting of Southey's longer poems; but to others *Roderick, the Last of the Goths* (1814) is the best because closest to the realities of life; and Southey himself so regarded it. The heroes of his previous poems had been relatively faultless beings; but in *Roderick,* called "A Tragic Poem," the titular hero began his career with wrongdoing, and brought down upon his people the calamities of the Moorish invasion. The main theme is that of an erring leader who succeeds in liberating his nation only after he has purified his soul through bitter penitence and self-sacrifice, and has renounced all forms of personal ambition, not even permitting his people to know who it was that saved them.

Coleridge found charm in *Thalaba;* and Shelley, whose *Queen Mab* it influenced, admired it. Scott read *Madoc* thrice with delight; and Charles James Fox was fond of reading it aloud, his company being spellbound by it until long after midnight. In *Kehama* Scott declared that he found passages as grand as any he had ever known. Landor likewise praised *Roderick* and the other epics. In modern days, however, they are almost unread. Their length is discouraging: none of them is much shorter than one hundred pages, and all told the four poems cover nearly five hundred—more than all the poems of Milton. It would gravely disappoint Southey to learn that his unpretentious ballads, metrical tales, and shorter poems like "The Battle of Blenheim," "The Holly Tree," and "My Days Among the Dead Are Passed" (*Anth.,* 477–9), are known to thousands who have never read a line of what he thought would prove to be his masterpieces.

In 1813, after Scott had declined the office, Southey was appointed Poet Laureate. The verses which he wrote in that capacity were much ridiculed, his elegy on the death of George III provoking Byron's deadly satire, *The Vision of Judgment* (1821; *Anth.,* 724). A complete contrast to the verses which official obligations forced him to write was the *Ode Written During the Negotiations with Buonaparte in January, 1814,* which Dowden calls "perhaps the loftiest chaunt of political invective, inspired by moral indignation, which our literature possesses," and which will always be inspiring whenever, as so often during our own times, craven appeasers incline to make peace with despotism.

His Prose Writings.—In 1807 it was suggested by Scott that Southey contribute to the *Edinburgh Review;* but although the offer was pecuniarily tempting, he declined it because he disagreed with its Whig politics. A year later when the Tory *Quarterly Review* was begun, he found his opening; and thereafter he was for several decades one of the chief writers on the conservative side. Like most who permit themselves to be drawn into political controversy, he often displayed bitterness and blindness, and opposed some measures which time proved to be sound ones, such as Catholic Emancipation and the Electoral Reform Bill of 1832. His principles, however, were not those of a reactionary, and some of the proposals of this romantic Tory would have aroused Dr. Johnson's outspoken scorn. Southey was conservative in disbelieving that in his day the betterment of society could be attained by surrendering political power into the hands of an uneducated proletariat. This did not mean, however, that he was content with conditions as they were or had no faith in meliorism nor any program of improvement. On the contrary, he pointed out repeatedly the evils which modern conditions had brought to agricultural and industrial laborers ("I know not how a cotton-mill," he writes to Lord Ashley, "can be otherwise than an abomination to God and Man") ; and he insisted that the economists of the *laissez-faire* school, who said that to try to meddle with such conditions was futile, were as wrong as they were callous to human suffering. By indifference they were encouraging the victims of a bad social order to become the dupes of demagogues who promised them relief through violence and revolution. Humanity should not be regarded as if it were created to manufacture cotton goods, nor children as if they were born to feed power looms. It was the moral responsibility of the upper classes to make England a land in which factories and machines should be means to human ends rather than ghastly destroyers of human life. Not votes for an illiterate multitude, but a change of heart and conscience in the leaders of the people was the fundamental need. If that were brought about, there would follow such practical reforms as widespread popular education, more sincere and helpful activity by the churches, humanitarian factory legislation, protection of agriculture, the undertaking of public works for the relief of unemployment, the intelligent direction of emigration, and other steps toward the common welfare. The discourses in which he advocated such policies were in part collected in his *Colloquies on the Progress and Principles of Society* (1829) and his *Essays: Moral and Political* (1832).

Among Southey's other writings are his abridged versions of the medieval Spanish romances, *Amadis of Gaul* (1803), *Palmerin of England* (1807), and *The Cid* (1808). He wrote a *History of Brazil* (1810–19) and a *History of the Peninsular War* (1822–32; *Anth.,* 481), each in three volumes. Unfortunately for Southey, the latter soon found a powerful rival in a brilliant account of the same struggle by Sir William Napier, who had served in the campaigns.

The prose of Southey has always been praised for its clarity, correctness, and adaptability to its varied themes. Modern readers will find it most engagingly exemplified in his biographies, some of which are among the temporarily neglected treasures of our language. One of them is the *Life of Wesley* (1820; *Anth.*, 480) , wherein Southey, though belonging to a church most members of which looked with contempt upon Methodism, gave a magnanimously fair characterization of one of the greatest English worthies. "It is," said Coleridge, his fellow Anglican, "the favorite of my library; the book I can read for the twentieth time when I can read nothing else." Other noteworthy biographies are the *Lives of the Uneducated Poets* (1829), unintentionally a refutation of pre-romantic illusions; the *Life of Bunyan* (1830) of whose *Pilgrim's Progress* Southey edited the first approximately correct text since the days of its author; and the charming *Life of Cowper* (1835) , which contains a significant sketch of eighteenth-century literary history.

The most celebrated of the biographies is of course the *Life of Nelson* (1813; *Anth.*, 482) . Owing to unavoidable dependence upon sources which have since been proved to be not the best, it contains errors in fact; but it discerned those features of Nelson's life and character which were the most significant and which made him, despite his faults, the savior and the most beloved naval hero of the greatest maritime empire. Here Southey had found in actual life a personality even greater than the champions glorified in his epics, and beset with not dissimilar difficulties. The devotion of Nelson to his country was felt to be an inspiration to patriotism in other lands than his own, and a special edition of Southey's *Life* was published by the government of the United States and presented to each officer and seaman of our navy.

His last long work, *The Doctor,* is a prose fiction almost as loose and digressive as *Tristram Shandy.* It centers about the experiences and reflections of a country physician, but includes scholarly curiosities, criticisms, indecorous jocosities, and even a nursery tale, "The Three Bears" (*Anth.*, 488) , which is likely to outlive most of the graver works of its author, and which illustrates the kinship of his mind with that of the other Romantics in suffering little children to participate in the pleasures of the imagination. His "Memoirs of the Cats of Greta Hall" is in a similar vein.—Like Lamb and De Quincey, he felt there must be some kind of significance in dreams; and he systematically recorded his own, though he says apologetically "not superstitiously, but for their strange combinations."

The works which have been mentioned are only a few of the many volumes, amounting in all to over one hundred, that Southey wrote. The single-mindedness of his devotion to literature was one of the most admirable traits of his character. He repeatedly declined opportunities to engage in less arduous or more remunerative activities. He refused the Librarianship of the famous Advocates' Library in Edinburgh; declined to serve when elected to Parliament in 1826; and would not accept a professorship of history at Durham University in 1832. Those who suppose he was a Tory for worldly reasons may ponder the fact that in 1815 he might have become Sir Robert Southey, but refused to accept the proffered baronetcy. Of the many honors offered him, the only one he accepted was a Doctorate of Laws from his alma mater, the University of Oxford.

The chief domestic events of Southey's later years were the death of his eldest son in 1816, the mental illness of his wife in 1834, and her death in 1837. Two years later he married Caroline Bowles, a literary woman whom he had known for over twenty years. Shortly afterwards he grew feeble in mind and body: Wordsworth gives a sad picture of him in his library, among the fourteen thousand books that he had collected, aimlessly taking some of them from their shelves, "patting them with both hands affectionately like a child." In 1843, he died, aged sixty-nine.

His Relation to Other Romantics.—If the greatness of a man of letters depended wholly upon his moral character, Southey would be foremost among the Romantics, for he was as unselfish as Charles Lamb and more diligent in his calling. Not that he was impeccable: even as Lamb had a weakness for gin, Southey was intemperately fond of black currant rum, strong ale, and Rhenish wine (not to mention gooseberry tarts). Of the worldliness of Scott, he had not a trace. His entire life was devoted to the dissemination of truth as he saw it.

He pioneered in several kinds of romantic writing, an historically noteworthy fact which has been forgotten because Wordsworth and Coleridge a little later did the same kind of work even better. The three companions of youthful days unfortunately grew away from one another. Southey, as Griggs says, "at first loved Coleridge, then pitied him, came to condemn him, and finally, as far as he was able, tried to forget him." Coleridge condescendingly referred to Southey as "the bibliographer." Wordsworth regretfully said, "he never enquires on what *idea* his poem is to be wrought, what *feeling or passion* is to be excited; but he determines on a subject, and then reads a great deal" (to Crabb Robinson, May 13, 1812). Before 1817 Shelley, eighteen years younger than Southey, admired him; thereafter, like Byron, he condemned him violently as an "apostate" and "hireling." Even his fellow Tory, Sir Walter Scott, thought some of Southey's strong prejudices too extreme, and once was moved to remark, "in point of reasoning and political judgment he is no better than a wild bull"—a comment certainly not true of most of Southey's political principles, which were those of one who earnestly pleaded that society should become conscientious.

Southey ranks at the present time, in spite of what can be justly said on his behalf, among those Romantics who are historically interesting, but have become intrinsically of secondary importance. For this, two reasons may be given—one doubtfully valid, the other more nearly certain. The first, and admittedly doubtful, reason is that, misled by his own estimate of the relative value of his works we have judged him too much by his poetry, and have not yet sufficiently valued his admirable works in prose. The second and less doubtful reason is that, in devoting so much of his energy to an interpretation of the past, he overlooked a principle which Scott never left out of account—namely, that those aspects of past history are most important to us which have left a permanent impress upon our Anglo-American civilization. Southey's poetical interpretation of Hindu, American Indian, and Spanish history are of interest in so far as any conspicuous variety of human experience is interesting; but in comparison with the experiences depicted by Scott, they come less directly home to our own feelings and circumstances.

His political and social ideals were influential upon Carlyle, but the indebtedness was forgotten because Carlyle expressed them in so individual a manner that they seemed entirely original with him.

SELECTED BIBLIOGRAPHY

OF FIRST IMPORTANCE

Selections

Poems, ed. Edward Dowden (Golden Treasury Series), 1930.
Select Prose of Robert Southey, ed. Jacob Zeitlin (Macmillan), 1916.
Letters: A Selection, ed. M. H. Fitzgerald (World's Classics), 1912.

Best Biography

Simmons, Jack; Southey, 1945. — Especially good on Southey's many relationships with the other Romantics.

Good Introductory Criticisms

The prefaces to the selections listed above, and the essay "The Industrious Poet: In Southey's Workshop," TLS, Apr. 21, 1945.

FOR ADVANCED STUDENTS

Important Additional Texts

No complete edition of the poetry and prose exists. The poetry which Southey chose to preserve is collected in Poetical Works, 10 vols., 1837–38. — The Poetical Works, with a Memoir, ed. H. T. Tuckerman; 10 vols., 1860; 5 vols., 1880.

A convenient one-volume edition is Poems of Robert Southey, ed. M. H. Fitzgerald (Oxford Univ. Press), 1909; but it does not contain some of the historically important works, e.g., Joan of Arc and A Vision of Judgment.

A Vision of Judgment, ed. R. Ellis Roberts (with Byron's Vision), 1932.

Life of Horatio, Lord Nelson, ed. Emma Gollancz (Temple Classics), 1896; ed. G. A. R. Callender, 1922. — Cf. J. A. R. Jones "Corrigenda," N&Q, CXLVII, 62; 1924.

Life of Wesley, ed. M. H. Fitzgerald, 2 vols., 1925.

Lives and Works of the Uneducated Poets, ed. J. S. Childers, 1925.

The Doctor, ed. J. W. Warter, 7 vols., 1848, etc.; ed. and abridged, M. H. Fitzgerald, 2 vols., 1930.

Journal of a Tour in Scotland in 1819, ed. C. H. Herford, 1929.

Selections from the Letters of Southey, ed. J. W. Warter, 4 vols., 1856. — Correspondence with Caroline Bowles, ed. Edward Dowden. — Previously unpublished letters are edited by I. K. Fletcher, TLS, Nov. 20, 1937; E. R. Seary, RES, xv, 412 (1939); C. L. Cline, RES, XVII, 65 (1941); and Roland Baughman, Huntington Libr. Quart., VII, 247 (1944). — Kenneth Curry is preparing an edition of the unpublished letters.

Chiefly Biographical

Southey, Cuthbert C.; *The Life and Correspondence of Robert Southey*, 6 vols., 1849–50. — By his son. — Basic.

Dowden, Edward; *Southey* (English Men of Letters). Readable brief biography, criticized as too favorable by Leslie Stephen, "Southey's Letters," *Studies of a Biographer*, 1898. — A vivid sketch is Dowden's "The Early Revolutionary Group," *The French Revolution and English Literature*, 1897.

Haller, William; *The Early Life of Southey*, 1917. — Thorough and detailed account of the 1774–1803 period. — Supplemented by "Southey's Later Radicalism," PMLA, xxvii, 281; 1922.

Macaulay, Rose; *They Went to Portugal*, 1946. — Cf. her essay in *Orion: A Miscellany*, 1945. — On his visits to Portugal.

Elwin, Malcolm; *The First Romantics*, 1947. — Preoccupied with defense of Coleridge; Southey held chiefly responsible for abandoning Pantisocracy.

Criticism

Macaulay, T. B.; "Southey's Colloquies on Society," *Edinburgh Rev.*, Jan., 1830. — Rptd. in *Essays, Critical and Historical*, 1843. — Hostile.

Carlyle, Thomas; *Reminiscences*, ii, 309; 1881. — At first hostile, later not without admiration.

Saintsbury, George; *Essays in English Literature*, 1895. — A good review of Dowden's *Southey*, and discussion of the decline of his vogue.

Symons, Arthur; *The Romantic Movement in English Poetry*, 1909. — Condemns his verse.

Graham, Walter; "Robert Southey as Tory Reviewer," PQ, ii, 97; April, 1923. — Emphasizes the narrowness and intolerance of his politics.

Kaufman, Paul; "The Reading of Southey and Coleridge," MP, xxi, 317; Feb., 1924. — Based on the record of their loans from Bristol Library, 1793–98.

Knowlton, E. C.; "Southey's Eclogues," PQ, vii; July, 1928.

Feiling, Keith; "Southey and Wordsworth," *Sketches in Nineteenth Century Biography*, 1930.

Wright, Herbert G.; "Three Aspects of Southey," RES, ix, 37; 1933. — Influence of Coleridge on *Madoc*, etc.

Brown, Wallace C.; "Southey and English Interest in the Near East," ELH, v, 218; 1938.

Hoadley, Frank T.; "The Controversy over Southey's *Wat Tyler*," SP, xxxviii, 81; 1941.

Cameron, K. N.; "Shelley vs. Southey," PMLA, lvii, 489; 1942.

Sousa-Leão, J. de; "Southey and Brazil," MLR, xxxviii, 181; 1943. — By a Brazilian, on Southey's *History of Brazil*.

Anon.; "Southey, A Problem of Romanticism: Poet Who Lost His Way," TLS, March 20, 1943. — Occasioned by the centenary of his death; explains the decline of his fame.

Havens, R. D.; "Southey's *Specimens of the Later English Poets*," PMLA, lx, 1066; 1945.

Griggs, E. L.; "Southey's Estimate of Coleridge," *Huntington Libr. Quart.*, ix, 61; 1945.

Shamburger, Mary I., and Lachmann, Vera R.; in *Journal of American Folklore*, Oct., 1946. — On "The Three Bears." Cf. E. B. Vest, *Sat. Rev. Lit.*, May 24 and Sept. 6, 1947 (Phoenix Nest).

CHAPTER 10

THOMAS CAMPBELL

(July 27, 1777–June 15, 1844)

His Early Years.—Thomas Campbell was of Highland ancestry, and spent part of his youth amid Highland scenes; but he was born in Glasgow, where his father was a merchant, and was educated at the University of Glasgow. In his college days, he was enthusiastically in favor of the French Revolution, and when two Scotch sympathizers were indicted for sedition at Edinburgh, he journeyed there on foot in order to attend their trial. In due course he became anti-Napoleonic; but he continued to adhere to many doctrines of the School of Sensibility. He was ingenious enough to perceive that most of these might be associated with expectations of a happier future for mankind, and he made that thought the basis of his poem, written in the Popean couplet, *The Pleasures of Hope* (1799). Here he expatiated upon those hardships and wrongs which could find consolation only in an optimistic belief that the conditions of life would improve, and thus had an opportunity to deal with almost any topic that occurred to him from ideal love to the abolition of negro slavery and (taking a hint from Coleridge's sonnet on Kosciusko) the liberation of Poland. A line or two of his poem became proverbial—for example,

'Tis distance lends enchantment to the view;—

and its fluency and agreement with the general sentiments of the time made it very popular. The superficiality of its thoughts, and the very fact that its enchantment was due to keeping at a distance from the realities of life, were defects that were at first not perceived.

His Best Period.—Campbell used the money received from the original edition of the *Pleasures of Hope* (*Anth.*, 491) to defray his expenses on a visit to Germany. At Ratisbon in Bavaria, he had his first sight of battle, standing on the ramparts of the Scottish college there, and seeing the French troops capture the city. He did not remain in Bavaria long enough to witness the battle of Hohenlinden, which took place some weeks after he had gone to Northern Germany; but he obtained very clear and strong impressions of what warfare and the military spirit meant. He also tried to understand the literature of German

Romanticism, and became personally acquainted with some German authors; but a close examination of the so-called German influence upon him shows that it was confined to secondary matters. He was not sufficiently serious or profound to be affected by the deeper aspects of the German movement. The important result of his sojourn abroad, besides his already mentioned glimpse of warlike scenes, was to arouse his love of England and her navy. This was to be the one steadfast and ardent sentiment in his otherwise rather commonplace nature. His feelings were like those of many an American visitor in Europe nowadays: while at home he may have experienced no exalted emotions of patriotism, but, happening to catch sight of the Stars and Stripes upon a vessel in a foreign port, he suddenly realizes what his native land means to him. In Campbell's case this kind of sentiment was enhanced by the realization that in the last resort the only force that stood between the growing might of Napoleon and such nations as still remained independent was the British fleet. As he sailed homeward after his winter in Germany, Nelson and that fleet were on their way to check at Copenhagen the chief menace to British control of the seas.

Campbell's visit to Germany inspired the three poems by which he is best known—*Ye Mariners of England,* which was written in that country, *Hohenlinden,* and *The Battle of the Baltic (Anth.,* 493). Owing to the extravagant praises accorded the *Pleasures of Hope,* Campbell fancied that he had a genius for long and pretentious poems, and not only considered these shorter pieces unimportant but spoke scornfully of *Hohenlinden* as "a mere drum and trumpet thing." Today, however, it is recognized as one of the best battle poems in our language, swift in action, skilful in its choice of characteristic details, and unforgettably picturesque in its contrast between the unsullied purity of the snowclad landscape and the bloody, sulphurous horror of battle.

To appreciate the merits of *Ye Mariners of England* one needs only to compare it with the earnest but crude verses which were in part its source. There is in its pauses and its onward rushes—its sweep through the deep—something unerringly suggestive of the waters and the winds that its seamen ruled. Written in a dark hour of English national history, it expressed as no other poet had succeeded in doing the confidence of the people that the traditions and personnel of their navy would be their bulwark, a confidence justified by the event. More than a century later, it likewise helped to sustain the national courage during the two world wars.

The Battle of the Baltic is marred by a meaningless phrase or two, such as "flushed to anticipate the scene," and some lines of needless haughtiness; but here, too, we have an air of sublimity and of an unconquerable spirit. The metre, subsequently influential upon Tennyson's martial poem, *The Revenge,* is splendidly adapted to the subject. "Campbell," says Professor Saintsbury, "holds the place of the best singer of war in a race and language which are those of the best singers and not the worst fighters in the history of the world,—in the race of Nelson and the language of Shakspeare. Not easily shall a man win higher praise than this."

His Decline.—Campbell wrote a few other short poems, such as *Lochiel's Warning,* that have merit; but nearly all the rest of his work has fallen into oblivion. His most ambitious later effort was *Gertrude of Wyoming, a Pennsylvanian Tale* (1809), in Spenserian stanzas. Here he imitated James Fenimore Cooper in some parts of his accounts of Indian life, and Wordsworth in the descriptions of nature. He referred in notes to many works written by explorers in America, but his knowledge of them did not save him from introducing into this romance of border life the most ludicrously unrealistic details. In his battle pieces, so he himself says, he had tried to tell "when, where, and how the event happened— without gaud or ornament but what the subject essentially and easily affords"; but in *Gertrude* he relapsed into the idyllic and fantastic.

He had become celebrated and prosperous through his war songs, received a royal pension, and was elected Lord Rector of Glasgow University. He continued to write verses—but ceased to be a poet, except in brief moments. Themes which might be treated with sublimity still attracted him—"The Dead Eagle" who had been lord of the North African wildernesses; "The Last Man" (*Anth.,* 495) who, unlike Byron's, died defiantly protesting his faith in immortality. But too often his verses were merely talented, "elegant," rhetorical efforts. It was, however, admiringly remembered that he had taken a stand in favor of Polish and of Greek independence; and when he was buried in Westminster Abbey a grateful Pole cast earth from Kosciusko's grave upon Campbell's coffin. The nationalistic strain, which in the greater Romantics is only one of many themes, is in Campbell almost the only note that is struck resonantly.

SELECTED BIBLIOGRAPHY

OF FIRST IMPORTANCE

Selected Poems, ed. Lewis Campbell (Golden Treasury Series), 1904.

Complete Poetical Works, ed. J. Logie Robertson (Oxford Univ. Press), 1907.

Hadden, J. Cuthbert; *Thomas Campbell,* 1899. — The best biography.

Dixon, W. Macneile; "Thomas Campbell," in *An Apology for the Arts,* 1944. — Good general introduction.

FOR ADVANCED STUDENTS

Campbell, Thomas, ed.; *Specimens of the British Poets,* 7 vols., 1819; ed. P. Cunningham, 1841.

Bierstadt, A. M.; "Unacknowledged Poems by Campbell," MLN, xxxvii, 343; 1922.

Hazlitt, William; *The Spirit of the Age,* 1825; in *Complete Works,* xi (1932).

Beattie, William; *Life and Letters of Thomas Campbell,* 3 vols., 1849, 1850. — The standard biography.

Redding, Cyrus; *Literary Reminiscences and Memoirs of Thomas Campbell,* 2 vols., 1859. — Supplements Beattie.

Saintsbury, George; "The War Songs," *Essays in English Literature, Second Series,* 1895. — Praise.

Symons, Arthur; *The Romantic Movement in English Poetry,* 1909. — Judicious.

Elton, Oliver; *Survey of English Literature: 1780–1830;* 1912. — Best treatment of his relation to his times.

Bierstadt, A. M.; "Gertrude of Wyoming," JEGP, xx, 491; 1922. — Shows indebtedness to Chateaubriand; possibly exaggerates it.

Graham, Walter; "Byron and Campbell," N&Q, x, 45; 1922. — Borrowings from Byron.

Turner, A. M.; "Wordsworth's Influence on Campbell," PMLA, xxxviii, 253; 1923.

Shumway, D. B.; "Thomas Campbell and Germany," *Schelling Anniv. Papers,* 1923. — Studies his visits, and slight influences upon his writings.

Forsythe, R. S.; "Freedom's Shriek," N&Q, cl, 23; 1926. — Borrowing from Coleridge in *Pleasures of Hope.*

CHAPTER 11

WALTER SAVAGE LANDOR

(January 30, 1775–September 17, 1864)

His Early Life and Works.—Landor was the eldest son of a Dr. Landor of Warwick (a physician of irascible temper) and of his second wife, Elizabeth Savage. Both his father and mother were descended from old and well-to-do families. He was sent to Rugby School, where he displayed excellent scholarship in Latin as well as a pugnacious disposition toward boys larger than himself. When his master reproved him for writing bawdy verses, he replied so impudently that he was removed from the school. At eighteen he entered Oxford, where he soon offended the conservatives. Landor was even more openly enthusiastic about the French Revolution than Southey: he appeared with his hair unpowdered, and was called "the mad Jacobin." A Tory undergraduate having jeered at him, he fired, with no intention of doing bodily harm, a shot through the scorner's window; and was thereupon expelled. Over this escapade, he had a quarrel with his father, and left his home, as he vowed, "for ever." At twenty he published a volume of poems. Friends persuaded his father to give him a sufficient allowance, and he settled in South Wales, devoting himself to the reading of Greek, Latin, Italian, and English literature, but also enjoying the natural loveliness of the countryside and the society of the local gentry. Among the young ladies of his acquaintance was Rose Aylmer. There was no love affair between them, but her girlish beauty made an indelible impression upon his memory. She went to India with an uncle stationed there, and died in Calcutta. To her niece and namesake Landor in his later years wrote many delightful letters.

It was Rose Aylmer who lent to Landor *The Progress of Romance* by Clara Reeve, in which he found an outline of the Indian romance on which he based his epic *Gebir*. The motivation of the tragical outcome of the action was too trivial for epic purposes, but the young Landor was attracted by the opportunity which the legend afforded to attack despotism. He contrasted Gebir, a ruler who, despite divine warnings, entered upon a war of aggression and met his downfall, with Tamar, his peace-loving brother, who with a beloved nymph, found happiness in pastoral retirement. In point of view, this was a product of the Pre-Romantic Movement. The style, however, was superior to the substance; and already showed the beneficent influence of ancient classical authors and of Milton. On that account *Gebir*, which appeared in 1798, seems to some modern critics almost as indicative of the revival of poetry as were the *Lyrical Ballads* of the same year. Except for a few beautiful passages, it is little read today; for the plot is vague, and the majestic sound grows monotonous.—Stronger Miltonic influence upon his style appeared four years later, in the short narrative poem *Chrysaor*. Here, too, despotism is the object of the attack: a Titan rebels against Jupiter, and is supinely accepted as ruler of Spain. He is ultimately destroyed by Jupiter, but has in the meantime begotten a daughter, Superstition, who, because the people submitted to a king that pretended to be a god, is allowed for ages to oppress them. The idealism of these poems won for Landor the admiration of Southey; they met in 1808, and became personal friends.

At thirty, upon his father's death, Landor found himself wealthy. His generous sympathy for the oppressed was, however, not diminished. The subjugation of Spain by Napoleon seemed to him the blackest of crimes; and, although without any military knowledge, he hastened to the Peninsula and offered to equip a regiment of volunteers at his own expense. A small band gathered around him, but his temperament was too tactless and unpractical to succeed in such an undertaking. He decided he could help the Spanish cause better by returning to England and devoting himself to a denouncement of the Convention of Cintra (cf. Wordsworth; *Anth.*, 240). On his return, however, he became absorbed in the improvement of an estate which he had purchased, Llanthony Abbey, in Wales, and tried to make it a model of agricultural and social improvement. With the most unselfish recklessness he spent more than £70,000 upon this scheme, only to see it also defeated, after five years' effort. His Welsh tenants were suspicious of him, and his lawyers were either disloyal or not wise enough to moderate his quarrelsome temper. He became involved in lawsuits, and his idealistic plans eventuated in failure. He put the crown upon his impulsive and imprudent acts by marrying at the age of thirty-six, Julia Thuillier, who had "wonderfully beautiful golden hair," but was nineteen years younger than himself and not only totally obtuse to his intellectual interests but unskilful in helping the generous sides of his nature to overcome the obstreperous. Within three years she quarreled with him, because against her wishes he wanted to visit France. She made his seniority to her a point of reproach, whereupon he left her. Some months later, however, she rejoined him; and they went to Italy, settling at Fiesole, near Florence, in a villa traditionally associated with Boccaccio. This marked the end of his years of extremest inward storm-and-stress.—For the next twenty years, those of his intellectual and artistic prime, he remained in Italy, a voluntary exile. He loved Italy passionately, especially Florence, though he wished the

Florentines had "as much as one heart among them." Characteristically he was irritated by their excessive use of superlatives; he scornfully termed them "issimi." His dislike of certain individuals was always strong, and his personal relationships were often vexatious.

The Latter Half of His Life.—His tragedy, *Count Julian* (1812), which grappled with a more realistic aspect of life than his previous works, had already indicated that his powers were maturing; but it was not until his settlement in Italy, at the age of forty-six, that he found the right vehicle for his powers in the *Imaginary Conversations* (1824 ff.), two thirds of which were composed at Fiesole. Indifferent to pecuniary rewards, he entrusted their publication to friends in England, stipulating that any profits were to be given to charities. In 1835, another quarrel with his unfaithful wife led him to return to England, where he lived peaceably, chiefly at Bath, until 1858, when scandalmongers involved him in an action for libel. Partly because he was advised that the libel suit was likely to be decided against him, and partly because he was always generous to his family, he now settled his fortune upon them. When, somewhat like King Lear, he again found it impossible to live with them, he was reduced almost to destitution. The ungratefulness of his children was the hardest burden he had to bear in his declining years. His disciple, Robert Browning, was a great help and comfort to him; he administered the income provided by Landor's brothers, which supported Landor until his death at Florence, at the age of eighty-nine, in 1864. Fortunately his interests and powers remained unabated, and almost to the day of his death he was energetically devoted to his studious and literary pursuits. He lived to be the last of the great Romantics, outliving not only the younger group—Byron, Keats, and Shelley—by more than forty years, but surviving his own contemporaries—Scott by twenty-two years, Coleridge and Lamb by thirty, Southey by twenty-one, and even the aged Wordsworth by fourteen. When Landor died, the great Victorians, Browning and Tennyson, were already famous.

His Personality.—Landor was a man of great physical strength and impetuous emotions, but he had many of the gentler traits. He was exquisitely courteous toward women, adored children, and treated the so-called lower animals, especially dogs, almost as if they were human beings. Of flowers he was passionately fond: upon one occasion, it is said, when a servant spoke impudently to him, he threw him out a window into the garden; and then, bethinking himself, exclaimed "My God, I forgot the violets!" "Landor," said Leigh Hunt, "is like a stormy mountain pine that should produce lilies." All who have studied his personality admit that he was remarkably kind and generous, but what preoccupies their attention is his violent temper. It is indeed difficult in a brief sketch to avoid the impression that he was quarreling constantly, and the incidents which his irascibility caused are the most entertaining that can be related. In judging his character, the long periods during

which he lived peaceably should not be forgotten. He had a gift of in-
fectious laughter. When Dickens asked him what he would like most
as a memento from Italy, Landor said "an ivy-leaf from Fiesole"; Dickens
brought one home to him; and when Landor died, twenty years later, it
was found treasured among his belongings. It was not his fame, but his
essential lovableness, which kept him attractive to a host of friends and
visitors, English and American, even when he was very old. Dickens'
exasperating yet endearing Boythorn in *Bleak House* is much like Landor,
but with the genius left out.—The disappointments and domestic unhappiness which he had suffered because he had occasionally failed to restrain his wrath, led him in his writing to place self-control high among
the virtues.

The Works of His Maturity.—The best poems of Landor are mostly
either brief lyrics or epigrams, or somewhat longer narrative poems like
the *Hellenics*. Among the former are "Rose Aylmer," "The Maid's
Lament," "Death Stands Above Me," and "I Strove with None, For None
Was Worth My Strife," (*Anth.*, 497 ff.), in which the feeling is as pure
and intense as the form is beautiful. The *Hellenics* were written as a rule
in blank verse, and upon themes drawn from Greek myths or legends. If
such a poem was based upon a Roman subject, he called it an *Idyllium
Heroicum*. Some of the *Hellenics*, for example "Agamemnon and Iphi-
geneia," are dialogues in verse; others are narratives, such as the exquisite
"Hamadryad" (*Anth.*, 514), in which the youth Rhaicos loses his love, a
tree nymph, because he carelessly injures a bee, her messenger. These
poems are well described in Swinburne's lines:

> . . . Through the trumpet of a child of Rome
> Rang the pure music of the flutes of Greece.

Even more important than his flawless poems, are the *Imaginary Conversations* (*Anth.*, 501), the *Pentameron* (*Anth.*, 511), consisting of conversations between Petrarch and Boccaccio, and *Pericles and Aspasia*, a
long work of prose fiction in the form of letters (*Anth.*, 509). In lighter
vein is *The Citation and Examination of William Shakspeare Touching
Deer-Stealing*. Although the imaginary dialogue was a type of literature
that had been employed by Greek, Roman, and modern writers, Landor
made it peculiarly his own, finding possibilities in it that had not been developed. Like previous writers, he used it sometimes to express his ethical
views, sometimes to satirize evils, and sometimes to criticize literature;
but he was especially interested in making it a means of interpreting
varieties of human character as displayed in illustrious historical personages. He made the conversations strictly imaginary, i.e., he did not introduce into them, *verbatim*, remarks which the speakers had actually made,
nor did he employ archaic language; but he endeavored to be true to the
general spirit of the respective periods and to the known traits of the
famous men and women who were the interlocutors. In a few instances,
Landor's prejudices gave a bias to his characterizations. Sometimes—

e.g., in "Florentine, English Visitor, and Landor"—he modified later editions of a Conversation to accord with his changes of opinion. Contemporaries appeared in a few of the Conversations, such as "Landor and Marchese Pallavicini," "Southey and Landor," and "Porson and Southey"; but the large majority dealt with characters from the past.

Landor himself considered "Dante and Beatrice" his best Conversation. (Students of the early Italian Renaissance also admire his dramas "Andrea of Hungary," "Giovanna of Naples," and "Fra Rupert.") But of the more than one hundred and fifty Imaginary Conversations, the twenty-eight listed below are considered by most critics to be the best. In order to show what epochs Landor was especially interested in, they are arranged chronologically by subject matter; and the *Examination of Shakspeare* (not one of the best) and *Pericles and Aspasia* (not a Conversation) have been included.

Century B.C.	Title	Date of Publication
	Achilles and Helena	1853
	Aesop and Rhodope	1843-44
5th	Pericles and Aspasia	1836
3rd	Epicurus, Leontion, and Ternissa	1829
3rd	Marcellus and Hannibal	1828
2nd	Metellus and Marius	1829
1st	Lucullus and Caesar	1829
1st	Cicero and Quintus Cicero	1824
1st	Tiberius and Vipsania	1828

A.D.		
1st	Epictetus and Seneca	1828
11th	Leofric and Godiva	1829
12th	Tancredi and Constantia	1845
13th	Dante and Beatrice	1845
14th	Pentameron (Boccaccio and Petrarch)	1837
15th	Maid of Orleans and Agnes Sorrel	1846
15th	Filippo Lippi and Pope Eugenius IV	1846
16th	Henry VIII and Anne Boleyn	1824
16th	Roger Ascham and Lady Jane Grey	1824
16th	Princess Elizabeth and Princess Mary	1846
16th	Lord Brooke and Sir Philip Sidney	1824
16th	Examination of William Shakspeare	1834
16th	Essex and Spenser	1834
17th	Galileo and Milton	1839
17th	Admiral Blake and Humphrey Blake	1853
17th	Walton, Cotton, and Oldways	1829
17th	Lady Lisle and Elizabeth Gaunt	1829
17th	Andrew Marvell and Parker	1846
17th	William Penn and Lord Peterborough	1829
18th	Peter the Great and Alexis	1828
18th	Empress Catherine and Princess Dashkoff	1829

His Views of Life.—Critics have vied with one another in praising Landor as one of the greatest masters of English prose. They rightfully declare that none surpasses him in combining purity, lucidity, calm strength, and stateliness. But they seem to suppose that his activity was merely aesthetic, and that, as Leslie Stephen declares, he had no basis of serious thought. In point of fact, Landor himself asserted:

> Principles and ideas are my object; they must be reflected from high and low; but they must also be exhibited where people can see them best, and are most inclined to look upon them [i.e., through individual characters].

Accordingly, a knowledge of the chief principles and ideas that motivate his works is helpful toward a full appreciation of their value.

Landor believed that man was meant to be reasonably happy in his universe, because although imperfect he was endowed with certain noble tendencies the fulfillment of which would ensure his happiness. But in surveying human history, one made the sad discovery that there were forces blunderingly created by man himself which too often deprived him of his destined felicity. In the field of government he had set up kings and tyrants, thus destroying that state of liberty in which alone the individual can grow as he should. Landor was an aristocrat in revolt against monarchy; he was a republican when to be so meant to defy social ostracism. If his writings have any *one* dominant motif, it is the exaltation of freedom. He fulminated against whatever seemed to him autocracy in his own day—against Napoleon, against the Bourbons, against Austrian despotism over Italy, and other suppressions of national independence; and he pleaded the cause of Poland and of Ireland. On the other hand he was not a believer in pure democracy, holding that it was jealous of merit, suspicious of enlightenment, incapable of giving thoughtful consideration to public problems, and therefore likely to defeat the purpose of government, which should be to order affairs so that truth and virtue might flourish. The best constitution was one which should encourage the election of sagacious and honest governors who were reluctant to solicit a public trust, slow to accept it, and resolute never to betray it.

Another way in which man had cheated himself out of happiness was by perverting religion. Landor believed in God and immortality; but he thought that priests had fostered dogmatism concerning points which human reason could not solve, as well as bigoted sectarianism, gross superstitions, and too elaborately formal worship. He declared

> It would grieve me to foresee a day when our cathedrals and our churches shall be demolished or desecrated; when the tones of the organ, when the symphonies of Handel, shall no longer swell and reverberate along the groined roof and painted windows. But let old superstitions crumble into dust; let faith, hope, and charity be simple in their attire; let few and solemn words be spoken before Him to whom all hearts are open, all desires known.

In conceiving of God as wrathful, men had not only misrepresented Him but also harmed themselves:

> Nothing is holy to me that lessens in my view the beneficence of my creator. If you could show him ungentle and unkind in a single instance, you would render myriads of men so throughout the whole course of their lives. The less that people tell about God, the better. He has left us a design to fill up; he has placed the canvas, the colors, the pencils within reach; his directing hand is over us incessantly; it is our business to follow it, and neither to turn around and argue with our master nor to kiss and fondle him. If any man would do all the good he might within an hour's walk of his own door, he would live the happier and the longer, for nothing is so conducive to longevity as the union of activity and content.

To achieve happiness, man must rid himself of certain false ideas and bad motives. Here Epicurus was the most helpful of sages, because he showed that most of our fears and worries might be reasoned away, that death might be disarmed of its terrors, that vice was inevitably painful and vindictive, and that worldly ambition was childish and illusory. But Epicurus was not sufficient; he could cast out evil, but other forces were needed to stimulate active good. One of these was nature. Landor did not interpret nature mystically; but he found in gardens and peaceful woods places where the finer parts of man's mind freely expanded, and it seemed to him that flowers understood the human heart and how its feverishness might be allayed. Another beneficent force was our sympathy for the unhappiness of others, especially when they were unjustly used. "Whoever is wronged," said Landor, "is my fellow-creature, were he never so before"; and the cultivation of that feeling was needful to moral growth. Another essential virtue was self-control, mastery over oneself being as necessary as arbitrary mastery over others was harmful. If to compassion for others and governance of self, there were added fortitude, the highest virtues were attained. The ideally good man, however, would not be content, as a pagan saint might be, with improving his own char· acter; he would want to impart his experience and knowledge to others as a means of their attaining happiness also; and the marks of the true hero are his thus persuading and leading his fellows.

These partly Stoic and partly Christian principles were the standards by which Landor measured the worth of the historical characters presented in his works; and the noblest among those characters were to him witnesses that the experience of mankind had shown that such ideals were realizable. Even love, in its higher forms the most sensitive and fragile of human joys, had actually been realized in noble hearts like those of Pericles and Aspasia, Dante and Beatrice, Boccaccio and Fiammetta (*Anth.*, 511). For those immortal dead who in some way or other manifested the essential integrity of human nature, he felt a solemn awe; not only were they happier and more glorious than any living being, but their influence over the living might be more benign and powerful than that of any contemporary. His task should be to make us feel as intimately as possible the temper of their souls, and our kinship with them. In this spirit he scanned the records of history from the days of Homer to modern times. More than previous composers of imaginary conversations, he appreciated the place of woman in the development of civilization; and it is strange that such admirable characterizations as those of Aspasia, Vipsania, Godiva, Beatrice, Lady Jane Grey, and Lady Lisle have been so largely ignored by the sex to which they are a tribute. In male characters, he especially delighted to portray the powers of thoughtful reflection, frankness, tolerance, courtesy, and fortitude. *Pericles and Aspasia* is his longest and most elaborate study of the past because in the Periclean age he found the nearest approach to the noblest human ideals of domestic and national happiness. The Greeks of that era had been fortunate because they had dwelt in small independent communities under laws made by the people, had avoided the evils of centralization, and were guided by unselfish and enlightened leaders. And the love of Pericles and Aspasia was all the nobler because it placed duty to the commonweal higher than personal affection. As Landor said elsewhere:

> Love is a secondary passion in those who love most, a primary in those who love least. He who is inspired by it in a high degree is inspired by honor in a higher. (*Ascham and Lady Jane Grey*)

His Literary Principles.—In Landor's judgment the first requisites of an author were knowledge of the human heart and an ability to discriminate characters. "Enter the mind and heart of your own creatures," he wrote, "think of them long, entirely, solely,—never of style, never of self, never of critics, cracked or sound" (*Pentameron*). His emotional reactions should be strong, but stronger yet should be control over them; moderation and composure were qualities of the greatest literature. If his work lacked intensity, it was not literature; but without selection and coherence, it fell short of greatness. This was the flaw in Byron's work, which had energy, and a large grasp of phenomena, but without selection and unity. Landor stressed the importance of choosing great themes, but he disliked the fanciful, mystical, and allegorical; the defect of Spenser was that in him the idea and the form did not cohere in vital interpenetration. He admired Addison, Johnson, Fielding, Richardson, and Sterne; and among contemporaries Wordsworth, Southey, Browning, and Dickens; but the greatest authors were Pindar, Dante, Shakspeare, Bacon, and Milton. The presence of Bacon in this list is indicative of the realism of Landor's temper.

His Relation to Other Romantics.—It is customary, because Landor admired Greek and Roman subjects, to describe him as "a classic writing in a romantic age" (Colvin), just as historians of music call Mendelssohn "a classicistic romanticist" (Paul Henry Lang). His own insistence upon his solitariness—"I am alone, and will be alone as long as I live, and after"

—has strengthened the impression that he stands radically apart from the Romantics. The above statement of his views should, however, show that, although he had his individual peculiarities of sentiment and purpose, he was in fundamental harmony with the general trend of the Romantic Movement.

His works were not as imaginative as those of Blake, Coleridge, and Shelley. His style is marmoreal in contrast with the pictorial of Keats. Sublimity he attains, but it differs from the transcendental sublimity of Wordsworth, though on other levels they had much in common. Their conceptions of the manly and heroic character were closely similar, as well as their ideals of womanhood; but Landor's ability to characterize individual women was greater than Wordsworth's. Their ideas of the relation of love to duty were identical, and it is not surprising that Landor greatly admired Wordsworth's *Laodamia*. Although in one of the Conversations he ranks Wordsworth with the very greatest poets (*Anth.*, 502), in another he severely condemns the prosiness of many lines in the *Lyrical Ballads* ("Southey and Porson," 1842). He admired Coleridge, especially as a critic, and thought him "worthy fifty Hazlitts" in that respect. He was angered by Byron's sneers at Southey and Wordsworth, and denounced him as a profligate and poseur; but, though Byron had ridiculed him in *The Vision of Judgment* and *Don Juan*, Landor expressed regret for his denunciation when Byron died in the cause of liberty (*Anth.*, 501). He refused to meet Shelley, having been misled by false gossip; but later he likewise repented that mistake, and he defended the virtues of Shelley against the "unco' guid" (*Anth.*, 503). The works of Landor and those of Scott supplement one another. Scott had, of course, the much more popular appeal. While Landor restricted himself to characterization and sentiment, Scott included the narration of stirring actions. Moreover, as a comparison of the works of Scott and Landor listed on pp. 142 and 173 will show, the author of *Waverley* restricted himself as a rule to those historic events and historic types of character that had a more close and obvious relation to the Great Britain of his own times, whereas Landor included in his scope remoter cultural traditions that had contributed to British civilization, including those Greek, Roman, and Renaissance heritages not represented in the work of Scott. His disciple, Robert Browning, richly developed this tendency. These traits of Landor's works—his dispensing with action, and his preoccupation with less familiar tracts of history—are perhaps sufficient to explain why he is not as widely appreciated as he might be; but the insistence of those who ought to know better that he was a mere stylist with no definite message has also postponed due recognition of his genius. "I shall dine late," he said; "but the dining-room will be well lighted, the guests few and select." It is to be hoped that this prediction will prove false so far as the fewness of guests is concerned; for Landor is one who should ultimately appeal to all who love truth and beauty.

SELECTED BIBLIOGRAPHY

OF FIRST IMPORTANCE

Selections

Selections from the Writings of Walter Savage Landor, ed. Sidney Colvin (Golden Treasury Series) , 1882. — Still, on the whole, the best selection of the poetry and prose.

Imaginary Conversations and Poems, ed. Havelock Ellis (Everyman's Libr.) , 1933. — The "Southey-Porson" is cut.

The Shorter Poems, ed. J. B. Sidgwick, 1947. — Regrettable omissions are noted in TLS, Feb. 1, and SRL, Aug. 2, 1947.

The Sculptured Garland, ed. Richard Buxton, 1948. — From the lyrical poems only.

Imaginary Conversations, ed. Ernest De Selincourt (World's Classics) , 1915. — Good introduction.

Imaginary Conversations, ed. F. A. Cavenagh and A. C. Ward, 1934. — Good annotations.

Best Biography

Elwin, Malcolm; *Savage Landor,* 1942. — Admirable, though a little too partial and often too positive. Good rev., TLS, May 16, 1942. — In literary appreciation of the works, the brief *Landor* (Engl. Men of Letters Series) by Sidney Colvin is preferable, but not in points of biographical fact.

Good Introductory Studies

Stephen, Leslie; "Landor's Imaginary Conversations," *Hours in a Library*, III, 1879. — Representative of those criticisms which emphasize that Landor was inconsistent and had no important message, being a mere stylist.

Saintsbury, George; *Essays in English Literature*, II, 1895. — High lights on both the personal faults and the literary merits. — Cf. Saintsbury's "The Landors, Leigh Hunt, De Quincey," in *Cambr. Hist. of Engl. Lit.,* XII; 1916.

Bailey, John; "Some Notes on the Unpopularity of Landor," in *Essays by Divers Hands*, v, 63; 1925. — Attributes it to his air of erudition and aloofness.

"Landor and Boythorn" and "The Independence of Landor." — These two articles, in TLS, May 16, 1942, and Jan. 27, 1945, the second of which is rptd. in Charles Morgan, *Reflections In A Mirror,* 2nd Series, 1947, taken together, provide probably the best brief introduction to Landor's character and works.

FOR ADVANCED STUDENTS

Additional Texts

The Complete Works of Walter Savage Landor, ed. T. E. Welby and Stephen Wheeler, 16 vols., 1927–36. — Despite some controversy as to its alleged defects (see TLS, May 15, 29, June 5, 19, 1930) , this supersedes the editions of the collected works edited by John Forster, 8 vols., 1874–76; and by C. G. Crump, 10 vols., 1891–93. — Cf. R. H. Super, "Forster as Landor's Literary Executor," MLN, LII; 1937; and Edmund Gosse on the difficulties besetting an editor of Landor, *Books on the Table,* 1921.

The Poetical Works from the Welby-Wheeler edition are published separately, 3 vols., 1937.

Some previously unpublished pieces are edited by M. F. Ashley-Montagu in *Nineteenth-Century,* CVII, 836 (1930) ; CX, 353 (1931) ; CXXV, 93 (1939) ; and RES, VIII, 44 (1932).

Chiefly Biographical

Dickens, Charles; "Landor's Life," in *All the Year Round*, July 24, 1869; rptd. in *Miscellaneous Papers*, II, 241. — Kindly interpretation of his character. Of interest because Boythorn in Dickens' *Bleak House* is much like Landor, with the genius, however, left out.

Wheeler, Stephen; "Landor's Llanthony," *Nineteenth Century*, LXXXIX, 445; 1921. — Corrects Forster regarding Landor's quarrels with tenants, etc. — Cf. P. F. Baum, "Landor and Betham," *Sewanee Rev.*, XXX, 411; 1922.

Hawkes, C. P.; "The Spanish Adventure of Landor," *Cornhill Mag.*, LXXIV, 551; 1933. Rptd. in *Authors-at-Arms*, 1934.

Minchin, H. C.; *Landor: Last Days, Letters, and Conversations*, 1934. — A kind of Lear in his old age.

Super, R. H.; "An Unknown Child of Landor's," MLN, LIII, 415; 1938. — Perhaps by Nancy Jones.

Super, R. H.; "Extraordinary Action for Libel: Yescombe *v.* Landor," PMLA, LVI, 736; 1941. — Includes Landor's pamphlet in which he defends himself.

Super, R. H.; "Landor's 'Dear Daughter,' Eliza Lynn Linton," PMLA, LIX, 1059; 1944.

Criticisms

Dowden, Edward; *Studies in Literature*, 1878. — The usually accepted paradox of an ill-regulated personality that loved classical form.

Swinburne, A. C.; "Landor" (1886), in *Miscellanies*. — A panegyric.

Woodberry, G. E.; "Landor," in *Makers of Literature*. — Interprets his work as beautiful but without vital significance.

Schlaak, Robert; *Entstehungs- und Textgeschichte von Landor's 'Gebir,'* 1909. — A source-study; cf., below, Bradley (1914) and Williams (1921).

Bradley, William; *The Early Poems of Landor: A Study of His Development and Debt to Milton*, 1914. — Thinks influence of Milton a development of slow growth, disagreeing with Schlaak (1909).

Williams, Stanley T.; "The Sources of Landor's 'Gebir,'" MLN, XXXVI, 315; 1921; and "The Story of Gebir," PMLA, XXXVI, 615; 1921. — Cf. above, Schlaak (1909) and Bradley (1914).

Wheeler, Stephen; "Landor: The Man and the Poet," *Nineteenth Century*, XCI, 236; 1922. — Based on his letters; states his views on art and religion.

Williams, Stanley T.; "Landor as a Critic of Literature," PMLA, XXXVIII, 906; 1923. — Also "Landor's Criticism in Poetry," MLN, XL, 413; 1925.

Mason, August H.; *Landor, Poète Lyrique*, Paris, 1924.

De Selincourt, Ernest; "Classicism and Romanticism in the Poetry of Landor," *England und die Antike*, Berlin, 1932.

Richards, I. A.; "Landor," *Criterion*, April, 1933. — How undergraduates understood fifteen lines of his poetry.

Elkin, Felice; *Landor's Studies of Italian Life and Literature*, 1934.

Becker, George J.; "Landor's Political Purpose," SP, XXXV, 446; 1938. — Chiefly the exaltation of freedom.

Bradner, Leicester; *Musae Anglicanae*, 1040. — Landor's high rank among English writers of Latin poetry.

Ashley-Montague, M. F.; "Imaginary Conversations," TLS, Jan. 27, 1940. — Their form suggested by "conversations" in Clara Reeve's *Progress of Romance*, 1785.

Pfeiffer, K. G.; "Landor's Critique of *The Cenci*," SP, xxxix, 670; 1942. — An unpublished letter. — Cf. R. H. Super, "Landor's Critique: A Correction," SP, xl, 101; 1943.

Chambers, E. K.; "Some Notes on Landor," RES, xx, 147; 1944.

Super, R. H.; "Landor and the 'Satanic School,' " SP, xlii, 793; 1945.

De Selincourt, Ernest; "Landor's Prose," in *Wordsworthian and Other Studies,* 1947.

Anon.; "In Landor's Dining-Room," TLS, Feb. 1, 1947. — Judicious appreciation of his poetry.

Bibliographies

Wise, T. J.; and Wheeler, Stephen; *A Bibliography of the Writings in Prose and Verse of Landor,* 1919.

Wise, T. J.; *A Landor Library,* 1928.

CHAPTER 12

THOMAS MOORE

(May 28, 1779–February 25, 1852)

1800 Odes of Anacreon   1817 Lalla Rookh
1807–34 Irish Melodies   1827 The Epicurean
1830 Life of Byron

His Early Life and Work.—Moore was born in Dublin, Ireland, above the grocery store and wineshop kept by his father. The Moores were moderately prosperous; and the tone of their household was cheerful, affectionate, and sociable. He early displayed a talent for singing and for playing the piano, as well as proficiency in his studies. His mother supervised his lessons, in what he afterwards called his "boudoir education"; and his parents were glad to give him the best schooling obtainable. When he entered the University of Dublin at the age of fifteen, he was already scribbling verses and dabbling with other youths in political conspiracies against the British rule. Among his friends was Robert Emmet, the Irish patriot who some years later was to be executed as a revolutionist, and whom Moore commemorated in his poems, "Oh, Breathe Not His Name" (*Anth.*, 520), and "She Is Far from the Land Where Her Young Hero Sleeps." While in college, Moore was accused by the academic authorities of being a member of the proscribed United Irish Society; but he was acquitted of the charge, and never really demanded for Ireland any greater degree of freedom than the English Liberals of his time were ready to grant.

An even greater interest to him than politics was his attempt to translate into English verse the Odes of Anacreon. From the point of view of some of his elders this was almost as reprehensible an addiction as political radicalism would be; for Anacreon sang erotically of wine and of women. "Between Bacchus and Venus," says John Addington Symonds, "Anacreon spent his days in palaces; and died at the ripe age of eighty-five, choked, it is reported, by a grape-stone,—a hoary-headed roué." This was not an end that would have appalled young Thomas Moore, whose greatest joys were flirtation and conviviality. Before he graduated he had finished his translation. He thought the faculty should be proud of his feat; and when most of them met it with indifference, he called them "a corporation of boobies, without even sense enough to thank Heaven for anything like an effort of literature coming out of their leaden body."

He proceeded to London, taking his manuscript with him, and intending to study law at the Middle Temple. Within a year, this youth of twenty-one, with no advantages of birth or fortune, had made such distinguished friends that his *Odes of Anacreon* were published under the patronage of the Prince Regent. This was but the beginning of that personal popularity which he enjoyed all his life. In stature he was short; but his handsome countenance, brilliant dark eyes, curly brown hair, and gay and vivacious manner, were admired by all, as was his unpretentious cordiality of manner. The chief reason for his becoming such a favorite, however, was his talent for singing. He had a charmingly sweet voice, and rendered his own songs as well as those composed by others with unaffected sincerity and warmth of feeling. Soon he knew nearly everybody worth knowing, not only in literary but also in general society; and the *Journal* or *Diary* which he kept for many years, not being confined like Henry Crabb Robinson's to contacts with men of letters, gives us a wide survey of the life of his generation. The excitement and glory of being taken up by the great in London did not cause Moore to forget or neglect his parents, whom he continued to treat with deep respect and fondness: more than four thousand letters to his mother witness his filial devotion.

His second volume, *Poems by the Late Thomas Little* (1801), contained erotic verses which in later years he regretted. In 1803 he was given a government appointment as registrar for the naval court in Bermuda, and he spent some months there at the uncongenial task of examining the accounts of vessels. Finding the post less profitable than he had expected, he hired a deputy to perform its drudgery, and visited the United States from September, 1803, to November, 1804. Like so many young optimists of his time, he thought of the new world as a Utopia, "seduced into the belief," as he put it, "that innocence, peace, and freedom had deserted the rest of the world for Martha's Vineyard and the banks of the Ohio." The natural scenery he found sublimely beautiful, especially Niagara Falls, concerning which he wrote in thoroughly romantic fashion (*Anth.*, 519); but as for noble savages, or citizens blissfully and innocently living the simple life, or a government purer than those of effete Europe, they were sadly to seek. He writes to his sister:

> Oh! Ask me not, if Truth have yet
> Her seal on fancy's promise set;
> If even a glimpse my eyes behold
> Of that imagined age of gold;—
> Alas, not yet one gleaming trace!

He expressed his bitter disappointment in satirical verses that were published in *Epistles, Odes, and Other Poems* (1806).

Irish Melodies and Lalla Rookh.—A year later he published the first volume of *Irish Melodies* (*Anth.*, 520). His friend Sir John Stevenson assisted him by adapting the music of well known Irish airs to Moore's poems, and as the poems themselves drew upon Irish memories and feelings, the appeal to the national sentiment of his country was doubly strong. Their artistic distinction is the perfect adaptation of the words and the music to each other; fully to be appreciated, they should be sung. The *Melodies* proved as popular in England as at home, for Moore tactfully succeeded in making the Irish cause an appealing one without belligerently offending the British. For longer than a quarter of a century he continued to add songs to his collection; and they were in such demand that in the end he earned more than £12,000 by their composition. He spent money, however, at least as fast as he earned it, was repeatedly in debt, and often did hack work to make both ends meet.

In 1811, at the age of thirty-two, he married an actress aged sixteen, Elizabeth Dyke. The union proved a very happy one, Moore remaining faithfully devoted to his "darling Bessie" during the rest of his life. Five children were born to them, three of whom died in infancy.

Although the poems of Scott and Byron were beginning to rival Moore's in popularity, he was paid the astonishingly large sum of £5,000 for his next work, *Lalla Rookh* (1817; *Anth.*, 523). The prose framework of *Lalla Rookh* tells of the journey which the titular heroine, a daughter of the Emperor Aurengzebe, takes from Delhi to the vale of Cashmere, where she is to meet her betrothed, the prince of Bucharia. She is attended on her way by a minstrel, Feramorz, who recites the four romances which constitute the poem, and with whom she falls in love. At the end of her journey she discovers that the minstrel is her royal bridegroom in disguise. The first of the four romances is a tragic story of a maiden who was seduced by the Veiled Prophet of Khorason and inadvertently slain by her true lover. The second tells of a Peri who tried to win admission to Paradise by bringing the gift dearest to Heaven: first she offered the blood of a patriot who died to liberate his people, and next the sigh of a maiden who died for love; but she did not gain her entrance until she brought a tear of repentance shed by a criminal in response to the prayer of a child. The third, like the first, is a story of ill-fated love, in which the daughter of a Mohammedan emir falls in love with a devotee of the ancient Persian religion and is destroyed in the sectarian warfare between them. The last relates how the Sultana Nourmahal, the "Light of the Harem," regained her husband's love by learning to sing a magic song. It was all very graceful and charming, and would thrill the gentlest bosom without ever shocking or violently agitating it. Unlike Southey, Moore was not critical of Oriental manners and religion.

Lalla Rookh likewise was enthusiastically received, six editions being sold within six months; and its appearance marks the high tide of Moore's reputation. Admired and courted by notables like Lord Lansdowne, Canning, and Sir Robert Peel; beloved by men of letters like Samuel Rogers, Sydney Smith, Sir Walter Scott, and Lord Byron, petted and idolized by fashionable ladies, he basked in the sunshine of celebrity.

Later Works.—After Byron's death it was Moore who was chosen as his official biographer; and he performed the delicate task with characteristic suppleness, sometimes hinting that there were things that might be told, but never committing any real indiscretion. His *Letters and Journals of Lord Byron, with Notices of His Life* (Jan. 1, 1830) is not a masterful biography like Lockhart's *Scott* or Southey's *Nelson*. It does not give a vivid characterization of Byron; but Moore did accomplish what he was charged to do, i.e., he set Byron in as favorable a light as possible, mainly by letting him speak for himself through his letters and journals. Only by defying those who had assigned him the work, and speaking the truth, cost what it might in the loss of friends or of reputation, could Moore have produced a great *Life of Byron,* and he was not the man to do anything so unwary and genuinely romantic.

His later writings were of varied kinds. For the Whig, or Liberal, party, he composed facile verse satires on contemporaneous politics. In prose, he satirized the Englishman abroad in *The Fudge Family in Paris* (1818). In *The Memoirs of Captain Rock* (1824) and the *Travels of an Irish Gentleman in Search of a Religion* (1834) he wrote in support of the Roman Catholic church. His extensive knowledge of books about the Orient he utilized in another long poem *The Loves of the Angels* (1823), which proved a complete failure, and in an historical novel, *The Epicurean* (1827), which dealt with a pagan philosopher's conversion to Christianity.

In 1835, he was granted an annual pension of £300. His closing years were saddened by the loss of his two remaining children. "The last of my five children is gone," he wrote in his journal; "and we are left desolate and alone; not a single relation have I in this world." Two years before his death at the age of seventy-two, he lost his mind.

General Estimate.—There is no doubt that "Tom" Moore was one of the most agreeable and amiable of companions, but the history of his fame shows the vanity and evanescence of social triumphs. His *Irish Melodies* will always have an honored place in the history of his country's liberation. As Oliver Wendell Holmes wrote,

> The land of fair maidens and heroes undaunted
> Where the shamrock grows green from the cliffs to the shore,
> The land of fair maidens and heroes undaunted
> Shall wreathe her bright harp with the garlands of Moore.

But patriotic service is not synonymous with literary greatness; and Moore, although he had a lively intelligence and some talent in expression, lacked certain traits which are essential for the achievement of the truest fame. His opportunities were as favorable as those of any of the Romantics, and superior to those of several who surpassed him. His visit to the United States gave him an exceptional opportunity to deepen his insight into the problems of life, but he returned from it little wiser than before. In America he had seen some of the sublimest scenes of nature, and in Europe some of the noblest remains of civilization; but he was unable to grasp and express their grandeur. His mind was shallow, and he lacked seriousness of purpose. His chief concern was how tc entertain his contemporaries without offending them and without requiring from them any intellectual effort. Hence his poetry was at best melodious and pretty, but not beautiful in the highest sense of the word. And the kind of fame which he gained has been well called "a breezy immortality."

SELECTED BIBLIOGRAPHY

OF FIRST IMPORTANCE

Selections

Selected Poems, ed. C. L. Falkiner (Golden Treasury Series), 1903.
Tom Moore's Diary: A Selection, ed. J. B. Priestley, 1925.

Texts

Poetical Works, ed. A. D. Godley (Oxford Univ. Press), 1910; or rptd. from 1840–41 ed., Boston, 1930.

Standard Biography

Jones, Howard Mumford; The Harp That Once: A Chronicle of the Life of Thomas Moore, 1937. — Good on both his personality and his relation to his times; a little overenthusiastic about his lesser works.

Introductory Essays

The prefaces of the Godley and the Priestley editions listed above, and George Saintsbury's study in Essays in English Literature, 1890.

FOR ADVANCED STUDENTS

Additional Texts

Works, 6 vols., Golden Cockerel Press, 1923. — Very beautiful and expensive.

Irish Melodies and Songs, ed. Stephen Gwynn (Muses' Libr.), 1908.

Memoirs, Journals, and Correspondence, ed. (Lord) John Russell, 8 vols., 1853–56; abridged, 1860.

———

Brandes, Georg; Main Currents in Nineteenth Century Literature, 1871 ff.; transl. 1901 ff. — Because of Moore's liberalism, Brandes, in vol. IV, devotes much attention to him.

Vallat, Gustave; Etude sur la Vie et les Œuvres de Thomas Moore, 1876. — Detailed and judicious.

Symington, A. J.; Thomas Moore: His Life and Works, 1880. — More about the works than in Gwynn, below.

Gwynn, Stephen; Thomas Moore (English Men of Letters), 1905; 2nd ed., 1924. — More about the life than in Symington. — Rev. in Catholic World, cxx, 296; 1924.

Thomas, A. B.; Moore en France, 1911.

Preis, Anton; Moore's Belesenheit, 1921.

Strahan, J. A.; "Byron's Biographer," Blackwood's, ccxv, 574; 1924.

Strong, L. A. G.; The Minstrel Boy: Portrait of Tom Moore, 1937.

Brown, Wallace C.; "Moore and the English Interest in the East," SP, xxxiv, 576; 1937. — Important for *Lalla Rookh*.

Schneider, Elisabeth; "Moore and the *Edinburgh Review*," MLN, lxi, 177; 1946. — The article on "Irish Novels" in the *Review*, Feb., 1826, probably by Moore.

Kirby, T. A.; "Irving and Moore: Anglo-American Relations," MLN, lxii, 251; 1947.

Bibliographical

Muir, P. H.; "Moore's Irish Melodies," *Colophon*, No. 15; 1933.

MacManus, M. J.; *Hand-List of First Editions*, Dublin, 1934. — Rptd. from *Dubl. Mag.*, viii; 1933.

CHAPTER 13

LORD BYRON

(January 22, 1788–April 19, 1824)

1809 English Bards and Scotch Reviewers
1812 Childe Harold, I and II
1813–14 Turkish Tales (The Giaour, The
    Corsair, etc.)
1815 Hebrew Melodies
1816 Childe Harold, III; IV, 1818
1816 The Prisoner of Chillon
1817 Manfred

1818 Beppo
1819 Mazeppa
1819 Don Juan, I and II; III–V, 1821
1821 Sardanapalus
1821 Cain
1822 The Vision of Judgment
1822 Heaven and Earth
1823 The Island

1823 Don Juan, VI–XIV; XV–XVI, 1824

His Early Life and Works.—George Gordon, Lord Byron, was unfortunate in his ancestry. On the paternal side, his family, of Norman descent, was noted for its energy, rebelliousness, and self-indulgence. His father, a spendthrift and libertine, who was known as "Mad Jack" Byron, had eloped with the Marchioness of Carmathen, married her after she had been divorced, and had by her a daughter, Augusta, born in 1783. Upon the death of his first wife he married, in 1785, Catherine Gordon of Aberdeenshire, Scotland. It was of this unhappy union that Byron was born, in London, in 1788. His father died within two years; his half-sister was sent away to her grandmother's; and Byron was taken by his mother to live in a shabby apartment in Aberdeen. His mother was violently impulsive and capricious, sometimes overindulging him, and sometimes unjustly storming at him. One of his feet was deformed, probably owing to infantile paralysis, and she knew no better than to employ quacks in vain and excruciating attempts to cure the trouble. At times she taunted him with being a "lame brat." His Scottish schooling gave him a thorough grounding in the Bible, and a Calvinistic interpretation of Christianity. At an early age he took an interest in the colorful Orient, and read much about the Near East in histories and books of travels. In his vacations, he obtained unforgettable impressions of the grandeur of the scenery of the Highlands.

At the age of ten, by the death of his great-uncle, he became Lord Byron and owner of the ancestral estate of Newstead Abbey, Nottinghamshire. It is said that when first addressed by his title, he burst into tears. Although he and his mother visited Newstead, they did not at that time make it their home, it being in a half-ruinous condition, and the family income being small. Byron's education continued to be irregular; but on his own initiative he read widely, devouring among other volumes a set of the English poets from Chaucer to Churchill. Although he lacked the usual preparation, his mother insisted that he enter Harrow School; and the headmaster there, understanding what a humiliation to the lad's proud spirit it would be to have his ignorance exposed in the classroom, assigned him to no grade until he had made up his deficiencies in Greek and Latin through private tuition. It was at Harrow, where Byron stayed from the age of thirteen to seventeen, that he lived for the first time under normal and favorable circumstances, and that he had the opportunity of forming wholesome friendships, an opportunity which he seized with delight. Although he had moods of solitariness, and spent much time with books, he was a favorite and a leader among the boys; and in later years he felt it as another manifestation of a malign fatality that the closest friends he made at this time were soon severed from him by death or other mischances. In his school work, he was most proficient in the composition and delivery of speeches, the bold and impassioned nature of which excited attention, and caused a general feeling that the young lord was destined to become an orator.

At fifteen, he fell in love with Mary Chaworth, who was two years older, and distantly related to him. She was the heiress of an estate adjoining Newstead; and, although engaged to a squire of the neighborhood, for a while found his boyish ardor a thrilling pastime. When she finally dismissed him, he felt "alone, on a wide, wide, sea." He poured out his grief in several poems, including "Hills of Annesley, Bleak and Barren"; and he alluded to her passionately in "The Dream" thirteen years afterwards. The theory of Richard Edgcumbe that in later years she had an intrigue with him, and bore him a child, is, however, untenable.

The year after he had lost Mary Chaworth, Byron met his half-sister Augusta, who had been separated from him since infancy. It pleased him to have one creature in the world who would look to him for protection, and when he gave her his affection and confidence she responded. Though they were again to be separated for long periods, there was no one else whom he thought of quite so fondly as of her.

Byron entered Trinity College, Cambridge, at seventeen, and was graduated three years later. He continued to read voraciously, and made a few friends, but on the whole derived little benefit from his college years. He took to gambling and other dissipations, was often in debt, and, when he could not obtain sufficient funds from his mother, resorted to money lenders. His most amusing escapade (if authentic) was to bring to the university a tame bear to be a candidate for an instructorship. He wrote much verse, and at eighteen published a small volume, but was persuaded to withdraw the edition, because some of the contents were indecent. A revised edition appeared in June, 1807—*Hours of Idleness,* "by George Gordon Byron, a minor." Some of the critics treated it more kindly than it deserved; but the *Edinburgh Review,* which, like the bargeman in Thackeray's *Codlingsby,* "liked whopping a lord," attacked it insultingly. Byron bided his time, read Pope's *Dunciad* diligently, and a year later, at the age of twenty-one, gave the first hint of his dangerous powers as a satirist in *English Bards and Scotch Reviewers* (1809). Herein he expressed a contempt for Wordsworth, Coleridge, and Southey, which time has proved ill-judged; but he also showed ingenuity in discerning weaknesses and epigrammatic power in lampooning them.

On coming of age, Byron, having borrowed money for the purpose, restored portions of Newstead, which for some years had been rented, and, with a keen sense of the dramatic significance of the event, assumed his rightful dignities. His ancient estate, despite dilapidation, was still of noble appearance, with its beautiful Gothic buildings and lordly woods. From the windows of his room he looked out upon a noble forest, lake, and waterfall, associated with the historic tradition of his ancient house. That he celebrated the event with a dinner consisting of nothing more festive than bacon and eggs and a bottle of ale, is an instance of the intermingling of the romantic and the commonplace which was characteristic of his life.

His Travels, and Childe Harold I and II.—To settle down to the existence of an ordinary English lord was, however, impossible to Byron. He had long wished to see the Mediterranean lands about which he had read so extensively, and in the summer of 1809, with his college friend John Cam Hobhouse (afterwards Lord Broughton), he sailed for Portugal, and began the journey of two years which was to be poetically described in the first two cantos of *Childe Harold's Pilgrimage*. The traveler of today finds it difficult to realize how hazardous and adventurous Byron's journey was, undertaken when roads were either nonexistent or indescribably bad, when disease lurked on every hand, and when warfare was rendering all Europe insecure. Byron and Hobhouse rode five hundred miles on horseback across Portugal and Spain, admiring the grandeur of the scenery but dejected by the helplessness of the people. Napoleon was conquering Spain, and Byron was out of sympathy with the British effort to preserve her independence. From Gibraltar he sailed to Malta, where a love affair arrested him for one month; and then proceeded to the almost unvisited Albania, "the rugged nurse of savage men." Here was a land which, though only a few score miles from Italy, was even more primitive than the Highlands of Scotland. It was the scenery of Albania that he had in mind when he wrote of Nature:

> Oh! she is fairest in her features wild,
> Where nothing polished dares pollute her path.

The Albanian chieftain, Ali Pasha, entertained the noble British traveler; and Byron, although not glossing over the barbarity of the Albanian feuds, praised the courage and hospitality of the people. He journeyed to Greece, stayed in Athens ten weeks, and to his landlady's daughter wrote the amorous farewell:

> Maid of Athens, ere we part,
> Give, oh give me back my heart!

He visited Constantinople, and was received by the Sultan. Emulating the feat of the legendary Leander, he swam across the Hellespont from Sestos to Abydos, a distance of three or four miles, an exploit of which he was especially proud. A portion of his time abroad he lived in a Franciscan monastery where he studied modern Greek. After spending two years in this unforgettably interesting journey, Byron returned to England, intending soon to continue his travels.

In February, 1812, Byron delivered his maiden speech in the House of Lords, in which he pleaded the cause of the poor weavers who were being ruined by the introduction of machinery. He was an ardent Liberal, and might have won fame in parliamentary debate. His sharpness of tongue is illustrated by the scornful comparison which he drew in his speech on behalf of the Irish Catholics. The negroes, he pointed out, had been freed from oppression, but not the Irish. "I pity," he remarked, "the Catholic peasantry for not having had the good fortune to be born black." He wrote "Lines to a Lady Weeping," in which he pitied the Prince Regent's daughter for having such a disgraceful father; and he visited Leigh Hunt in the prison to which that champion of liberty had been consigned for similar audacities. The political career which he might have entered upon was, however, turned aside by the unexpected outcome of his literary activities. He had brought back to England with him a satire upon current literary tendencies, entitled *Hints from Horace;* and although he scorned to deal with publishers himself, he was willing to let an admiring friend of his, Robert Charles Dallas, do so. At first he said nothing about the two cantos of *Childe Harold;* but Dallas found out that he had them, and was permitted to seek a publisher for them also. He secured one in John Murray, whose name was thenceforth to be inseparably linked with Byron's.

The experiences of Byron on his journey had strengthened his impression that life was predominantly painful. Upon his return, he met with a series of bereavements. His mother passed away, so suddenly that he was unable to reach her before she died; and, although they had often quarreled tempestuously, he mourned her loss. Before she was buried, the news came to him that one of his closest friends, a schoolmate, had been drowned; and two others had died within a few months. He was therefore not merely affecting the melancholy he expressed at this time in his "Epistle to a Friend," "To Thyrza," and the closing lines of the second canto of *Childe Harold:*

> What is the worst of woes that wait on age?
> What stamps the wrinkle deeper on the brow?
> To view each loved one blotted from life's page,
> And be alone on earth, as I am now.

This tone of gloom harmonized well with the leading themes of *Childe Harold*—the laments over what he thought to be the dolorous destiny of Spain, in the first canto; and his preference of the virtues of Albanian outlaws to the corruptions of European "civilization," in the second.

His Popularity and Downfall.—The piquancy of such an attitude on the part of a young nobleman was instantly felt; and, immediately after the publication of *Childe Harold,* Byron became popular so suddenly as to justify his celebrated words, "I awoke to find myself famous." Every door was now open to him, and his company was sought not only by men of letters like Rogers, Moore, and Campbell, but also by the leaders of fashionable society. His popularity, especially among women, was enhanced by his extraordinarily handsome person, and also by a shy taciturnity which came upon him when surrounded by company, and which was interpreted as a sign that he was gloomy, lonely, and lost in noble thoughts. His loneliness not a few ecstatic ladies did their best to dispel, and they courted him with such abandon that they might have overwhelmed the resistance of a youth who was most austere and anaemic. Byron was neither, and during the next two or three years reveled in libertine intrigues, being sometimes the pursuer and sometimes the pursued—probably the latter more often than the former. Of those who pursued him, the most indiscreet was the golden-haired, brilliant, and wayward Lady Caroline Lamb, who sometimes disguised herself as a page to seek him out, and who a few years later based her novel *Glenarvon* upon their amour. He discarded her for Lady Oxford, although the latter was more than twenty years older than himself.

His relations with these and his other mistresses, however, were to sink into insignificance in comparison with those that arose between him and his half-sister Augusta in 1813. For about eight years he had scarcely seen her. In the meantime (1803) she had been married to her first cousin, Colonel George Leigh—and not very happy in that relationship. She took life rather easily and superficially, tried to avoid anything unpleasant, was willing to be dominated by as strong-willed and fascinating a man as Byron; in short, she was unmoral rather than immoral. To Byron she had become almost a stranger. That she was a Byron meant much to him; and he found her complete confidence in him, and uncritical acceptance of his intellectual superiority, delightful. There grew between them an essential sympathy, lacking in most of Byron's other affairs with women: and, partly because of that fondness, and perhaps partly because of his excessive craving to experience the forbidden, he entered into incestuous relations with her, and became the father of her child, Medora Leigh. It was this abhorrent guilt and dread secret that burdened the rest of their lives and involved others in bitter consequences.

During this agitated period, he wrote (1813–14) the four Turkish Tales, *The Giaour, The Bride of Abydos, The Corsair,* and *Lara,* in the second of which the subject of incest is touched upon. These poems, upon the accurate local color of which Byron had bestowed much care, were received with even greater acclaim than *Childe Harold,* and outrivalled Scott's in popularity. They struck a note of passion deeper and more violent than expressed by the author of *Marmion,* and their heroes had that mood of pride and gloom which was regarded as peculiarly By-ronic. Today they are little read, owing to the superficiality of their characterization and the commonplace melodramatic quality of their plots.

Like most young libertines, Byron was not entirely contented with his course of life, and believed that marriage with an innocent young girl would be an easy and pleasant way of saving himself. He proposed to Miss Anna Isabella Milbanke, four years younger than himself, the heiress to a baronetcy, and a strictly reared and highly accomplished young lady. Because of his scandalous reputation she rejected him. But presently he persuaded her that her refusal would be his ruin, and that as his wife she could reform him. She had no real knowledge of his character; but she took life very seriously, and the idea of having a moral mission in saving so brilliant a man from wickedness, strongly appealed to her. In September, 1814, she accepted him. The tone of his letter (*Anth.,* 737) to Thomas Moore, announcing his engagement shows what a miracle Byron expected to take place, as well as a consciousness that others might be apprehensively skeptical about its likelihood.

The marriage, entered into on January 2, 1815, proved a disappointing and horrible experience. Even before his wedding, Byron seems to have felt resentful, possibly because Miss Milbanke had not accepted his first proposal and thus saved him from the incest (which occurred be-tween that and the marriage) , or because this was a union which he could not, like his liaisons, dissolve at his pleasure; and every now and then he shocked his bride with outbursts of hatefulness. By an irony of fate, it was Mrs. Leigh that bestowed upon her the only real love and comfort that she experienced during her frightful months with Byron. On De-cember 10 she gave birth to a daughter, Augusta Ada. Byron had sav-agely expressed the hope that both mother and daughter would die; and his conduct had become more violent and indecent. He even gave his wife reason to suspect that before their marriage (not afterwards) he had been his half-sister's lover. It is remotely possible that some other woman, less rigid in her moral views, might have tamed him; but Lady Byron is not to be blamed for being unable to do so. She endured his brutalities with patient loyalty until (January 15, 1816) she feared that he might be dangerously insane, whereupon with her infant daughter she sought ref-uge in her father's house. When, upon medical authority, she learned that he was sane, and responsible for what he said and did, she refused to return to him. A deed of separation was signed on April 21. He pro-tested that he could not learn what her specific charges against him were, and a few of his friends took his part. The overwhelming public senti-ment, however, was against him; and he, the proudest of the proud, ex-perienced the fickleness of popularity. In the circles where he had been idolized, he was shunned; when he appeared in company, some ladies fainted, and others left the room. He did not mend matters by writing the poem

Fare thee well! and if forever,
Still forever, fare thee well,
Anth., 539

in which he expressed love for Lady Byron and his daughter, and pity for himself. Some thought the poem hypocritical; others felt that, however sincere, Byron showed his vulgarity in publishing, even privately, so intimately personal an appeal. He felt that England, with unjustifiable self-righteousness, hated him; and on April 25, 1816, he scornfully left his native land, never to return. His career as a British lord was wrecked; but ruin and agony now raised his talent into genius.

His Exile and Death.—The exile, not being permitted owing to his anti-Bourbon sentiments to enter France, passed through Belgium, where he visited the field of Waterloo, and up the Rhine to Geneva, Switzerland. Here he met Shelley, who was living there with Mary Godwin and was also ostracized from England. The latter's half-sister [1] Claire Clairmont, likewise brought up in Godwinian contempt for the institution of matrimony, had determined to win at any cost the love of Byron, whose poetry she adored; and, after his wife had left him, he half-contemptuously accepted her as his mistress. She rejoined him in Switzerland, and copied out many of his poems for him including the third canto of *Childe Harold;* but when he learned that she was to become a mother, he sent her back to England. Her child, Allegra, was born in January, 1817. Byron spent the summer of 1816 at Geneva, in a villa near Shelley's; and together they visited the castle of Chillon (*Anth.*, 536). At Geneva he also foregathered with Monk Lewis and with that female incarnation of the European romantic movement, the celebrated Mme. de Staël. With his friend Hobhouse he toured the Bernese Alps, described them glowingly in a journal written for Mrs. Leigh, and he was inspired by their grandeur while composing *Manfred*. It is significant that, as he confesses, even in the presence of the majesty and the power and the glory of Nature he could not forget his "own wretched identity."

When Shelley returned to England, he took with him for publication *The Prisoner of Chillon* and the third canto of *Childe Harold*. Byron proceeded to Venice, where he remained for about three years, producing a large portion of his best work, including the last canto of *Childe Harold, Beppo,* and the beginning of *Don Juan*. He also devoted himself to a study of Venetian history and the Italian language and literature. His amusements continued to be deliberately and frankly licentious; and in his vivid letters to Moore and to Murray (*Anth.*, 738) he described his liaisons with his landlord's wife and with a Venetian wench whose tigerish passion and complete lack of sophistication amused his jaded taste. In his moral history this was probably the lowest point to which he sank.

From this abyss he was saved by the young and beautiful Countess Teresa Guiccioli, whom he met in the spring of 1819. At the age of six-

---

[1] On the Godwins, Clairmonts, etc., see, above, p. 30.

teen, she had been given in marriage to a husband more than sixty years old, and by Italian custom would not lose caste by receiving the attentions of a young cavalier. She and Byron fell in love at first sight, and during the next four years, which were also the period of his supreme poetical achievement, he was her faithful lover. The Guicciolis moved to Ravenna, and Byron lived there from June, 1819, to October, 1821. When her husband grew more insistent in his objections to Byron, Teresa procured a separation from him. She was an ardent Italian patriot, and increased Byron's already strong interest in freeing Italy from Austrian rule: his *Prophecy of Dante* was composed at her request. His literary production at Ravenna was enormous—including three cantos of *Don Juan*, as well as *Sardanapalus, Cain, The Vision of Judgment, Heaven and Earth,* and many other poems. Both he and Teresa were deep in revolutionary conspiracies and were compelled by the authorities to leave Ravenna.

At Pisa (October 1821–September 1822) he met Shelley again, and entered into a plan to establish an unfettered periodical, *The Liberal,* in which several of his poems first appeared. Not long after this project had been decided upon, Shelley was drowned. Byron was present at the cremation of Shelley's body on the seashore. Another grievous event of his stay at Pisa was the death of Allegra, his daughter by Claire Clairmont, at the age of five. Her mother had given her into Byron's charge, and he delighted in the child's unusual personality; but apparently he neglected to investigate with sufficient care the conditions at the convent where he sent her to be educated, and where she died of typhus. Her mother had protested against her being there, but Byron treated the protest with contumely.

Again at the command of the government, which more and more realized that Byron was a dangerous foe to autocracy, he was obliged to change his residence. The Countess Guiccioli and he thereupon went to Genoa. Here his chief interest became the rebellion of the Greeks against Turkish rule. A group of liberals in England were organized to assist in the securing of Greek independence, and they elected Byron to membership in the London Committee. Despite some misgivings, he threw himself into the cause. In July, 1823, accompanied by Teresa's brother and a number of English and Italian friends of liberty, he sailed for the western coast of Greece. He found that the insurgents were divided into hostile factions, and that the likelihood of success was remote; but he persevered against the most discouraging obstacles. He raised and drilled troops, and hoped to fall gloriously in action; but he never had the opportunity. He died of a fever at Missolonghi, on April 19, 1824, aged thirty-six; and there his heart was buried. His body was borne to England, refused burial in Westminster Abbey because of his defiant immorality, and laid to rest in the parish church of his ancestral home. The Greeks, who knew little of his literary work, mourned him as a brave man and true friend of liberty; and to all of Europe except England, it seemed that there had passed away the very incarnation of the spirit of liberty. To contemporaries, his life and death seemed even more romantic than his poetry.

The Aftermath.—The story of Byron's life is almost matched in sensationalism by the history of the attempts to get that life truthfully told. Five years before his death, Byron had generously made Thomas Moore a present of his manuscript autobiography, entitled his *Memoirs.* He suggested that the publisher Murray would probably lend him £2,000 if Moore gave him the right to publish it upon Byron's death; and this bargain was made. What we know of Byron's candor makes it not unlikely that his autobiography stated the truth about his relations with his half-sister. When he died, upon consultation of those concerned, including Mrs. Leigh, it was agreed that the manuscript ought not to be published; and on May 17, 1824, it was burned. Moore was authorized to write the "official" biography, and his publishers, Longmans, repaid Murray the loan. In Moore's *Life* (1830) there were no indiscreet revelations.[2] In 1868, the Countess Guiccioli, then in her sixties, published her *Recollections of Lord Byron.* She had known him at his best, and her testimony was extremely favorable to his character.

The difficulty in the situation was that, since the whole truth was not exactly known, any testimony in favor of Byron seemed indirectly a condemnation of his wife for leaving him. She was still living when the *Recollections* of the Countess Guiccioli appeared, and had become a leading light in many movements for educational progress, ethical uplift, and social betterment. Her friends were indignant at the criticism of her which seemed implied in praises of Byron. Within a year of the publication of the Countess Guiccioli's eulogy, Mrs. Harriet Beecher Stowe, the author of *Uncle Tom's Cabin,* who, likewise interested in reform movements, had become acquainted with Lady Byron and had gathered some particulars of her experiences from conversation with her, burst forth with *Lady Byron Vindicated,* in which she declared that Lady Byron left her husband because he had committed incest with Mrs. Leigh. This half-truth was easily refuted by the admirers of Byron because they could show that, even after leaving Byron, Lady Byron had written affectionate letters to Mrs. Leigh (a fact intelligible enough when it is known that the incestuous relations were not continued after Byron's marriage, and that Mrs. Leigh had proved herself a loyal and extremely affectionate friend to Lady Byron).

In this uncertainty the matter rested until 1905, when Byron's grandson, the Earl of Lovelace, in vindication of Lady Byron, issued *Astarte: a Fragment of Truth,* in which evidence was brought forward that ought to have made the truth clear to any unprejudiced reader. Mr. Murray, however, the publisher in succession to his grandfather of the standard edition of Byron's works, and Mr. R. E. Prothero (later

[2] See pp. 183–184.

Lord Ernle), one of its editors, endeavored to refute *Astarte* in *Lord Byron and His Detractors* (1906). In that effort they failed: but their criticisms of certain weaknesses in the Earl of Lovelace's work may have helped to make the presentation of the case much stronger in the second edition of *Astarte* (1921), which included important additional letters. A year later there was published *Lord Byron's Correspondence, Chiefly with Lady Melbourne, etc.,* in which further indiscreet admissions by Byron appeared. The new evidence was hotly discussed in many articles in the leading British magazines in 1921–22. A few writers (especially one interested in a movement to get permission to place a bust of Byron in Westminster Abbey) insisted that he was innocent of incest; but most of his defenders saw that the best that could be said was that the evidence was not strong enough to convict him in a court of law. Finally Sir John Charles Fox, in *The Byron Mystery* (1924), brought the powers of a highly competent and legally trained mind to bear upon the evidence, and concluded that although Byron and Mrs. Leigh had not continued their offense after his marriage, they were guilty of it previously.

Thus the attempts to conceal part of the truth about the life of Byron proved ultimately futile, but for a century they allowed mistaken impressions of his personality and work to pass current. The conspiracy of silence permitted overzealous admirers of the melancholy exile to represent him as an ill-used and misunderstood man, who had, to be sure, committed youthful follies and excesses, but was not exceptionally reprehensible. Those opposed to Byronism, on the other hand, might fall into errors like Mrs. Stowe's.

Today there are those who plead that it would be best to ignore the problem of Byron's personal morals and confine attention to his poetry, but this is an attitude of superficiality. His poetry and his views of life were profoundly influenced by his experiences, and without a knowledge of them his work cannot be adequately understood and judged.

His Character.—In his childhood Byron displayed naive simplicity and remarkable love of truth, growing on one occasion very indignant while watching the performance of a play, because one personage in it tried to misrepresent something to another. His hatred for lies, evasions, and shams remained one of his strongest virtues. Another was his courage in denouncing them without regard for the displeasure of political and ecclesiastical powers. By nature he was deeply affectionate. Haughty toward equals and superiors, his sympathy for the poor and the oppressed was unfailing. In personal relations with men, he could be unselfish, considerate, and generous. Intellectually he was as energetic and intense as he was emotionally, and his powers of observation were those of a genius.

Heredity planted certain evil tendencies in him, and an unwholesome upbringing fostered them. He was unduly proud of his rank and family. He was vain about unessentials: he tried to conceal his deformity;

he was so afraid of becoming corpulent that he almost wrecked his health by undereating; and despite the fact that he had no real respect for public opinion, he liked to attract general attention by parading his woes or posing as satanically wicked. The abnormal sensuality which he had inherited, he gratified to the utmost limits of licentiousness. When the inevitable consequences followed, he sometimes felt remorse; but, even after the period had passed when his incontinence might be extenuated on the plea of his youth, he did not reform his conduct. The least pardonable trait of his character, however, will to some minds be his heartlessness toward the women who had ministered to his lusts, and were discarded with scornful contempt. Even Shelley, no Pharisee, became at last disgusted by the brutality of Byron's attitude toward the forsaken Claire Clairmont and his callous neglect of their daughter Allegra. Nominally Byron was a nobleman, but at times no vulgarian could sink lower than he did.

No service is rendered to truth by characterizing Byron otherwise than as a thoroughgoing sensualist. His importance lies, in the first place, in that very fact. He systematically pursued that life of indulgence in the pleasures of sensation which most human beings, at some period of their existence, secretly yearn after but are deterred from following far because of economic or social restrictions. Moreover, he was a sensualist who, unlike most, was starkly honest and outspoken about his experiences and sentiments, highly sensitive in his perceptions, and stupendously powerful in his utterances.

His Views of Human Life and History.—Goethe qualified his high praise of Byron by asserting that when he reflected he seemed like a child; and in comparison with philosophical poets like Goethe himself or Wordsworth, Byron is not profound. But he had thought keenly and independently about certain aspects of life. He was not always consistent—as will appear presently in our survey of his works; but the general tenor of his beliefs is sufficiently definite.

He began with a sincere love of the good, the true, and the beautiful. He was enthusiastic about the grander features of nature, an enthusiasm which he never lost. He loved youth, femininity, freedom, and glory. He fancied that in life he would meet on every hand with true and noble values. But his own experience brought him doubt and disillusion, and he inferred that the actual life of mankind displayed no manifestation of those ideals that he loved.

He was much interested in history, particularly in that of Greece, Rome, modern Italy, and Turkey; and he greatly admired Gibbon, whose influence upon him was extensive. He read the historians skeptically, thought most of them prejudiced, and wished they had given less space to indecisive battles and conquests, and more to the noble deeds of heroes and liberators. He tried to find lessons in history, and those which he found were melancholy. On rare occasions a truly noble character had appeared. One was Epaminondas, who had defended Thebes and died penniless; others were the savior of Greece and the founder of the United States:

> Leonidas and Washington,
> Whose every battle-field is holy ground,
> Which breathes of nations saved, not worlds undone.
> How sweetly on the ear such echoes sound!
> While the mere victor's may appal or stun
> The servile and the vain, such names will be
> A watchword till the future shall be free.
>
> *Don Juan,* VIII, 5

But such heroes were exceptions to the dismal rule. What the general weight of historical evidence showed was the futility of patriotic endeavors. A nation would achieve its freedom, rise from indigence to wealth, from wealth to luxury, then become corrupt and emasculated, and finally, conquered by a virile oppressor, decline into ignominious subjection. Perhaps, Byron sometimes hoped, mankind might achieve a permanently secure independence; but heretofore nothing had occurred but this succession of futile attempts. Such is the burden of his celebrated laments over Greece, Rome, and Venice.

Some who have judged the past a failure have been confident about the promise of their own times. Not so Byron. Like Hazlitt, he hoped much from Napoleon, scourge of kings; but the Corsican disappointed him in the end, abjectly relinquishing power only because he was forced to. Yet the opponents of Napoleon, including Great Britain, were unqualifiedly contemptible. Wellington was a mere drill master and a miscreant; Waterloo was a victory that established tyrants and crushed peoples. Wordsworth, Coleridge, and Southey were satisfied with the post-Napoleonic settlement of Europe; but Byron and Shelley were as discontented with it as the elder romantics in their younger days had been with the régime that the French Revolution overthrew. They had become patriots and nationalists; Byron could see nothing in England that deserved his wholehearted admiration. Its nominal freedoms were well enough, like beefsteaks, pots of beer, and the so-called fair "English weather" which occurred so rarely; but in honest truth it meant heavy taxes, a high cost of living, a cloudy climate, and chilly women (*Anth.,* 613). As for the national over-soul, its better self and higher destiny, that was nothing but illusive chatter. In the only instance when Byron approaches the idealistic conception of nationality, *The Prophecy of Dante,* it was not England but Italy that he had in mind. As for politics, they were not a rational process of the reconciliation of opposites, but merely the strife of selfish politicians.

Byron had been indoctrinated with Calvinistic Christianity, but in his college days he came under the skeptical influence of Voltaire and Gibbon. He remained a Deist, and thought that a purified Christianity was the best of religions; but the God in whom he believed was not the God of some Christian dogmatists. Life had acquainted him with not a few persons who were not Christians but whose conduct was admirable, as well as with many professed Christians who were evildoers, and he refused to believe that the real God would condemn the good pagans to everlasting perdition. As for the purpose the Almighty had in creating our world, that seemed to Byron an inscrutable mystery, in which there was something sinister: for it was obvious that mankind was miserable, and God seemed to be entirely indifferent to the wretchedness of his creatures.

Since the final intention of the universe was thus shrouded in darkness, it was hard to know what should be one's object in this futile and ludicrous existence of ours. The magnanimous might say one should pursue fame, but no one who knew the black ingratitude of mankind would deny that fame was a mockery. The only thing a man could be sure of was the throb and urge of his senses. "To feel that we exist—even though in pain" was a genuine reality; and the gratification of the senses was to mortals the only indubitable pleasure.

One of the many paradoxes in Byron's beliefs was that while he passionately and unceasingly urged that mankind should be free, and theoretically believed that human nature was good, he was as contemptuous of democracy as he was enthusiastic over liberty. He despised and hated men and women as they actually existed. His notion of women was Turkish rather than English: as means of pleasure they were rapturously desirable, but intellectually and ethically they were not to be taken seriously—most of them, if not all, having, as Pope had sapiently remarked, no character at all.

Fortunately Byron's detestation of mankind in general was concentrated, for personal reasons, upon a portion of it which in large part deserved contempt—namely upon fashionable society. Here was a set of men and women who had the good fortune to be born with advantages that lifted them far above the poor and ignorant masses. In their hands lay the preponderance of the wealth and the political power of the nation. The highest professional careers of every kind were open to them. They had been educated in the best schools and universities and by foreign travel. Reared in the Church, they professed to be Christians and to believe in morality. Surely their aims in life and their standards ought to be of the highest. In fact, however, although they prided themselves on their aristocratic position, there was nothing noble in their views or motives. They were unintellectual and unenlightened. Their literary and artistic tastes were vulgar. They intrigued for power, and married for money or rank. Their courtesy was mere etiquette, their religion mere form. They were addicted to the silliest follies, and, stealthily, to the grossest vices. Most despicable of all was their cant and hypocrisy. They smugly considered English standards of society more moral than the continental, and they pretended to be horrified when anyone violated the code; but the plain truth was that they ostracized not all who were immoral but only those who were careless enough to be publicly found out. That the realm should be ruled by such as they seemed to Byron a preposterous mockery.

His Poems from 1816 to 1819.—The poetry which Byron wrote after the agonizing experiences that led to his exile was much superior to his earlier work. The first two cantos of *Childe Harold* (*Anth.,* 546) had picturesqueness and sadness, but in the third and fourth cantos (1816–17), he sounded more powerfully the notes of remorse and rebelliousness. It is in these cantos that the most celebrated passages occur—the self-portraiture of the unhappy wanderer, the descriptions of Waterloo, Lake Leman, Venice, and Rome, and the apostrophe to the ocean. Throughout he utilized nature and history to enhance the expression of his passionate personality, not untouched with remorse but defying the censure of the world.

In the next three poems, he turned to historical incidents for his themes. *The Siege of Corinth* (1816) described the attack upon that city by the Turks in 1715, and the manner in which the old Venetian governor, realizing that further resistance was hopeless, exploded his powder magazine, thus carrying down to death with him hundreds of his enemies. It is possible that Byron had in mind a contrast between that defiant and glorious death, and what he considered the ignominy of Napoleon in abjectly surrendering himself to captivity. In *Parisina* (1816), based on a story related by Gibbon, Byron dealt with a horrible episode of incest and revenge. In the best-known of these historical pieces, *The Prisoner of Chillon* (1816; *Anth.,* 536), a dramatic monologue, he illustrated the sufferings which those have endured who tried to liberate mankind from oppression.

In the dramatic poem *Manfred* (1817; *Anth.,* 585), he touched upon his relations with his half-sister. Manfred, who dwells in a Gothic castle in the Alps, is haunted by remorse for a crime, the precise nature of which is not disclosed. He has sought forgetfulness in the indulgence of the senses, but has found only ennui. He loathes himself and all mankind. Possessed of necromantic powers, he calls up the spirit of the dead Astarte, the victim of his crime ("I loved her—and destroyed her!"), and implores her to assure him that,

> though it were
> The deadliest sin to love as we have loved,

she has not been doomed to punishment and does not loathe him. But she gives no direct answer to his question.

> *Manfred:* Yet one word more,—am I forgiven?
> *Astarte:* Farewell!
> *Manfred:* Say shall we meet again?
> *Astarte:* Farewell!
> *Manfred:* One word for mercy! Say thou lovest me.
> *Astarte:* Manfred! (*She disappears.*)

Thereupon he craves nothing but complete oblivion. An abbot attempts to move him to repentance, and demons try to terrorize him by threats of eternal punishment; but he defies both, certain that death ends all. The contrast is a striking one between Goethe's Faust, who ultimately finds happiness in the service of humanity, and Byron's seeker, who despairingly longs for total extinction.

In 1818, with *Beppo* (*Anth.,* 612), Byron returned to satire. He had recently happened upon John Hookham Frere's *The Monks and the Giants* (1817), a burlesque poem in the *ottava rima,* i.e., in eight-line stanzas, with rhymes as ababab cc. Formerly he had used the heroic couplet in satire, but in Frere's stanzas he instantly perceived the perfect vehicle for the expression of one of his dominant moods. The subtitle of *Beppo* was "An Italian Story," but even more amusing than his main narrative of an intrigue in Venice, were his digressions on the differences between Italian people and manners and British, comparisons highly unfavorable to the latter. There was for example, his portrait of the typical English débutante:

> 'Tis true, your budding Miss is very charming,
>   But shy and awkward at first coming out,
> So much alarmed, that she is quite alarming,
>   All Giggle, Blush; half Pertness, and half Pout;
> And glancing at *Mamma,* for fear there's harm in
>   What you, she, it, or they, may be about,
> The nursery still lisps out in all they utter—
> Besides, they always smell of bread and butter.

In *Mazeppa* (1819; *Anth.,* 614), based upon Voltaire's *History of Charles XII,* he vividly told the story of the youth who, having been caught in an intrigue with the wife of a Polish nobleman, was bound naked upon a wild horse and turned loose into the wilderness to perish; but was rescued, half-dead from fatigue and hunger, and subsequently rose to be the chieftain of the Cossacks.

His Historical Dramas and Mysteries.—In his last years, Byron's powers were manifested in two strikingly diverse forms, in his satirical masterpieces, *The Vision of Judgment* and *Don Juan,* and in his historical dramas. In the former, he spoke his own mind; in the latter, he tried to prove to a world which accused him of egotism and cynicism that he could give an objective and austere interpretation of virtues as well as vices. He was at pains to ascertain accurately the historical incidents and circumstances upon which his dramas were based; but he felt free to introduce particulars not found in his sources, provided they did not contradict the known facts, and his imaginative inventions proved to be not the least interesting elements in these works.

In *Marino Faliero, Doge of Venice* (1821), an historical tragedy in five acts, he closely followed the chronicle of Marin Sanudo, who related how the doge had been insulted by a youth who wrote upon his official chair the legend: "Faliero, husband of a fair wife; others kiss her, but he keeps her," and that the Council of Forty had dealt so lightly with the gibe that the doge entered into a conspiracy to overthrow the constitution of the city. The conspiracy was promptly discovered, and the doge and his cabal were put to death. To this source, Byron made two additions. He invented the character of the doge's wife, Angiolina, describing her as young, beautiful, and impeccably virtuous. It is said that, except in the last respect, the Countess Guiccioli was his model; but Angiolina, unlike the countess, is too nearly perfect to be interesting. Byron's other addition to his source consisted in the sentiments which he attributed to the conspirators. Their aim is not mere revenge for insulted dignity, but the good of the commonwealth. Venice is a lazar house of tyranny, her citizens are oppressed, and the conspirators will disregard any and all personal considerations in order to win her liberty:

> We must forget all feelings save the *one*,
> We must resign all passions save our purpose,
> We must behold no object save our country,
> And only look on Death as beautiful,
> So that the sacrifice ascend to Heaven,
> And draw down Freedom on her evermore.

In such passages, Byron was encouraging the Venice of his own day to revolt against Austrian rule.

For his next tragedy he turned to the history of the great Assyrian monarch, Sardanapalus, as related by Diodorus Siculus. History represented Sardanapalus as an effeminate debauchee, who was finally goaded by insurrections into taking up arms against his opponents and after a vigorous resistance avoided his forcible deposition by killing himself. Byron's interpolations into the traditional accounts bore the marks of his own experience. He gave Sardanapalus some amiable traits, which appear in the words with which he checks his flatterers:

> I feel a thousand mortal things about me,
> But nothing godlike—unless it may be
> The thing which you condemn: a disposition
> To love and to be merciful, to pardon
> The follies of my species, and (that's human)
> To be indulgent to my own.

He thought of him as regretting his estrangement from his queen Zarina and as awakening too late to the priceless value of her love. Sardanapalus says to her:

> Zarina!
> I must pay dearly for the desolation
> Now brought upon thee. Had I never loved
> But thee, I should have been an unopposed
> Monarch of honoring nations. To what gulfs

> A single deviation from the track
> Of human duties leads even those who claim
> The homage of mankind as their born due,
> And find it, till they forfeit it themselves!

Byron also invented the character of Myrrha, for whom Sardanapalus deserted his queen, and who died with him upon his funeral pyre. It was not surprising that contemporaries identified Byron with Sardanapalus, Zarina with Lady Byron, and Myrrha with the Countess Guiccioli.

   The Two Foscari (1821) Byron based upon a Venetian incident related by the historians Daru and Sismondi. The aged doge Foscari was in duty bound to preside over the Council of Ten on two occasions when his only son was put to torture and condemned to exile for alleged crimes against the state, these sufferings being brought down upon him by the machinations of an enemy. Byron added the character of Marina, the devoted wife of the younger Foscari, again borrowing traits of the heroine's character from that of the Countess Guiccioli. He emphasized the younger Foscari's passionate love for Venice, and, in thinly veiled allusion to his own condition, dwelt upon the wretchedness of an exile's lot. To the aged doge, as to Byron, existence in this world seemed a state of infernal frustration of the individual will:

> All is low,
> And false, and hollow—clay from first to last,
> The prince's urn no less than potter's vessel.
> Our fame is in men's breath, our lives upon
> Less than their breath; our durance upon days,
> Our days on seasons; our whole being on
> Something which is not *us!*—So, we are slaves,
> The greatest as the meanest—nothing rests
> Upon our will; the will itself no less
> Depends upon a straw than on a storm;
> And when we think we lead we are most led,
> And still towards death, a thing which comes as much
> Without our act or choice as birth, so that
> Methinks we must have sinned in some old world,
> And *this* is hell: the best is, that it is not Eternal.

   In *Cain, a Mystery* (1821; *Anth.*, 720), Byron conceived of the eldest son of Adam and Eve as rebelling against having to endure the curse of toil and the horror of death for an act committed not by himself but by his parents. Lucifer takes Cain on a flight through the abyss of space and shows him that the God whom his pious parents and his devout brother Abel worship is a sardonic tyrant who creates beings only to destroy them and who tries to keep them ignorant. He urges him to believe in nothing except himself:

> *One good* gift has the fatal apple given—
> Your *reason:*—let it not be overswayed
> By tyrannous threats to force you into faith

'Gainst all external sense and inward feeling:
Think and endure,—and form an inner world
In your own bosom—where the outward fails;
So shall you nearer be the spiritual
Nature, and war triumphant with your own.

Subsequently Cain is further revolted by the idea of a God who is sup-
posed to take pleasure in painful and bloody sacrifices upon his altars.
Thus the quarrel with his brother Abel, and the murder, are motivated.
To some contemporaries it seemed that Byron had here undone himself
in heresy and blasphemy, justifying fratricide and proselytizing for
Satanism.

His other mystery, *Heaven and Earth* (1821), was a less sensational
and in some respects a more admirable work. Its characters were Noah,
his sons and daughters, and heavenly spirits; and the action took place
just before the flood. Few other poems of Byron, if any, show so impressively his powers of describing vast spaces and the grander features
of nature. His imaginary scenes form a sublime setting for the wretched
human beings who by divine decree are to suffer destruction. In the
characterization of the personages Byron did not stress gloomy or frantic
rebelliousness, as was his wont. They face their bitter fate in a proudly
stoical mood:

Let us resign even what we have adored,
And meet the wave, as we would meet the sword,
If not unmoved, yet undismayed,
And wailing less for us than those who shall
Survive in mortal or immortal thrall.

Heaven and Earth, in some ways the most impressive of Byron's serious
poems, suggests that if he had lived longer, he might have taken an attitude of mind somewhat different from that which predominates in the
works by which we know him.

Among his nonsatirical poems, the last noteworthy one was *The Island*
(1823). It is inferior in quality to his historical tragedies and his mysteries; but it illustrates the persistence in Byron to the very end of a
tendency which it is important not to overlook—viz., the tendency
towards primitivism and idyllicism. He had read Lieutenant William
Bligh's account of the mutiny in the South Seas of the sailors on the
naval vessel, the "Bounty," who, in 1789, seized the vessel and set their
commander and those who remained loyal to him adrift in an open boat.
Bligh's *Narrative of the Mutiny* makes it quite clear that the mutineers
were actuated by no higher motives than to enjoy the lazy and lascivious
life of which they had had a taste at Tahiti. As Bligh says,

It ought hardly to be the subject of surprise that a set of sailors, most of
them void of connections, should be led away, where they had the power
of fixing themselves, in the midst of plenty, in one of the finest islands in
the world, where there was no necessity to labor, and where the allure-
ments of dissipation are beyond any conception that can be formed of it.

Byron attributed to the native women innocence and constancy, and to
the sailors exalted ideas about humanity's right to live untrammeled by
conventions. To him they were

> Men without country, who, too long estranged,
> Had found no native home, or found it changed,
> And, half uncivilized, preferred the cave
> Of some soft savage to the uncertain wave—
> The gushing fruits that nature gave untilled;
> The wood without a path but where they willed;
> The field o'er which promiscuous plenty poured
> Her horn; the equal land without a lord;
> The wish—which ages have not yet subdued
> In man—to have no master save his mood.

Their life with their native loves was not only blissful but uplifting,—

> Did more than Europe's discipline had done,
> And civilized civilization's son.

The Vision of Judgment and Don Juan.—The height of Byron's
powers was shown not in his serious poems and dramas but in those of
his works which were wholly or partly satirical. His *Vision of Judgment*
(1821) was provoked by Southey's panegyric upon George III, in the
preface of which the poet laureate had attacked the Satanic School. Byron
saw that Southey could not with safety take the position that the publishing of radical sentiments on religious or political subjects was a sure
sign of personal depravity, because Southey had himself published such
sentiments in *Wat Tyler* and many other youthful writings. As for
George III, Byron strengthened his case by granting that the king had
many private virtues; but he was outraged by Southey's attempt to represent him as a great monarch. From the Whig or Liberal point of view, a
king who had tried to strengthen the authority of the Crown at the expense of the House of Commons was a despot; and one who had opposed
the American Revolution and the French was an enemy of liberty. With
great skill, however, Byron in his satire did not depict George III as a
terrible oppressor, but as a poor creature whose former opponents Wilkes
and Junius scorned wasting further words upon him; in short, he made
him something worse than odious, namely futile and ridiculous. Since
the days of Swift and Pope, there had been no satire so perfect in ease
of execution and so scathing in effect.

Byron's masterpiece, however, is *Don Juan* (*Anth.*, 622). To it he gave
a large part of his energies during the last five years of his life, and in
length it extends to more than one fourth of all his poetical works. For its
form, he turned again to the stanza which he had used in *Beppo,* and
which had its remoter origin in the serio-burlesque poem *Morgante Mag-
giore* (1485), by Luigi Pulci, the first cantos of which Byron translated
during the period when he was engaged upon *Don Juan*. As a motto for
Don Juan Byron chose Shakspeare's taunt to Pharisees:

Dost thou think, because thou art virtuous, there shall be no more cakes
and ale? Yes, by St. Anne, and ginger shall be hot i' the mouth, too!

He prefixed a dedication in verse, in which he ironically offered his poem
as a tribute to Southey, and also gibed at the other "Lakers," Wordsworth
and Coleridge, especially for their political conservatism.

The hero of the poem is named after the Don Juan who for two centuries had been the type of skeptical libertinism, but otherwise there is
little connection between Byron's narrative and the older treatments of
the theme. His Don Juan begins his amorous career as a handsome youth
aged sixteen, who seduces Donna Julia, an old grandee's wife. Having
been sent into exile, he is shipwrecked in the Mediterranean (here the
poet drew upon some of the hardships endured by his grandfather, Ad-
miral John Byron), and is cast half-dead upon the shore of an island
ruled over by a pirate, Lambro. Haidee, the beautiful daughter of Lambro, and Juan fall in love, and are idyllically happy; but Lambro, whom
they supposed dead, returns, and sells Juan into slavery, whereupon
Haidee dies. At Constantinople, the Sultana purchases him, has him
clad in woman's apparel, and brought into her palace. When she discovers, however, that he prefers another to herself, she commands that
he be put to death. He escapes, and joins the Russians, who, under the
great General Suvaroff, are engaged against the Turks in the famous
siege of Ismail. Having borne himself bravely here, he is sent to the
court of the Empress Catherine the Great, and becomes her lover. She
sends him on a diplomatic mission to England; and, at a house party,
he has the opportunity to study the manners and morals of the British
aristocracy. In the last stanzas penned by Byron, Juan is being sought
at midnight by the noble Duchess of Fitz-Fulke, she being disguised in
the garment of a friar. The poem is unfinished; and Byron, when
asked how it was to be concluded, remarked that he had not decided
whether to make Juan end in hell or in an unhappy marriage.

The moods of Byron were so various and intense that he needed for
complete expression a theme as many-sided as Don Juan's career. In his
serious poems, only one part of his nature could find utterance; and in
Childe Harold the main character permitted less variety than in *Don
Juan*. In the latter, he deals with the adventurous, the sentimental, the
amorous, and the satirical. In the serio-comic poem, the chief rule was
to avoid the regular; digression and change of tone were merits. Anything that he had seen or experienced or felt might be admitted—the
scenery of his wanderings, his yearnings for beauty and innocence, the
raptures and illusions of his amours, the sordidness of his baser indul-
gences, his knowledge of past history and present fads and fashions, his
ardors on behalf of liberty, his disillusionments, his questionings of religious dogma, his scorn of cant and hypocrisy, his ridicule of the general
pettiness of human life. With the possible exception of prose fiction
(what a novel of manners *Don Juan* would have made!) there is no conceivable form of literature in which Byron could have found so good an

outlet for his personality as that afforded by these stanzas, now hurrying onward in the full career of action, now caressing a beloved, now thrusting rapier-like through the heart of false dignities, and now pealing with laughter over the folly of mortals. Byron achieved not only an unforgettable description of the fashionable society of his own time, but, since that kind of society changes only in external ways and not at all at heart, his *Don Juan* is applicable to the corresponding social group of our own day.

Byron the Poet of Action.—Although Goethe praised Byron as "a personality such as in eminence has never yet been, and such as is not likely to come again," he added, "the way out of the false state of things which enraged him he did not see; he had not the patience, knowledge, self-discipline, and virtue, requisite for it." His poetry is the poetry of the actual. His pages are a fiery volcano pouring forth the desire for freedom, and that dynamic vitality in which all the important manifestations of life originate—deeds, feelings, thoughts, arts, and religions. Life to him means first the instincts, the senses, sometimes eroticism; but it reaches blindly upward, through lamentable sufferings and strange feelings of guilt, toward a mysterious infinite and eternal. In reading Byron, as in reading Shakspeare, one feels in intimate contact with throbbing life. Even the so-called dead are alive, the past breathes in the present, in the historic places of human civilization we feel the thrilling nearness of what has gone before.

His Relation to Other Romantics.—The place of Byron in the Romantic Movement is far from obvious, and there is much difference of opinion concerning it. In some respects he seems an opponent rather than an ally of romanticism; and certain modern critics who are as a rule hostile to romantic authors—Paul Elmer More, for example—incline favorably toward Byron. Byron attacked some of the leading Romantics —wished that Coleridge would "explain his explanation" of his philosophy, and sneered at both the thought and the style of Wordsworth. He regarded mysticism and transcendentalism as mere nonsense. The only great Romantic whom he praised was Sir Walter Scott, who was palpably nontranscendental. He would not join in the customary romantic clamor against Pope, and in opposition to William Lisle Bowles wrote vehement polemics in Pope's defense. He proclaimed his belief that the neo-classic law of the three unities was a sound principle of dramatic construction, and tried to observe it in his own dramas. What was more important, there appeared in his writings certain outstanding qualities which were not usually associated with Romanticism—namely, clearness, concreteness, and an addiction to the satirical. He never indulged in "verbal magic" at the cost of lucidity. His letters (*Anth.*, 737) are among the most brilliant in English. In them Byron is as vigorous as in his poetry, and not rhetorical or playing for effect, but completely and genuinely himself, frank, keen, and hard-hitting. It was apropos of his letters that Hobhouse exclaimed: "God bless him for a gallant spirit and a kind one!" Their sparkling realistic style is as different from the prose of Coleridge, Lamb, and De Quincey as high noon from starlit midnight.

Shelley disliked the cynicism of *Childe Harold,* and attributed it to Byron's addiction to the lowest kind of life.

> The spirit in which *Childe Harold* is written is, if insane, the most wicked and mischievous insanity that ever was given forth. . . . I remonstrated with him in vain on the tone of mind . . . Nothing can be less sublime than the true source of these expressions of contempt and desperation. The Italian women with whom he associates are perhaps the most contemptible who exist under the moon,—the most ignorant, the most disgusting. . . . Well, Byron is familiar with the lowest sort of these women. . . . He is heartily and deeply discontented with himself.
>
> Shelley to Peacock; Dec. 22, 1818

Shelley thought and wrote of mankind, Byron of men and women. More than any other Romantic he was a cosmopolitan man-of-the-world; he was not Universal Man, nor Representative Man.

These distinctions between Byron and other Romantics are not, however, irreconcilable differences. His quarrels with them about contemporaneous politics and literary technique sink into insignificance in comparison with the essential relationship between them. His love of ideals was as deep as theirs—his love of truth, virtue, and beauty. But whereas they had learned to perceive the manifestations of their ideals in various aspects of the actual life of mankind, past or present—had, in other words, become believers in concrete idealism—Byron was disappointed with the world as it is, and his idealism remained abstract. His most famous portrayal of happy love, that of Haidee, does not show it existing among the actualities of life but in a temporarily idyllic situation. Actual life, as he saw it, was devoid of present bliss or future promise. The glory that was Greece and the grandeur that was Rome had no modern successors. Love and happiness might visit us in youth, but the rest of life was disillusion. Perhaps this was the most tragic penalty of his libertinism, that he supposed his half-knowledge of women and of love to be the entire truth.

The moralist may rail against some of Byron's sentiments, but the literary critic, even though he does not share all of them, must remind us that the vigorous and beautiful expression of those sentiments is justifiable. Byron voices, with the clarity and intensity that only genius commands, that melancholy and pessimism which are inescapable moods of any human life that has run the gamut of experience. The youth whose mind has not passed through the Byronic stage is unlikely to attain wisdom; for either he has not a sufficiently intense love of the ideal, or he has not sufficient powers of observation to discern that in many respects the actual falls far short of that ideal. The fortitude of Wordsworth and of Landor, and the hopefulness of Shelley, are higher stages of insight;

but they are not likely to be sincerely attained without passing through the passionate despair and mocking scorn of Lord Byron. Historically his chief works followed those of some other Romantics, but logically they represent an earlier phase in the development of the romantic attitude toward life. Coleridge, Wordsworth, and Southey during their years of storm and stress lived through Byronic moods; but before they acquired the power to express them, they passed onwards to another state of mind.

Byron's work was a needed weapon in the armory of Romanticism because that reform of the standards and ways of living which the Romantics desired could not be effected as long as the sway of worldliness over human minds remained so strong. Wordsworth and Lamb and Landor might turn away from such worldliness and find delight in nature, in simplicity of life, or in noble traditions; but power and prestige and common sense still seemed to remain on the side of the worldlings. To ridicule their pretensions, show the selfishness of their politics, and unmask the hypocrisy of their religion and their moral codes, was the most valuable service of Byron to the romantic cause.

SELECTED BIBLIOGRAPHY

OF FIRST IMPORTANCE

Selections

The Poetry of Byron, ed. Matthew Arnold (Golden Treasury Series) , 1881.
Poems of Lord Byron, ed. H. J. C. Grierson, 1922.
Letters, ed. R. G. Howarth (Everyman's Libr.) , 1933.
The Best of Byron, ed. R. A. Rice, 1933. — Both verse and prose, including Letters; the most comprehensive of the selections.

Texts

One-volume editions of the poems: *The Poetical Works*, ed. E. H. Coleridge, Murray, 1905; and *Complete Poetical Works*, ed. Paul Elmer More (Houghton) , 1906.

Best Short Biography

Quennell, Peter; *Byron*, 1934; but almost as good for introductory purposes are the longer biographies by Ethel C. Mayne (1912) and John Drinkwater (1925) listed below.

Best Introductory Critical Discussions

See Quennell, above.

Brandes, Georg; *Main Currents in Nineteenth Century Literature*, IV, Chs. 17–21 (1875) . — Byron as the inspirer of the liberal movement throughout Europe.

Arnold, Matthew; *Essays in Criticism:* Second Series, 1888. — Wordsworth and Byron the two surpassingly important English poets of the nineteenth century, — Byron on account of his personal force.

More, Paul Elmer; "The Wholesome Revival of Byron," *Atlantic Monthly*, LXXXII, 801; 1898; also his Introduction to Byron's *Poetical Works*, 1906. — Stresses the value of the classical element in Byron's work, i.e., the predominance of intellect over emotion, and the interest in human life.

Elliott, G. R.; "Byron and the Comic Spirit," PMLA, xxxix, 897; 1924. — A study of Byron's rising above the personal toward the poetic.

Knight, G. Wilson; *The Burning Oracle: Studies in the Poetry of Action*, 1939. — Incarnate poetic energy — fiery sense of life, love, and liberty; master of tragedy.

FOR ADVANCED STUDENTS

Important Additional Texts

The Works of Lord Byron: Poetry, ed. E. H. Coleridge, 7 vols.; *Letters and Journals*, ed. R. E. Prothero [Lord Ernle], 6 vols.; 1898–1903; reissue, 1922. — The standard edition; annotated.

Lord Byron's Correspondence, Chiefly with Lady Melbourne, Mr. Hobhouse, the Honorable Douglas Kinniard, and Percy B. Shelley, ed. John Murray, 2 vols., 1922.

A Vision of Judgment. By Robert Southey. *The Vision of Judgment.* By Lord Byron. Ed. R. E. Roberts, 1932.

On the Byron MSS at the University of Texas, and publications based thereon by T. G. Steffan and W. W. Pratt, see Willis W. Pratt, *Lord Byron and His Circle*, 1948, and the reviews in ELH, March, 1948, and TLS, June 26, 1948.

On the apparently forged notes in the copy of *Ossian* (2 vols., 1806) at the Harvard Library, see Herbert Greenberg, "Two Versions of Byron's Poem, 'Ossian's Address to the Sun,'" N&Q, cxc, 256; 1946.

Chiefly Biographical

Moore, Thomas; *Letters and Journals of Lord Byron, with Notices of His Life*, 2 vols., 1830. — See above, p. 183. — Reviewed by T. B. Macaulay, *Edinburgh Rev.*, June, 1831; rptd. in *Critical and Historical Essays*.

Among the many other contemporaneous accounts, the following are noteworthy: Thomas Medwin, *Journal of Conversations*, 1824; John Galt, *Life of Byron*, 1830; the Countess of Blessington, *Conversations of Lord Byron*, 1834; and Teresa Guiccioli, *Lord Byron Jugé par les Témoins de sa Vie*, Paris, 1868; transl., 1869, as *My Recollections of Lord Byron*.

Stowe, Harriet Beecher; "The True Story of Lady Byron's Life," *Macmillan's Magazine*, xx, 377; 1869; and *Lady Byron Vindicated*, 1870. — The charge of incest brought against him. Cf. Catherine Gilbertson, *Harriet Beecher Stowe*, 1937.

Lovelace, Ralph, Earl of; *Astarte: a Fragment of Truth*, 1905. — By Byron's grandson. Evidence that Byron had committed incest with his half-sister, Lady Augusta Leigh. — Second ed., much superior to the first, by Mary, Countess of Lovelace, 1921.

Murray, John; Prothero, R. E., et al.; *Lord Byron and His Detractors*, 1906. — An attempt to refute *Astarte*.

Edgcumbe, Richard; *Byron: The Last Phase*, 1909. — Holds that Medora Leigh was the child of Byron by Mary Chaworth. Unconvincing. — See Andrew Lang, in *Fortnightly Review*, xciv, 268; 1910.

Mayne, Ethel C.; *Byron*, 2 vols., 1912; abridged and revised, 1924. — Excellent, well-documented. See also her *Life of Lady Byron*, 1929; 2nd ed., 1932.

Fox, (Sir) John Charles; *The Byron Mystery*, 1924. — An able lawyer's analysis of the evidence on the incest.

Nicolson, Harold G.; *Byron, the Last Journey: April, 1823–April, 1824*, 1924; 2nd ed., with new chapter, on Hobhouse, 1948. — Admirable.

Drinkwater, John; *The Pilgrim of Eternity: Byron — A Conflict*, 1925. — Tries to be fair, but puts Byron's conduct into the most favorable light.

Maurois, André; *Byron,* transl. Hamish Miles, 1930. — Accepts his wrongdoings with Gallic unconcern; sprightly. Believes the incest proved; see "Ethics of Biography," *Engl. Inst. Annual for 1942,* p. 14.

Massingham, H. J.; *The Friend of Shelley: A Memoir of Trelawny,* 1930. — Unfair to Byron.

Quennell, Peter; *Byron, the Years of Fame,* 1935. — The most detailed account of the 1811–1816 period; brilliant. — Cf. below, 1941.

Origo, Iris.; *Allegra,* 1935. — Well-written account of the Claire Clairmont episode. — Cf. R. Glynn Grylls, *Claire Clairmont,* 1939, which is "semi-fictionalized."

Cecil, (Lord) David; *The Young Melbourne,* 1939. — Vivid, unfavorable portrait.

Erdman, D. V.; "Byron's Stage Fright," ELH, VI, 219; 1939. — On his "ambition and fear of writing for the stage."

Quennell, Peter; *Byron in Italy,* 1941. — Sequel to the *Years of Fame,* 1935, above; vivid narrative of 1816 to 1823.

Erdman, David V.; "Lord Byron and the Genteel Reformers," PMLA, LVI, 1065 (1941) ; "Lord Byron as Rinaldo," PMLA, LVII, 189 (1942) ; and "Byron and Revolt in England," *Science and Society,* XI, 234 (1947) . — His career as a liberal peer, and a force for political and social reform.

Gray, Austin K.; *Teresa, or Her Demon Lover,* 1945. — Subtitle of British edition, "The Story of Byron's Last Mistress." Slightly fictionalized, but on the whole reliable and percipient.

Aldonov, Mark; *For Thee the Best,* 1945. — An historical novel, centering around Byron at Missolonghi; vivid, but uneven; rather cynical.

Vulliamy, C. E.; *Byron: With a View of the Kingdom of Cant and a Dissection of the Byronic Ego,* 1948. — His life as "romantic expressionism" in revolt against an age of hypocrisy.

Chiefly Critical

Noteworthy early criticisms are Hazlitt's "Lord Byron" (*Anth.,* 407) ; Landor's satirical sketch of "Mr. George" in *Bishop Burnet and Humphrey Hardcastle* (*Anth.,* 501) ; and, recently identified as Lockhart's, *John Bull's Letter to Lord Byron* (on *Don Juan*) , well edited by Alan L. Strout (Univ. Okla. Press) , 1947.

Taine, Hippolyte; *History of English Literature,* 1864–65. — Byron described as the greatest and most English of the Romantics.

Morley, John; "Byron," *Critical Miscellanies,* I, 203; 1871. — Plea for divorcing his poetry from his life; and assertion of his importance as a leader of the spirit of revolt.

Swinburne, Algernon Charles; "Byron," *Essays and Studies,* 1875. — Eulogy.

Nichol, John; *Byron* (Engl. Men of Letters) , 1887. — Well balanced introduction.

Elton, Oliver; *Survey of English Literature, 1780–1830,* 1912.

Chew, Samuel C.; *The Dramas of Lord Byron,* Göttingen, 1915.

Goode, Clement T.; *Byron as a Critic,* 1923.

Grierson, H. J. C.; "Byron and English Society," in W. A. Briscoe, ed., *Byron the Poet,* 1924.

Symons, James D.; *Byron in Perspective,* 1924. — Maintains that the Scottish influences upon Byron have been too much neglected, but exaggerates them.

Chambers, R. W.; *Ruskin (and Others) on Byron,* Engl. Asso. Lect., 1925; rptd. in *Man's Unconquerable Mind,* 1939. — A spirited defense against Byron's and Shelley's exaggerations of the evils in the England of their day.

Robertson, J. G.; *Goethe and Byron,* Publ. Engl. Goethe Soc., II, 1925.

Van Rennes, J. J.; *Bowles, Byron, and the Pope-Controversy,* 1927.

Du Bos, Charles; *Byron and the Need of Fatality,* Paris, 1929; tr. and enlarged, 1932. — The effect of the incest on his mind and work; somewhat too speculative for the matter-of-fact critics; but tries to fathom the real depths. Cf. TLS, March 13, 1930.

Calvert, William J.; *Byron: Romantic Paradox,* 1935. — The combining of Romanticism and Classicism.

Eliot, T. S.; "Byron," in Bonamy Dobrée, ed., *From Anne to Victoria,* 1937. — Byron's "a disorderly mind, and an uninteresting one"; cf. Edmund Wilson, *Axel's Castle,* 1931, p. 117.

Brown, Wallace C.; "Byron and the English Interest in the Near East," SP, XXXIV, 55; 1937. — Cf. H. S. L. Wiener, "Byron and the East: Literary Sources of the 'Turkish Tales,'" *Nineteenth-Century Studies* (Cornell), 1940.

McElderry, B. R. Jr.; "Byron's Interest in the Americas," *State Coll. Wash. Research Studies,* V, 145; 1937. — Cf. Joseph J. Jones, "Lord Byron on America," *Univ. of Texas Studies,* 1941.

Marjorum, Edward W.; *Byron as a Skeptic and Believer,* Princeton, 1938.

Russell, Bertrand; "Byron and the Modern World," JHI, I, 24; 1940. — Praised as an aristocratic rebel against political tyranny and against basing moral standards merely on social conventions. Russell gives Byron a whole chapter in his *History of Western Philosophy,* 1946.

Morgan, Charles; "The English View of Byron," TLS, Jan. 22, 1944; rptd. in *Reflections in a Mirror,* Second Series. 1046. — "The English look, in poetry, for a quality that he is almost without," — yet acknowledge his greatness as a personality.

Hudson, A. P.; "Byron and the Ballad," SP, XLII, 594; 1945.

De Ullmann, Stephen; "Romanticism and Synaesthesia: Sense Transfer in Keats and Byron," PMLA, LX, 811; 1945.

Faulkner, C. W.; *Byron's Political Verse Satire* (Abstr. Univ. of Ill. Thesis), 1947. — Confirms Hazlitt's charge of lack of serious purpose.

Strout, Alan L.; Introduction to ed. of (Lockhart's) *John Bull's Letter to Lord Byron,* Univ. of Okla. Press, 1947. — Best account of contemporaneous critics of Byron.

On Separate Works

Amstel, A. von; "The True Story of The Prisoner of Chillon," *Nineteenth Century,* May, 1900; p. 821.

Evans, Bertrand; "Manfred's Remorse and Dramatic Tradition," PMLA, LXII, 752; 1947. — Influence of Gothic novels and dramas.

Boyd, Elizabeth F.; *Byron's "Don Juan,"* 1945.
Steffan, T. G.; "Byron at Work on Canto I," MP, XLIV, 141; 1947.
MacKay, Dorothy E.; *The Double Invitation in the Legend of Don Juan* (Stanford Univ. Press), 1943.
Johnson, E. D. H.; "Don Juan in England," ELH, XI, 135; 1944. — The satire just only as to "high society."
Trueblood, P. S.; *The Flowering of Byron's Genius,* 1945. — *Don Juan,* an attack on "all insincerity which obstructs individual and national freedom."
Madariaga, S. de; *Don Juan as a European Figure,* 1946.
On *Don Juan,* see also Alan L. Strout, ed., *John Bull's Letter,* above, 1947. — A study of the MSS and versions is planned by Guy Stephan; see TLS, June 12, 1948.

Messac, R.; "Cain et le Problème du Mal dans Voltaire, Byron, et Leconte de Lisle," RLC, IV, 620; 1924.

On the History of the Interpretations of Byron

A good brief account is Richard A. Rice's *Lord Byron's British Reputation* (Smith College Studies), 1924. — The detailed history of all the important English work on Byron is Samuel C. Chew's *Byron in England: His Fame and After-Fame,* 1924, an indispensable work for thorough study. Cf. R. W. Chambers, *Ruskin (and Others) on Byron* (Engl. Asso. Pamphlet, LXII), 1925.

Leonard, William Ellery; *Byron and Byronism in America,* 1905. — Finds less influence than might be expected; but see Samuel C. Chew, "Byron in America," *Amer. Mercury,* I, 35; 1924; and Desmond Powell, below.

For the vast influence of Byron on continental literature, see the studies, such as Edmond Estève, *Byron et le Romantisme Français,* 1907, 1929; listed under "Literary Relations with the Continent" in *Cambridge Bibliography of English Literature,* III, 23–24, as well as Pollard's Byron Bibliography, do., III, 187–212. — A good introduction is Desmond Powell, "Byron's Foreign Critics," *Col.-Wyo. Journal of Letters,* Feb., 1939 (includes American). — Add, for Scandinavia, Sigmund Skard, "Byron i Norsk Litteratur," *Edda,* XXXIX, 67–144; 1939; and, for Germany, Cedric Hentschel, *The Byronic Teuton: Aspects of German Pessimism,* 1939, which shows Byronism throttled by Nazis (rev. TLS, Jan. 27, 1940).

Bibliographical

Wise, T. J.; *A Bibliography of the Writings in Verse and Prose of Lord Byron,* 2 vols., 1932–33. — Cf. TLS, Sept. 15, 29, 1932; April 27, May 4, Sept. 21, 1933 (Notes by John Carter).

Chew, Samuel C.; *Byron in England,* 1924, pp. 353–407. — Byronia.

Pollard, H. G.; "Bibliography of Byron," *Cambridge Bibliography of English Literature,* III, 187–212; 1941.

Quintana, Ricardo; *Byron, 1788–1938: An Exhibition at the Huntington Library,* San Marino, 1938.

CHAPTER 14

JOHN KEATS

(October 31, 1795–February 23 [or 24], 1821)

1817 Poems: I Stood Tiptoe, Chapman's Homer, Sleep and Poetry, etc.
1818 Endymion

wr. 1819 The Fall of Hyperion: a Vision (publ. 1856)
1820 Lamia, Isabella, The Eve of St. Agnes, and Other Poems

His Childhood and Schooling.—In the last quarter of the eighteenth century, one John Jennings was prosperously conducting a livery stable at the Swan and Hoop Inn, a short distance north of the center of London. He had in his employ a young man named Thomas Keats, who had come up to the city from the west of England and proved himself so industrious and capable that he became the chief hostler. Presently Thomas Keats married his master's daughter, Frances, and succeeded to the business. His wife was as sensitive, affectionate, and emotional as he was steadfast. Of this union, and seemingly inheriting the traits of both parents, was born in 1795 John Keats. None of the other great Romantics had an origin so humble and apparently so unpropitious to poetical genius.

The parents of John Keats were more desirous of giving their children the best education than people of their class usually were in those days, and at one time they hoped to be able to afford to send John to the celebrated Harrow School; but, this proving impossible, they placed him at eight years of age in a private school kept by John Clarke at Enfield, north of London, where he remained until 1811. This chanced to be a fortunate choice, for the tone of the school was in many ways exceptionally good; and Keats was very happy there. In his first years at school, he showed no signs of any unusual gifts: he seemed an entirely normal, carefree schoolboy, rather pugnacious in disposition, devoted to sports, interested in all kinds of natural phenomena, and fond of animals. The death of his father, when Keats was only nine years old, made little impression upon him; but at the age of fourteen he was deeply affected by the loss of his mother. He had three brothers and a sister, all younger than himself. The orphans were placed under the guardianship of Richard Abbey and Rowland Landell, merchants; and a small inheritance from their grandfather was left for their support.

At about this time Keats began to take an interest in reading, which was carefully fostered by his schoolmaster's son and assistant teacher, Charles Cowden Clarke. Clarke, eight years older than Keats himself, was an enthusiastic devotee of literature and music, and had remarkable skill in communicating his enthusiasm to his pupils. He encouraged Keats to browse in the school library, which was not a large one, but well chosen. Here, during his last eighteen months at school, Keats read many histories, voyages, tales, and poetical works; but what fascinated him most of all were books like Tooke's *Pantheon,* Lemprière's *Classical Dictionary,* and Spence's *Polymetis,* which gave him glimpses of the art and literature of classical antiquity. He now won several prizes for his scholarship, and seemed in a fair way toward an academic career, when Abbey, his matter-of-fact guardian, judging that a boy with such small resources ought to acquire as soon as possible a means of livelihood, withdrew him from school before he was sixteen and apprenticed him to a surgeon and druggist.

His Apprenticeship to Surgery.—For four years Keats served in that apprenticeship, and for a year thereafter he studied in London at Guy's Hospital and St. Thomas'. During the earlier part of this period, his grandmother provided a home for his brothers and sister; but Mrs. Jennings died in 1814, Fanny Keats went to live at their guardian's, and the brothers were left to shift for themselves. To Keats, whose nature was extremely affectionate, this breaking of the family ties was a dismal event. He was also depressed by the fact that, although he had dutifully pursued his studies, had passed his final examinations, and had been licensed in 1816 as an apothecary, the thought of a medical career had grown more and more distasteful to him.

What really interested him was that world of literature and art to the existence of which he had awakened during his last months at school. Most youths in their teens, placed as Keats was, would have felt that it was useless for them to try to maintain an interest so remote from their regular work. They would soon have solaced themselves with the companionship of other apprentices, and have sunk to the level of their narrow outlook and their commonplace pleasures. Keats, however, with dogged determination, used his scanty leisure in self-cultivation, and seized upon such opportunities for cultural improvement as remained open to him. Whenever he could find time to do so, he would trudge to his former school at Enfield to borrow books and to keep in touch with Charles Cowden Clarke. He had already made a prose translation of Virgil's *Æneid,* when, in his nineteenth year, there occurred that incident which decisively settled what was to be his vocation. Clarke, seated in the school garden, read aloud to him Spenser's *Epithalamion.* It was his first introduction to him who is termed the poet's poet. Says Clarke:

> He certainly appreciated the general beauty of the composition, and felt the more passionate passages; for his features and exclamations were ecstatic. . . . That night he took away with him the first volume of the "Faerie Queene," and he went through it . . . as a young horse would through a spring meadow—ramping! Like a true poet, too—a poet born,

not manufactured, a poet in grain, he especially singled out epithets, for that felicity and power in which Spenser is so eminent. He *hoisted* himself up, and looked burly and dominant, as he said, "What an image that is—'*sea-shouldering* whales'!"

His first extant attempt in verse was his *Imitation of Spenser* (*Anth.*, 746).

He now read with avidity the Spenserians of the eighteenth century; and—to his greater advantage—those of the seventeenth, Fletcher, Browne, and the early poems of Milton. Clarke also stimulated his former pupil's interest in contemporaneous authors, especially in Leigh Hunt, whose journal, *The Examiner,* helped to make Keats a liberal in politics. Hunt had been imprisoned from February, 1813, to February, 1815, for publishing a libel against the Prince Regent; and when he was released Keats wrote a *Sonnet on Hunt Leaving Prison* (Feb., 1815). In the fall of 1816, Clarke showed this and other attempts by the young aspirant to Hunt, to whose literary circle Keats, then twenty-one years old, was thereupon admitted. It was natural that Keats should look up to Hunt, who was eleven years older than himself and already of some reputation, with not a little awe; and that he should admire him both as a modern poet of the Spenserian school and a martyr to the cause of liberty. It is not to be supposed that Hunt was at first deeply impressed with the young medical student's efforts in verse, but he and his friends liked him personally. At this time Keats became acquainted with the artist Haydon, and with Shelley, Hazlitt, and Lamb. Haydon, with his virile personality and his lofty ideas about the sublime mission of art and literature, was a valuable counterpoise against Leigh Hunt's occasional nambypambiness. The young portrait-painter, Joseph Severn, who was to prove one of his most devoted friends, he had come to know somewhat earlier. Keats's ability to learn from his friends was as noteworthy as his intelligence in making the right choice of books. Clarke continued his mentorship, and in October, 1816, introduced Keats to the Elizabethan poet Chapman's noble and spirited version of Homer, which immediately inspired Keats to write that sonnet in which for the first time he manifested unmistakable poetic genius (*Anth.*, 751). This was also one of the first of his productions that received public notice, Hunt quoting it in *The Examiner* in December of the same year.

The Beginning of His Literary Career.—Keats's income from his grandfather's estate was not enough to support even his modest wants, and from the worldly point of view it was unthinkable that he should not enter upon the occupation for which he had been trained. His guardian, Mr. Abbey, naturally expected him to do so, frowned upon his unprofitable interest in poetry, and was not cordial on occasions when he called to visit his sister Fanny. Temporarily Keats thought of taking a post as a surgeon, but he did not delude himself with the notion that he could do so and at the same time achieve his cultural and literary aspirations. In the autumn of 1816, he finally decided to devote himself entirely to poetry. Through Shelley and Hunt, he found a young publisher named Ollier who was willing to take the risk of issuing his poems; and the little volume, with a dedicatory sonnet to Leigh Hunt, appeared in March, 1817. It received six reviews, all recognizing Keats as a poet of promise; and Hunt's review in *The Examiner* was full of judicious praise. The sale, however, was so slight that the publisher voiced his disappointment in an angry and insulting manner. The poet gained by its publication, however, a few valued personal friends, including Benjamin Bailey, who was a devotee of Wordsworth and was presently to influence Keats in notable ways.

The artists Severn and Haydon introduced Keats to those remains of the sculptures of the Greek Parthenon which had been brought to London not many years previously by the Earl of Elgin, and which were therefore known as the Elgin Marbles. Haydon was particularly enthusiastic over these masterpieces, which he rightly regarded as even more beautiful than those of Michelangelo, because they united idealism with realism, i.e., unity of significance with fidelity to minute details. This introduction to Greek art Keats commemorated in *On Seeing the Elgin Marbles* (*Anth.*, 758) and in his sonnet *To Haydon* beginning

> Haydon! forgive me that I cannot speak
> Definitively of these mighty things.

He passed many evenings in Haydon's studio, where he heard brilliant conversation by romantic artists and authors. He was more and more impressed with the feeling that his era was one of great intellectual and aesthetic achievement. In this mood of enthusiasm he wrote his sonnet "Great Spirits Now on Earth Are Sojourning" (*Anth.*, 757), which he addressed to Haydon, who declared that he would send it to Wordsworth. Keats replied:

> The idea of your sending it to Wordsworth put me out of breath,—you know with what reverence I would send my well-wishes to him.

Haydon, who in his own art loved large canvases, urged Keats, against Hunt's counsel, to undertake a poem of considerable length, and this advice may have influenced him to attempt the poetic romance in four books, *Endymion*. He began its composition in April, 1817, and finished it in November of that year.

One of the most admirable traits of Keats, surprising in one so young, was that despite the appreciative comments which his friends made upon his verses, he felt very strongly that before he could achieve great poetry he must grow in knowledge, culture, and self-discipline. In the spring of 1817 he left London to seek a quieter environment in the country, first on the Isle of Wight, and later at Margate and Canterbury. Although daily spending a portion of his time upon the composition of *Endymion*, he was as persistently devoted to the study of the great poets, particularly Shakspeare, whose works he read, reread, reflected upon, and marginally annotated, with the deepest devotion. It was not that he wished to imitate Shakspeare closely, but that he hoped through the supreme master to develop in himself a state of mind and feelings, a temper of the soul, which should be more and more genuinely poetical. He also gave much attention and thought to Milton and to Wordsworth, the latter especially while visiting his new friend, Benjamin Bailey, at Oxford in the autumn. On his return to London, he heard Hazlitt lecture on the English Poets,[1] and wrote a few reviews of plays, which somewhat show the influence of that critic. Late in December, Keats was introduced to Wordsworth by Haydon, and the young poet, upon Haydon's urging, recited his *Hymn to Pan*. Wordsworth's dry comment was, "A very pretty piece of paganism!" Keats felt hurt; and though he dined with Wordsworth at Haydon's soon afterwards, and saw a good deal of him during the next two months, he could never quite forgive Wordsworth's asperity.

The Attacks by Reviewers.—In April, 1818, *Endymion* was published. Unlike most poets of the age of twenty-two, Keats did not suppose that his work was flawless, but he might reasonably have hoped that the reviewers would try to discover a few merits in it as well as the faults. The Tory *Blackwood's Magazine,* however, was determined to see in Keats merely a hanger-on of Leigh Hunt, who was obnoxious to it for political reasons. Already before the publication of *Endymion, Blackwood's* had contained an article on "The Cockney School of Poetry" (Oct., 1817) in which Keats had been contemptuously alluded to; and now in continuation of that subject (Aug., 1818) its reviewers made it a reproach to him that his early training and associations had been so plebeian and unpoetical. In the *Quarterly* (Sept., 1818) an anonymous writer, now known to have been John Wilson Croker, jeered at Keats's modest preface and quoted the feeblest passages he could find in the poem, to justify his sweeping condemnation. What must have irritated Keats especially was the general assumption that the author of *Endymion* was merely a disciple of Leigh Hunt's, when, in point of fact, he had therein been reacting against Hunt's influence. The friends of Keats— Shelley, Benjamin Bailey, and J. H. Reynolds (in *The Champion,* March 9, 1817)—did what they could to offset these dispraises; but their commendations were either made in private letters, or published in journals too obscure to be widely influential. In the circumstances the young poet might have been expected to show himself embittered or discouraged. The remarkable common sense, modesty, and courage of Keats, however, displayed itself in his readiness to learn whatever could be learned from his hostile critics and in his reluctance to overvalue the praises of his friends. In a letter (Oct. 9, 1818) to his publisher, he wrote:

> I cannot but feel indebted to those gentlemen who have taken my part,— as for the rest, I begin to get a little acquainted with my own strength and

---

[1] See above, p. 127.

weakness. Praise or blame has but a momentary effect on the man whose love of beauty in the abstract makes him a severe critic on his own works. My own domestic criticism has given me pain without comparison beyond what *Blackwood* or *The Quarterly* could possibly inflict; and also when I feel I am right, no external praise can give me such a glow as my own solitary reperception and ratification of what is fine. J. S.[2] is perfectly right in regard to the slip-shod *Endymion*. That it is so is no fault of mine. No! though it may sound a little paradoxical. It is as good as I had power to make it,—by myself. Had I been nervous about its being a perfect piece, and with that view asked advice, and trembled over every page, it would not have been written; for it is not in my nature to fumble —I will write independently. I have written independently *without judgment*. I may write independently and *with judgment* hereafter. The genius of poetry must work out its own salvation in a man. It cannot be matured by law and precept, but by sensation and watchfulness in itself. That which is creative must create itself. In *Endymion* I leaped headlong into the sea, and thereby have become better acquainted with the soundings, the quicksands, and the rocks, than if I had stayed upon the green shore, and piped a silly pipe and took tea and comfortable advice. I was never afraid of failure; for I would sooner fail than not be among the greatest.

The notion which was current after his death, that the reviewers had killed him, was false.[3]

What the enemies of Keats did not know was that he was more conscious of his imperfections, more pained by them, and more aware of their cause, than anyone else. He knew that what he needed was still further study and meditation. Even before the reviewers had jeered at his faults, he was writing (April 24, 1818) to a friend:

I know nothing, I have read nothing—and I mean to follow Solomon's directions of "Get wisdom, get understanding." I find cavalier days are gone by; I find that I can have no enjoyment in the world but continual drinking of knowledge. I find there is no worthy pursuit but the idea of doing some good for the world. . . . There is but one way for me. The road lies through application, study, and thought. I will pursue it. . . . I have been hovering for some time between an exquisite sense of the luxurious, and a love for philosophy,—were I calculated for the former I should be glad. But as I am not, I shall turn all my soul to the latter.

In this spirit, he steeped himself in Milton and in Dante, Cary's translation of the latter being the only volumes that he took with him on his walking tour through the Lake district and Scotland in the summer of 1818.

His Last Years.—It was in the two and a half years that remained to Keats that nearly all of his supremely great poetry was composed—including *The Eve of St. Agnes, La Belle Dame Sans Merci, Lamia,* the odes

[2] J. S.—A writer in the *Morning Chronicle* of Oct. 3, 1818.
[3] The legend was believed because of Reynolds' report that Keats had at the time decided to give up poetry, the over-modest epitaph on his tomb at Rome, Shelley's *Adonais,* and Byron's *Don Juan,* xi, 6.

On a Grecian Urn, To a Nightingale, and *To Autumn,* and both versions of *Hyperion.* In the same period, however, while poetically he was rising to his greatest heights, his personal existence was sinking toward a fatal end. On his tour in Scotland, he contracted a severe soreness of the throat which became chronic; and when he returned to London, he exposed his hereditarily frail health (his mother had died of tuberculosis) to further danger by devotedly nursing his brother Thomas, who likewise was consumptive, and who died in December, 1818. His other surviving brother, George Keats, had emigrated to the United States half a year previously.

In his loneliness, and not knowing how precarious was the state of his health, Keats now fell in love with a young, attractive, cheerful girl named Fanny Brawne. After a brief courtship, they were engaged. His growing illness, as well as his financial difficulties, which were aggravated by his generosity to his brother George, made their immediate marriage impossible. On July 25, 1819, he wrote to Fanny:

> My sweet girl,—I have two luxuries to brood over in my walks, your loveliness and the hour of my death. O that I could have possession of them both in the same moment!

(Compare "And so live ever—or else swoon to death" in the "Bright Star" sonnet, *Anth.,* 817, which has been called "perhaps the most marvelous short poem in our language.") He knew that his passionate hopes would be frustrated, and sometimes in his morbid state he uttered jealous and desperate sentiments not characteristic of his real nature. To censure either him or Fanny Brawne for their distraught feelings under such circumstances is either fatuous or cruel.

In July, 1820, there appeared Keats's third volume, *Lamia, Isabella, The Eve of St. Agnes, and Other Poems.* Its reception was not marred by such blunders and outrages of criticism as had affronted his earlier works. Not only did his friends Leigh Hunt and Charles Lamb praise it, but even Francis Jeffrey in the dreaded *Edinburgh Review* spoke of it with respect.

Under medical advice, Keats, in September, 1820, accompanied by his friend Joseph Severn, sailed to Italy in the hope of restoring his health in a milder climate. His physicians had told him that what he was suffering from was a disease of the digestive organs, and not of the lungs. Their diagnosis was wrong. He had laryngeal and pulmonary tuberculosis; and the autopsy showed that before his death both of his lungs were almost wholly destroyed. Attended by the faithful Severn, he died at Rome on February 23 (or 24), 1821, aged twenty-five; and his remains were buried in the Protestant Cemetery of the Eternal City. In the purblind view of the world, it was an incident of little importance; but Shelley, learning of it at Pisa, composed his *Adonais,* an elegy more noble and beautiful than has been bestowed upon any other author. Keats revered great poets; and one may wish that he could have known that the hand of genius was to lay such a tribute upon his grave. Nothing else would have so assuaged the wretchedness of his last days, when he felt that he must die without leaving behind him works which approached that perfection for which he had yearned.

During his last illness he wrote to Fanny Brawne:

> Now I have had opportunities of passing nights anxious and awake, I have found other thoughts intrude upon me. "If I should die," said I to myself, "I have left no immortal work behind me—nothing to make my friends proud of my memory—but I have loved the principle of beauty in all things, and if I had had time I would have made myself remembered."

Keats's over-modest view of his achievement is also seen in the words engraved at his request on his tombstone:

HERE LIES ONE WHOSE NAME WAS WRIT IN WATER

His Personality.—As long as Keats was known only through his earlier poems, it was natural to suppose him to be a rather feeble character, sensitive to beauty, but dreamily indolent. Except as to the sensitiveness, this impression was a false one, as has been gradually revealed by closer study of his letters and of the details of his life. From his mother he had inherited not only his tubercular tendency but some perilous emotional traits. When he became conscious of his ego, he found it impulsive, vehement, luxury-loving, wilful, irritable, proud, and suspicious of others, also given to self-analysis and self-pity, with moods of depression which showed what he himself termed his "horrid morbidity of temperament." The outstanding fact about his moral history is that he so rarely permitted such qualities to win control over him. It was not until the last months of his life, when his fatal disease was undermining his will power, that he was unable to refrain from outbursts of ill-temper or jealousy.

To a degree remarkable in so young a man, he knew what his weaknesses were, as his letters show so clearly, and he resolutely tried to master them and to build up within himself a manly and generous spirit. Thus when the crucial test of his character came, i.e., when the critics jeered at his poems, and when he knew that their attacks would discourage publishers from accepting his poems, he lost neither his temper nor his courage, but doggedly applied himself to the improvement of his work. Unlike Haydon, whose self-confidence was so arrogant that he felt sure that adverse criticism must be entirely mistaken, Keats was even more conscious of his imperfections than his enemies were.

In his personal relationships he displayed many lovable traits. Clarke testifies to his popularity from his school days onwards:

> He was not merely the "favorite of all," like a pet prize-fighter, for his terrier courage; but his high-mindedness, his utter unconsciousness of a mean motive, his placability, his generosity, wrought so general a feeling in his behalf, that I have never heard a word of disapproval from anyone, superior or equal, who had ever known him.

The qualities which those who knew him best dwelt upon in characterizing him were on the one hand his sense of honor, his unselfishness, and the warmth of his sympathy; and on the other, his sanity of judgment and his sense of humor. Severn's devotion to Keats at Rome was only the most conspicuous instance of that deep affection which all his friends felt for him.

His Idea of Poetry.—The thoughts which Keats regarded as the most precious had come to him not through philosophers but through poets, and the relations between poetry and truth, and between poetry and life, were to him a matter of the highest importance. He realized of course—how could anyone so sensitive have walked the hospitals of London without realizing it?—that there was much in life that to ordinary perception appeared utterly unpoetical. He had seen his full share of the pain, sickness, sorrow, wretchedness, and frustration that burden human existence. But, unlike Byron, he did not deem it fitting to make such aspects of life the chief theme of poetry. It was only too true that our existence seemed but weariness, fever, and fret (*Ode to a Nightingale*), and that the loveliest things in life must pass away (*Ode on Melancholy* and *On a Grecian Urn*), but this was not the sum of wisdom. In that same world, so dismal to superficial observation, there stood out Beauty. To this the average purblind man was oblivious because he was absorbed in things of directly practical value; but artists and poets were consecrated to the worship of beauty, and to the revelation of its reality, its glory, and the significance of its presence in our universe.

Poets gave something to mankind which philosophers could not give, because to confine oneself to what the logical understanding could prove was to ignore other means of access to truth, especially the imagination. To poets, imagination, or intuitive apprehension, was the necessary means of perceiving beauty; and the instinctive human impulses, when not diverted from their normal and wholesome channels, were tributaries of the imaginative stream. To minds darkened by confinement within merely practical concerns, poems and works of art seemed as unreal as dreams,—perhaps amusing as a pleasant way of escaping from the burden and dullness of life, but not to be taken seriously. To poets, however, to find something beautiful meant to find something true. To discern and to reveal the beauty of a phenomenon, or of some aspect of human experience, did not mean merely to represent it in a manner which might strike contemporary taste as pretty in color, sound, or form; it meant to disclose its inward nature and purpose in the light of eternal values. Thus beauty, being that quality of an object which was discerned when its essential nature was seen, was a mode of truth. The immortality of great works of art rested upon that fact: they survived not because they happened to please the generation in which they were produced, but because the interpretation which they gave of their subjects proved permanently true.

Such being the real nature of poetry, certain qualities were necessary in a poet. He must desire above all things to attain a sympathetic apprehension of the Infinite. He could not obtain it, however, by mere ratiocination, by "any irritable reaching after fact and reason," by reducing the intricate and mysterious universe to a readily understandable logical and systematic pattern. Nor could he obtain it by supposing that his own selfish feelings and individual fancies were significant. That was the error of Byron, whose egotism and violence made him one of the

> self worshippers
> And careless Hectorers in proud bad verse.
> *Fall of Hyperion*, 208; *Anth.*, 833

The true poet would find himself by losing himself. He would make his way toward a comprehension of the Infinite by a self-forgetful observation of the finite. His would be "a life of sensations rather than of thoughts" because it would be a search not for formulae but for vivid objects and concrete experiences that were beautiful because they suggested the real nature of the universe. The poet would especially endeavor to understand the most relevatory of all finite entities, the heart and mind of man, and would try to cultivate the intuitive insight which is deepened by actual contact with the joys and pains of human existence. Imagination was the poet's highest faculty, but he must also studiously acquire knowledge and wisdom. He must not expect to attain a poet's soul speedily; it was a process of development that passed, not without error and pain, through several stages. If he reached the highest stage, as Shakspeare did supremely, he would have that attitude of mind which Keats obscurely called "negative capability." On this he wrote (Dec. 21, 1817) as follows:

> I had, not a dispute, but a disquisition with Dilke on various subjects; several things dove-tailed in my mind, and at once it struck me what quality went to form a man of achievement, especially in literature, and which Shakspeare possessed so enormously—I mean *negative capability*, that is, when a man is capable of being in uncertainties, mysteries, doubts, without any irritable reaching after fact and reason.

The true poet, in other words, refused to adhere to any system of thought which would ignore that life was in part a mystery. To him the best way to lift "the burden of the mystery" from man's spirit was to reveal to man that his universe was replete with beauty. Full of tolerance and wise acceptance, he might disclose the presence of beauty even in some things which to prosaic view seemed painful or ugly; as Shakspeare did, for example, with folly and madness in *King Lear*.

His Views of Life.—In a letter of February 27, 1818, Keats stated some of his principles as follows:

> In poetry I have a few axioms, and you will see how far I am from their centre.
> 1st. I think poetry should surprise by a fine excess, and not by singu-

larity; it should strike the reader as a wording of his own highest thoughts, and appear almost a remembrance.

2d. Its touches of beauty should never be half-way, thereby making the reader breathless, instead of content. The rise, the progress, the setting of Imagery should, like the sun, come natural to him, shine over · him, and set soberly, although in magnificence, leaving him in the luxury of twilight. But it is easier to think what poetry should be, than to write it. And this leads me to

Another axiom—that if poetry comes not as naturally as the leaves to a tree, it had better not come at all.

Keats could not have consistently believed in such theories of poetry unless he also believed that the universe is fundamentally a beneficent one. He was, to be sure, far from being satisfied with things-as-they-were in all respects. He was an ardent liberal in politics, and the reader of his letters will discover that he was much more interested in political and social issues than perusal of only his poetry would suggest. He was rather hostile toward institutional Christianity, opining that the history of its founder had been "written and revised by men interested in the pious frauds of religion"; and he refused to accept its theology.

The religion of Keats, like his aesthetics and his philosophy, was chiefly derived from poets, especially from Spenser's *Four Hymns* and from the poems of other Elizabethan Neo-Platonists. Hence the Deity to him was the ultimate source of that ideal and absolute beauty which was the true reality. God, beholding and loving his own beauty, willed its extension; and thus arose a world which was a series of emanations from the Creator, each being or object reflecting in the degree of its nearness to him, its divine origin. Thus our world was linked together by love and by beauty, and the human manifestations of them were imperfect but precious reminders and assurances that Heavenly Love and Beauty were realities with which we might come into communion. All things that endured were not only created but also preserved by those two principles: the beauty which animated each being with its essential character or nature, and the love which desired to perpetuate that beauty. On every hand the phenomena of this world betrayed the imprint of eternal and divine laws. But only those who were willing to exercise that imagination with which they were gifted could behold these great truths.

Unimaginative and narrow-minded men were discontented not merely with those evils of our existence which were artificially and unnecessarily introduced into it (a righteous discontent) but also with its apparently inherent and irremediable woes and limitations. They fancied that, if they had been given charge of the matter, they could have contrived a world superior to the one which God had created, a world in which man would have been endowed with perfect mental and moral powers, in which there would be neither pain nor death, and in which consequently we should all be entirely happy. In his notable letter of April 28, 1819 (*Anth.*, 849), he rejected both the dream of perfectibilitarians and the discontent of the pessimists. We might, and we should, improve the conditions of life to the extent that it was possible for us to do so; but so long as our world and our human nature remained essentially what they were, man would not find life perfect nor would he become entirely happy. But this was, on deeper reflection, and on one's trying to grasp the total scheme of things, not a cause for lamentation and despair. If all unpleasantness and pain were removed from life, death would become inconceivably more horrible than it now is. The Creator in making man and his world what they were had a purpose more sublime than making him happy without effort and without self-respect.

God gave to man not a soul, but the capacity and opportunity for developing one. He endowed him with mind and heart, the mind with its powers of perceiving and understanding, and the heart with its desires and intuitions. If in an individual life these two powers mutually cooperated—but not otherwise—there would be gradually developed what God desired for each, a soul, i.e., a personality conscious of its individual integrity. And for the self-development of such individuals our world was the best conceivable environment. It was therefore not to be groaned over as "a vale of tears" but delighted in as "the vale of soul-making" (*Anth.*, 849).

Even as Keats's neo-Platonic ideas concerning cosmic beauty and love were derived from Spenser, so his belief that man should accept the conditions of life was Wordsworthian. He was a devoted reader of Wordsworth's *Excursion*, despite the fact that its style and manner were so different from his own, because its theme was the overcoming of despondency.[4] His conception of the way in which happiness might be pursued likewise showed the influence of Wordsworth in two notable respects. In the first place, he too represented that pursuit as no sudden leap from misery to joy, but as a gradual process of readjustments between the human mind and its environment, the mind becoming successively aware of new values in life. In the second place, Keats followed his contemporaneous master in giving a prominent place among those values to human sympathy and love, without which the attainment of happiness seemed to him impossible.

When Keats finally succeeded in clarifying what were to him "the gradations of happiness," or "a pleasure thermometer," he sent to his publisher a revision of the famous passage in *Endymion* (*Anth.*, 768; ll. 777–842), urging him to substitute it in place of the first version, and declaring

> I assure you that when I wrote it, it was the regular stepping stone of the Imagination towards a truth.

Probably the most important lines in this confession of his faith are these:

> Wherein lies happiness? In that which becks
> Our ready minds to fellowship divine,
> A fellowship with essence . . . (ll. 777–779)

[4] See, above, p. 100.

because properly understood, they disclose that principle which gave unity to Keats's ethical and literary ideas. The "essences" or absolute realities which, if we would be happy, we must learn by preference to commune with, are phenomena which reveal their divine or ideal origin and their own significance—aspects of nature, art, friendship, love, etc. Only the Imagination can thus behold them as they really are, and when they are thus beheld they are beautiful. Hence

> Beauty is truth; truth, beauty.

And hence the poet who imaginatively discovers and communicates whatever is beautiful is a revealer of truths otherwise inaccessible.

Themes and Style in the Poems of 1817.—The fact that Keats died so young, yet left us so many poems of supreme loveliness, is apt to give rise to the impression that perfection must have been natural and easy to him. As a matter of fact, however, a considerable part of his work was feeble or uneven, and he learned to master his art only through intense effort and after many missteps. He had to teach himself not only to overcome his own faults but also to recognize those of the writers whom he admired at the outset of his career, and he succeeded in doing so with astounding rapidity.

Of these the chief was Leigh Hunt, who, in the years when the young Keats fell under his spell, was engaged upon the *Story of Rimini.*[5] In the preface of that poem, Hunt, with the best of intentions, pleaded that the heroic couplet should be used in a much freer form than that to which the Neo-Classicists confined it: there should not always be a pause in the sense at the end of a line or couplet, run-on lines should be permitted, as well as occasional triplets, double rhymes, feminine rhymes, half-lines, and Alexandrines. And the diction of poetry ought to be much more natural and familiar than customary. Although Hunt's theory was perhaps sound, in practice it led him into mannerisms which were to have an undesirable influence upon his disciple. Too often Hunt confused with the natural what was merely the unprecise, loose, obscure, and common language of careless and thoughtless talk. He was too fond of nouns like "doings" and "measurings," adjectives like "rooty" and "scattery," and adverbs like "poutingly" and "smilingly." And he was capable of such stylistically vulgar phrases as that which he wrote concerning Dante's noble Francesca—"she had strict notions on the marrying score." Such expressions seemed to contemporaneous critics to justify the charge that the Cockney School was ill-bred. What was perhaps worse, Hunt's poetry was superficial in observation and thought. All these weaknesses left their impress upon some of Keats's earlier poems.

The most important of the poems in the volume of 1817 are "I Stood Tip-toe Upon a Little Hill," "Sleep and Poetry," and the sonnet on Chapman's Homer (*Anth.,* 748–51). In the first two, Keats showed his fealty

[5] See, below, p. 270.

to the Huntian romantic couplet, but used its freedom rather cautiously. The motto of "I Stood Tip-toe" was appropriately taken from the *Story of Rimini (Anth.,* 996); and the sentiment which rather loosely united the descriptive passages, was that what gave rise to poetry was the beauty of nature. Its loveliness had stimulated the imagination of the ancient Greeks to create their beautiful myths, and its movements and tones had suggested the rhythms and harmonies of verse. Between man and nature there was the instinctive sympathy of kinship, he being a part of nature distinguished from it only by his powers of self-consciousness and expression.

In *Sleep and Poetry (Anth.,* 752), written after a night in Hunt's library, Keats voiced his reverence for the awe-inspiring greatness and value of true poetry as the revealer of the mystery of life. He expressed his fears that he would not live to achieve poetic eminence, and he attacked the Neo-Classicists, handicraftsmen who were insensitive to nature, and with their heroic couplets

> Swayed about upon a rocking-horse
> And thought it Pegasus.

In these two poems it is not difficult to find effeminacies—"Kisses" rhyming with "blisses," and an inclination

> to pluck a posey
> Of luxuries bright, milky, soft, and rosy.

But there are also lines informed with Keats's true genius, like the sublime description of the ocean which

> Heaves calmly its broad swelling smoothness o'er
> Its rocky marge, and balances once more
> The patient weeds; that now unshent by foam
> Feel all about their undulating home.

In this volume, however, the clearest promise of his future power might be seen in the sonnet *On First Looking into Chapman's Homer (Anth.,* 751), with his superb association of what was most bold and glorious in ancient life and literature with one of the most adventurous and marvelous enterprises of the modern era.

Endymion.—The influence of Hunt upon Keats's style was gradually superseded by that of others. Among these, besides Chapman, were William Browne, author of *Britannia's Pastorals* (1613), a charming descriptive poem in romantic couplets; and George Sandys' translation of Ovid's *Metamorphoses* (1626), the folio edition of which, with annotations, was one of his favorite books. It is important to bear in mind that Keats's conception of that ancient Greek world in which he was so much interested came to him neither through a direct knowledge of the language, nor—as used to be thought—through prosaic dictionaries of antiquities, but through the Elizabethan or Jacobean poets—that is, through a "dome of many-colored glass" which conferred indeed a new beauty upon the ancient tradition but a beauty different from its own "white radiance." In other words, what Keats directly appreciated and found congenial was the Elizabethan temper; from the Greek he could take over only those elements which are universally human.

Far more important to Keats than Chapman, Browne, Sandys, or even Spenser, especially during the months when he was writing *Endymion*, was Shakspeare. In that poem, and thereafter, the Shakspearian influence is pervasive. To him even Spenser, as too pale and wan, must take a second place:

> O Golden Tongued Romance with serene lute!
>   Fair plumed Syren! Queen of faraway!
>   Leave melodizing on this wintry day
> Shut up thine olden pages and be mute:
> Adieu! for once again the fierce dispute,
>   Between damnation and impassioned clay
>   Must I burn through; once more humbly assay
> The bitter-sweet of this Shaksperian fruit.
>   On *King Lear*

Shakspeare was to Keats the greatest master of poetry as a creative art, even as Wordsworth was among philosophic poets the wisest and most humane. The former quickened his soul and style, the latter affected his beliefs and purposes.

These influences helped to make *Endymion* (*Anth.*, 758) a poem more serious in purpose and higher in achievement than his earlier works. Keats took the ancient myth of Endymion's love for Cynthia, the goddess of the moon, as he found it in Drayton's *Endimion and Phoebe*, in Sandys, and elsewhere, and retold it with an allegorical meaning. Some of the faults of his first volume he was still unable to overcome. As a narrative poem it was too digressive and much too obscure, the course and connection of the incidents being at times so uncertain as to result in tediousness. Partly because of that vagueness, the meaning of the allegory has been in dispute; but Keats's main intent was probably to set forth the quest of the soul for the ideal. The shepherd Endymion is drawn away from his people by his extraordinary love of nature, and presently aspires to win the goddess Cynthia. He undergoes the experience of discovering that for a human being there is no happiness in turning away from the love of humanity in order to pursue an ideal unrealizable by man. In the end he turns back to earthly scenes and affections, sadly supposing that he thereby has lost his heavenly love, only to find in the human also the divine. In many utterances Keats successfully seized opportunities which this parable gave to express his yearning for ideal love, his perception of the beauty of nature, and his sense for the claims of human affection; and therefore *Endymion*, defective as a whole, contains many passages of lovely poetical description and sentiment.

Lamia, Isabella, and The Eve of St. Agnes.—It was his last volume (1820) that contained (except for the final version of *Hyperion*) his greatest work. It began with three tales—*Lamia, Isabella,* and *The Eve of St. Agnes*—which showed a decided advance in narrative skill, Keats having learned to avoid excessive digression, and undesirable intrusion of his personal feelings. In this improvement he was aided by his study of two masters of narration, Boccaccio and Dryden.

. *Lamia (Anth.,* 821) was based upon a story told by Robert Burton in *The Anatomy of Melancholy* (1621), who in turn had derived it from Philostratus' biography of Apollonius Tyanæus, a Greek philosopher of the first century. It related that a pupil of Apollonius had been fascinated by a lamia, i.e., by a serpent in the guise of a beautiful woman; but that Apollonius, coming to their wedding feast, had discerned her true nature, whereupon she vanished. This legend Keats versified in the manner of Dryden's *Fables,* which were the best tales in verse written in the heroic couplet between the age of Chaucer and that of Keats himself. Under Dryden's influence he took fewer liberties with the couplet form, and caused his action to march forward with greater rapidity and clearer aim. But unlike Dryden, he told his story not solely for its own sake, but suggested that in the conflict between old Apollonius' pitiless science and the passion of his pupil and the beautiful Lamia there was typified the tragic conflict between intellect and feeling—

> Do not all charms fly
> At the mere touch of cold philosophy?

And repeatedly he rose to a pitch of emotional and imaginative intensity not characteristic of his predecessor, as in the description of Corinth at midnight, and in the passage describing the god Hermes wooing his beloved nymph:

> Upon the nymph his eyes he bent
> Full of adoring tears and blandishment,
> And towards her stept: she, like a moon in wane,
> Faded before him, cower'd, nor could restrain
> Her fearful sobs, self-folding like a flower
> That faints into itself at evening hour:
> But the God fostering her chilled hand,
> She felt the warmth, her eyelids opened bland,
> And, like new flowers at morning song of bees,
> Bloomed, and gave up her honey to the lees.
> Into the green-recessed woods they flew;
> Nor grew they pale, as mortal lovers do.

What point it was that Keats intended to stress in *Lamia* is disputed; but probably he wanted to show the tragic conflict between two extremes, both being falsities—false illusions in the lovers, and false, coldly factual knowledge in Apollonius. By contrast, the true ideal of Keats would later be shown in the Apollo of *Hyperion* and the Poet of the *Fall of Hyperion.*

Keats found the source of his *Isabella, or the Pot of Basil* (*Anth.*, 785) in the fifth novel of the fourth day of Boccaccio's *Decameron* (1353) . The summary of the sixteenth-century English translation read as follows:

> The three brethren of Isabella slew a gentleman that secretly loved her. His ghost appeared to her in her sleep, and showed her in what place they had buried his body. She, in silent manner, brought away his head, and putting it in a pot of earth, such as flowers, basil, and other sweet herbs are usually set in, she watered it a long while with her tears. Whereof her brothers having intelligence, soon after she died with mere conceit of sorrow.

The Italian master related this as a realistic tale of terror, and dwelt upon the action; Keats entirely changed its atmosphere by imaginatively elaborating the feelings and sentiments of Isabella and her lover. He used the *ottava rima,* which was often employed by Italian poets for tales in verse, and which had been recently reintroduced into English by Frere and by Byron.[6] But whereas they had made it a vehicle of mockery, Keats made it one of pathos. Byron, in *Beppo,* described Laura's grief in this manner:

> And Laura wailed long, and wept a little
> And thought of wearing weeds, as well she might;
> She almost lost all appetite for victual,
> And could not sleep with ease alone at night.

Keats on the same instrument voiced Isabella's grief in a different tone:

> She weeps alone for pleasures not to be;
> Sorely she wept until the night came on,
> And then, instead of love, O misery!
> She brooded o'er the luxury alone.

Keats rose to an even more beautiful achievement in *The Eve of St. Agnes* (*Anth.*, 806) . This was likewise based upon Boccaccio, but again the action was elevated into a higher atmosphere. It is the grosser Renaissance seen through the purifying medium of Spenser, to whose stanza Keats here returned, managing it with wonderful felicity.[7] Love as here described is reminiscent of Spenser in uniting a feeling for sensitiveness of form with chastity of spirit, for example, in the famous passage:

> Full on this casement shone the wintry moon
> And threw warm gules on Madeline's fair breast,
> As down she knelt for heaven's grace and boon;
> Rose-bloom fell on her hands, together pressed,
> And on her silver cross soft amethyst,
> And on her hair a glory, like a saint.

Briefer, but even more nearly perfect in every respect, was *La Belle Dame Sans Merci.*

---

[6] See, above, p. 201.
[7] There was also some influence of Chatterton.

In each of these four poems Keats had shown what love may make of life. In *Lamia*, it was love that spent itself upon a false and monstrous object; in *Isabella* it was love in bereavement and tears; in *The Eve of St. Agnes*, it was chivalrous love happily triumphant; in *La Belle Dame Sans Merci* (*Anth.*, 815), it was love hopeless and woe-begone; but whatever its circumstances or its issue, Keats garlanded its brow with beauty, placed it amid settings exquisitely appropriate to whatever aspect he desired to present, and always made us feel it, whether it created misery or joy, as an intense power. Historically *La Belle Dame Sans Merci* was to become important for its influence on the Pre-Raphaelites, especially Rossetti and Morris.

The Sonnets and Odes.—Although in his verse tales Keats could keep his lyrical impulses under control, he needed outlets for them, and found them in the sonnet and the ode. In the sonnet, Shakspeare was again his chief inspiration and model; and not a few critics place Keats's sonnets next to those of his master. Robert Bridges, author of the noble *Testament of Beauty*, appreciated in them especially the absence of that self-consciousness which sonneteers have difficulty in avoiding; and he listed the following eight in order of merit, as nearly flawless and among the best in our language:

"Much Have I Traveled in the Realms of Gold"
"When I Have Fears That I May Cease to Be"
"Come Hither All Sweet Maidens Soberly"
"Four Seasons Fill the Measure of the Year"
"Bright Star, Would I Were Steadfast as Thou Art"
"O Soft Embalmer of the Still Midnight"
"I Cry Your Mercy—Pity—Love! Ay, Love!"
"As Hermes Once Took to His Feathers Light"

to which should be added, by general consent of the best critics,

"The Day Is Gone and All Its Sweets Are Gone."

(These nine sonnets are all in the *Anthology*.)

The lyric form, however, which was most congenial of all to Keats was the ode. Here he surpassed his predecessors so much, and was so individual, that he cannot be said to have had a master. In his odes, those strong personal feelings and preferences which he rightly suppressed in his verse-tales found direct, not allegorical, utterance—his delight in the loveliness of autumn and the song of the nightingale, his melancholy over the evanescence of beautiful things, and his enthusiasm over their achieving a new and immortal life in art and literature. The feelings and thoughts are harmonious, but so rich and varied that critics have erred by stressing only one strain in the harmony and by supposing that the other strains were contradictory. But, as R. H. Fogle says of the *Ode to a Nightingale,* and as is also true of the other great odes, they "express an exquisite awareness of the existence of joy and melancholy, pleasure and pain, and art and life. They express a feeling that these are inseparable, although not identical, and they express acceptance of the inseparability of the elements of human experience." The informal ode, with its spaciousness, its dignity and exaltation of tone, and its freedom and variety of metre and lines, was exactly suited to express the temper of Keats, his high seriousness, his meditativeness, his leisurely and caressing manner of approaching a thought, and his fondness for developing and enriching it with abundance of concrete imagery. Brisker and balanced measures, requiring the nimble and sprightly, would have been unsuited to him who saw beauty chiefly in its intricate or undulating forms.

The Two Versions of Hyperion.—Necessary as the lyric was to Keats for personal expression, he rightly felt that the greatest poetry was dramatic or epic. His most ambitious final effort was to compose an epic, *Hyperion,* originally planned to extend to about ten books, of which only two and a half were finished. The subject was that overthrow of the Titans by the true gods of which he had read in Chapman's *Homer* and *Hesiod* and in Sandys' *Ovid.* Characteristically, he intended to interpret the downfall of the primordial rulers of the universe as being due to the fact that their power was that of mere brute force. They were therefore fated to fall when there arose, in Apollo, a nobler type of power— a god whose strength lay in beauty, enlightenment, and poetry, and who had attained his godhead through becoming acquainted with grief and tears.

In his endeavor to write this epic, Keats's chief inspiration was Milton. Milton's earlier poems, especially *Comus,* had from the first influenced him; but what now deeply impressed him was the style of *Paradise Lost.* Indeed in his first version, published as *Hyperion: a Fragment (Anth.,* 793), the occurrences of Miltonic diction, syntax, and mannerisms were so frequent that Keats decided to recast the poem. He wrote to Reynolds (Sept. 22, 1819):

> I have given up *Hyperion;* there are too many Miltonic inversions in it. Miltonic verse cannot be written but in an artful, or rather an artist's humor. I wish to give myself up to other sensations.

Since the actions he intended to relate were not as traditional as those of an epic were supposed to be, but were almost entirely his own invention, he entitled the second version of *Hyperion "A Vision" (Anth.,* 831).

In this version the poet, in his dream, passes from a garden where he "ate deliciously" (19–40) and drank an enchanted draught (41–59), through the richly stored temple (60–85) to the altar, where the true nature of poetry is disclosed to him (87–215). It is an allegory of the stages in the highest development of human character. It should be compared with Wordsworth's ages of man, for similarities in substance and contrasts in style. The garden is the youthful period of merely sensuous delight; the temple, that of knowledge, art, and philosophy, serves the period of intellectual curiosity, in which likewise one may wander purposeless; the altar, that of inspired truth and unselfish dedication, marks the hour when true self-knowledge is attained. Keats felt that up to this time his work had been too largely that of a dreamer, a self-indulgent wanderer in the garden and through the temple, too detached from his fellow beings and of too little service to them. (This self-condemning opinion was either entirely mistaken or a considerable exaggeration, but it was sincerely and strongly held.) The poet imagines that at the altar he is given a last opportunity to rise to a higher understanding of a true poet's functions, and by a most painful effort he succeeds in mounting the first step (105–133). He is rewarded by new strength, and by the disclosure to him through the prophetess, Moneta, of the secret of great poetry—its sympathy with human suffering, a sympathy which dreamers and self-worshippers [Byron] lack (134–210). After this prelude, the poet is privileged, under Moneta's guidance, to behold the Fall of Hyperion, one of Saturn's Titans, who, when the action of the poem begins, is still the ruler of the sun but who is to be overthrown by Apollo. In Keats's view, Hyperion fell because he was a god of mere power. Apollo won because he was a god of enlightenment, of beauty, and of beneficence to mankind.

Critics differ as to the relative merits of the two versions of *Hyperion*. Since both are fragments, it is difficult to compare and judge them. Artistically, the first version has the advantage of being more nearly homogeneous and sustained, and the changes made in some of the lines were usually not improvements. In content, however, the second version is distinctly the more important, for it includes Keats's maturest and fullest expression of his feelings concerning a problem which always seemed to him crucial—namely, what were the highest functions of a poet, and what should be his attitude toward his fellowmen. The introduction of *The Fall of Hyperion: A Vision* described the stages in the development of a true poet; moreover, in so doing, since in Keats's mind the poetic spirit and the human spirit at its best were identical, it likewise disclosed his conceptions of the phases through which all of us must pass if we are to attain culture and happiness.

The Development of His Poetic Style.—To Keats the aim of poetry was on the one hand the discovery of the real, and on the other its complete and intense expression. Always there was the hard problem of mastering the most appropriate expressional means. W. J. Bate's recent studies, based upon detailed scrutiny of metrical and other data, show how Keats worked out increasingly skilful methods of utterance, metrical, phonetic, etc. His constant effort was to find a prosody really congenial to poesy:

> So if we will not let the Muse be free,
> She will be bound with garlands *of her own*.

It was a valiant struggle against errors of taste and judgment, some traditional errors, some subjective; and it reached as nearly complete a victory as human fallibility allows. At first, in *Endymion,* Keats sought unprecedented freedom in prosody, and fell into excessive luxury and laxness. In *Isabella* his diction and rhythm grew less soft and liquescent, and its stanzas were not so loosely knit as the earlier couplets. Thereafter intensity, harmonized with its apparent opposite, restraint, became the goal. The most profound and precise truth about every actuality—including its relationships to its origins—became, when passionately expressed, beauty, i.e., the poetry in which truth and beauty coexist. In *Hyperion* Keats further developed his tendency toward restraint of expression and integrity of the blank-verse line; and in *The Eve of St. Agnes* he succeeded in combining impassioned richness of diction, sounds, and metaphors, with firm patterns of stanzaic form. In his later sonnets he sought a movement with a slow and satisfying rise, and a close which "sets soberly although in magnificence" (above, p. 224). In the *Odes* his stylistic achievement reached its height—dynamic diction, effulgence of imagery and sound, held within "forms of strict sobriety and classical restraint." It was the union of power and grace—

> Might half-slumbering on its own right arm.

Lamia, in form more nearly Augustan than any other couplet-poem of the century, seemed to mark a departure toward an uncertain and never-reached goal; but in *To Autumn,* his last great poem, Keats returned to the style of his earlier odes. There is a poignant contrast during the years 1816 to 1820 between the decline of his health and happiness, and the upward surge of his stylistic power. Toward the end he achieved an unperturbed assurance of expression, a priest-like self-forgetfulness like that of a celebrant before a sacred altar.

His Relation to Other Romantics.—Keats differs markedly and obviously from the Romantics studied in the preceding chapters. He is almost the antithesis of Byron, whose gloom and mockery he equally disliked; and his concern is not that reanimation of the historic past which was a leading purpose with Scott, Southey, and Landor. He was not a critic of everyday life like Charles Lamb; and although none of the Romantics had a greater reverence for poetry and poets, he was not a critic of literature like Coleridge, Lamb, and Hazlitt. His opinions on politics, and on prose literature, were often similar to those of Hazlitt, whom he admired. His views on poetry were in harmony with those of Wordsworth, but he did not convey them in a didactic or philosophical manner. He veiled his thoughts in allegory, or suggested them through imagery. Hence he seemed to Leigh Hunt (Essay on Keats; *Anth.,* 1013), and to many others, "a poet of the most poetical kind"—so beautiful in style that he was mistakenly supposed to be unconcerned about purpose or meaning.

Not even Wordsworth responded emotionally to sights and sounds as palpitatingly as Keats. Joseph Severn testifies to his intense delight in them as follows:

> Nothing seemed to escape him, the song of a bird and the undernote of response from covert or hedge, the rustle of some animal, the changing of the green and brown lights and furtive shadows, the motions of the wind —just how it took certain tall flowers and plants—and the wayfaring of the clouds; even the features and gestures of passing tramps, the color of one woman's hair, the smile on one child's face . . . Certain things affected him extremely, particularly when "a wave was billowing through a tree," as he described the uplifting surge of air among swaying masses of chestnut or oak foliage, or when, afar off, he heard the wind coming across the woodlands. "The tide! The tide!" he would cry delightedly, and spring on to some stile, or upon the low bough of a wayside tree, and watch the passage of the wind upon the meadow-grasses or young corn, not stirring till the flow of air was all around him, while an expression of rapture made his eyes gleam and his face glow till he would look sometimes "like a wild faun waiting for some cry from the forest depths," or like "a young eagle staring with proud joy," before taking flight.

To impart such enthusiasms to others was his aim—to make us feel more joyously than we have ever felt that this world of ours is full of beauty— the beauty of nature, of love, of art, and of poesy. None of the other Romantics surpassed him in sensuousness of appeal, richness of colors, exquisiteness of rhythm, and stateliness of forms.

SELECTED BIBLIOGRAPHY

OF FIRST IMPORTANCE

Selections

Complete Poems and Selected Letters, ed. C. De W. Thorpe (Doubleday) , 1935. — Exceptionally well edited and annotated.

Autobiography, ed. Earle V. Weller (Stanford Univ. Press) , 1933. — Compiled from his Letters.

Texts

The Poetical Works of John Keats, ed. H. W. Garrod (Oxford) , 1939. — Textually the best.

The Poems of John Keats, ed. Ernest De Selincourt (Dodd Mead) , 1905; 5th ed. revised, 1926. — Excellent annotations and commentary.

The Letters of John Keats, ed. H. Buxton Forman (Oxford) , 1895; 3rd ed., 1947. — Best complete edition.

Best Biography

This is a disputed question — the choice, for introductory purposes, lying between the next two, viz.:

Colvin, Sidney; *John Keats: His Life and Poetry, His Friends, Critics, and After-Fame,* 1917. — By some regarded as sounder in taste and in judgment than Miss Lowell's.

Lowell, Amy; *John Keats,* 2 vols., 1925. — Valuable new data, and vigorous original opinions.

Finney's *Evolution of Keats's Poetry*, 1936, is listed under "Advanced," below. — A good *brief* biography is B. I. Evans' *Keats* (Great Lives) , 1934.

The Best Introductory Criticisms

Until about fifteen years ago, the critics belonged to opposite schools: (1) those who assumed that Keats was (for better or worse) preoccupied with the creation of beauty; and (2) those who believed that he also was evolving some kind of philosophy. The chief critics of the first school were:

Rossetti, W. M.; *Life of Keats*, 1887.

More, Paul Elmer; *Shelburne Essays;* IV, 1906. Unsympathetic.

Symons, Arthur; in *Keats Memorial Volume*, 1921.

Lowell, Amy; *John Keats*, 2 vols., 1925.

The chief critics of the second school were:

Arnold, Matthew; *Essays in Criticism: Second Series*, 1888.

Bridges, R. S.; Introduction of the Muses Library edition of Keats, 1896; rprtd. in *Collected Essays*, IV, 1929.

De Selincourt, Ernest; Introduction and Notes to *Poems of Keats*, 1905.

Murry, J. Middleton; *Keats and Shakespeare*, 1925. — Penetrating criticism, rich in suggestions. Sometimes draws from Keats's statements inferences which the poet himself did not actually express.

Thorpe, C. De W.; *The Mind of John Keats*, 1926. — The ideas of Keats, especially on art and poetry. Cf. Thorpe's Introduction to edition of *Poems and Letters*, 1935.

The best introductory criticisms since c. 1926 are:

Ridley, M. R.; *Keats's Craftsmanship: A Study in Poetic Development*, 1933. — Careful study, poem by poem; their beauty the main interest.

Bate, W. J.; *The Stylistic Development of Keats*, 1945. — Carefully traces the increasingly skilful methods of expression which Keats evolved in his search for Truth and Reality. See rev., MLN, LX, 476; 1946.

FOR ADVANCED STUDENTS

Important Additional Texts

The Poetical Works and Other Writings of John Keats, ed. with Notes and Appendices by H. Buxton Forman, revised by Maurice Buxton Forman (Hampstead Ed.) , 8 vols., 1938–39. — A handsome edition, limited to 1,025 copies.

Poems [of 1817] (The English Replicas) , 1934. — Facsimile.

Endymion, ed. H. Clement Notcutt (Oxford) , 1927. — Facsimile.

Lamia, Isabella, etc. (The English Replicas) , 1934. — Facsimile of the Poems of 1820.

Hyperion: A Facsimile of Keats's Autograph Manuscript, ed. Ernest De Selincourt (Oxford) , 1905.

Biographical and Critical

Hunt, Leigh; Proem to Selections from Keats's Poems, in *Imagination and Fancy*, 1844. (*Anth.*, 1013) . — Cf. Hunt's *Lord Byron and Some of His Contemporaries*, 1828.

Brown, Charles Armitage; *Life of Keats*, ed. Dorothy H. Bodurtha and W. B. Pope, 1937. — Probably the earliest written biography now extant; important for 1818–20. Cf. Finney, ELH, v, 16; 1938.

Milnes, Richard Monckton (Lord Houghton) ; *Life, Letters, and Literary Remains of John Keats*, 2 vols., 1848; rev. 1857. — In Everyman's Library, 1927; in World's Classics, 1931. — The first published biography; still valuable. The inclusion of the letters was especially important because they offered indications of those intellectual interests of Keats which Hunt and the Rossettis tended to ignore, and which were to be recognized later.

Clarke, C. Cowden; *Recollections of Writers*, 1878. — By Keats's teacher and early friend.

Shelley and Keats as They Struck Their Contemporaries, ed. Edmund Blunden, 1925. — Partly from manuscript sources. — Cf. C. De W. Thorpe on an early review, JEGP, XLIII, 336; 1944.

Letters of Fanny Brawne to Fanny Keats, ed. Fred Edgcumbe, 1937. — Should silence the detractors of Fanny Brawne.

———

Owen, Mrs. Frances Mary; *John Keats: A Study*, 1880. — One of the first serious attempts to analyze the meaning of Keats's poems.

Bridges, Robert; Introduction to Muses Library ed. of Keats's *Poems*, 1896.

Bradley, A. C.; "The Letters of Keats," *Oxford Lectures on Poetry*, 1909.

Wolff, Lucien; *John Keats: Sa Vie et Son Oeuvre*, 1910. — A detailed study of the life and the literary qualities. — Shortened and improved ed., 1929.

Elliott, G. R.; "The Real Tragedy of Keats," PMLA, XXXVI, 315; 1921. — Holds that Keats's artistic powers and his original poetic gusto did not keep pace with his intellectual development, and that he would have achieved greater work if he had lived longer.

The John Keats Memorial Volume, 1921. — Among the more important essays are those by E. De Selincourt and Lascelles Abercrombie, and especially that by A. C. Bradley on "Keats and Philosophy."

Havens, R. D.; *The Influence of Milton on English Poetry*, ch. 10, 1922.

Fausset, Hugh I'A.; *Keats: a Study in Development*, 1922. — Maintains that he advanced "from sensationalism to vision, from idealization to idealism" and died "on the very threshold of absolute truth." — Not careful enough about chronology and documentation, but stimulating.

Garrod, H. W.; *Keats*, 1926. — Represents a return to the Pre-Raphaelite tendency in the criticism of Keats. Admits that he evolved a philosophy, but thinks he ruined his poetry whenever he allowed philosophy to affect it, and is at his best when he allows his senses to rule. — Cf. Royall Snow, below, 1928.

Thorpe, C. De W.; "Wordsworth and Keats," PMLA, XLII, 1010; 1927.

Spurgeon, Caroline F. E.; *Keats's Shakespeare: A Descriptive Study Based on New Material*, 1928; 2nd ed., 1929. — Valuable discussion of the marginal annotations in Keats's copy of Shakspeare, now in the Princeton University Library.

Murry, J. Middleton; *Studies in Keats*, 1930; 2nd ed., with three new essays, 1939. — Sensitive, thoughtful, sometimes opinionative. — Attacked by Lord Gorrell, *Keats* (1948).

Roberts, John H.; "Poetry of Sensation or of Thought," PMLA, XLV, 1129; 1930. — At the end, Keats surrenders to sensuous beauty.

Fairchild, H. N.; *The Romantic Quest*, 1931. — On Keats's medievalism, and on his aesthetics.

Thorpe, C. De W.; "Keats's Interest in Politics," PMLA, XLVI, 1228; 1931.

Crawford, Alexander W.; *The Genius of Keats: An Interpretation*, 1932. — Finds and vindicates a philosophy in his work.

Marsh, G. L., and White, N. I.: "Keats and the Periodicals of His Time," MP, xxii, 37; 1934. — Reviews of 1816–21; majority favorable.

Olney, Clarke; "Keats and Haydon," PMLA, xlix, 258; 1934.

Havens, R. D.; "Unreconciled Opposites in Keats," PQ, xiv, 289; 1935.

Finney, Claude L.; *The Evolution of Keats's Poetry,* 2 vols., 1936. — Admirably thorough in relating the life to the work, but too systematic. Cf. Thorpe's rev., ELH, iv, 12; 1937.

James, D. G.; *Scepticism and Poetry,* 1937.

Hewlett, Dorothy; *Adonais: A Life of John Keats,* 1937. — Sometimes naive; but spirited, and good on the effects of the reviewers and on the contemporary background.

Haber, T. B.; "The Unifying Principle of Love in Keats's Poetry," PQ, xvi, 192; 1937.

Wagenblass, J. H.; "Keats's Roaming Fancy," *Harvard Studies and Notes,* xx, 123; 1938. — His interest in Herrick, etc. Cf. "Keats and Lucretius," MLR, xxxii, 537; 1937.

Hale-White, William; *Keats as Doctor and Patient,* 1938. — Cf. M. B. Forman, ed., *Keats's Anatomical and Physiological Note Book,* 1934.

Bate, W. J.; *Negative Capability: The Intuitive Approach in Keats,* 1939. — Cf. his *Stylistic Development,* 1945, above, under "Of First Importance."

Zillman, L. J.; *John Keats and the Sonnet Tradition,* Los Angeles, 1939. — His relation closer to the Petrarchan and Shakspearian than to the Wordsworthian sonnet. Cf. Thorpe's rev., ELH, viii, 15; 1940.

Wright, Walter F.; "A Sudden Development in Keats's Poetic Method," *State Coll. of Wash. Studies,* viii, 113; 1940.

Du Bos, Charles; *What Is Literature?,* 1940. — Keats one of the three greatest poets.

Pershing, J. H.; "John Keats: When Was He Born and When Did He Die?" PMLA, lv, 802; 1940; and "Reply" by H. E. Briggs, PMLA, lvi, 592; 1941. — Cf. ELH, ix, 15; 1942.

McLuhan, H. M.; "Aesthetic Pattern in Keats's Odes," *Univ. Toronto Quart.,* xii, 167; 1943.

Ford, George H.; *Keats and the Victorians: 1821–95,* 1944. — His rise to fame and his great influence on Tennyson, Rossetti, etc. — Cf. Clarice Short, in PMLA, lix, 513, 1944, on Morris; and Rollins, below, 1946.

Spender, Stephen; "The Sensuous World of Keats," *Penguin New Writing,* 1944.

Caldwell, J. R.; *John Keats' Fancy,* 1945. — Good on his relation to associationist aesthetics, but exaggerates the importance of "wild spontaneous ranging." — Cf. reviews of Bate and Caldwell, MLN, lx, 466; 1945.

Tate, Allen; "A Reading of Keats," *Amer. Scholar,* xv, 55; 1945–46. — Pompous; too obscure for brief comment; but see ELH, xiv, 15; 1947.

Rollins, H. E.; *Keats's Reputation in America to 1848,* 1946. — His increasing vogue, especially after 1829, fostered by Willis, Lowell, etc.

Miles, Josephine; *Major Adjectives in English Poetry* (Univ. of Cal. Publ.) , 1946. — With Spenser, Milton, and Collins, Keats one of the greatest users of magnificent adjectives.

Fogle, Richard H.; "Empathic Imagery in Keats and Shelley," PMLA, lxi, 163; 1946. — The projection of the poet into the object is found more in Keats than in Shelley, and Keats is more successful in drawing the reader into intimacy with the object.

Beyer, William W.; *Keats and the Dæmon King,* 1947. — The influence of the German poet Wieland's romantic epic, *Oberon,* on many of Keats's poems. — Cf. Thorpe's rev., ELH, xiv, 10; 1947.

Thorpe, C. De W.; "Keats and Hazlitt," PMLA, LXXII, 487; 1947. — Their admiration for each other. Hazlitt "a sort of self-appointed champion" of Keats.

Stallman, R. W.; "Keats the Apollinian," UTQ, XVI, 143; 1947. — A poet who is a painter of the sensuous here-and-now; not like Shelley of the moving world-that-is-to-be.

On Individual Poems

These references are *supplementary* to the important general works listed above, by Colvin, De Selincourt, Amy Lowell, Ridley, Finney, Murry, Thorpe, Bate, etc., which discuss most of the chief poems.

On First Looking into Chapman's Homer: Grace Landrum, PMLA, XLII, 986 (1927); B. I. Evans, *Essays and Studies*, XVI, 26 (1930); J. L. Lowes, TLS, Oct. 12 (1933); J. W. Beach, PMLA, XLIX, 246 (1934); K. G. Pfeiffer, N&Q, CLXXV, 203 (1938); H. E. Briggs, PMLA, LIX, 184 (1944); and especially Harris, Mabbott, and Walcutt, EXP, March and Dec. (1946), and June (1947).

On Seeing the Elgin Marbles: Hyder Rollins in *Studies in Honor of A. H. R. Fairchild*, 1946.

Endymion: Leonard Brown, "The Genesis, Growth, and Meaning of Endymion," SP, XXX, 618 (1933); E. S. Le Comte, *Endymion in England*, (1944); H. E. Briggs, "Keats's Conscious and Unconscious Reactions to Criticism," PMLA, LX, 1106 (1945); and W. W. Beyer, *Keats and the Dæmon King* (Wieland's influence) (1947).
N. F. Ford, "Endymion — A Neo-Platonic Allegory?" ELH, XIV, 64 (1947), and "Fellowship with Essence," PMLA, LXII, 1061 (1947) maintains that the theme is merely the "quest of an everlasting erotism," and that "essence" signifies "things." This is out of accord with most critics, except Miss Lowell, who termed the poem an "idealization of sexual love." — See Thorpe's rev., ELH, XV, 20; 1948.

Hyperion and *The Fall of Hyperion:* On the question which was the earlier, C. L. Finney, JEGP, XXVI, 304 (1927), following Amy Lowell, held *The Fall* the first; but this is disproved by J. M. Murry, *Keats and Shakespeare* (1925) and Douglas Bush, MLN, XLIX, 281 (1934). — On the stylistic differences, W. J. Bate, *Stylistic Development* (1945), pp. 171–182; also Ridley, *Craftsmanship* (1933). — On other points: Helen Darbishire, "Keats and Egypt," RES, III, 9 (1927); J. M. Caldwell, "The Meaning of Hyperion," PMLA, LI, 1080 (1936); and J. L. Lowes, "Moneta's Temple," PMLA, LI, 1098 (1936).

The Eve of St. Agnes: EXP, Nov. and Dec., 1942; June, 1943; Oct., 1944. — *The Eve of St. Mark:* W. E. Houghton, ELH, XIII, 64; 1946. — *La Belle Dame Sans Mercy:* EXP, Oct., 1946; Feb., May, and Dec., 1947. — *Ode to Psyche:* T. S. Eliot, *Use of Poetry*, p. 91; R. F. Rashbrook, N&Q, CLXII, 385; 1947.

Ode to a Nightingale: Charles Williams, *Reason and Beauty in the Poetic Mind*, 1933, pp. 63–81; A. W. Crawford, *The Genius of Keats*, 1932; S. P. Pitcher and C. S. Kilby, EXP, March, 1945, and Feb., 1947; and especially Richard H. Fogle "A Note on the Ode to a Nightingale," MLQ, VIII, 81; 1947.

Ode on a Grecian Urn: R. H. Snow "Heresy Concerning Keats," PMLA, XLIII, 1142 (1928), stressing the sensory elements; refuted by Mary E. Shipman, "Orthodoxy Concerning Keats," PMLA, XLIV, 929 (1929). — "Keats and Ourselves," TLS, Nov. 10, Dec. 22 (1945), Jan. 26, Feb. 2 (1946). — Especially notable is Cleanth Brooks, *The Well Wrought Urn* (1947); cf. Kenneth Burke, "Symbolic Action in a Poem," *Accent* (Autumn, 1943); and S. C. Wilcox, EXP (Oct., 1947). See also H. Pettit, "Scientific Correlatives," SP, 1943.

Ode on Melancholy: On Relation to *Grecian Urn*, R. D. Havens, MP, XXIV, 209 (1926); also R. H. Fogle, MLQ, VIII, 81 (1947). — A strained interpretation in William Empson, *Seven Types of Ambiguity* (1930), p. 272.

Lamia: J. H. Roberts, PMLA, I, 550 (1935) , and Finney, *Evolution* (1936) , give interpretations that do not seem as acceptable as Thorpe's Introduction to *Complete Poems* (1935) , p. xliv, and Bate's *Stylistic Development* (1945) , pp. 146–171.

To Autumn: Admirable appreciation by Anna J. Mill, TLS, Feb. 2, 1946.

Concordance

Baldwin, D. L., Broughton, L. N., et al.; *A Concordance to the Poems of John Keats*, 1917.

Bibliographies

Finney, C. L.; *The Evolution of Keats's Poetry*, 1936, vol. II. — List of manuscript material.

Forman, H. B. and Forman, M. B., eds.; Hampstead Edition of the *Works* (1938–39) , vol. I, pp. xcix–cxxviii, "List of Principal Works Concerning Keats."

There is need of an up-to-date critical bibliography of Keats. The English Association Leaflet, No. 23 *(Short Bibliographies)* , 1912, is obsolete; and Warren L. Perry's thorough *Bibliography of Keats*, Urbana, Ill., 1933, is available in typescript in only a few libraries.

Addenda (appeared too late to be inserted above in their proper place)

The Keats Circle: Letters and Papers: 1816–1878, ed., Hyder E. Rollins (1948) . — Review by C. D. Thorpe, NYT, Dec. 19, 1948.

Lord Gorrell, *John Keats: The Principle of Beauty* (1948) . — Review, TLS, Nov. 27, 1948.

CHAPTER 15

PERCY BYSSHE SHELLEY

(August 4, 1792–July 8, 1822)

His Early Life.—Bysshe Shelley, the grandfather of the poet, was a well-to-do squire, romantic in his youth and eccentric in his old age, who was knighted for political services to the Duke of Norfolk. Sir Bysshe's eldest son, Timothy, a member of parliament, was an adherent of the Liberal party, but narrowly conventional in most respects, as well as vain, hot-headed, and obstinate. He married Elizabeth Pilfold, whose disposition was gentle and kindly, but whose views were no broader than his own. Of this union was born at Field Place near Horsham in Sussex, as the eldest son and heir, on August 4, 1792, Percy Bysshe Shelley, whose temperament could hardly have found a more unsuitable environment than that of the British squirearchy. If he had been like others of his class, he would have passed through Eton and Oxford, without unusual perturbations, and would have settled down to the sensible performance of the responsibilities, and the whole-hearted enjoyment of the privileges and sports, of the society into which he was born. He was sent to Eton and Oxford, but his conduct there was incomprehensible to his family.

As a child, he had been very happy, playful, mischievous, gentle, and affectionate. When, at the age of ten, he was sent away to school, however, and had his first experience of the so-called fagging system, under which the younger boys were at the beck and call of the older, and might be thrashed for disobedience, his fiery temper caused him to revolt. The tyrannous attitude and methods of the teachers were likewise provocative to him: as a gesture of protest, he blew up the boundary-palings of the schoolyard with gunpowder. From tormentors young and old he sought refuge in a world of fancy. He lost himself in the romances of Mrs. Radcliffe and "Monk" Lewis. He was fascinated by those aspects of science which the Tales of Terror dwelt upon—namely, the spectacular and apparently magical, and attempted physical and chemical experiments which were not part of the regular courses. His only sympathizer during his Eton days was a shrewd old physician, Dr. Lind, of Windsor, who had traveled in the East and was regarded as eccentric. It was perhaps Lind who, little realizing what a decisive course of events he was initiating, introduced Shelley to William Godwin's *Political Justice*. At fifteen Shelley vowed himself to the cause of reform, which he was never to desert, in these lines:

> I will be wise
> And just and free, and mild, if in me lies
> Such power; for I grow weary to behold
> The selfish and the strong still tyrannize
> Without reproach or check.

In the summer vacation before entering Oxford, he was attracted by his cousin Harriet Grove; and his parents, approving of the union, were pleased to regard them as engaged. He, however, was more deeply interested in the publication of some verses which he and his sister had composed, and which were privately published as *Original Poetry, by Victor and Cazire*. At this time he also wrote a poem on the Wandering Jew, and a novel *Zastrozzi*, which showed the effect of the Tales of Terror upon his youthful imagination.

In October, 1810, Shelley entered Oxford, where rigid conservatism was dominant among the faculty. At first, however, he found the freedom which the students were allowed, after the constant supervision that had galled him at Eton, delightful and stimulating. Here he could, without objections, indulge his interest in scientific experimentation; and his rooms soon became cluttered with chemical materials and instruments. His efforts were directed toward the more spectacular possibilities of science rather than toward plodding research. The regular courses did not interest him, and the professors and dons seemed to him contemptible holders of ecclesiastical sinecures. The students he despised because they were wholly absorbed in athletics, amusements, and dissipation. He found only one friend—Thomas Jefferson Hogg, the first recognizer of his genius, and just as much opposed to conventionalism as Shelley himself. Together they read the great skeptics—Locke, Hume, and Voltaire —and acquired the zeal of rebellious reformers.

In the innocence of his heart, Shelley expressed some of his unorthodox views in letters to Harriet Grove. Being an entirely conventional maiden, she was alarmed by them; and when he returned home on his Christmas vacation, he found that she would no longer encourage his attentions. Shocked by the discovery that his search for truth resulted in estrangement from those who took their standards from society, he returned to college in a mood of fiery indignation against the established order. It seemed to him that the bases of conventionalism, intolerance, bigotry, and tyranny, rested upon the dogmas of the established church, and that therefore faith in God, whom the priests professed to know, was the root of all error. In that state of mind, he and Hogg wrote *The Necessity of Atheism* (what it actually advocated was agnosticism). The pamphlet was put on sale in the college book-store. A horrified don brought it to the attention of the authorities, who promptly expelled Shelley and Hogg from the university.

The disgraced friends went to London; and Shelley's irate father, sputtering in rage and perplexity, descended upon him. Shelley refused to recant his beliefs, and his parent declared that unless he did so no support would be given him. He lived frugally and was helped by friends and by his loyal young sisters, who were at school at Clapham, a few miles north of the city, and whom he often visited there. One of their schoolmates was Harriet Westbrook, aged sixteen. Her father had been the proprietor of a coffee house. She had a sister, Eliza, much older than herself and not unaware of what advantages Harriet might reap from an acquaintance with a prospectively wealthy young aristocrat. Shelley did not fall in love with Harriet; but, as he did in the case of all whom he met, he talked and wrote to her about his radical ideas in the hope of making her a convert to them.

He pursued his scientific interests by taking a course in anatomy and by beginning the study of medicine at St. Bartholomew's hospital. After a few months, however, the quarrel between him and his father was patched up, and he returned home. His father agreed to give him an allowance of c. £200 a year, and to let him live wherever he chose. Shelley went to Wales, and there met Elizabeth Hitchener, a schoolmistress aged twenty-nine (ten years older than himself), who had sufficient education to talk intelligently with him about his scientific and philosophical enthusiasms, and to whom he wrote voluminous letters on such themes, intermingled with indiscreet expressions of his admiration and affection for her as his "image of intellectual beauty."

In August, 1811, Shelley received word from Harriet Westbrook that her father insisted upon her returning to school and that this was nothing less than persecution since at school she had become "universally hated" because of her acquaintance with "Shelley the atheist." Would he not protect her from such cruelty? To Shelley she seemed a victim of that system of parental tyranny and religious bigotry which was so odious to him. Quixotically he hurried to London, and eloped with Harriet to Edinburgh. In theory he was opposed to the institution of matrimony, but "because of the disproportionate sacrifice which the female was called upon to make" in defying social conventions, he married Harriet on August 28, 1811, she being then sixteen and he barely nineteen. Shelley's friend Hogg was with them in Edinburgh; and when, in October, he had to return to York, they followed him thither.

On learning that his son had married without his parents' consent, Timothy Shelley stopped his allowance. Hoping to assuage his father's wrath Shelley journeyed home, leaving Harriet at York, where her sister Eliza came to visit her. On his return, after an unsuccessful conference with his father, Shelley discovered that Hogg had tried to seduce Harriet. Although Hogg's frank confession of his impulsive misdemeanor moved Shelley to forgiveness, this loss of faith in his closest friend was a deep shock to him. The Shelleys left York immediately, went to Keswick, and took a cottage near Southey. Shelley at first respected Southey as "a man of virtue," although he disapproved of his political conservatism.

What Shelley desired to devote his life to was the service of all kinds of liberal causes, including the improvement of the living conditions of the common people, but such unremunerative crusading would obviously be impossible unless he could obtain an income sufficient for his support. His father and grandfather, interested only in the perpetuation of the family name and wealth, now tempted the young idealist with a splendid offer of c. £2,000 a year, on condition that he would consent to entail the Shelley property upon his eldest son. He had previously horrified them with what seemed to them the insanely generous statement, that, if he had his way, the estate upon his father's death should not go to himself alone but should be divided equally among himself, his mother, and his sisters. And self-sacrificingly true to his principle that the method of bestowing property by primogeniture was socially evil, he rejected his elders' proposal. For the time being he was helped by an allowance of c. £200 annually from Mr. Westbrook; and finally his father grudgingly allowed him an equal amount.

The problem of support thus being temporarily solved, Shelley promptly threw himself into the first cause he could find—that of Catholic Emancipation, then being strongly agitated in Ireland. Going to Dublin, and having his *Address to the Irish People* (1812) printed there, he and Harriet distributed the pamphlets broadcast. In this campaign against sectarian intolerance, he also spoke at a public meeting. After two months, failing to effect any results (the cause was not won until years later), Shelley returned to England, continuing there his pamphleteering on behalf of liberty, writing his *Declaration of Rights* and launching copies of it into the air, attached to small balloons, and into the sea in sealed bottles. When a printer was prosecuted for publishing Paine's agnostic *Age of Reason,* Shelley expostulated in his *Letter to Lord Ellenborough.* His friend Miss Hitchener, whom, with Harriet's cheerful approval, he had invited as "the sister of his soul" to visit them, was with them during a portion of these exciting days; but presently she became so objectionable that he spoke of her as the "brown Demon," and brought about her departure, not without considerable expense in the way of gifts of money to her. He found new friends in an eccentric family named Newton, who, like Shelley himself, believed that many of the evils of humanity were due to the drinking of alcoholic beverages and the eating of meat, a theory which he expounded in his *Vindication of Natural Diet* (1813). His intense pity for the sufferings of dumb animals led him, while sojourning in Wales, now and then to put an ailing sheep out of its misery; and some shepherds, angered thereby, made a nocturnal assault upon him in his cottage, in order to frighten him away from their neighborhood. In later years, because there seemed to be no certain evidence of the attack, this was set down as one of Shelley's hallucinations.

In the spring of 1813, he published his poem, *Queen Mab*. In June his first child, Ianthe Elizabeth was born. Up to this time his marriage had not been unhappy. Harriet, who, though fond of reading, was not deeply interested in intellectual and political matters, had done her best to develop such an interest and to sympathize with Shelley's ardor for reforming the world. After she became a mother, however, she abandoned her studies and began to yearn for new bonnets, silverware, and a carriage. Shelley's financial circumstances were embarrassed, his allowance being far from sufficient for one as generous as himself in subscribing to causes he thought worthy. He had bestowed loans upon William Godwin, whom he regarded as one of the noblest of mortals and who was constantly in a needy condition. Nevertheless Harriet obtained her carriage, Shelley borrowing money, at ruinous rates, on his future expectations, as he often did in these years; and they made a holiday journey in it to Scotland. On their return the relations between them continued little by little to grow cooler, Shelley becoming more and more interested in his studies and doctrines, and finding her unsympathetic toward them.

His Views in His Early Period.—Shelley from boyhood onwards was an insatiable reader of all kinds and schools of literature, ancient and modern; but the works which dominated his thoughts before the age of twenty-one were, with the exception of Rousseau, the writings of materialists, Epicurus, Lucretius, Helvetius, Holbach, Voltaire, Hume, Paine, and especially Godwin's *Political Justice*,[1] of which treatise, twenty years after Wordsworth, Coleridge, and Southey had emancipated themselves from it, he was a devoted student. Godwin it was who chiefly taught him to hate institutions, to exalt reason as the only basis of morality, and to believe in the doctrines of necessity and of perfectibility. The youthful author of *The Necessity of Atheism* and *Queen Mab* held that nothing could be true which was not attested by the senses or by logical deduction from the evidence which they gave, and that religion, incapable of enduring that test, must be false. He doubted the existence of God, and the divinity of Christ. The Christian religion, professing to be one of love, had set up a god who was vengeful and tyrannous, and who predestined innocent children to everlasting torture. The Christian church had become an ally of obscurantism, intolerance, and oppression, darkening the illumination which had arisen in pagan Greece. "The only true religion," he thought, "is the religion of Philanthropy." Let faith be ousted and reason re-established, and mankind would speedily rid itself of such artificial institutions and customs as governments, laws, the use of force, private property, and matrimony. And since these, together with certain unnatural appetites like those for meat and alcohol,

---

[1] See, above, p. 29.

account for all follies, crimes, and miseries, man would, upon their abolition, become morally perfect.

History, which, on Godwin's recommendation, he read in both the ancient and the modern historians, seemed to him chiefly a "record of crimes and miseries." In *Queen Mab*, he set forth his views of the past, present, and future. By nature mankind was virtuous and peaceful; but it had allowed priestcraft, kingcraft, and commerce to govern the world, and the consequent evils were superstition, selfishness, greed, lust, and animal diet. Hence came savage wars and conquests, and the general suppression of individual liberties through such tyrannous institutions as matrimony. Ultimately, however, by Necessity, the real omnipotence, there would arise an era of freedom, universal love, and happiness. To political radicals, Robert Owen, G. B. Shaw, etc., *Queen Mab* seemed the most admirable of Shelley's works, and they made it famous in circles which are not interested in Shelley's later and better poetry. Shelley himself, ten years after he wrote it, thought it of little importance.

His Transitional Period: c. 1814–1817.—The young materialist was now to undergo experiences far more trying than any he had heretofore faced. In the summer of 1814 he became seriously involved with Godwin's daughter, Mary, then seventeen, an unusually talented and intellectual girl, deeply interested in the causes to which he was devoted.[2] He fell violently in love with her, and she with him. It was the first time that he had known love in its most passionate form—his feelings for Harriet having been predominantly those of pity, protectiveness, and affection rather than this consuming ardor. He made a clean breast of the matter to Harriet, seemingly expecting that she would accept the situation sensibly, and bow to the inevitable without resentment. Apparently her first attitude was evasive, for he came away with the impression that she was acquiescent. She felt that Mary was the pursuer, and perhaps she hoped that Shelley was only temporarily infatuated. When she realized the full truth, she reproached Shelley and denounced Mary; and he replied with bitter recriminations. On July 28, 1814, he eloped with Mary to France. Claire Clairmont joined them, and from Switzerland, Shelley wrote Harriet the amazing proposal that she come and live with them as a sister. This, of course, she refused to do. When Shelley and Mary returned to London in the autumn of 1814, the tone of the correspondence between him and Harriet grew more and more angry. Pecuniarily he was in bad straits until, in January 1815, his grandfather died, whereupon his debts were settled and he received an income of c. £1,000 a year, a portion of which he at once set aside for Harriet.

A year later, in January, 1816, his and Mary's son, William, was born. The summer of that year, they spent in Switzerland, partly in the company of Byron and Claire Clairmont.[3] In the course of a boating tour

[2] See the table of relationships, above, p. 30.
[3] See, above, p. 193.

around Lake Geneva, when they were near shipwreck in a storm, Shelley, who could not swim, displayed great courage and refused to allow Byron to take risks on his account.

After their return to England, Shelley and Mary were shocked by the suicide of her half-sister, Fanny Imlay, who was very dear to them. Two months later, in December, Shelley learned to his horror that Harriet had drowned herself. The precise reasons for her act are not known; but the world, justly or unjustly, deemed that his desertion of her was at least partly the reason. Shelley immediately wrote to Harriet's sister, asking that his children might be given into his care; but the Westbrooks refused to surrender them, and a court of law decided that his views on religion and on morality made him an unfit guardian of children. The recriminatory letters which he had written after he had left Harriet were also submitted in evidence, and probably helped to form an unfavorable judgment. Even if one does not deny the fact that Shelley's conduct had been wrong, one may nevertheless pity him because of the severity of the punishments that fell upon him. Not only did he have to bear public obloquy and be deprived of his children, but remorseful thoughts burdened the rest of his years.

His Changing Views: c. 1814–1817.—It was during this agonized period of his life that he began to be metamorphosed from a materialistic reformer into a poet, less insistent on immediate revolutionary action. The change was not sudden nor steady; it required several years, and various causes cooperated to bring it about. One of the most powerful of those causes was doubtless his acquaintanceship with misfortune, grief, and remorse; but since, unlike Byron, he restrained his expression of it, it is not definitely demonstrable. There is no greater chastener of intellectual pride than such sorrow as Shelley's; and he who, although he had considered himself enlightened, had nevertheless fallen into such errors and calamities, might well begin to question the materialistic doctrine that reason is a sufficient guide. Another cause of the change in him was his visit to the Alps in 1816, especially to the vale of Chamouni (*Mont Blanc; Anth.*, 864), the majestic scenery of which stimulated in him that sense of natural beauty which had hitherto not been very strong, and evoked feelings vaguely resembling the religious.—After he gave up vegetarianism, his health improved.

Various personal influences were also at work upon him. Thomas Love Peacock, later to become a well-known satirical novelist, encouraged his studies in Greek literature; and at Leigh Hunt's house, which he frequented in 1817–18, his interest in the literary rather than the scientific approach to life was also intensified. He now read much in Wordsworth, Coleridge, and Southey. Both he and Mary lived studious lives, reading many hours daily in the classics of Greek and modern literature, always with the intent of thereby becoming of service in the causes of enlightenment and social reform. In philosophy Shelley was turning more and more away from the skeptics to the idealists—to Plato, to

Berkeley (whom Southey had previously praised to him), and to Spinoza. Of the latter, he planned to make a translation.

The result was not that all his views during this transitional period were in flat contradiction to those of his younger days, but that they were modified in significant ways. He ceased to make sweeping attacks upon religious concepts. The former "atheist" admitted the existence of a spirit of Nature not very different from a divine power. In his *Essay on Christianity*, while still hostile to the church, he spoke with respect of Christ. The French mechanistic philosophers lost their hold upon him. He writes:

> This materialism is a seducing system to young and superficial minds. It allows its disciples to talk and dispenses them from thinking.
>
> *Essay on Life*

He began to recognize the presence of forces in life which seem mystical but are real, not entirely comprehensible to the reason but knowable nevertheless. Phenomena were not merely physical but had a mental or psychological principle within them. As to the practical problems of our existence in this world, he became less certain that a state of perfection could be quickly brought about. Evil now seemed to him a primordial power, not speedily to be eliminated. Good will ultimately prevail, but

> Know then that from the depths of ages old
> Two powers o'er mortal things dominion hold,
> Ruling the world with a divided lot,
> Immortal, all pervading, manifold,
> Twin Genii, equal Gods—when life and thought
> Sprang forth, they burst the womb of inessential
>   Nought . . .
>
> *Laon and Cythna*

Kingship and priestcraft, injustice and poverty, were still evils to him; but he now saw that their supersedure would come only gradually; and it required not only the enlightenment of man's understanding but a refinement of his feelings. The latter consideration modified Shelley's attitude toward literature. As long as he remained a Godwinian he looked upon literature as a means of teaching truth, saying:

> All poetical beauty ought to be subordinate to the inculcated moral. . . .
> Metaphorical language ought to be a pleasing vehicle for useful and momentous instruction.
>
> *To Miss Hitchener; June 6, 1811*

In the second period, however, he was beginning to value literature, and especially poetry, as a unique means of awakening those feelings and that imagination which were quite as necessary as reason for the redemption of mankind. A bare and merely logical style now seemed to him unsuited to persuade mankind; symbols were the more potent forces—streams, vessels, clouds, eagles, serpents, etc.

Among the works which show the effects of his changing views at this time, was his political tract, *A Proposal for Putting Reform to the Vote Throughout the Kingdom* (1817), the moderation and good judgment of which was to be proved by subsequent events. Ages of slavery had made men too torpid to be perfected at once; "many gradations of improvement" were required. In 1817 also appeared *Laon and Cythna*, a poem in Spenserian stanzas, later to be recast as *The Revolt of Islam* (1818). This described what may be called Shelley's idea of a revolution as it should be, entirely unselfish on the part of its leaders, and bloodless in its methods, and in those respects in contrast with the French Revolution. As a work of art, it is imperfect, because again and again Shelley was swept away into furious outbursts that were not in harmony with the serenity he aimed at; but as a document illustrating his transitional period, its very faults are illuminating.

The best poems of Shelley in this period were *Alastor* (1816) and the *Hymn to Intellectual Beauty* (1817). *Alastor (Anth., 855) reflects* his distraught state of mind. His youthful attempts at bringing about swift reforms had been baffled. He had been driven into exile. "I am," he wrote Leigh Hunt, "an outcast from human society; my name is execrated,—by those very beings whose happiness I ardently desired." The tragedy of the idealist who vainly seeks the embodiment of his ideals in actuality, weighed upon his mind. He showed the influence of Wordsworth in his implied criticism of those idealists, however, who turn away from the world to seek elsewhere their ideal, while his preface to *Alastor* also condemned those of the opposite extreme, the worldlings who are sunk in earthly concerns. In the *Hymn to Intellectual Beauty* (*Anth.*, 863) he expressed his yearning for that ideal realm which as mortals we do not behold, but the existence of which is manifested to us by the loveliness of those things which even in this life we may come to know. To Shelley, as to Keats, Truth imaged itself in Beauty.

His Last Period: c. 1818–1821.—The verdict, given in the spring of 1818, that Shelley was to be deprived of his and Harriet's children, was in effect, though not in intention, a sentence of exile; for he and Mary (who were married at the end of 1816) feared that similar action might possibly be taken with respect to their children, William and Clara Shelley. The poor state of his health was another reason why in March, 1818, they left England, to which he was never to return, and went to "the paradise of exiles," Italy. During the summer they lived at Bagni di Lucca, upon the forested heights of Tuscany, and later in the year sojourned at Venice, Este, and Naples. He was with tireless avidity continuing his studies in literature—Greek, Italian, and English—and acquiring a new interest in the treasures of classical art. His vivid letters from Italy (*Anth.*, 990) combine the aesthetic delights of a percipient lover of nature with the historical enthusiasms of a scholarly antiquary. At Venice, he saw a good deal of Byron; and their conversations inspired his poem *Julian and Maddalo*. Further sorrows came to him and Mary in the deaths of both their children,—Clara's in 1818, and William's early in 1819. In the summer of 1819, Shelley was stirred by the news of the so-called Manchester massacre, labor troubles in that city having resulted in the dispersal of a public meeting by troops and the deaths of several persons. This incited him to write his *Mask of Anarchy* and *Songs for the Men of England* (*Anth.*, 881). At Florence in the autumn of 1819 was born his son Percy Florence Shelley, who was destined to succeed to the baronetcy in 1844. In 1820 and 1821 they lived much of the time at Pisa, where there was a large colony of English visitors, including Mr. and Mrs. Edward Williams, to whom they became deeply attached. They also formed the acquaintance of the young Italian Countess Emilia Viviani, who was immured in a convent while her father was seeking her an elderly husband. For her Shelley conceived a Platonic affection, the enthusiastic expression of which in *Epipsychidion* must have been rather painful to Mrs. Shelley, although years later she loyally included the poem in her edition of his works (1839), without, however, there making any comment upon it. She might have recorded that Shelley presently discovered that Emilia was after all not going to approach his ideal of womanhood quite so closely as he at first had supposed; or, as he put it, she became "a cloud, instead of a Juno."

Byron and Shelley conceived the idea of establishing at Pisa a journal of protest and enlightenment, *The Liberal;* and Shelley invited Leigh Hunt to Pisa, with a view to his undertaking the editorship. The winter of 1821 Shelley and Byron saw much of each other there. Shelley, like Byron, was interested in the plans for a revolution in Greece; and inspired by his hopes for it, wrote the drama, *Hellas.* Hunt arrived at Leghorn in July, 1822; and Shelley, with his friend Williams, sailed thither in his little boat, the Ariel. After seeing the Hunts settled at Pisa, Shelley and Williams, who were living at Lerici, sailed homeward on July 8, 1822 in the Ariel. They encountered a storm, and perished in it. Their bodies were cast up by the sea; and were cremated in the ancient Greek fashion upon the shore. Shelley's ashes were borne to Rome and buried in the same cemetery where Keats, in the previous year, had been laid to rest. Upon his gravestone were graven the Shakspearian lines he loved:

> Nothing of him that doth fade
> But doth suffer a sea-change
> Into something rich and strange.

The Aftermath.—Unfortunately for Shelley's personal and literary reputation, he died before the greatness of the works written during his Italian period was widely recognized. A few writers, notably Leigh Hunt (*Anth.*, 1007) and Horace Smith, pleaded his cause; but they were overborne by those to whom he was a bad man and a bad poet, a deserter of his wife, a seducer, an atheist, a blasphemer, and a revolutionist. "His works," said the *Quarterly,* "exhale contiguous mischiefs," and "his poetry contains the most flagrant offenses against morality and religion." His style, said the *London Literary Gazette,* was "merely opposition of words, phrases, and sentiments, so violent as to be utter nonsense."

The approach to a just estimate of Shelley was long delayed by obstacles which his family put in the way of a full disclosure of all the facts about him. Mary Shelley was warned by Sir Timothy Shelley that her allowance would be cut off if she published anything indiscreetly revelatory concerning the life and character of her husband, and this restriction hampered her when she composed the notes for her edition of Shelley's works in 1839. When Thomas Jefferson Hogg, in the first volume of his biography (1858), wrote quite frankly about Shelley's faults, Lady Jane Gibson Shelley, the wife of the new head of the family, Sir Percy Florence (Mary's son), recalled the papers she had loaned him, and herself issued *The Shelley Memorials,* in which nothing was permitted that would not glorify Shelley and Mary, and in which too much blame was cast upon Harriet.

The important effect of this family pride and hostility to truth, shown in many cases other than those just mentioned—besides encouraging forgers and blackmailers—was to leave biographers in the dark on crucial points, and to permit both those who admired Shelley and those who disliked him to misconceive and misrepresent his conduct and views. For decades after Shelley's death, biographical and critical works concerning him might be divided into two classes: those which praised him as angelic; and those which, even if they admitted that he was an angel, denounced him as ineffectual in a world such as ours. The only respect in which those hostile schools agreed was in their tacit and erroneous assumption that Shelley's character and work was a static thing. It was not until comparatively recent days that there arose a third school of criticism, marked by a tendency to distinguish between the several stages of his life and art; and therewith a juster appreciation of their nature and value was attained.

His Personality.—The gravest charges against Shelley's character rest upon his conduct toward Harriet. His desertion of her may be understood, without being condoned, if we bear in mind that he believed that to continue a marriage without love was wrong; and that in other situations he had consistently acted up to what he regarded as the soundest principles, even when to do so was disadvantageous to himself. On the other hand, some passages in his letters to her after the separation display a petulance and unkindness irreconcilable with his own ideals, and are excusable, if at all, only on the ground that at his age contradictory behavior was to be expected. Throughout his life he occasionally failed to control himself or to bear in mind how different were his views from those commonly held, and consequently how readily his motives might be misconstrued when he was acting in accordance with those views. This was particularly true with respect to his attitude toward women: and he may plausibly be charged with fickleness, or else with self-deception, in cases like those of Emilia Viviani or Mrs. Williams, where his delight in perceiving what he thought ideal perfections led him into expressions of rapture which ordinary mortals might consider not entirely Platonic.

Epipsychidion (*Anth.*, 948) arose out of poignant personal experiences, in which passion intruded upon ideals; but it is nevertheless a sincere, though in some passages an obscure, expression of what Shelley believed to be the highest kind of love, the most intense expression thereof in all his works. It was inspired chiefly by Plato's exaltation (in the *Symposium*, which Shelley had been translating) of spiritual love above physical; and by Dante's and Petrarch's glorifying of romantic love between man and woman as the highest fulfillment of human life. The main theme is spiritual affinity.

Except for the weaknesses mentioned above, Shelley during his last five years (who is the really important Shelley) displayed few faults and follies, and many virtues. Retaining that unselfishness, that courageous and independent spirit, and that enthusiastic devotion to the intellectual life, which he had already shown in his adolescence, he now tried manfully to adapt himself better to the actualities of life, and to a remarkable degree succeeded in doing so. He became less hasty in his judgments of other men, and more percipient of their real characters. Not even Byron carried him off his feet; for while admiring Byron for his boldness and poetic power, he saw through his conceit and his poses. He developed an unexpected sense for practical affairs, as is shown in his negotiations with Leigh Hunt, and in the fact that he managed to indulge his generosity by supporting many dependents and nevertheless made both ends meet. His letters during this period furnish abundant evidence of maturity and sound judgment.

Shelley's Mature Views, c. 1818–1821.—A glance at the chronology of Shelley's work will show that nearly all of his famous works were produced during his last four years. It is therefore his views during that period which are the important ones. Criticism has, however, persisted in reading into the works of this period either moral traits or intellectual tendencies which had ceased to be characteristic of him at that time.

As we have seen, his youthful views had already undergone changes in the years between 1814 and 1817, changes of an anti-materialistic kind. Italy, with its wealth of natural and artistic beauty, helped to complete this cultural process. More and more his studies centered upon literature and art, and upon those contemporaneous aspects of science which were non-mechanistic in their interpretation of the physical world.

Although he never became a Christian, as Browning thought he would had he lived longer, and although he still regarded institutional Christianity as antipathetic to the true Christ, he spoke in praise and reverence of Him whose mission was love and regeneration: in *Hellas* Jesus was represented as the liberator of mankind. He enthusiastically admired the ancient Greeks, especially those of the Periclean Age; but he now recognized that the ideals of Christianity had advanced civilization by causing the abolition of slavery and by revealing a nobler concept of love. At the summit of what to him was the greatest literature (his list included Plato, Greek Tragedy, Dante, Petrarch, Boccacio, Calderon, Shakspeare, Milton, Goethe, and Schiller) he placed the Bible. And if he did not profess a belief in God, he assumed the existence of a Universal Spirit manifested in nature as beauty and in humanity as love. Nature to him no longer was dominated by inhumane Necessity but by a spirit of love which was the moving cause of all things, and which through a process of evolution would ultimately, despite periods in which evil was dominant, result in the ascendency of good. Social and political progress was likewise to be evolutionary, not cataclysmic. Even the noblest of ends would not justify forcible or violent means: reforms must never be achieved by the sword. In his *Philosophical View of Reform* (1819), his last important pronouncement on such a subject, he proposed nothing more extreme than the gradual broadening of the suffrage. His views as to private property had likewise changed. He still opposed economic injustices which made it difficult for men to find work and to get fair wages, but he was neither a socialist nor a communist, although some modern adherents of those systems regard him as their forerunner and although, even when his maturer sentiments favorable to gradualism are remembered, he may still be called "the greatest radical voice in poetry since Lucretius."

The most important statement of his position, however, is to be found not in his political writings nor in his occasional comments on religion, but in that splendid *Defense of Poetry* (wr. 1821; *Anth.*, 975) in which, provoked by Peacock's contemptuous belittlement of the art, he set forth his maturest and profoundest beliefs. Here his juvenile notion that poetry should be a mere means of inculcating moral rules which the understanding had excogitated, was scornfully rejected. Poetry had an indirect moral effect by exercising those powers of the imagination and of sympathy without which no kind of morality is conceivable; but it should never be a direct didactic preachment. Its appeal was not to the understanding, "the owl-winged faculty of calculation." That faculty could never see the universe as it truly is; to it the real relationships and values were inapprehensible. The commonplace world which alone it knew was not substance, but shadow; not life, but death. The poet's faculty was imagination, by which he "lifted the veil from the hidden beauty of the world," and recalled that things apparently finite had a connection with the infinite and eternal. He presented us, to be sure, with images taken from actual life; not, however, with those images as the eye of common sense beheld them, but in their eternal truth. Without the poet, the truest and most precious things in life would not be revealed to us—neither the beauty of nature, nor love, nor patriotism, nor friendship, nor "our consolations on this side of the grave, nor our aspirations beyond it." It was the poet who was the true priest, for he gave us our most appealing approach to "that partial apprehension of the agencies of the invisible world which is called religion." In short, the former Godwinian rationalist had become a mystic and transcendentalist.

His Chief Works.—*The Cenci (Anth.,* 874) , a tragedy in blank verse, was intended to be performed at Covent Garden; but was not acted upon a stage until the Shelley Society produced it in 1886. Shelley said:

> It is written without any of the peculiar feelings and opinions which characterize my other compositions. I have attended simply to the development of such characters as it is probable the persons really were.

Because of that purpose it is, although too declamatory to be suitable for presentation, the most objective of his works. Shelley let his characters speak for themselves in starkly realistic terms. Nevertheless the subject was one which gave him an opportunity to place some of his own sentiments in a strong light. It dealt with a Roman Count, Francesco Cenci, who outraged his daughter Beatrice and was murdered at her instigation. Modern investigation has shown that Beatrice and her accomplices were less justified in their act, and much less admirable personally, than he, knowing only a fictitious version of the incidents, supposed. He treated the episode as a horrible example of the cruelties which women and children were exposed to under the *patria potestas,* i.e., the autocratic power of a father; and characteristically he motivated the Pope's refusal to pardon Beatrice on the ground that the Holy Father feared that thereby attacks on his own power might be encouraged. The terror, horror, and pathos of the situations are powerfully conveyed, and the dignity of high tragedy is throughout sustained. Although untrue to history, it was much more nearly true to human nature than were the preromantic tragedies of terror; and in various passages there might be discerned the influence of such masters of tragedy as Sophocles, Shakspeare, Ford, and Webster. By coming closer to actual life than in his other works, Shelley hoped to win public favor; but the incest theme defeated that hope. He regarded *The Cenci* as much less important than his "idealisms of moral excellence," *Prometheus Unbound* and *Adonais;* but Mary Shelley thought it his masterpiece, and some critics agree with her judgment.

Lyrical poems and dramatic visions offered Shelley better outlets than realistic or historical dramas for the expression of his ideas and aspirations. His lyrics of nature, though vivid, are never descriptions; in one way or another they are quickened by his abiding sense of the contrast between the world of appearance and the world of reality, between the present and the future. Often, as in "Stanzas Written in Dejection" and the beginning of "Lines Among the Euganean Hills" *(Anth.,* 869, 872) , it is the world of appearance that weighs heavily upon his spirit—the life of care which we have to endure here, the sea of misery and waters of agony, the Venice now ingloriously enthralled, the Pavia whose lamp of learning has been extinguished by tyranny. But the mood of melancholy evoked by the actualities of the here and the now is usually superseded by recognition of the ideal realities and future promise that lie behind the veil. The West Wind, which is the harbinger of Winter and Death, will come, the poet himself like the leaves of the forest will be swept away, but just as certainly Spring and the fruition of his hopes for humanity will not be far behind (*Anth.*, 873). The clouds of heaven are witnesses to the validity of hope: to the prosaic they are emblems of the evanescence of beauty, but in truth they but change and never die; they "silently laugh at their own cenotaph" (*Anth.*, 940). We are earthbound and our sweetest songs are sad; but the strains of the skylark suggest the reality of perfect love and joy (*Anth.*, 941). What we must believe in are the veiled and underlying things: a garden is not constituted by a collection of plants but by the personality of her who makes and tends it ("The Sensitive Plant"; *Anth.*, 936).

It is this confidence that material and present things are not the precious ones that animates *Adonais* (*Anth.*, 954) and is uttered in its sublimest stanzas. Poets other than Shelley might have made much more of the actual facts concerning Keats's life and character. They might have given us a clearer idea of the young poet's personality, his high resolves, his gallant struggles against circumstances, the longings and disappointments of his last months; and they might thus have written an elegy arousing deeper sympathy and pity. It has indeed been made a reproach against *Adonais* that it is not human and pathetic enough, that it is too coldly beautiful. It must be granted that Shelley's strength did not lie in the treatment of such aspects of a theme. Indeed, as to the only concrete incident in Keats's life that he made much of—the effect of the hostile reviewers—he was quite mistaken. What Shelley did deeply comprehend and superbly express was what the life of such a genius, and his death at such an age, signified. To the reviewers, who typified the calculating and insensitive intellect, his work was nothing; and the world would regard his death as a defeat. But those who recognized beauty would feel otherwise; at first they would grieve at his departure, as would the lovely things which he had worshiped and disclosed, but presently they would be consoled with the reflection that he was with the immortals and that to him his death was victory, an awakening from the feverish dream of life into the unstained radiance of Eternity. This was an elegy not voicing the grief of the heart so much as the exaltation of the soul.

The lyrical drama, *Hellas* (*Anth.*, 964), was inspired by Shelley's hopes for the ultimate liberation of Greece, and contains several famous passages expressing the poet's confidence that ultimately the freedom of the entire world would be achieved.

His other lyrical drama, *Prometheus Unbound* (*Anth.*, 883), is Shelley's greatest work, because here he expressed with more intensity and breadth than anywhere else those conceptions upon which his hope of the future of mankind rested. He had, as he confessed in his brilliant preface, "a passion for reforming the world," although his drama was not intended to do so except indirectly, for didactic poetry was his abhorrence. His purpose was, he said,

> to familiarize the highly refined imagination of the more select classes of poetical readers with beautiful idealisms of moral excellence; aware that until the mind can love, and admire, and trust, and hope, and endure, reasoned principles of moral conduct are seeds cast upon the highway of life, which the unconscious passenger tramples into dust, although they would bear the harvest of his happiness.

In this particular instance his "beautiful idealisms of moral excellence" illumined the deepest of human problems—why man was enslaved, and how he would be freed. Never would he achieve true liberty until he overcame that passion for revenge which now held him captive.

To express his feelings on this theme, Shelley did not go to history, but to myth, which could be more easily molded to his purpose. The most powerful Greek dramatist, Aeschylus, had represented the Titan Prometheus as offending Zeus (Jupiter) by giving to man the use of fire, and as chained to a rock in punishment; but ultimately Prometheus was to have been reconciled to Zeus by disclosing the secret of a danger to his empire. Shelley declared that he was "averse from a catastrophe so feeble as that of reconciling the Champion with the Oppressor of mankind."

When Shelley's drama opens, Prometheus, who at the beginning of his torture had pronounced a frightful curse against Jupiter, has suffered ages of pain and gained insight and wisdom. Hatred has now left his soul, he despises revenge, and would recall his curse. Jupiter, mistakenly supposing that this means feebleness, demands that Prometheus disclose the secret; and when Prometheus refuses to bow to unjust power, inflicts further tortures upon him. Far away, in an Indian vale, dwells Asia, the beloved of Prometheus, and the very spirit of Love. She is, however, passive and ineffectual until, roused by messengers from Prometheus, she yearns for enlightenment, whereupon she is borne through the dark forest of human experience into the presence of the most dread of beings, Demogorgon, that Eternal Fate which is greater even than the gods of Olympus. She implores him to disclose the fate of Prometheus, and their future is shown to her in a vision, culminating in his adoration of her. There follows the downfall of Jupiter, who has incurred the secret danger by marrying Thetis. Their child, Hercules, overthrows Jupiter and frees Prometheus, whereupon all the spirits of the universe chant a paean of rejoicing over the downfall of tyranny and the victory of forgiveness, love, and unconquerable resistance to force, ending with the noble lines

> To suffer woes which hope thinks infinite;
> To forgive wrongs darker than death or night;
> To defy Power, which seems omnipotent;
> To love, and bear; to hope till Hope creates
> From its own wreck the thing it contemplates;
> Neither to change, nor falter, nor repent;

This, like thy glory, Titan, is to be
Good, great and joyous, beautiful and free;
This is alone Life, Joy, Empire, and Victory.

Prometheus Unbound is not an allegory in the sense that every detail has a double meaning; the cosmic characters have an individualized existence often entirely freed from any general implications. Nevertheless the course of action and the utterances of the personages clearly suggest more than lies on their surface. Both Prometheus and Jupiter typify certain human traits. Prometheus represents the temper and the methods which will in the end save mankind. But he has permitted Jupiter, who represents the lower sides of human nature, to become his master; and under Jupiter's sway there have consequently arisen institutions and customs obnoxious to humanity at its best:

> Those foul shapes, abhorred by god and man,
> Which, under many a name and many a form,
> Strange, savage, ghastly, dark, and execrable,
> Were Jupiter, the tyrant of the world.

And Demogorgon is not merely the victor in a combat of gods, his victory suggests that while time may be on the side of man's oppressors, Eternity will bring triumph to his saviors.

Prometheus Unbound was condemned by many contemporary critics as blasphemous, as immoral, and (not quite so unjustly) as obscure. Its later admirers included, besides Robert Browning and Francis Thompson, political radicals like Robert Owen, Karl Marx, and Bernard Shaw. But the youthful *Queen Mab* was much nearer Marxian philosophy than is *Prometheus Unbound*, in which Shelley moves closer toward Christian ethics, especially in the key thought that Evil is not inherent in creation originally, but has existed only by the weak consent of the human mind and will.

The main purpose of *The Triumph of Life* (*Anth.*, 967), which Shelley unfortunately left unfinished and unrevised, and which therefore has gaps and obscurities, may probably be, in the words of the Preface to *The Cenci*, "to make apparent some of the most dark and secret caverns of the human heart." Although fragmentary, it is a powerful pageant of the alluring yet evil attractions of the world, which enchain, degenerate, or destroy human character. The mass of mankind succumb; they become selfish, deceitful, or cruel. Only a few (Socrates? Christ? see l. 128) have escaped to Light and Love. Even love may in weak souls contribute to the moral collapse; but on the whole, as in Dante, it is the only force that can pass through Hell without foul metamorphosis (l. 475, "All things are transfigured except love"). In short "Life" is worldliness; and its "Triumph" is a tragedy. There is a splendor and impetus in this Rembrandt-like vision, partly inspired by Dante's *Divina Commedia* and Petrarch's *Trionfi* ("The Triumph of Love over Man"). The resemblance to the contemporary Leopardi's *Appres-*

samento alla Morte (a vision of the omnipotence of Death) is striking. Of all Shelley's works, it is the most Italian in manner and spirit.

Form and Style.—Shelley's art was not, as the apparent ease and inevitability of his utterances might suggest, an unpremeditated one. He gave great care to the choice of his verse-forms and his diction, as is shown by his much corrected manuscripts. He was the master of a nobly eloquent prose, and in verse commanded many meters and forms, some of them technically very difficult. The shimmering beauty of *Prometheus Unbound* is largely due to his frequent and skilful variation of lyric forms. In *Epipsychidion* he used the heroic couplet; in *The Witch of Atlas,* the *ottava rima;* in the *Ode to the West Wind,* the *terza rima;* and in *Adonais,* the Spenserian stanza; always with appropriateness and potency. His favorite metaphors were felicitously chosen—the "veil" for ordinary life, the "boat and stream" for the ego and its experience, and the "eagle and serpent" for good and evil. His verse was not reposeful and soothing like Keats's, but intensely energetic and swift, seemingly spontaneous, and extraordinarily musical.

His Relation to Other Romantics.—Of all the great Romantics, Shelley was the least interested in the world as it actually was or as it had been in the historic past. He agreed with Byron that the world of his day was on the whole contemptibly bad; and did not disagree with Scott or Landor that in the past one might find manifestations of the good; but his preoccupation was with the future. He tried to stand, as he himself said, upon a promontory and to descry what lay in the far distance. Even when he wrote of the present or the past, it was chiefly to disclose what forces had hindered the coming of a better day and what forces would hasten its arrival. While Keats found reality and delight in the present beauties of nature and art, Shelley found reality only in the rudimentary tendencies toward moral perfection and delight, only in foreseeing their fruition. Since his main theme was a condition of life that has not yet been brought to pass, his poetry has been condemned more than that of any other great Romantic as attenuated, indistinct, unreal, and ineffectual. Matthew Arnold spoke pityingly of it in those respects; and Carlyle, after he had ceased to be a Romantic, spoke savagely of Shelley as "a poor, thin, spasmodic, hectic, shrill, and pallid being." When Aldous Huxley was a cynical realist, he derided Shelley as a pretentious poseur and liar (*Point Counterpoint,* p. 119), not foreseeing that after his curious conversion he was to embrace a kind of religion in some points very like Shelley's own (see *The Perennial Philosophy,* 1945).

If the world is never to be a better abiding place for the soul of man than it has been, the contemners of Shelley will stand approved. But that verdict only the distant future has a right to pronounce confidently. For the time being, Shelley is not ineffectual, since he keeps hope and determination alive in the hearts of those reformers who believe that by far the greater part of man's past follies and vices is avoidable, and who yearn to see society reorganize itself, without compulsion or bloodshed, in such a way that each individual might enjoy equal opportunity of access to enlightenment, beauty, and happiness.

SELECTED BIBLIOGRAPHY

OF FIRST IMPORTANCE

Selections

The Best of Shelley, ed. Newman I. White, 1932. — Selections from the poetry and the prose; valuable introduction and interpretive comments.

Poetry and Prose, ed. A. D. M. Hughes, 1931. — With essays by Bagehot, Swinburne, etc.

The Reader's Shelley, ed. Carl H. Grabo, 1942. — Poems only.

Selected Poems, Essays, and Letters, ed. Ellsworth Barnard, 1944.

Texts

The best one-volume edition of the poems is the *Complete Poetical Works*, ed. Thomas Hutchinson, Oxford, 1904; rev. B. P. Kurtz, 1934. — This should be supplemented with *A Defense of Poetry*, either in A. S. Cook's ed., 1891; or H. F. B. Brett-Smith's, 1921; both of which contain Peacock's *Four Ages of Poetry*.

Best Biography

The best introduction to both the life and the works is Newman I. White's *Portrait of Shelley*, 1945, a condensed and revised version of his two-volume *Shelley* of 1940.

Other Critical Discussions of Introductory Importance

Arnold, Matthew; "Shelley," *Essays in Criticism: Second Series*, 1888. Originally a review of Dowden's eulogistic life. Unintentionally damned Shelley in the famous sentence, "In poetry, no less than in life, he is a beautiful and ineffectual angel, beating his luminous wings in vain." — Very influential.

Thompson, Francis; "Shelley," wr. 1889; publ. 1909. In *Collected Works*, III. Leans toward the "eternal child" interpretation; nevertheless "perhaps the finest appreciation of Shelley" (N. I. White).

Yeats, W. B.; "The Philosophy of Shelley's Poetry," *Ideas of Good and Evil*, 1903. — Shelley the supreme poet-philosopher, especially in *Prometheus Unbound*.

More, Paul Elmer; "Shelley," *Shelburne Essays*, VII, 1910. — The anti-romantic reaction. Shelley and his poetry represent dangerous emotionalism unchecked by reason.

Strong, Archibald T.; *Three Studies in Shelley*, 1921. — On "Faith," "Symbolism," and "The Sinister." Thoughtful.

Campbell, Olwen Ward; *Shelley and the Unromantics*, 1924. — Enthusiastic appreciation of Shelley's manliness and effectiveness, marred by unwillingness to admit his faults and by uncritical scorn of the other Romantics. The most stimulating of introductions, but afterwards to be checked by other accounts.

Solve, Melvin; *Shelley: His Theory of Poetry*, 1927.

Grabo, Carl H.; *The Magic Plant: The Growth of Shelley's Mind*, 1936. — The steps from science, materialism, and political radicalism to poetical mysticism. Prolix, not very original, but thorough. — Reviews by George Whicher, *N. Y. Herald Tribune Books*, Dec. 27, 1936; N. I. White, ELH, v, 21; 1938.

Knight, G. Wilson; "The Naked Seraph," *The Starlit Dome*, 1941. — See General Bibliography: The Value of Romanticism, Appreciative Enthusiasts; below, p. 320.

Fogle, Richard H.; "Romantic Bards and Metaphysical Reviewers," ELH, XII, 221; 1945. — A defense of Shelley against the New Critics.

Baker, Carlos; *Shelley's Major Poetry: The Fabric of a Vision*, 1948. — The best modern interpretation; succeeds in its purposes, "to live the inner life of these poems" and "to achieve a balanced and judicious estimate."

FOR ADVANCED STUDENTS

Important Additional Texts

The Complete Works of Shelley (The Julian Edition), eds. Roger Ingpen and Walter E. Peck, 10 vols., 1926–30. — If this limited and costly edition is not available, use *The Works in Verse and Prose*, ed. H. B. Forman, 8 vols., 1880; or *The Complete Poetical Works*, ed. G. E. Woodberry, 4 vols., 1892.

The Poems, ed. C. D. Locock, 2 vols., 1911, with a good Introduction by A. Clutton-Brock, has valuable notes and commentaries.

Prose Works, ed. R. H. Shepherd, 2 vols., 1912.

Literary and Philosophical Criticism, ed. John Shawcross, 1909.

The Cenci, ed. G. E. Woodberry (Belles Lettres Series), 1909.

Prometheus Unbound, ed. Vida D. Scudder, 1897.

Adonais, reproduced from 1821 ed. (Columbia Univ. Press), 1935.

A Philosophical View of Reform, ed. T. W. Rolleston, 1920.

An Essay on the Vegetable System of Diet (Linden Press, Newport, Essex), 1941.

Notebooks, ed. H. B. Forman, 3 vols., 1911. — *The Shelley Notebook in the Harvard Library*, ed. G. E. Woodberry, 1930. — *Verse and Prose from MSS.*, eds. Shelley-Rolls and Ingpen, 1934.

Letters (besides the Ingpen and Peck edition above), ed. Roger Ingpen, 2 vols., 1915; and Shelley's *Lost Letters to Harriet*, ed. Leslie Hotson, 1930.

The Letters of Mary Wollstonecraft Shelley, ed. F. L. Jones, 2 vols., 1944; and *Mary Shelley's Journal*, ed. F. L. Jones, 1947.

Scott, Walter S., ed.; *Correspondence of Shelley* (Golden Cockerel Press), 3 vols., 1944–45. — I, *The Athenians*; II, *Harriet and Mary*; III, *Shelley at Oxford*. Unpublished correspondence between Shelley, Hogg, Peacock, Hunt, etc.

Early Biographical Accounts

Moore, Thomas; *Letters and Journals of Byron*, 2 vols., 1830.

Hunt, Leigh; *Autobiography*, 1850; (World's Classics), 1928.

Medwin, Thomas; *Life of Shelley*, 2 vols., 1847; ed. H. B. Forman, 1913. — Apologetic and inaccurate.

The Life of Percy Bysshe Shelley, as Comprised in Hogg's "Life," Trelawny's "Recollections," and Peacock's "Memoirs." — Introduction by Humbert Wolfe, 2 vols., 1933. — Rev. TLS, March 30, 1933.

Hogg, Thomas J.; *Life of Shelley*, 2 vols., 1858, ed. R. A. Streatfield, 1904; ed. Edward Dowden, 1906. — Especially for Shelley at Oxford; unreliable.

Trelawny, Edward J.; *Recollections of the Last Days of Shelley and Byron*, 1858; ed. E. Dowden, 1906. — Hero worshipping.

Peacock, Thomas Love; "Memoirs of Shelley" and "Shelley's Letters to Peacock," *Fraser's*, 1858; ed. H. F. B. Brett-Smith, 1909. — Fairest of the early memoirs, but Peacock was too anti-romantic to understand some of Shelley's qualities.

Shelley, (Lady) Jane Gibson; *Shelley Memorials*, 1859; 3rd ed., 1875. — Intended to offset revelations by Hogg., etc.; apologetic.

Biographical and Critical

On the *history of the biography and criticism*, see section thus entitled below.

Browning, Robert; "Essay on Shelley," prefixed to *Letters*, 1852; rptd, in H. F. B. Brett-Smith's ed., 1921, of *A Defense of Poetry*.

Rossetti, William Michael; "Memoir," prefixed to Shelley's *Works*, 1870; rptd. by Shelley Society, 1886. Admiring, but judicious.

Swinburne, A. C.; in *Essays and Studies, 1875.* — Rapturous praise of Shelley's lyrical powers; depreciates Byron.

Symonds, John Addington; *Shelley* (Engl. Men of Letters) , 1878. Long one of the best brief introductions. Preceded Dowden's biography; rev. 1887.

Jeaffreson, J. C.; *The Real Shelley: New Views of the Poet's Life*, 2 vols., 1885. — An attack like a prosecuting attorney's: Shelley guilty and abnormal. Of value in warning against forgeries, and against undue family influence.

Dowden, Edward; *Life of Shelley*, 2 vols., 1886; revised and condensed, 1896. — Long the standard life, and still valuable, but tries to explain away all of Shelley's weaknesses by blaming his connections, including Harriet; his reading of romances of terror and of Godwin; etc. — Should be supplemented with his "Last Words on Shelley" and "Shelley's Philosophical View of Reform," in *Transcripts and Studies*, 1888. — Dowden's Life provoked Mark Twain's outburst, *Defense of Harriet Shelley*.

Blind, Mathilde; "Shelley's View of Nature Contrasted with Darwin's," *Shelley Society Papers*, 1888. — Nothing of the ruthlessness of nature in Shelley's conception of development. — Cf. Grabo's studies below, 1930 ff; and A. M. D. Hughes, *No. Amer. Rev.*, CCVIII, 287; 1918.

Patmore, Coventry; "Principle in Art," 1889, p. 87. — Shelley "a beautiful, effeminate, arrogant and ignorant boy."

Salt, Henry S.; *Shelley: Poet and Pioneer*, 1896. — By a disciple, whose *Shelley Primer* (1887) was published by the Shelley Society, and who was among the first to deal with him as a developing personality.

Robertson, John M.; "Shelley," *New Essays Towards a Critical Method*, 1897. — The attitude of the materialistic school: Shelley "turns life into a dream," his poetry is mere fantasy.

Locock, C. D.; *An Examination of the Shelley Mss. in the Bodleian Library*, 1903. — Shows Shelley's care in revision.

Croft, Margaret L.; "A Strange Adventure of Shelley's and Its Belated Explanation," *Century*, LXX, 905; 1905. — Tends to prove Shelley's truthfulness.

Droop, Eduard J. A.; *Die Belesenheit Shelleys*, 1906. — Lists of his reading. — Cf. E. E. Burriss, who, in *Classical Journal*, XXI, 344, 1926, records from the Letters the references to Greek and Latin authors.

Bradley, A. C.; "Shelley's Views of Poetry," *Oxford Lectures on Poetry*, 1909. — "Coleridge Echoes," "Odours and Flowers," and "Arnold's Critique," *A Miscellany*, 1929.

Koszul, A. H.; *La Jeunesse de Shelley*, 1910. — Detailed study of his youth; the first part of the book is the better one.

Brailsford, Henry N.; *Shelley, Godwin, and Their Circle*, 1913. — The personal relationships. For another lively account, cf. A. E. Newton, "Skinner Street News," *The Greatest Book in the World*, 1925.

Santayana, George; "Shelley," *Winds of Doctrine,* 1913. — Polite skepticism; Shelley incapable of understanding reality. Mistakenly supposes he had not read Spinoza (cf. Campbell, 1924; pp. 146, 184).

Elliott, George R.; "How Poetic Is Shelley's Poetry?" PMLA, xxxvii, 311; 1922. — On the whole the answer is, "Not very."

Maurois, André; *Ariel: a Shelley Romance,* Fr., 1923; transl., 1924. — An historical fiction, based on good sources; delightfully vivid. The interpretation is worldly wise.

Liptzin, Solomon; *Shelley in Germany,* 1924. — After 1830 his works aided the ill-fated liberal movements.

Carpenter, Edward, and Barnefield, George; *The Psychology of the Poet Shelley,* 1925. — Pretentious but adds little. — On this kind of criticism see Louis Cazamain, "La Psychoanalyse et la Critique Littéraire," *Rev. Litt. Comp.,* iv, 449; 1924.

Walker, A. Stanley; "Peterloo, Shelley, and Reform," PMLA, xl, 128; 1925. — On the Manchester massacres.

Peck, Walter E.; *Shelley: His Life and Works,* 2 vols., 1927. — Many new facts. Superseded by N. I. White, 1940.

Bald, Marjory A.; "Shelley's Mental Progress," *Engl. Asso. Essays and Studies,* x, 112; 1928. — He was "a man who grew," and "his mind repeated itself in spirals, not circles."

Grabo, Carl; *A Newton Among Poets: Shelley's Use of Science in Prometheus Unbound,* 1930. — See his *Magic Plant,* 1936, above, in "Of First Importance."

Fairchild, H. N.; "Shelley and Transcendentalism," *The Romantic Quest,* 1931. — Believes his faith grew weaker.

Stovall, Floyd; *Desire and Restraint in Shelley,* 1931. — Believes his development culminated in adjustment between extremes. Cf. "Doctrine of Love," PMLA, xlv, 283; 1930.

Weaver, Bennett; *Toward the Understanding of Shelley,* 1932. — Influence of the Bible.

Propst, Louise; *An Analytical Study of Shelley's Versification,* Univ. of Iowa Humanistic Studies, 1932.

Sickels, Eleanor M.; *The Gloomy Egoist: Moods and Themes of Melancholy from Gray to Keats,* 1932.

Croce, Benedetto; *The Defense of Poetry: Variations on the Theme of Shelley* (Oxford), 1933. — A lecture.

Kurtz, Benjamin P.; *The Pursuit of Death: A Study of Shelley's Poetry,* 1933. — Tries to make his attitude toward death the key to his whole work.

Read, Herbert; *In Defense of Shelley, and Other Essays,* 1935. — Against T. S. Eliot's contempt. But unsoundly based on psychoanalytic guesswork. See the brilliant rev., TLS, Feb. 22, 1936.

Peyre, Henri; *Shelley et la France: Lyrisme Anglais et Lyrisme Français au xixe Siècle,* Paris, 1935. — Far-reaching study of Shelley as for the French the exemplar of the spiritual quality of English poetry; his influence on Baudelaire, the Symbolists, and critics like André Chevrillon.

Barnard, Ellsworth; *Shelley's Religion,* 1937. — A serious attempt to clarify an obscure subject. Stresses Shelley's recognition of the persistent evil in the universe. — Cf. A. M. D. Hughes, *The Theology of Shelley,* 1939.

Firkins, O. W.; *Power and Elusiveness in Shelley,* 1937. — Analysis of dominant ideas in the poetry; exhaustively illustrated.

Grylls, R. Glynn; *Mary Shelley,* 1938. — Supersedes Mrs. J. Marshall's *Life and Letters,* 2 vols., 1889.

Grylls, R. Glynn; *Claire Clairmont,* 1939. — "Semi-fictionalized." — Cf. J. H. Smith, "Shelley and Claire Clairmont," PMLA, LIV, 785; 1939; F. L. Jones, "Mary Shelley," SAQ, XLII, 406; 1943; and J. H. Smith, SP, XLI, 94; 1944.

Clark, David L.; "Shelley and Shakespeare," PMLA, LIV, 261; 1939. — Cf. F. L. Jones, PMLA, LIX, 591; 1944.

Lewis, C. S.; "Shelley, Dryden, and Mr. Eliot," in *Rehabilitations and Other Essays,* 1939. — Noteworthy defense of Shelley against T. S. Eliot.

White, Newman I.; *Shelley,* 2 vols., 1940. — The standard account of the life and works, based partly on new materials. Thorough and judicious treatment of the many dark problems. Shelley is brought nearer to reasonableness and moderation without loss of his genius and highmindedness. Most questionable point is the treatment of Shelley's religion. — Rev., D. L. Clark, ELH, VIII, 19; 1941. — The one-vol. condensation, *Portrait of Shelley,* 1945, is a revised ed. — Some difficulties are pointed out by Carlos Baker in *Engl. Inst. Essays: 1946,* 1947.

Clark, D. L.; "What Was Shelley's Indebtedness to Keats?" PMLA, LVI, 479; 1941.

Cluck, Julia; "Elinor Wylie's Shelley Obsession," PMLA, LVI, 841; 1941.

Cameron, K. N.; "Shelley vs. Southey: New Light on an Old Quarrel," PMLA, LVII, 489; 1942. — Did Shelley in Adonais have Southey in mind as the critic?

Cameron, K. N.; "The Social Philosophy of Shelley," *Sewanee Rev.,* L, 457; 1942. — Cf. JEGP, XLII, 197; 1943; and ELH, XII, 62; 1945.

Notopoulos, J. A.; "The Dating of Shelley's Prose," PMLA, LVIII, 477; 1943. — Ingenious.

Smith, Robert Metcalf; *The Shelley Legend,* 1945. — Sensational attack on the Shelley family and on Mary Shelley for intentionally concealing or distorting the truth about the poet. "Circular argument, incomplete, inadequate, or biassed use of data, misunderstanding of the poetry, and unbased imputation of motives" are frequent (N. I. White, ELH, XIII, 15; 1945). — Reviews by N. I. White, SP, XLIII, 522; F. L. Jones, PMLA, XLI, 848; K. N. Cameron, JEGP, XLV, 369; and TLS, Oct. 26, 1946.

Fogle, R. H.; "The Abstractness of Shelley," PQ, XXIV, 362; 1945; and "Empathic Imagery in Keats and Shelley," PMLA, LXI, 163; 1946. — Cf. Fogle's "Romantic Bards," above, 1945, under "Of First Importance."

Jones, F. L.; "The Vision Theme in Shelley's *Alastor* and Related Works," SP, XLIV, 108; 1947; and "Shelley's *On Life,*" PMLA, LXII, 774; 1947.

Blunden, Edmund; *Shelley: A Life Story,* 1946. — A smooth performance by a practised hand; nothing distinctively new; evades passing judgment. Rev. TLS, May 4, 1946.

Hughes, A. M. D.; *The Nascent Mind of Shelley,* 1947. — Condemns his bewildered thinking, in 1811–13, culminating with *Queen Mab,* after which he ceased to think at all; a poet only of "unordered intuition."

Barrell, Joseph; *Shelley and the Thought of His Time: A Study in the History of Ideas,* 1947. — The mingling of the eighteenth-century Enlightenment, and of Greek philosophy, with the emotionalism of his own nature and of his times. — For weaknesses, see Grabo's review, JEGP, XLVII, 313; 1948.

Weeks, Donald; "Image and Idea in Yeats' *The Second Coming,*" PMLA, LXIII, 281; 1948. — Strong influence of *Prometheus Unbound.*

Laser, Marvin; "Poe's Concept of Beauty," ELH, XV, 69; 1948. — Influence of Coleridge, and of Shelley's *Defense of Poetry.*

Notopoulos, J. A.; *The Platonism of Shelley,* 1948. — By a scholar in Greek literature.

On Individual Poems

These references are supplementary to the books and articles listed above, by White, Grabo, Kurtz, Firkins, Carlos Baker, G. Wilson Knight, Cameron, Fogle, etc.

Alastor: R. D. Havens, PMLA, XLV, 1098 (1930); H. L. Hoffman, *An Odyssey of the Soul* (1933); A. E. Du Bois, JEGP, XXV, 530 (1936); M. Kessel, PMLA, LI, 302 (1936); F. L. Jones, ELH, XIII, 291 (1946) and SP, XLIV, 108 (1947) and E. K. Gibson, PMLA, LXII, 1022 (1947).

Hymn to Intellectual Beauty: J. A. Notopoulos, on the Platonic sources, PMLA, LVIII, 582 (1943); F. L. Jones, "Shelley's *On Life,*" PMLA, LXII, 774 (1947); and Elizabeth Nitchie, PMLA, LXIII, 752 (1948).

Mont Blanc: I. J. Kapstein, PMLA, LXII, 1046; 1947.

Ozymandias: D. W. Thompson, PQ, XVI, 59; 1937.

Ode to the West Wind: F. A. Pottle, TLS, June 20, 1936; Mead, Wormhoudt, and Fogle, EXP, May and Oct., 1947; and Fogle, "Imaginal Design," ELH, XV, 219; 1948.

The Cenci: Sara R. Watson on *Othello* and *The Cenci;* PMLA, LV, 611 (1940); K. G. Pfeiffer, "Landor's Critique," SP, XXXIX, 670 (1942); and Cameron and Frenz, "Stage History," PMLA, LX, 1080 (1945).

Prometheus Unbound: Besides N. I. White (1940 and 1945) and Grabo (1930 and 1936), see Stovall (1931), K. N. Cameron "Political Symbolism," PMLA, LVIII, 728 (1943), and J. L. Thomson, "The Unbinding of Prometheus," UTQ, XV, 1 (1945).

To a Skylark: E. W. Marjarum, PMLA, LII, 911; 1937.

Ode to Liberty: EXP, June, 1944; Dec., 1946.

Epipsychidion: Stopford Brooke, *Studies in Poetry,* 1920; P. N. Roy, *Shelley's Epipsychidion: A Study,* Calcutta, 1938, which utilizes an Italian *Life of Emilia Viviana* (1936); G. Wilson Knight, *Christian Renaissance* (1933), p. 305; and J. H. Roberts, EXP, April, 1943.

Hellas: R. D. Havens, "Hellas and Charles the First," SP, XLIII, 545; 1946.

Lines: When the Lamp Is Shattered: EXP, March, April, May, Oct., 1943; Nov. 1944.

The Triumph of Life: F. Melian Stawell, *Engl. Asso. Essays and Studies,* V, 112 (1919), and William Cherubini, "Shelley's Own Symposium," SP, XXXIX, 559 (1942).

A Defense of Poetry: Editions by A. S. Cook (1891) and H. F. B. Brett-Smith (1929). — A. C. Bradley, "Shelley's Views of Poetry," *Oxford Lectures on Poetry* (1911); A. C. Bradley, MLR (1914); M. T. Solve, *Shelley: His Theory of Poetry* (1927); Lucas Verkoren, *A Study of Shelley's Defense* (1937); K. N. Cameron, "A New Source," SP, XXXVIII, 629 (1941); and B. R. McElderry, Jr., "Common Elements in Wordsworth's *Preface* and Shelley's *Defense,*" MLQ, V, 175 (1944).

History of the Biography and Criticism

N. I. White, ed.; *The Unextinguished Hearth: Shelley and His Contemporary Critics,* 1938. — 240 notices in 83 books and periodicals in Shelley's lifetime, showing him "known and feared."

Cf. Edmund Blunden, *Shelley and Keats as They Struck Their Contemporaries* (1925); Walter Graham, "Shelley's Debt to Leigh Hunt and 'The Examiner,'" PMLA, XL, 185 (1925); G. L. Marsh, "The Early Reviews of Shelley," MP, XXVII, 73 (1929); W. S. Ward, MLN, LIX, 539 (1944); and F. C. Mason, *Shelley Criticism* (1929).

N. I. White; "The Beautiful Angel and His Biographers," SAQ, XXIV, 73; 1925.

J. W. Beach; "Latter-Day Critics of Shelley," YR, XI, 718; 1922.

William White; "Fifteen Years of Shelley Scholarship: 1923–1938," ESt, XXI, 8; 1939. — Supplemented by L. Verkoren, ESt, XXI, 120; 1939.

Julia Powers; *Shelley in America,* Univ. of Nebr. Studies; 1940.

For Shelley criticism in Germany and France, see, above, under Biography and Criticism, Liptzin (1924) and Peyre (1935).

Concordance

Ellis, Frederick S.; *A Lexical Concordance to the Poetical Works of Shelley,* 1892.

Bibliographies

Forman, H. B.; *The Shelley Library,* 1886. — Limited to works by Shelley himself.

Wise, Thomas B.; *A Shelley Library,* 1924. — Supplements Forman's; includes some works on Shelley; good descriptions and quotations.

De Ricci, Seymour; *A Bibliography of Shelley's Letters, Published and Unpublished;* Paris, 1927.

CHAPTER 16

LEIGH HUNT

(October 19, 1784–August 28, 1859)

His Life.—The father of Leigh Hunt was a lawyer in Philadelphia. When the American Revolution broke out he took the loyalist side, and went to England, where he became an unsuccessful Unitarian minister. For some time he was the tutor of a young nobleman named Leigh, after whom his son was named. Leigh Hunt's mother had a strong love of nature and of books, and also a strong tendency to defy and resist injustice—qualities which, like his father's impracticability, reappeared in her son. From the age of seven to fifteen he was at school at Christ's Hospital, where Coleridge and Lamb had preceded him by about ten years. He had little interest in his studies, but precociously delighted in the poetry of Spenser, Thomson, Gray, and Collins; and at seventeen published a volume of verse, *Juvenilia.* He was not enabled to attend a university, but persevered in his self-culture while working as a clerk. For some years he wrote dramatic criticisms for newspapers. In 1808 his brother John Hunt established a journal, *The Examiner,* and appointed him editor. Unfortunately this brought him into the vortex of political controversy, the *Examiner,* though not owned by a party, being intended to support the policies of the Whigs or Liberals, or as Hunt said,

> to assist in producing reform in Parliament, liberality of opinion in general (especially freedom from superstition), and a fusion of literary taste into all subjects whatsoever.

It advocated Catholic emancipation, Parliamentary reform, the freedom of the press, popular education, the relief of unemployment, and the abolition of the slave trade, of child labor, and of imprisonment for debt.

It was a period when, as not infrequently in politics, personal vituperation was employed as argument. When in 1811, George III became insane, his son, afterwards George IV, was appointed Prince Regent. He was a middle-aged man, fat and fifty, and of notoriously dissolute habits;

but the Tory press spoke of him as if he were a patron of letters like Mæcenas and as handsome as Adonis. Thereupon *The Examiner,* unable to restrain itself, exclaimed

> What person, unacquainted with the true state of the case would imagine . . . that this "glory of the people" was the subject of millions of shrugs and reproaches! . . . That this "conqueror of hearts" was the disappointer of hopes! That this "exciter of desire," . . . this "Adonis in loveliness," was a corpulent gentleman of fifty! In short that this "delightful," "blissful," "wise," "pleasurable," "honorable," "virtuous," "true," and "immortal Prince," was a violator of his word, a libertine over head and ears in debt and disgrace, a despiser of domestic ties, the companion of gamblers and demi-reps, a man who has just closed half a century without one single claim on the gratitude of his country or the respect of posterity!

All this was true enough, but no government could permit its publication; and John and Leigh Hunt were found guilty of libel and sentenced to two years' separate imprisonment.

Leigh Hunt bore his incarceration (February 3, 1813–1815) cheerfully. It was not confinement at hard labor. Owing to his weak health, he was assigned a room in the prison hospital. He decorated its sides with a wallpaper showing trellises of roses, colored the ceiling with clouds and sky; and, surrounded with his books and piano, made the very best of the predicament. Charles Lamb opined that nothing like it had ever been known out of a fairy tale. Hunt thus became a graceful martyr to the cause of liberalism and freedom of speech, and was visited in prison not only by Charles and Mary Lamb but also by Hazlitt, Moore, Byron, Shelley, and many other notables. When he was released, Keats wrote a sonnet in celebration of the event, beginning

> What though, for showing truth to flattered state
> Kind Hunt was shut in prison, yet has he,
> In his immortal spirit been as free
> As the sky-searching lark, and as elate.

On regaining his freedom, Hunt published his poem *The Story of Rimini* (1816). Keats, who was over ten years younger than himself, now became his admiring friend and temporarily his disciple. He won an even more ardent friend in Shelley, whose feelings and opinions were in many respects sympathetic with his own. In his article "Young Poets," in *The Examiner* Hunt, a lone voice in the wilderness, first uttered that approval of the poetry of Keats and Shelley which he was to reiterate throughout his long life.

The Tory reviewers looked upon Hunt's poetry as that of a man who had been found guilty of slandering his king and must therefore be contemptible in every way. *Blackwood's Magazine* (October, 1817), in an article on the "Cockney School," attacked him as follows:

> His poetry is that of a man who has kept company with kept-mistresses. He talks indelicately like a tea-sipping milliner girl. Some excuse for him

there might have been, had he been hurried away by imagination or passion. But with him indecency is a disease, and he speaks unclean things
from perfect inanition. The very concubine of so impure a wretch as
Leigh Hunt would be pitied, but alas! for the wife of such a husband!
For him there is no charm in simple seduction; and he gloats over it only
when accompanied with adultery and incest. . . . How such a profligate
nature as Mr. Hunt can pretend to be an admirer of Mr. Wordsworth, is
to us a thing altogether inexplicable.

When Hunt threatened to bring action against this outrageous vilifica-
tion, a new edition of the number was issued, in which the article was
toned down; but for decades Hunt had to fight his way, and that of his
friends, against such political malignity.

Keats, before leaving for Italy, was a guest of Hunt's at Hampstead;
and when he lay dying at Rome, Hunt wrote to Joseph Severn:

Tell that great poet and noble-hearted man that we shall all bear his
memory in the most precious part of our hearts, and that the world shall
bow their heads to it, as our lives do.

Hunt's own health was failing at this time, he had an ailing wife and a
large family, and was as usual in pecuniary straits. Hence he was delighted to receive Shelley's suggestion in 1821 that he come to Italy and
edit *The Liberal,* as an organ in which Byron's and Shelley's writings
would appear. With characteristic confidence that his future was assured,
he sold his belongings, and arrived in Italy in July, 1822, expecting that
Shelley would support him until *The Liberal* should bring returns. No
doubt Shelley, whose gifts to Hunt had already been generously large,
would have done so; but his death made Hunt a dependent on the par-
simonious Byron, who looked upon the Hunt family as a distressing in-
cubus. In the circumstances, *The Liberal,* though extraordinarily brilliant, survived only one year. When Byron, in 1823, departed for Greece,
he left Hunt to shift for himself. Hunt, as usual writing voluminously,
struggled along in Italy until 1825, when his publisher loaned him sufficient money to return home.

Three years later, tempted by desperate need of money, he wrote his
*Lord Byron and Some of His Contemporaries, with Recollections of the
Author's Life and of His Visit to Italy.* He included in it appreciative
sketches of Lamb, Keats, and Shelley; but it was mainly devoted to a
detailed account of the departed Byron, which dwelt upon his major and
minor weaknesses, not omitting his fear of growing fat and his disinclina-
tion to settle debts. Hunt's bitterness was natural enough; and, as he
protested in answer to reproofs, he had not said anything which he did
not believe absolutely true. But since it was in the capacity of a dependent and guest that he had learned much of what he disclosed, its
publication was met with a storm of disapproval from Thomas Moore
and others; and Tory critics saw in it a new proof that the Cockney
School had no sense of propriety. This was indeed the greatest blunder

of Hunt's life, almost as regrettable a mistake as his friend Hazlitt made in publishing the *Liber Amoris*.[1]

The rest of Hunt's long life was spent in a prodigious amount of literary and journalistic labor of many different kinds. He wrote much dramatic criticism for the daily press, and has been called "the first critic of the theater worthy of the name," for he preceded Hazlitt. He scrupulously abstained from knowing any actor personally, and "would as lief have taken poison as accept a ticket from the theaters." He was considered "a newspaperman"; but in that age, when journalists were looked down upon as licentious, dishonest, unprincipled, and vulgar, Hunt's idealistic and scholarly standards helped to make journalism respectable. Until he was nearing sixty, he was always harassed with debts and repeatedly on the verge of absolute destitution. In his later years, when the enmities aroused by his politics and by his *Byron* had grown feebler, and when he was recognized as a veteran who had performed valuable services to the world of letters, he was aided by a government pension and by gifts from some who, like Mary Shelley, felt grateful toward him. The most unpleasant incident of his old age occurred when, on the publication of Dickens' *Bleak House* (1852), a character in that novel, Harold Skimpole, a cheerful borrower and sponger, was supposed to be intended as a satire upon him. Dickens, however, indignantly denied the accusation, declaring Hunt "the very soul of truth and honor." Among the friends of Hunt in his last years, besides Dickens himself, were Carlyle, Browning, and Thackeray. His last notable work was his *Autobiography* (1850), a delightful record of literary and personal experiences, which candidly discloses his own weaknesses, and which has been praised in one of the best modern autobiographies, William Henry Hudson's *Far Away and Long Ago*.

His Personality.—Hunt's greatest weakness was, so to speak, his willingness to live up (or down) to what Godwin preached,—viz., that property should be distributed according to individual needs. He had no sense of responsibility in matters of money, ran into debt without hesitation, borrowed more money to pay off former debts, and accepted the bounty of friends as freely as he would have bestowed wealth upon others, had he ever possessed it. Except that he was the extreme opposite of a lazy person, he displayed, in some of his unpracticalities, what popular ignorance supposes to be the real "literary temperament" (though it is not ordinarily found in great authors). His finer qualities are best described by Shelley, who, in dedicating *The Cenci* to him, wrote:

Had I known a person more highly endowed than yourself with all that it becomes a man to possess, I had solicited for this work the ornament of his name. One more gentle, honorable, innocent, and brave; one of more exalted toleration for all who do and think evil, and yet himself more free from evil; one who knows better how to receive, and how to confer

[1] See, above, p. 127.

a benefit though he must ever confer far more than he can receive; one of simpler, and, in the highest sense of the word, of purer life and manners, I never knew: and I had already been fortunate in friendships when your name was added to the list.

Carlyle, who was not a lenient judge of anyone, especially not of those who possessed chiefly the gentler virtues, called Hunt "a man who can be other than *loved* only by those who have not seen him, or seen him from a distance through a false medium."

His Poems.—Hunt wrote many poems that described nature prettily, and he was ingenious and facile in verse narrative. His limitations as a poet have already been set forth in connection with their influence upon Keats.[2] His *Story of Rimini* was based upon one of the most nobly tragic episodes in Dante, that of Paolo and Francesca; but his treatment of it was often inappropriate or incongruous because he fell into the tone of careless, airy, and familiar conversation. This fault sprang out of his praiseworthy revolt against the rule of the stiff and stilted Popean couplet. The fact that he thereby initiated a change in taste constitutes his chief claim to a place in the history of poetry, although it was not he, but Keats and Shelley, who wrote the romantic couplet in its perfection. His departure from the fashion of the day was not a sign of his absolute originality, but rather of his good taste in imitation: he had recognized the superiority, for narrative purposes, of that form of the couplet which was employed by Chaucer and Dryden.

His Miscellaneous Work and Familiar Essays.—Hunt had a sincere interest in raising the level of general culture. In his many journalistic and editorial enterprises, he tried to heighten popular appreciation of literature and of refined ways of life. He was influential in a wholesome democratization of newspapers and other journals; and, when not exasperated by the brawling temper of contemporaneous controversy, discussed public questions with an urbanity then unusual.

His religious views he stated in a privately issued pamphlet, *Christianism* (1832), admired by Carlyle, and afterwards published under the characterizing title *The Religion of the Heart* (1853). "Nothing," he opined, "again will ever be universally taken for Christianity but the religion of Loving Duty to God and Man." His pacifism was expressed in the poem, *Captain Sword and Captain Pen* (1835), written "to show the horrors of war, the false ideas of power produced in the minds of its leaders, and, by inference, the unfitness of those leaders for the government of the world." All his work, whatever the subject, rests upon a sincere and humane religious faith.

In *The Indicator,* a weekly magazine, and elsewhere, he published innumerable familiar essays, such as "Getting Up on Cold Mornings," "The Old Gentleman," "The Old Lady," "A Few Thoughts on Sleep," and "Deaths of Little Children." In this art he did not rise to such heights

[2] See, above, p. 226.

as Lamb or Hazlitt; but there are some gentle readers who enjoy him even more than those masters, for he does not deal as much as they do in frankly voiced antipathies, and he indulges in no archaic diction or difficult allusions. He pleases the kindly, forgiving, or mildly humorous mood. The best of his essays were collected in book form, e.g., in *The Seer,* and *Men, Women, and Books.*

For fifty years Hunt fostered English interest in the best Italian literature. He made many graceful translations, e.g., of Tasso's *Amyntas* (1820), Redi's *Bacchus in Tuscany* (1825), and *A Jar of Honey from Mount Hybla,* the Sicilian pastoral poets (1848). He produced numerous anthologies, still of value because of his excellent taste in selection and his appreciative commentaries. Among the best of these books are *Imagination and Fancy* (1844; *Anth.,* 1009–13), *Wit and Humour* (1846), and *The Book of the Sonnet* (1867).

His Criticisms and His Relations to Other Romantics.—Hunt's method of criticism was largely based upon his conviction that analyses of a literary work and generalizations concerning its qualities were not so likely to convey a sense of its beauty as quotations from it or as an account of the critic's feelings in reading it. He said:

> Taste is the very maker of judgment. Put an artificial fruit in your mouth, or only handle it, and you will soon perceive the difference between judging from taste or tact, and judging from the abstract figment called judgment. The latter does but throw you into guesses and doubts.
>
> *Imagination and Fancy*

In his own case the method was safe enough, for his skill was extraordinary in choosing quotations that happily illustrated an author's traits, and, although his own creative powers were not great, his appreciation of them in others was wide and sound. Time has shown him nearly always right in his opinions about poetry from Chaucer to Browning. This is not to say that as a critic he approached in greatness Coleridge, or Hazlitt, or Lamb, or De Quincey. They surpassed him in philosophical profundity, or originality of application of ideas, or subtlety, or scholarship, or in the discernment of faults.

The greatest distinction of Leigh Hunt was the twofold service which he rendered to the leading Romantics. In the first place, in writing *What Is Poetry?* (1844; *Anth.,* 1009) he popularized the romantic theory of poetry. Here he explained, without any flights above the heads of the ordinary reader into the realm of the Infinite, or of the One and the Many, just what poetry meant; and he made its principles clear with the most apt illustrations. His essay remains one of the best elementary introductions to an important and difficult subject. Here as elsewhere his apparent lightness of manner disguises the seriousness and integrity of his thought.

Hunt's other service to the movement lay in his encouragement, and in his intelligent, brave, and persistent advocacy, of Romantics greater than himself. He fostered the reputations of Wordsworth, Coleridge, and Lamb, and founded those of Keats and Shelley (*Anth.*, 1012–13). In *The Liberal* he published Byron's *Vision of Judgment,* Shelley's "Song for an Indian Air," and Hazlitt's *My First Acquaintance with Poets* and *Shakspere's Fools.* In *The Examiner* of December 1, 1816, he published an article, "Young Poets," in which he greeted Shelley as "a very striking and original thinker," and Keats as a poet whose lines "fairly surprised us with the truth of their ambition and ardent grappling with nature." When the *Eve of St. Agnes* appeared, he praised it as "full-grown poetry of the rarest description, graceful as the beardless Apollo, glowing and gorgeous with the colors of romance." He did not shrink from vindicating Shelley's character and ideas. As early as 1818–19, he wrote of him as "no doubt destined to be one of the leading spirits of his age." In 1822 he wrote a superbly indignant defense of *Prometheus Unbound* and other Shelleyan poems against the bigoted attacks of the *Quarterly Review (Anth.,* 1007). He declared *The Cenci* "the greatest dramatic production of the day," and defended *Adonais* against those who called it cold and insincere. Shelley was, he said, a poet for whom "if for any poet that ever lived, the beauty of the external world has an answering heart, and the very whispers of the wind a meaning." To realize the value of such utterances, one must bear in mind that, at the time when they were made, indifference or misunderstanding or opposition to the Romantics was the rule, and that the general recognition of their greatness might have been much retarded if Leigh Hunt had not appreciated them and praised them so well.

SELECTED BIBLIOGRAPHY

OF FIRST IMPORTANCE

Selections and Texts

    Essays and Poems, ed. R. B. Johnson (Temple Libr.) , 2 vols., 1891.

    Prefaces, Mainly to His Periodicals, ed. R. B. Johnson, 1927.

    Essays, ed. J. B. Priestley (Everyman's Libr.) , 1929.

    The Autobiography of Leigh Hunt, ed. Edmund Blunden (World's Classics) , 1928.

Best Biography

    Blunden, Edmund; *Leigh Hunt and His Circle,* 1930.

Good Introductory Criticism

    In addition to the two preceding items: George Saintsbury, "Leigh Hunt," *Essays in English Literature,* 1890.

FOR ADVANCED STUDENTS

Important Additional Texts

    There is no complete, or approximately complete, edition; it would probably require c. 50 volumes. A four-volume collection appeared in 1857; a seven-volume, in 1870.

Poetical Works, ed. H. S. Milford (Oxford Univ. Press) , 1923. — Good Introduction and Bibliographical List.

Dramatic Essays, ed. William Archer and R. W. Lowe, 1894.

Dramatic Essays, ed. C. W. and L. H. Houtchens (Columbia Univ. Press) , announced for 1948.

Essays and Sketches, ed. R. Brimley Johnson (World's Classics) , 1907.

Leigh Hunt's 'Examiner' Examined: 1808–1825, ed. Edmund Blunden, 1928. — Essays on Shelley, Keats, Lamb, etc.

Imagination and Fancy: With an Essay 'What Is Poetry?' 1844; ed. Edmund Gosse, 1907.

What Is Poetry? ed. A. S. Cook (Ginn) , 1893.

The Months, Descriptive of the Successive Beauties of the Year, 1821; ed. R. H. B[ath], 1929.

Brewer, Luther A.; *My Leigh Hunt Library: The Holograph Letters* (Univ. of Iowa) , 1938. — *Leaves from a Leigh Hunt Note-Book* (Cedar Rapids) , 1932.

Biography and Criticism

Dickens, Charles; "Leigh Hunt: A Remonstrance," *All the Year Round,* Dec. 24, 1859; rptd. in *Miscellaneous Papers,* II, 206. — Denies that Harold Skimpole in *Bleak House* is like Hunt, except in manner of speaking. — Cf. M. B. Forman, *London Mercury,* XIV, 180; 1926.

Monkhouse, W. Cosmo; *Life of Leigh Hunt* (Great Writers Ser.) , 1893. — Good on facts; rather unsympathetic. Bibliographical Appendix.

Johnson, R. B.; *Leigh Hunt,* 1896. — Helpful on his journalistic and political writings.

Symons, Arthur; in *The Romantic Movement in English Poetry,* 1909. — Hunt as an innovator in diction and metre.

Miller, Barnette; *Leigh Hunt's Relations with Byron, Shelley, and Keats,* 1910. — Cf. Walter Graham, "Shelley's Debt to Leigh Hunt and 'The Examiner,' " PMLA, XL, 185; 1925.

Saintsbury, George; "The Landors, Leigh Hunt, and De Quincey," *Cambridge History of English Literature,* XII, 226; 1916. — Generous praise from a Tory.

Pierce, Frederick E.; "The Eddy Around Leigh Hunt," *Currents and Eddies in the English Romantic Generation,* 1918.

Gosse, Edmund; *More Books on the Table,* 1923.

Stout, G. D.; "Leigh Hunt's Money Troubles," *Washington Univ. Stud.,* XII, 221; 1925. — New evidence as to his attitude toward "sponging."

Stout, G. D.; "The Cockney School," TLS, Feb. 7, 1929. — Quotations from the suppressed edition of *Blackwood's Magazine,* Oct., 1817.

Wheeler, Paul M.; "The Great Quarterlies of the Early Nineteenth Century and Leigh Hunt," SAQ, XXIX, 282; 1930.

Brightfield, Myron F.; "Leigh Hunt," *Univ. of California Essays in Criticism,* Second Series, 1934.

Roberts, Michael; "Leigh Hunt's Place in the Reform Movement: 1808–1810," RES, XI, 58; 1935.

Landré, Louis; *Leigh Hunt: Contribution à l'Histoire du Romantisme Anglais, avec Bibliographie Nouvelle.* Vol. I: *L'Auteur;* Vol. II: *L'Oeuvre;* Paris, 1935–36. — One of the most thorough and valuable monographs on any of the Romantics. — Rev., TLS, May 9, 1936; MLN, LII, 534; MP, XXXV, 92 (1937) ; MLR, XXXIII, 592 (1938) .

Fischer, Erika; *Leigh Hunt und die Italienische Literatur*, Freiburg, 1936.

Strout, Alan L.; "Hunt, Hazlitt, and 'Maga': The Lighter Side of 'Cockney'-Killing," ELH, IV, 151; 1937.

Mineka, Francis E.; *The Dissidence of Dissent: The Monthly Repository: 1806–38*, 1944. — Hunt was the editor of this journal in its last years. — Rev., JEGP, XLIV, 323; 1945.

Aspinwall, Arthur; "The Social Status of Journalists at the Beginning of the Nineteenth Century," RES, XXI, 216, 1945.

Tyler, Henry; "Hunt and Shelley," TLS, Nov. 8, 1947. — How Hunt's essay on Shelley, c. 1825, was suppressed.

Bibliographies

Brewer, Luther A.; *My Leigh Hunt Library: The First Editions*, 1932. — This great collection is now in the Library of the University of Iowa.

Landré, Louis; *Leigh Hunt*, II, 483–595; Paris, 1936.

CHAPTER 17

THOMAS DE QUINCEY

(August 15, 1785–December 8, 1859)

His Life.—Thomas De Quincey was the fifth of eight children born to a prosperous merchant named "Quincey," in Manchester. He was a shy and sensitive child, craving affection and especially fond of one of his sisters, whose early death made a deeply melancholy impression upon him. His elder brother liked to torment or bully him. The death of his father in 1793 left his upbringing in the hands of a mother who, though very conscientious, displayed no warmth of affection toward him. He grew inclined to solitude and bookishness. He was given a good schooling, was precocious, and at fifteen could speak and write Greek with ease. "From my birth," he said, "I was made an intellectual creature." The restrictive routine of his school life, and the sedately respectable middle-class tone of his home and family, failed to satisfy his adolescent longings for emotional, mental, and imaginative stimuli: at sixteen, it pleased him to prefix a "homemade" "De" to his name; and a year later, having become involved in a petty difficulty about money, he ran away from school and home, and for some months led a half-starved existence in Wales and London, enduring great hardships in order to be his own master. The recently discovered diary which he kept about this time (1803) shows him a thoughtful youth, worrying over his own traits of character, and devoted to some of the great English poets, and, despite his youth, one of the first to appreciate the importance of the rising Romantics, especially Coleridge ("I begin to think him the greatest man that has ever appeared"). In his *Confessions*, he called this vagabond episode an "impassioned parenthesis of my life."

Reconciled to his family, he was allowed to enter Oxford, where he lived a studious life and attracted attention only through his charm as a conversationalist. When he was about twenty, he suffered from severe headaches, and, on the advice of a friend, began to take laudanum, an alcoholic tincture of opium. The relief from pain was so great and so pleasurable, and ill health tormented him so frequently, that he was unable to forego the use of this drug, and little by little became a slave thereto. Throughout his life this addiction had a harmful effect upon his habits, begetting unreliability and procrastination. Until recently little was known about the psychological effects of opium, and formerly there were sharp differences of opinion regarding De Quincey's use of it and of other stimulants. One of his physicians asserted that he suffered from a disease of the stomach, that only opium relieved his pains, and that his use of it prolonged his life. Another doctor declared that eye-strain or astigmatism was the cause of all his troubles. A third maintained that, because of the form in which De Quincey took the medicine, it was alcohol more than opium that affected him. Nowadays the following aspects of the matter are regarded as more important. In the first place, De Quincey during his life succeeded in freeing himself four times from slavery to opium, and some of his best work was composed during those periods of freedom. Secondly, he, like everybody else in his day, attached too much importance to the effect of opium on his dreams. It was not the cause of them, nor a shaping influence. His powerful imagination, and not laudanum, created his visions. The same doses might have been given to a thousand others, but unless they had been De Quinceys nothing like his achievements would have resulted. Years before he took to opium he was, so to speak, a connoisseur in dreams, reveries, and visions. Last, and most important, his originality lay in attaching great significance to dream experiences long before the days of Freud and Jung.

In college, De Quincey read widely in German philosophy and in classical and English literature, and grew more and more enthusiastic about the Romantic Movement. In later years he liked to believe that he was one of the first to quote freely from the *Lyrical Ballads*. After persistent effort, he contrived to make the personal acquaintance of Coleridge, whose disciple he was to become in many of his chief ideas. Through Coleridge, he met Wordsworth and stayed for a short time at his home. After he had been graduated from college, and had come of age and into a small inheritance, he moved to Grasmere in order to be near the Wordsworths. He saw Wordsworth's *Convention of Cintra* through the press, and supplied a *Postscript* to it. The death of little Kate Wordsworth aroused in him extraordinarily deep and eloquent grief, for he loved and understood children with unusual insight, being himself a childlike spirit.

At Grasmere, he also enjoyed the friendship of John Wilson, a young man of his own age, likewise an admirer of the Lake School, and later to become celebrated as Christopher North, the leading writer for *Blackwood's Magazine*. De Quincey spent most of his time in hard study, his only relaxation in these years being long rambles through the Lake district. At the age of twenty-eight he shocked the Wordsworth family by falling in love with an uneducated girl, Margaret Simpson, daughter of a farmer, and marrying her three months after a child had been born to them. De Quincey resented the attitude of the Wordsworths, which Dorothy vainly tried to make seem less harsh, and his bitterness was to show itself in some of his writings in later years. Margaret De Quincey proved to be a faithful, intelligent, and devoted wife; and the marriage, despite De Quincey's trying weaknesses and oddities, was a happy one. It is doubtful whether without her care, and that of his equally affectionate daughters, he would have lived to produce his masterpieces.

As late as 1821, when he was thirty-six years old, De Quincey was almost unknown. His ambition was to become a great scholar; dreaming that perhaps, as he said,

> . . . if I should be blessed with life sufficient, I should accomplish a great revolution in the intellectual condition of the world, . . . place education upon a new footing throughout all civilized nations, and be the first founder of a true philosophy.

But his scholarship hitherto had been absorptive only, not productive. Now, having let his little capital trickle away through mere laxness in money matters, he was almost destitute, and was obliged to earn his living by his pen. He moved to London where the Lambs and Hazlitt were among his friends. He was introduced to the owners of the new *London Magazine,* which was beginning its brief but brilliant career; and they accepted his *Confessions of an English Opium Eater, Being an Extract from the Life of a Scholar,* which appeared in their journal in 1821. Its marvelous prose style brought De Quincey immediate fame, and henceforth his contributions were welcome to the leading editors. In some respects his introduction to celebrity was unfortunate; for, owing to the strength of first impressions, the public thought of him too much as a man addicted to drugs and dreams, and too little as a scholar and prose poet whose work had very substantial qualities.

From this time onwards De Quincey was primarily a writer for the magazines—chiefly for *Blackwood's, Tait's Edinburgh Magazine,* and Hogg's *The Instructor* and *The Titan.* In the course of his long life, he wrote over one hundred and fifty articles, some of them much longer than the average length of such writings. Though there was mere hack work among them, in many cases their preparation required extensive study and note-taking; and wherever he sojourned, in country cottage or city lodgings, he was almost snowed under by chaotic heaps of books and papers. It was said that when the confusion grew too great he would depart to a new domicile, leaving the débris of his recent labors behind him. His daughters called his study "The Chaos."

His work for *Blackwood's* led him to make Edinburgh his home from 1826 onwards. He was a most affectionate father, and his daughters reciprocated his devotion throughout his life, although he was never out of debt and was in many ways a sore trial to their family life. His greatest sorrows were the deaths of two of his sons and, in 1837, of his beloved wife. The latter bereavement affected him so deeply that his mind for a time was almost unhinged. Thenceforth his intercourse with the world was still more infrequent than formerly. He continued to take his long solitary walks; but nearly all the rest of his time was spent in reading and writing. Not until 1846, when his mother died, leaving enough to provide for him and his family, did their harassments end. His work was as much appreciated in the United States as in Great Britain; and an American collected edition in more than twenty volumes, published by Ticknor and Fields in Boston, antedated the first English collected edition of 1853–60. In the fall of 1859, being in his seventy-fifth year, he grew so feeble that his daughters were unable to move him from his lodgings to their home, as they desired. He died on December 8, 1859, not from the effects of drug-taking, but of mere old age; and he was buried beside his wife in the West Kirkyard of Edinburgh.

His Personality.—The appearance and manner of De Quincey are described by his friend J. R. Findlay as follows:

> He was a very little man,—about five feet, three or four inches,—his countenance the most remarkable for its intellectual attractiveness that I have ever seen. His features, throughout regular, were aristocratically fine, and an air of delicate breeding pervaded the face. His forehead was un-usually high, square, and compact. At first sight his face appeared boyishly fresh and smooth, with a sort of hectic glow upon it that contrasted re-markably with the evident appearances of age in the grizzled and dim-looking eyes. He had the air of old-fashioned good manners of the highest kind; natural and studied politeness, free from the slightest ostentation or parade; a delicacy, gentleness, and elegance of demeanor that at once conciliated and charmed.

He looked and acted as, according to popular conceptions, a typical scholar or professor ought to look and act: his clothes were ludicrously ill-fitting; he was very absent-minded; he asked for nothing except to be left in peace with his books; he had an insatiable curiosity about facts and their meaning; and he wore an air of thoughtful abstraction; but if he could be inveigled into conversation, his talk proved astonishingly interesting in content and expression. It should be added, however, that, unlike some learned men, he was not haughty or unsympathetic toward ordinary mortals. He was shy and intruded upon no one, but he had not a trace of unkindness in his disposition; and he was not only deeply fond of his family and intimates but unaffectedly friendly toward men and women in the humblest walks of life, especially if they were in want or sorrow. None felt more deeply than he that since we were all born to a common heritage of suffering and sorrow, we should at least try to lighten one another's burdens by kindness and forbearance. His manners were studied and exquisite: he was as polite to a charwoman as to a lady—but a little aloof from either one.

His Views.—Because De Quincey's sentiments were expressed not in systematic treatises, but in magazine articles, or fragmentarily in bio-graphical writings, or allegorically in visions, the definiteness and consistency of his views have been disregarded. As a rule, he has been considered only as a great stylist. He held, however, certain firm convictions which are expressed either directly or indirectly in his works.

Unlike Coleridge, Wordsworth, or Southey, he underwent no revolutionary change in his attitude. He was probably the most conservative among the Romantics in his religion and philosophy. Liberty was not quite the sacred thing to him that it was to some of the other Romantics. His patriotism was occasionally blind to the rights or merits of foreign nations. He overlooked the anticipations of Christian ethics in pagan philosophers. His admiration for Greek and Roman literature did not extend to the religion of the ancients. He thought that it was Christianity alone that we had to thank for the best tendencies in political and social life—for democratic and humane laws, for the abolition of slavery, and for the efforts to abolish war. The teachings of Christ had often been misunderstood; and the possibilities of coming to a truer understanding of them were almost unlimited:

> The Christian theory and system are perfect from the beginning; in itself Christianity changeth not, neither waxing nor waning; but the motions of time and the evolutions of experience continually uncover new parts of its unchanging disk. Christianity, perfect from the beginning, had in its earlier stages a curtain over much of its disk, which Time and Social Progress are continually withdrawing.

Miracles might have been necessary in darker ages, but ought to be so no longer.

De Quincey's religious faith was the only ground of objection which he had against Kant, who did not include the existence of God and immortality among the intellectual certainties. In other important respects, De Quincey admired Kant, and in his *Autobiography* described Kant's "deep and abiding influence" upon his life. He believed that he was one of the first to interpret Kant to England; but actually his understanding of Kant was superficial and fragmentary, and his expositions of him were often erroneous. De Quincey delighted in all varieties of idealism, including that of the German Romantic, Jean Paul Richter. The inner life of the spirit was to him of the highest importance:

> I blessed God for my life upon earth, but much more for the life in those unseen depths of the universe which are emptied of all but the Supreme Reality, and where no earthly life or perishable hope can enter.
> *Analects from Richter*

This inner life God awakened and illumined in man's mind not in the crowded market-place but in solitude or in dreams. He spake not only in his temples, not only through the utterances of saints and sages, prophets and poets,

> . . . not by sounds that perish, or by words that go astray, but by signs in heaven, by changes on earth, by pulses in secret rivers, heraldries painted on darkness, and hieroglyphics written on the tablets of the brain.
> *Suspiria De Profundis*

To De Quincey our finite life was usually a state of pain and sorrow, alleviated only to the extent that we were conscious that it *was* finite and that our real destiny was glorious and eternal. The perception that human nature was partly divine was more or less dimly felt by all, and was manifested in their ordinary affections and better qualities. The minor faults and follies were common enough, but thorough villainy was abnormal. It required a stifling or suspension of the true course of human feelings. However frequent, it was an unearthly, inhuman, unnatural thing,—as he impressively showed it in *The Knocking at the Gate in 'Macbeth'*, and, in a grotesquely comic manner, in *Murder Considered As One of the Fine Arts*, where deeds of crime are represented as ghastly phantasmagoria rather than as events of characteristically human life. When the crime has been committed, the true world rushes back upon the villain's consciousness and he feels insufferable horror and remorse, his deed having struck not only at his victim but also at his own normal nature. In a larger sphere, all the movements toward world-wide peace and justice were expressions of man's real nature, which was essentially hostile to the discord of physical nature.

The latent idealism of man must be stimulated by education, a process in which De Quincey was deeply interested. The greatness of a nation was to be measured, not by its treasury or army, but by the amount of public effort bestowed upon its libraries and schools. Worse than no education at all, however, was one of the wrong kind—i.e., the too practical or the too dogmatic. A school which taught its pupils merely to earn a living was not an educational institution. A school which gave its pupils the impression that knowledge was a static body of information to be forced upon their uninterested minds and to be completely learned for examinations, and cast aside when they were graduated, was likewise misnamed. Unless the school aimed to create a *love* of knowledge, truth, and beauty, and unless the student helped to develop that love in himself, nothing worthy to be called education was going on. Man was to be saved not by teaching him how to become rich, nor by teaching him to learn by rote what his teachers believed, but by teaching him to desire to learn for himself the nature of his soul, of that world in which he was a sojourner, and of that universe of which he was a part.

In a genuine education, therefore, the study of literature, the content and method of which fulfilled the highest aim of culture, must have a leading part. Of all the fine arts, literature was the greatest. It not merely gave us knowledge, but communicated power; because it gave not only facts but also their significance in the light of the infinite and eternal. The so-called "classical education" of the leading English schools was admirable in centering the curriculum about literature. The Greek, and, to a less degree, the Roman literatures which they emphasized were admirable in many respects, especially in their depiction of those human traits which were universal; but the classical authors, being pre-Christian, lacked certain indispensable values. Among modern literatures, German was too intellectualistic, and French much too worldly and cynical. English literature was the greatest of them all, by virtue of its sincerity and its imaginative power. Of all authors, Shakspeare was supreme because his spirit was benign and his imagination discerned behind the apparent chaos of life proofs of design.

The imagination, which was the force that chiefly created and appreciated literature, was a universal instinct, subject to aberration, but susceptible of cultivation and self-discipline; and when thus refined, it truly discerned the underlying traits of separate phenomena and of the universe as a whole. Commonplace life was hostile to the exercise of the imagination. If one became absorbed therein, enslaved to drudgery and inane pursuits, it became difficult to discern ideal values. Hence men found it natural to escape out of the commonplace, sometimes through the aid of stimulants or sedatives, into the freedom of dreams, some of which were not illusions so much as revelations (*Anth.*, 1016).

His Chief Works.—The writings of De Quincey fill fourteen large volumes. In some of them he employed his analytical and argumentative skill upon economic, philosophic, educational, or literary themes. In *The Dialogue of Three Templars* (1824) and *The Logic of Political Economy* (1844) he attacked the system of Malthus and favored that of Ricardo on the ground that the former was materialistic and unphilanthropic; but he did not really understand the actualities of the industrial revolution nor the weaknesses of the *laissez-faire* school of economics. His metaphysical notions, which were amateurish, he set forth chiefly in several essays on various aspects of the philosophy of Immanuel Kant (1824-33). Of his discussions on education, the weightiest is his *Letters to a Young Man Whose Education Has Been Neglected* (1823).

As a critic, De Quincey had certain irritating weaknesses and prejudices. He could see no merits in French literature. In his discussions of contemporaries such as Wordsworth, Coleridge, Lamb, and John Wilson, he was often informative and penetrating; but here as elsewhere, he was subject to outbreaks of injudicious caprice. He was apt to digress into anecdotes. His worst blunder was the condemnation of Goethe's masterpiece of prose fiction, *Wilhelm Meister,* which he railed at because he thought the female characters were conceived by depraved taste and defective sensibility and the novel as a whole was too full of the loathsome aspects of human life. His best essays of applied criticism are probably those on Shakspeare (1838), Wordsworth (1845), and Goldsmith (1848). His special contributions to Shakspearian criticism were the reinforcement of the praise that others had bestowed on Shakspeare's heroines (he called him "the absolute *creator* of female character"); his emphasis on the complete naturalness of the dialogue; and his acute analyses of the dramatic situations. Of the latter, *On the Knocking at the Gate* (*Anth.*, 1018) is a perfect example; another notable one is his examination of the play-within-the-play in *Hamlet.* His essay on Pope (1848) may be denounced as "the most damning estimate of that

poet ever expressed by a reputable critic," and as unjust; but it is somewhat redeemed by including the admirable exposition of the distinction
between the literature of knowledge and the literature of power (*Anth.*,
1030). Coleridge and Wordsworth had established such a distinction
between the poetical and the unpoetical, but De Quincey made a valuable extension of it into the field of prose. In such general literary speculations he was more at home than in applied criticism; and his treatises
on Rhetoric (1828) and on Style (1840) are rich in generalizations, some
of them too dogmatic. He loved to expound the romantic doctrine that
style was not the "dress" of thought but its body. The literature of
knowledge could communicate what it had to say in plain unmeasured
language; but when the mind felt that contact with infinity which resulted in the literature of power its utterance naturally became rhythmical. "Mysterious," said De Quincey, "is the life that connects all forms
of passion with rhythmus."

Not a few of De Quincey's works were prose fictions translated or
adapted from German romances or influenced by them,—e.g., *The Fatal
Marksman* (1823), *The Incognito* (1824), and *Klosterheim* (1832) —the
last of these being an historical novel in which the tyranny of a land-
grave arouses the spirit of liberty among his subjects.

De Quincey was at his best in the treatment of historical, biographical,
or autobiographical themes. Some of his historical essays, like the
Toilette of the Hebrew Lady (1828), were largely of antiquarian interest; and, in accordance with that law of the ephemerality of the literature of knowledge which he himself set forth, have fallen into oblivion;
others he endued with such picturesqueness or eloquence that they survive among the glories of English prose. Among these is his *Revolt of
a Tartar Tribe* (1837), a brilliantly imaginative narrative based upon
dull French and German records, of the sufferings endured by the Kal-
mucks in their heroic retreat from the Caspian Sea to China.

Of greater general interest and importance is *Joan of Arc* (1847;
Anth., 1028). Here he drew the historic facts chiefly from the histories
of France by Anquetil, Michelet, and Kitchin; but his treatment of them
differed from such previous romantic interpretations as those of Schiller
and Southey, and was highly characteristic of his own views and
methods. His faults appeared in his occasional pseudo-humorous digressions upon the iniquities of French courts-of-law and French authors.
Attacking the liberalism of Michelet, he wrote:

> All these writers are of a revolutionary cast; not in a political sense merely,
> but in all senses, mad, oftentimes, as March-hares; crazy with the laughing
> gas of recovered liberty; drunk with the wine-cup of their mighty revolu-
> tion, snorting, whinnying, throwing up their heads, like wild horses in
> boundless Pampas, and running races of defiance with snipes, or with the
> winds, or with their own shadows, if they can find nothing else to challenge.

Another example of his eccentricity was his statement that the French
were not temperamentally capable of appreciating a character like Joan

of Arc, who was essentially more English than French! Despite such flaws, De Quincey's portrait of Joan of Arc was more admirable than any preceding one. Himself a visionary in the better sense of the word, he understood the real nature of her inspiration. He rejected those miraculous or melodramatic accessories which Schiller and others had thought necessary to display her greatness; he required no miracles to prove her a spiritual force and thought it unnecessary to invent a love story to make her seem human. He attributed her power to the influence of nature, to the awakening of her piety by the beautiful rites of her church, to her faith in God and in herself; he glorified her womanly capacity for patient suffering and self-sacrifice; and he touched the very heart of her sanctitude when he envisaged her as pleading upon the Day of Judgment for mercy upon him who had condemned her to death.

De Quincey's powers as an interpreter of apparently prosaic subjects are shown in his *English Mail-Coach* (1849; *Anth.*, 1031). Here he took what to common perception was merely a useful contrivance for speedy travel, and displayed it in the light of its national and patriotic significance.

Though De Quincey liked to range into fields remote from his own experience, he was not always successful in dealing with them. As an interpreter of themes as foreign to his own nature as German philosophy he was not as competent and important as other Romantics, such as Carlyle. But in writings based on his own life he was at his best. In them, he was not always trustworthy as to matters of fact, and sometimes he was malicious; but he had a childlike clearsightedness about people he had personally known, which gave an extraordinary vividness and depth to his recollections of Wordsworth, Coleridge, Southey, John Wilson, and other contemporaries. He described what was significant in their manners and characteristic of their inner life. But his deepest revelations were of his own self. His masterpieces are autobiographical: *Confessions of an English Opium-Eater* (1821), the *Autobiography* (1834–53), and *Suspiria De Profundis* (1845). Therein he dealt little with happenings and circumstances which were merely external or contingent, and lingered over those moments in which permanently significant visions of life had come to him. To call these works of his "fantasies" may be misleading, because it suggests that they are dreams having no reference to reality, when in point of fact they often interpret reality more vividly than accounts which conceal the essentials behind a mass of irrelevant details. He did not meet the Three Ladies of Sorrow in ordinary human intercourse but in dreams, yet more than volumes of realistic record they clarified and made poignant the varieties of human grief. He himself regarded these works as his most original, describing them as "modes of impassioned prose ranging under no precedents that I am aware of in any literature." He was trying to extend the psychological gropings of Romanticism, trying to fathom the mysterious lower depths of the subconscious, and to reach upward to the higher altitudes of the soul; he was wondering about their interrelationship, and about the possible governance of the lower memories and impulses by the higher will. In his own time, critics scoffed at these studies as mere opium dreams; in our age of Freud and Jung, we can see their real significance and originality. The traditional form of expression for such experiences and questings would have been poetry; and perhaps what was most characteristic of De Quincey was that he tried to make prose convey what was usually assumed to be too exalted for it. In his "impassioned prose" he used scarcely any word that might not be found in the diction of great poets, and he employed rhythm which, though not as regular as that of verse, was much more nearly regular than that of ordinary discourse. With Sir Thomas Browne, Jeremy Taylor, Dr. Johnson, and Edward Gibbon, he is one of the masters of ornate and balanced style.

SELECTED BIBLIOGRAPHY

OF FIRST IMPORTANCE

Selections

Selections from De Quincey, ed. M. H. Turk (Athenæum Press Series) , 1902. — Well annotated.

Selections, ed. M. R. Ridley (Oxford) , 1927. — With Essays by Leslie Stephen and Francis Thompson. Good Introduction.

Selections, ed. A. H. R. Ball (Ginn) , 1932.

Selected Writings of Thomas De Quincey, ed. Philip Van Doren Stern (Random House) , 1937. — The most comprehensive.

The Best Introduction

Sackville-West, Edward; *A Flame in Sunlight: The Life and Work of De Quincey,* 1936, although it is not as valuable and detailed factually as Eaton (1936) nor as vivid and concise as Metcalf (1940) , listed below. — Sackville-West's work is "exquisitely written, acute and sympathetic in perception of his character, as excellent as biography as it is as criticism" (S. C. Chew) .

Other Good Introductory Criticisms

Saintsbury, George; in *Essays in English Literature,* 1890; and C. T. Winchester, in *A Group of English Essayists,* 1910.

FOR ADVANCED STUDENTS

Important Additional Texts

The Collected Writings. New and Enlarged Edition by David Masson, 14 vols., Edinburgh, 1889–90.

A Diary of Thomas De Quincey: 1803, ed. H. A. Eaton, 1927.

De Quincey at Work: As Seen in One Hundred and Thirty New Letters, ed. W. H. Bonner, Buffalo, 1936.

"Some De Quincey Manuscripts," ed. Claude E. Jones, ELH, VIII, 216; 1941.

Confessions of an English Opium-Eater, First Edition (1821) , ed. R. Garnett, 1885. — Rpt. of Enlarged Edition (1855) , ed. Walter Jerrold, 1899 (Temple Classics) and many others. — Transl. into French by Baudelaire, 1860; by De Musset, 1878.

Recollections of the Lake Poets, ed. Edward Sackville-West (Chiltern Libr.) , 1948. — Good Introduction.

The Flight of a Tartar Tribe, ed. G. A. Wauchope, 1898.

The Nun-Ensign, ed. James Fitzmaurice-Kelly, 1918.

Biography and Criticism

Stephen, Leslie; "De Quincey," *Hours in a Library,* 1: 1874.

Masson, David; *De Quincey* (English Men of Letters) , 1881. — By the editor of the *Collected Writings;* long the standard biography.

"Page, H. A." [Japp, H. A.]; *De Quincey: His Life and Writings, with Unpublished Correspondence,* 2 vols., 1877; rev. and expanded, 1890. — Japp edited *De Quincey Memorials,* 1891 — family letters.

Findlay, J. R.; *Personal Recollections of De Quincey,* 1886. — He also contributed the article on De Quincey in *Encyclopedia Britannica,* 9th ed.

Hogg, James; *De Quincey and His Friends,* 1895.

Dowden, Edward; "How De Quincey Worked," *Saturday Review,* LXXIX, 246; 1895. — A study of his stylistic revisions.

Gould, George; *Biographic Clinics,* 1, 1903. — Diagnoses his ailments as due to eye trouble. — Cf. Marks, below, 1925.

Salt, Henry; *De Quincey,* 1904. — A brief and judicious biography.

Wells, John E.; "The Story of Wordsworth's *Cintra,*" SP, XVIII, 15 (1921) ; "De Quincey's Punctuation of Cintra," TLS, Nov. 3, 1932; "Wordsworth and De Quincey in Westmorland Politics," PMLA, LV, 1080 (1940) ; and "De Quincey and The Prelude in 1839," PQ, XX, 1–24 (1941) .

Fowler, J. H.; *De Quincey as Literary Critic* (Engl. Asso. Pamphlet, No. 52) , 1922.

Paull, H. M.; "De Quincey and Style," *Fortnightly Review,* CXVIII, 152; 1922.

Marks, Jeanette; *Genius and Disaster,* 1925. — Thinks his consumption of alcohol more important than that of opium. — Cf. Abrams, below, 1934.

Abrams, M. H.; *The Milk of Paradise,* 1934. — Characteristic images and effects in the works of four opium addicts. See Schneider, below, 1945.

Parsons, C. O.; "Woes of De Quincey," RES, X, 190; 1934. — Crises recorded in his correspondence with Lockhart and Robinson.

Eaton, Horace A.; *Thomas De Quincey: A Biography,* 1936. — The first thoroughly documented Life; sympathetic, judicious. The standard factual biography.

Sehrt, Ernst T.; *Geschichtliches und Religiöses Denken bei De Quincey,* Berlin, 1936. — His politics, philosophy of history, and religion; and his relation to Burke, Carlyle, Kant, Fichte, Hegel, etc. Cf. below, Proctor (1943) and Wellek (1944) .

Forward, Kenneth; " 'Libellous Attack' on De Quincey," PMLA, LII, 244; 1937. — The grossly personal attacks by the *John Bull Magazine,* etc., 1824. — "De Quincey's *Cessio Bonorum,*" PMLA, LIV, 511; 1939; recounts his legal involvements c. 1832–33.

Strout, Alan L.; "De Quincey and Wordsworth," N&Q, CLXXIV, 423; 1938. — Wordsworth's contributions to Westmorland Gazette during De Quincey's editorship.

V. R.; "De Quincey," N&Q, CLXXVI-CLXXIX; 1939–40. — Learned scrutiny discloses in his essays many errors due to ignorance, faulty memory, or haste.

Metcalf, John C.; *De Quincey: A Portrait,* 1940. — Brief, and delightfully written; but "too complimentary a portrait, and without cognizance of recent De Quincey literature" (H. A. Eaton) . Cf. Eaton in *Sewanee Rev.,* XLIX, 137; 1941.

Proctor, Sigmund K.; *De Quincey's Theory of Literature* (Univ. of Mich.), 1943.
— A thoughtful, but sometimes too conjectural, analysis and criticism. Appendix contains valuable survey by C. D. Thorpe of recent studies of this subject. Cf. Sehrt (1936); and, below, Wellek (1944).

Wellek, René; "De Quincey's Status in the History of Ideas," PQ, XXIII, 248; 1944. — Warns against oversystematizing De Quincey's views. Corrective of Sehrt (1936) and Proctor (1943), above. — Cf. Wellek, *Kant in England* (1931), pp. 171–180.

Schneider, Elisabeth; "The 'Dream' of Kubla Khan," PMLA, LX, 784; 1945. — Important rectification of De Quincey's mistaken, but influential, beliefs about the effects of opium.

Hendricks, Cecilia H.; "De Quincey, Symptomatologist," PMLA, LX, 828; 1945. — His illness in 1812 a "mild case of infantile paralysis."

CHAPTER 18

THOMAS CARLYLE

(December 4, 1795–February 5, 1881)

Carlyle is usually considered a Victorian author, and properly so; but he was less than ten years younger than Byron and Shelley, and was born in the same year as Keats. His earlier life and works (which alone will be considered here) are closely connected with the Romantic Movement, and to omit them would be to ignore a very forceful and important manifestation of the romantic spirit.

His Life.—The story of Carlyle's development is of particular interest to Americans because it shows what may happen when romantic ideas impinge upon a mind and character reared according to strict principles of Puritanism. Carlyle was born in the small town of Ecclefechan, in southern Scotland, the son of a farmer and mason who belonged to a sect called the Burghers. His father was honest, and as a rule, taciturn, but capable of pithy utterance, "his speech being filled with metaphors though he knew not what metaphor was." He was deeply religious, and he ingrained in his son the idea that a true sign of sincerity in religion was to work not only hard but with the utmost conscientiousness. His mother, a fond, anxious, Bible-reading parent, taught him to read at a very early age; and his father taught him arithmetic. They watched his progress through school with silent pride, hoping that he would become a minister of the Gospel, and at fourteen sent him away, to trudge the one hundred miles to the University of Edinburgh. "No man of my day," he wrote, "or hardly any man, can have had better parents." He declared that it was his father's brief and emphatic speech that had taught him his own style.

He found most of the subjects pursued at the university unattractive. He had been brought up to value (even in religious matters) only what was considered positive and demonstrable fact; and he turned away from most of the liberal studies because they seemed to deal largely with matters of opinion. The exception was mathematics, in which there were no uncertainties, and to which he therefore devoted himself ardently. His fellow students were impressed with his keenness of mind and harshness of temper: they nicknamed him "Jonathan" or "the Dean," as if he were to be a satirist like Swift. On graduating from college, he taught mathematics in various schools for some years, still half expecting to return to the university to study theology. But the course of his reading made this finally impossible to him. As is often the case with those whose religion rests wholly upon logical evidences, his beliefs could not withstand such arguments as those of Hume and Gibbon. After reading the latter, he said, he "first clearly saw that Christianity was not true." For the time being, materialism seemed to him the only honest and scientific philosophy; in ethical matters, the stoical Epictetus was his guide.

From the age of twenty-three to twenty-five, Carlyle was extremely unhappy. He was wretchedly poor, troubled with dyspepsia, worried because he saw no prospects of satisfying his literary ambition, and—worst of all—possessed by skeptical doubts which were quite out of harmony with his innermost nature. "I was," he said long afterwards, "entirely unknown, . . . solitary, eating my own heart, fast losing my health too, a prey to nameless struggles and miseries, which have yet a kind of horror to them to my thoughts." Out of this Slough of Despond he began, about 1820, to extricate himself by becoming acquainted, partly owing to the reading of Mme. de Staël's *L'Allemagne,* with German romantic literature. He threw himself into the study of the language with characteristic intensity, and was soon "living riotously," as he put it, with Schiller, Novalis, Richter, and, above all, Goethe. He was one of the first in Great Britain to appreciate the profounder aspects of Goethe's work, and his own growth was benefited by Goethe's broadminded doctrine that true culture requires the development in each individual not only of the moral powers but also of the intellectual and aesthetic. At the same time, Goethe's respect for the principles of duty, renunciation, and reverence, helped Carlyle to retain some of the fundamental Christian beliefs in which he had been reared. Under such influences, his deliverance from skepticism, or what he called the Everlasting No, was not long delayed. In June, 1821, as he was passing along a street in Edinburgh called Leith Walk, there occurred that experience which he was to describe in *Sartor Resartus* dramatically as a sudden "conversion" or "new birth," which determined his attitude for the rest of his life. It seemed to him as if the Everlasting No taunted him, saying:

"Behold, thou art fatherless, outcast, and the Universe is mine" (the Devil's), to which my whole Me now made answer, "I am not thine, but Free, and forever hate thee!"

Although this was the style of Scotch Calvinism, Carlyle never returned to the literal faith of his fathers; henceforth he gradually became more and more convinced of the truths of transcendental idealism, i.e., of the spiritual origin and nature of the Universe.

Goethe, who likewise had faced the dragon of doubt, and who had overcome him, now became more than ever his admired master. Carlyle, filled with zeal to communicate to others that inspiration which the Germans had been to him, in 1823 published his *Life of Schiller;* and a year later his translation of Goethe's *Wilhelm Meister.* To his great delight, his labors were appreciated by no less an authority than Goethe himself, who, apropos of the *Schiller,* paid his young disciple the following notable tribute:

> German literature has effected much for humanity in this respect, introducing not ascetic timidity, but a free culture in accordance with nature, and in cheerful obedience to law; and therefore I have observed with pleasure Mr. Carlyle's profound study of this literature, and I have noticed with sympathy how he has not only been able to discover the beautiful and the human, the good and the great, in us; but he has also contributed what was his own and has endowed us with the treasures of his genius. It must be granted that he has a clear judgment as to our aesthetic and ethic writers and, at the same time, his own way of looking at them, which proves that he rests on an original foundation and has the power to develop in himself the essentials of what is good and beautiful.

By his thirtieth year he had acquired very strong convictions upon many problems. He writes:

> This year I found that I had conquered all my scepticism, agonising doubtings, fearful wrestlings, with the foul, vile, and soul-murdering mud-gods of my epoch . . . and was emerging free in spirit, where, blessed be Heaven, I have, for the spiritual part, ever since lived, looking down upon the welterings of my poor fellow-creatures . . . still stuck in that fatal element, and have no concern whatever in their Puseyism,[1] ritualisms, metaphysical controversies, and cobwebberies, and no feeling of my own except honest silent pity for the serious and religious part of them, and occasional indignation for the poor world's sake at the frivolous, secular, and impious part with their universal suffrages, their nigger emancipations, sluggard and scoundrel protection societies,[2] and unexampled prosperities for the time being. . . . In a fine and veritable sense, I, poor, obscure, without outlook, almost without worldly hope, had become independent of the world. . . . I had a constant inward happiness that was quite royal and supreme, in which all temporal evil was transient and insignificant, and which essentially remains with me still, though far oftener eclipsed, and lying deeper down than then . . . I then felt, and still feel, endlessly indebted to Goethe in the business.

In the same year he married Jane Welsh, the daughter of a country doctor. She was an extraordinarily clever woman, vivacious, and highly sensitive; loyal to her husband, and proud of him, but often hurt by his

[1] High Church tendencies encouraged by the Rev. Edward Bowerie Pusey (1800–1882) , canon of Christ Church, Oxford.
[2] Societies for bestowing charity on the poor, and for aiding prisoners.

irritability and unintended thoughtlessness. For about a year and a half they lived in Edinburgh, Carlyle writing magazine articles on German authors. In May, 1828, feeling that he would never produce a great work except in peace and solitude, they moved to the lonely farm of Craigenputtock, which, with a few interruptions was their home for six years. It was their experiment in plain living and high thinking (Letter to De Quincey, Dec. 11, 1828; *Anth.*, 1037). At times he praised it as the place where he could work and meditate better than anywhere else, and then again he would rail against it as his "Devil's Den" or his "gaunt and hungry Siberia." In any case, it was at Craigenputtock that his genius matured; there he wrote some of his best essays, as well as his first long work, *Sartor Resartus;* and there he thought out those theories of biography and historiography upon which his later works were based.

In 1834, he moved to London. He had made the personal acquaintance of men of letters such as Jeffrey, Lamb, Leigh Hunt, and John Stuart Mill; but he had not yet had any recognition by the general public, and his prospects were extremely uncertain. Twice he had attempted to obtain a professorship, but in vain; for, then as now, college authorities were too timid to engage professors who were decidedly individual, not very sociable, and embarrassingly frank. *Fraser's Magazine,* which encouraged freedom of thought, accepted some of his first essays. *Sartor Resartus,* however, was too unconventional, and was submitted to various editors for several years before it was finally accepted. His next attempt was his *French Revolution;* and when, after months of toil, he sent the manuscript of its first volume to John Stuart Mill, it was burned by the carelessness of a servant. "Well," he said to his wife, "Mill, poor fellow, is terribly cut up; we must endeavor to hide from him how very serious this business is to us." As best he could he grimly set to work to write that volume anew, and when it was completed said that he felt "like a man that nearly killed himself accomplishing zero." While writing the other volumes, he staved off destitution by giving public lectures on German literature. On the evening when at last he finished the last pages of *The French Revolution,* he brought them to his wife, saying, "You have not had for a hundred years any book that comes more direct and flaming from the heart of a living man!" This marked the close of that poverty and obscurity which he and she had endured with uncompromising courage and independence of spirit. *The French Revolution* was immediately hailed as a masterpiece, publishers came forward with offers to reissue his *Sartor Resartus* (first appreciated, and first published, in the United States, through the influence of Emerson) and to collect his essays in book form; and his courses of lectures, culminating with *Heroes and Hero-Worship* in 1841, were brilliantly successful. Henceforth to the end of his long life, the greatness of Carlyle was everywhere acknowledged, especially in the United States, where *Heroes and Hero-Worship* had a huge vogue.

His Personality.—Carlyle was both moody and outspoken; hence his oral utterances often were contradictory. Mrs. Carlyle remarked that life with him was that of a weathercock in high winds. At times he seemed arrogant, scornful, and brutally harsh; but more than one of his friends felt, like Harriet Martineau, that his apparent savageness was a mask to conceal his almost unbearable sympathy with human suffering. His charities, though secretive, were numerous. His emotional intensity, whimsicalities, gruff tenderness, and uncompromising frankness, were bewildering; but he won the lasting affection of many friends. Emerson considered Carlyle's astounding conversation one of the three things that most impressed him in Europe. Even though in his conversation he sometimes indulged in angry or jocose exaggeration, the sincerity and earnestness of his writings are unquestionable: he had vowed never to set down a sentence which in his heart he did not believe to be true. As an author, he felt, as he wrote to his mother, that

> . . . we are ever in our great Taskmaster's eye, with whom are the issues, not of Time only, which is but a short vision, but of Eternity, which ends not and is a reality.

His Views.[3]—Carlyle's views were those of one who was educated in the Puritan tradition of conscientiousness of conduct, sincerity of speech, and literal acceptance of Biblical Christianity, and who retained the conscientiousness and sincerity while abandoning the literalness in favor of mystical faith. Like other Romantics, he came to believe that God spoke to man not only through the Scriptures but also through the world and its history. The universe was a vast symbol of a spiritual, just, and moral power struggling against evil, but sure to triumph in the end. Time and Space were not permanent realities, but world-enveloping appearances. Nature, organized society, government, the church, arts, poetry, and language, were merely signs or expressions, wrappings or vestures, of the only eternal being, God. The sole test of the merit of any human law was its conformity to divine law.

Speech was powerless to express the commingled greatness and little-ness of man. As a finite being, his lot was humble and dark:

> The course of Nature's phases in this our little fraction of a planet is partially known to us, but who knows what deeper courses these depend on; what infinitely larger Cycle of causes our little Epicycle revolves on? To the Minnow every cranny and pebble, and quality and accident, of its little native brook may have become familiar; but does the Minnow understand the Ocean Tides and periodic Currents, the Trade-winds, the Monsoons, and Moon's Eclipses, by all which the condition of its little creek is regulated, and may from time to time (unmiraculously enough) be quite overset and reversed? Such a minnow is Man; his Creek this planet Earth; this Ocean the unmeasurable All; his Monsoons and periodic currents the mysterious Course of Providence through Aeons of Aeons.

[3] Carlyle's views after 1844 are not treated here.

The infinitude of his soul prevents man from ever becoming entirely happy in this finite existence, yet only in faithful conformity to the bidding of his soul lies his salvation. Individuals differ widely in their intelligence, and still more in their moral purpose. The true man is he who has the eye to discern the divine meaning of life and history, and the will-power to further against adverse circumstances, at any sacrifice of his own desires, the divine purposes. Such a one is a hero, whom men instinctively worship, and allegiance to whom is their duty and their sole opportunity for happiness. Man's nature requires that he may not rest in speculation or in philosophical acceptance of truth: he must work strenuously, he must actively apply what he believes. In no other way can he raise his faith above doubt; in no other way can he develop in himself a real character:

> The great law of culture is: Let each become all that he was created capable of being; expand if possible to his full growth. There is no uniformity of excellence, either in physical or spiritual nature: all genuine things are what they ought to be.
>
> *Jean Paul Richter*

His Works: 1823–1832.—In the first decade of his literary activity, Carlyle's chief works consisted of essays which expounded and developed his fundamental principles. His essay on Voltaire was not inappreciative of the incisive power of that prose master, but condemned his failure to withstand the fashionable skepticism by which he was surrounded; in that inability to rise above his environment, Voltaire was inferior to Goethe. His *Schiller* (1823), *Novalis* (1829), *Richter* (1828; *Anth.*, 1038), and *Death of Goethe* (1832; *Anth.*, 1047), were admiring accounts of varieties of German idealism. In Richter he found not only the thoughts congenial, especially the concept that life was not mechanical but dynamic, but also a humor and ruggedness akin to his own. The style of this essay, influenced by the explosive abruptness of Richter's, attracted unfavorable comment. Novalis fascinated him as the most mystical of them all—a mind to whom the world was a magical phenomenon, and literature was nothingness unless it likewise was magical in its effect. Although the progress of knowledge requires some corrections of Carlyle's writings on the German Romantics in matters of fact, they still remain to the English reader stimulating introductions to an important group of authors, for they deal with essential and unchanging qualities of their work.

In *Signs of the Times* (1829; *Anth.*, 1044) he expressed the hope that henceforth the overvaluation of material and mechanical progress would be abated, for it was perilous to individual freedom and the sense of social responsibility.

Carlyle's *Burns* (1828; *Anth.*, 1040), evoked by Lockhart's *Life of Burns,* was the first study of the poet that was worthy of its subject. It was characteristic of Carlyle in that on the one hand it found the secret of Burns's poetic power in his singing with utter sincerity about the homely life which he actually knew, and in that on the other hand it candidly deplored that Burns failed in his personal life to conquer the temptations which beset him and to achieve moral manhood. Similarly in his *Sir Walter Scott* (1838), he praised Scott's lack of affectation, but regretted that he was given to worldliness in his conduct of life, and did not put more of prophetic fire into his works. The same point of view, stressing honesty in affections and truth to things-as-they-really-are, governs his *Boswell's Life of Johnson* (1832), in which he saw beneath the superficial littleness of Boswell the great and genuine power within him. In such studies Carlyle was beginning to develop what may perhaps be termed his X-ray-like power to penetrate into personalities that had been impervious to the vision of ordinary biographers. In his essay *History* (1830) he maintained that "history is the essence of innumerable biographies"; and in *Biography* (1832) he held that true narrative was superior to imaginative:

> Strange power of Reality! Not even the poorest of occurrences but now has meaning for us. Do but consider that it is true; that it did in very deed occur!

In this preference for the actual, his early training was still strong upon him.

His Works: 1833–1841.—*Sartor Resartus* (The Tailor Re-Tailored; *Anth.*, 1051) is the Carlyle of lonely Craigenputtock, denying doubt and denouncing everything that worldlings live by. The Psalmist had declared concerning the world of appearances, "As a vesture thou [the Lord] shalt change them, and they shall be changed; but thou art the same"; and Swift, in *A Tale of a Tub* had spoken of the world as a mere garment and of man as if made by his tailor:

> If certain ermines and furs be placed in a certain position, we style them a Judge; and an apt conjunction of lawn and black satin we entitle a Bishop.
> *Tale of a Tub*, Sect. II

These hints Carlyle elaborated in a discourse consisting of three parts. The introduction described an imaginary book by Diogenes Teufelsdröckh, German Professor of Things-in-General, entitled "Clothes: Their Origin and Influence," which set forth man's history as that of a being which had forgotten that it was spiritual and lived as if it were merely a clothed animal, basing all its distinctions upon externalities. In the second part (containing veiled autobiographical passages) Professor Teufelsdröckh told the story of his childhood and education, condemning the schools and universities for ignoring the greatest verities, and relating his painful self-education through doubt into a recognition of the presence of the ideal amid the actual (The Everlasting Yea). In the last part, even more unsystematic and digressive than the former ones, the object of life was set forth as a religious endeavor to rid ourselves of all the cant and hypocrisy and selfishness which is produced by materialism, and to come into contact with the mystery of life through reading its symbols aright—a religion of which the priests and prophets were men of letters like Goethe. This would lead us to value our fellow men not from their clothes and worldly possessions inwards, but from their souls out-wards.

At the summit of his powers, Carlyle produced *The French Revolu-tion* (1837; *Anth.,* 1052) , wherein he applied his principles to what was probably the greatest theme that was suited to his peculiar gifts. That Revolution, in agitated concentration, held all the passion and pictur-esqueness, all the comedy and tragedy, of which life was capable; and in it, as Carlyle saw it, were moral lessons which the world would in future ignore only at the peril of catastrophe. It was the outstanding event of modern history, and its reverberations still closely affected men's lives. If spiritual forces really ruled the universe, they must have been at work, however obscurely, in the Revolution; and if their omnipres-ence and omnipotence could therein be discerned and manifested, the truth and import of idealism might yet be brought home to men's bosoms.

He had no comprehensive and rigorous theory of just how the past had evolved, and precisely what the guiding aims of historiography ought therefore to be; but he had very definite, if not systematically related ideas, some of which he had met with in Goethe, Herder, and Novalis, and which proved pertinent and fruitful. He searched through eleven histories, more than forty memoirs, and innumerable other materials, to find what actually occurred and what it signified. Trying to keep scrupu-lously to his sources—though sometimes his wrath or admiration more or less distorted his vision—he selected from them whatever would most vividly recover the life of the past, taking one detail here, another else-where, and fitting them together without destroying their authenticity by reduction to a deadening uniformity. "While other historians had sought to blend their details into a smooth equable narrative, as rags are fashioned into a sheet of paper," says Richard Garnett, "Carlyle took the rags themselves and hung them forth gay or grimy or bloodstained, danc-ing in air or trailing in mud." As he saw it, the Revolution had not been an inevitable consequence of time and circumstances (as the materialist Taine was forty years later to try to show it) , but an event for which cer-tain human beings were chiefly responsible. Nor was it essentially a change in the external arrangement of society, in laws or constitutions. Its causes lay in the hearts and minds of definite groups of men, and the hearts and minds of other men determined its course. The early Ro-mantics had at first wholly admired the Revolutionists, and then utterly condemned them; Carlyle went to neither extreme.

He saw the causes of the Revolution in the fact that in eighteenth-century France those in the seats of power had become formalists and materialists, still going through the old governmental, ecclesiastical, and social conventions, but really caring nothing for the noble, religious, and chivalric ideals which once had given them life. Absorbed in worldliness, becoming skeptical, hypocritical, carnal, and cruel, they raised against them the Divine Fact, the overruling Righteousness, and thus became the authors of their own destruction. In such ways, History embodied the Divine. The Revolution therefore was not a merely national incident: the fate of the French aristocracy would surely be the fate of the ruling class in any people if it set its heart upon material things, became content with outward observances in its religion, and thought that the passing of laws was a substitute for personal rectitude.

The Revolution was just and necessary; but its course ended in failure (Carlyle brings the drama to a tragic close in 1795 with Bonaparte's seizure of power), and in that failure there was another fateful lesson. When those in power proved unworthy of their responsibilities, and the suffering of the people became unendurable, the mob would destroy the corrupt rulers and institutions; but the overruling Providence which approved the destruction left it to men's own efforts to upbuild new and better forms of government; and this no mob, but only true leaders, could accomplish. The Revolution failed, and every reform will fail, without heroes to lead it. If Carlyle underrated, as he probably did, the relative effects of organized groups in the past, and their possibilities in the future, as against the value of individual leadership, it was a natural corollary of his principle that ideas are nothing without a devoted personal will to put them into effect. To him History was a vital drama of individual successes and failures, a vivid illustration of the glory and the weakness that lies in our freedom of will and our power over circumstance.

Having been so much concerned in *The French Revolution* with leaders who had fallen short of success, it was natural for Carlyle to turn in *Heroes and Hero-Worship* (1841; *Anth.,* 1054) to those who had come nearer thereto. Among his heroes were Mahomet, Dante, Cromwell, Luther, Shakspeare, Knox, Rousseau, Johnson, and Burns. Diverse as they appeared to be, each of them was in his judgment a witness to the fact that the divine manifests its power in human beings. They differed widely in their interests and achievements, but had certain traits in common. They were wholly sincere, keeping themselves free from convention and hearsay, having a deep awe for the mystery of life and the wonder of the Universe, resolute to seek truth, notable for their insight into some aspect thereof, and absolutely devoted thereto when they found it. It was in this loyalty to truth that the secret of leadership was found: men worshipped heroes because heroes beheld and worshipped what was eternal.

Up to this time (1841), Carlyle's heroes were representative men, not demigods or supermen. Later, unfortunately, in his post-romantic period, he glorified forceful and successful men who could only be admired on the Machiavellian principle that the end justifies the means—Cromwell the Protector, and even Frederick the Great—and thus Carlyle became a false prophet, pleasing to the Italy of Mussolini and the Germany of Bismarck and Hitler. But for that corruption Romanticism was not responsible.

His Style.—Carlyle, especially in *Sartor Resartus*, felt that he was addressing himself to a world which doubted or ignored the truths he preached. Hence his style is vehement, indignant, abrupt, and explosive. But its prophet-like sincerity and force are superb. Few prose writers equal Carlyle in that kind of delineation of character which reveals the inner moral and spiritual life of a person through his outward appearance. As an historian, he aimed to "recover the life of things," and no one has revived the past with greater vividness and intensity. His moral preoccupations were sometimes injurious to his artistry, leading to needless outbursts of wrath, when beauty and grace fled and nothing but violence held sway.

His Relation to Other Romantics.—In the portraits which Carlyle has drawn of Coleridge (*Life of Sterling*, ch. 8), Lamb, Hazlitt, Keats, and Shelley (*Characteristics, Letters,* and *Reminiscences*), the delineation is very sharp, but there is too much prejudice and scorn. He acknowledged Wordsworth's genuineness, but did not perceive his greatness. The Romantics from whom he is farthest distant, however, are the most freely imaginative—Coleridge, Keats, Shelley, and, in prose, De Quincey. His complaint was that they had either been untrue to reality or had tried to escape from it altogether. He distrusted invention that was detached from fact and history, and he feared the gracefully beautiful, the ornate, or the obviously rhetorical. Byron he disliked on the ground that he was cynical and, except in *Don Juan*, insincere. From Scott, Carlyle learned not a little concerning the value of picturesque details; but he preferred to keep to history and biography, i.e., to "recover" the past rather than to imagine so much of it as an historical novelist felt free to do. Scott's purpose of giving readers pleasure aroused little sympathy in Carlyle: our business here below was not pleasure but truth and rectitude. From the general romantic faith, he drew its sternest lessons—to dread the pleasant, to obey the divine, and to work silently in its service without relaxation.

SELECTED BIBLIOGRAPHY

OF FIRST IMPORTANCE

Selections

> *The Best of Carlyle*, ed. Herbert LeS. Creek (Ronald Press), 1929.
> *Pen Portraits from Carlyle*, ed. R. Brimley Johnson, 1908. — Selected from the Works and the Letters.

Best Brief Biography

> Neff, Emery; *Carlyle*, 1932. — Discerning and judicious.

On Jane Welsh Carlyle, see the biography by Elizabeth A. Drew (1928), or that by Townsend Scudder (1939), preferably the former.

Good Introductory Criticisms

In addition to Creek and Neff:

Perry, Bliss; *Carlyle: How to Know Him*, 1915.

Johnson, W. S.; *Thomas Carlyle: A Study of His Literary Apprenticeship: 1814–31*, 1911.

Shine, Hill; *Carlyle's Fusion of Poetry, History, and Religion by 1834*, 1938.

FOR ADVANCED STUDENTS

Important Additional Texts

Works (Centenary Edition), ed. H. D. Traill, 30 vols., 1896–1901. — The most nearly complete.

Lectures on the History of Literature, ed. R. P. Karkaria (or J. R. Greene), 1892.

Sartor Resartus, ed. Archibald MacMechan (Athenæum Press Series), 1896; and ed. C. F. Harrold, 1937.

History of the French Revolution, ed. J. Holland Rose, 3 vols., 1902; or ed. C. R. L. Fletcher, 3 vols., 1902. — The notes give factual corrections. — The translation into French, Paris, 1912, has an Introduction by the celebrated authority, F. A. Aulard.

On Heroes, Hero-Worship, and the Heroic in History, ed. Archibald MacMechan (Athenæum Press Series), 1901.

––––

The Letters of Carlyle: 1826–1836, ed. C. E. Norton, 1889.

Correspondence Between Goethe and Carlyle, ed. C. E. Norton, 1887.

Correspondence of Carlyle and Emerson: 1834–1872; ed. C. E. Norton, 1883.

Biographical and Critical

Carlyle, Thomas; *Reminiscences*, ed. C. E. Norton, 2 vols., 1887. — Froude's edition of 1881 is untrustworthy.

Froude, J. A.; *Thomas Carlyle: A History of the First Forty Years of His Life*, 2 vols., 1882; and *Thomas Carlyle: A History of His Life in London*, 2 vols., 1884. — Until the appearance of D. A. Wilson's work (see below, 1923), the standard biography. Much assailed for its frankness and alleged misrepresentation. For a defense, see Waldo H. Dunn's *Froude and Carlyle*, 1929; checked by rev. TLS, March 6, 1930.

Caird, Edward; "The Genius of Carlyle," *Essays on Literature*, 1892. — Excellent on the strength and weakness of his philosophy.

More, Paul Elmer; "The Spirit of Carlyle," *Shelburne Essays*, 1904. — Interesting study of the conflict between the mystical ("Hindu") and the dogmatic ("Hebraic") in his teaching.

Brownell, W. C.; *Victorian Prose Masters*, 1909. — On the whole hostile.

Roe, F. W.; *The Social Philosophy of Carlyle and Ruskin*, 1921.

Schanck, Nikolaus; *Die socialpolitischen Anschauungen Coleridges und sein Einfluss auf Carlyle* (Bonner Studien, No. 16), 1924. — Coleridge's influence on Carlyle's views of society and its progress.

Wilson, David A.; *Carlyle Till Marriage: 1795–1826*, 1923; *Carlyle and the French Revolution: 1826–1837*, 1924; *Carlyle on Cromwell and Others: 1837–1847*, 1925; *Carlyle at His Zenith: 1848–1853*, 1927. — Detailed facts of his life. Not strong in interpretation.

Neff, Emery; *Carlyle and Mill*, 1924. — 2nd ed., 1926.

Geissendoerfer, Theodore; "Carlyle and Jean Paul Richter," JEGP, xxv, 540; 1926.

Thompson, Frank T.; "Emerson and Carlyle," SP, xxiv, 438; 1927.

Wellek, René; "Carlyle and German Romanticism," *Xenia Pragensia*, 1929.

Sagar, S.; *Round by Repentance Tower*, 1930. — A study from the Roman Catholic point of view.

Strachey, Lytton; in *Portraits in Miniature*, 1931.

Nichols, Elisabeth; *The Consistency of Carlyle's Literary Criticism* (Ann Arbor, Mich.) , 1931. — Made coherent by his admiration for northern primitive life.

Grierson, H. J. C.; *Carlyle and Hitler*, 1933. — Cf. Joseph E. Baker, *Sat. Rev. Lit.*, Nov. 25, 1933.

Harrold, Charles F.; *Carlyle and German Thought: 1819–1834*, 1934. — An important study. See his "The Mystical Element in Carlyle: 1827–34," MP, xxix, 459; 1932; on influence of Boehme, Kant, Novalis, etc. Cf. Hill Shine, below, 1935.

Thrall, Miriam M. H.; *Rebellious Fraser's*, 1934. — Carlyle's contributions to this magazine of revolt. — Cf. Hill Shine, MLN, March, 1936.

Shine, Hill; "Carlyle and the German Philosophy Problem: 1826–27," PMLA, l, 3; 1935. — Cf. Harrold, above, 1934.

Harrold, Charles F.; "The Nature of Carlyle's Calvinism," SP, xxxiii, 475; 1936.

Vance, W. S.; "Carlyle in America Before *Sartor Resartus*," *Amer. Lit.*, vii, 363; 1936. — Supplemented by George Kummer, *Amer. Lit.*, viii, 297; 1936.

Smith, Logan Pearsall; "The Rembrandt of English Prose," *Reperusals and Recollections*, 1936. (From TLS, June 7, 1934) .

Taylor, Alan C.; *Carlyle et la Pensée Latine*, Paris, 1937. — Comprehensive survey of his influence in France, Italy, etc., including that on Carducci and on Fascism.

Moore, Carlisle; "Carlyle and Fiction: 1822–34," *Nineteenth-Century Studies* (Cornell) , 1940. — His change of attitude from admiration of fiction to preference for historiography.

On "The French Revolution" and Carlyle's Theory of History

Aulard, F. A.; Introduction to the French translation of *The French Revolution*, 1912. — Cf. G. M. Dutcher, *Guide to Historical Literature*, 1931, p. 591.

Harrold, Charles F.; "Carlyle's General Method in 'The French Revolution,'" PMLA, xliii, 1150; 1928.

Young, (Mrs.) Louise M.; *Carlyle and the Art of History* (Univ. of Penn.) , 1939.

Lea, F. A.; in *Adelphi*, xviii, 20 and 36; 1941.

Shine, Hill; *Carlyle's Fusion of Poetry, History, etc.*, 1938; and *Carlyle and the Saint-Simonians: The Concept of Historical Periodicity*, 1941.

Wellek, René; "Carlyle and the Philosophy of History," PQ, xxiii, 55; 1944. — Rejects Mrs. Young's and Hill Shine's association of Carlyle with rationalistic schools, instead of romantic. Best account of his merits and weaknesses as an historian.

On "Heroes and Hero-Worship"

Lehman, B. H.; *Carlyle's Theory of the Hero*, 1929.

Smith, Fred M.; "Whitman's Poet-Prophet and Carlyle's Hero," PMLA, lv, 1146; 1940.

Hook, Sidney; *The Hero in History*, 1943.

Bentley, E. R.; *A Century of Hero-Worship*, 1944. — Carlyle, Nietzsche, etc. The menace of "Heroic Vitalism." — Rev. TLS, Aug. 23, 1947 (under the title, "The Cult of the Superman").

Weber, Max; *The Theory of Social and Economic Organization*, 1947.

Toynbee, A. J.; *A Study of History*, 1947.

"Hero-Worshippers Recalled," TLS, Aug. 23, 1947, a criticism of Bentley, is an important introduction to the whole problem.

Miscellaneous

Ralli, Augustus; *Guide to Carlyle*, 2 vols., 1920. — Analyses of the works and factual data concerning them.

Dyer, Isaac W.; *A Bibliography of Thomas Carlyle's Writings and Ana* (Southworth Press, Portland, Maine), 1929. — More than an ordinary bibliography, this includes reviews of his works and comments. Essential for an insight into the growth of Carlyle's fame.

CHAPTER 19

THE ROMANTIC MOVEMENT
AND SELECTED GENERAL BIBLIOGRAPHY

Differences Among the Romantics.—The chief Romantics differed from one another in origin, schooling, personality, conduct, and many other respects. Some, like Landor and Shelley, were of aristocratic birth; others, like Blake and Keats, of the humblest. Some had next to no formal schooling, others were forced to end theirs at an early age, and only about one half of their number attended a university. Some of them acquired sufficiently extensive knowledge to be considered scholars, e.g., Coleridge, Wordsworth, Lamb, Scott, Southey, De Quincey, and Carlyle; others died too young to amass much learning; and some, like Blake and Byron, were not scholars in the usual sense of the term. In their character and conduct, there were likewise great differences among them, from Byron at one extreme to Lamb, Blake, or Keats at the other. To some of them verse was the only or the chief medium of literary expression (Blake, Wordsworth, Byron, and Keats) ; others were mainly prosemen (Lamb, Hazlitt, De Quincey, and Carlyle) ; and a few found both forms congenial (Coleridge, Scott, Landor, and Shelley). In politics, they represented almost every shade of contemporaneous opinion, from the Toryism of Coleridge, Wordsworth, Scott, and De Quincey, to the Liberalism of Byron, Hazlitt, and Shelley.

Perhaps after their deaths, dwelling in Elysium under the aspects of Eternity, they may have reconciled their differences; but while they lived their disagreements and dislikes were more conspicuous than their congeniality. For longer or shorter periods two or three of them formed friendly alliances—e.g., Wordsworth, Coleridge, Southey, and Lamb—and Byron, Shelley, and Hunt—but even such groups were subject to disagreements or dissolution; and some Romantics, notably Blake, Hazlitt, and Landor, were solitary rather than companionable. Nearly all at some time uttered derogatory opinions about the views or writings of some of the others. Most of them—including Lamb, Southey, and Keats—disliked Byron's poetry, particularly *Don Juan*. Byron returned the dislike with interest; he respected only Scott and Shelley, and he ranked Wordsworth and Coleridge lower than the third-rate versifier, Rogers. Hazlitt thought Wordsworth a time-server and place-hunter; Shelley deplored his supposed apostasy; and even Keats, who loved his poetry, at times censured him for rudeness. Wordsworth was once heard to mutter something about Keats's "paganism"; he found the young Carlyle "an enthusiast and nothing more"; and he detested *Don Juan*.

These hostilities cannot be explained wholly on the ground that two generations of Romantics (those active before c. 1815, and those whose careers began thereafter) would naturally be at odds; for the young Carlyle spoke contemptuously of Keats's "maudlin sensibility," and scorned Shelley as one "filling the earth with inarticulate wail."

Attempted Definitions of Romanticism.—Despite their bickerings, the Romantics have long been thought of as a school of writers united by common tendencies. But just what are those tendencies? The attempt to reduce them to one formula was begun more than a hundred years ago, and has occupied an incredible amount of time and ingenuity. Hundreds of definitions of Romanticism have been excogitated. Among them are the following:

Romanticism is disease, Classicism is health.—*Goethe.*

A movement to honor whatever Classicism rejected. Classicism is the regularity of good sense,—perfection in moderation; Romanticism is disorder in the imagination,—the rage of incorrectness. A blind wave of literary egotism.—*Brunetière.*

Classic art portrays the finite, romantic art also suggests the infinite.—*Heine.*

The illusion of beholding the infinite within the stream of nature itself, instead of apart from that stream.—*More.*

A desire to find the infinite within the finite, to effect a synthesis of the real and the unreal. The expression in art of what in theology would be called pantheistic enthusiasm.—*Fairchild.*

The return to nature.

A sense of the mystery of the universe, and the perception of its beauty.—*Earnest.*

In general a thing is romantic when, as Aristotle would say, it is wonderful rather than probable; in other words, when it violates the normal sequence of cause and effect in favor of adventure. The whole movement is filled with the praise of ignorance, and of those who still enjoy its inappreciable advantages,—the savage, the peasant, and above all the child.—*Babbitt.*

The opposite, not of Classicism, but of Realism,—a withdrawal from outer experience to concentrate upon inner.—*Abercrombie.*

Liberalism in literature. Mingling the grotesque with the tragic or sublime (forbidden by classicism) ; the complete truth of life.—*Victor Hugo.*

The re-awakening of the life and thought of the Middle Ages.—*Heine, Beers, etc.* Abortive because premature.—*Ash.*

The cult of the extinct.—*Geoffrey Scott.*

The classic temper studies the past, the romantic neglects it.—*Schelling.*

An effort to escape from actuality.—*Waterhouse, Cabell, etc.*

Sentimental melancholy.—*Phelps.*

Vague aspiration.—*Phelps.*

Subjectivity, the love of the picturesque, and a reactionary spirit [against whatever immediately preceded it].—*Phelps.*

Romanticism is, at any time, the art of the day; Classicism, the art of the day before.—*Stendhal.*

Emotion rather than reason; the heart opposed to the head.—*George Sand, etc.*

A liberation of the less conscious levels of the mind; an intoxicating dreaming. Classicism is control by the conscious mind.—*Lucas.*

Imagination as contrasted with reason and the sense of fact.—*Neilson.*

Extraordinary development of imaginative sensibility.—*Herford.*

An accentuated predominance of emotional life, provoked or directed by the exercise of imaginative vision, and in its turn stimulating or directing such exercise.—*Cazamian.*

The renascence of wonder.—*Watts-Dunton.*

The addition of strangeness to beauty.—*Pater.*

The fairy way of writing.—*Ker.*

The spirit counts for more than the form.—*Grierson.*

Whereas in classical works the idea is represented directly and with as exact adaptation of form as possible, in romantic the idea is left to the reader's faculty of divination assisted only by suggestion and symbol.—*Saintsbury.*

To anyone who has read the Romantics, none of these definitions can be entirely satisfactory. Some are contradictory of each other (Beers, Scott, Schelling). Some (Brunetière and More) are obviously hostile, and as unfair to Romanticism as it would be to define Classicism by describing the worst tendencies of a neo-classic work. Some (Heine, Hugo, etc.) are applicable to a few Romantics, and inapplicable to others. Some consider chiefly the author's thought or feeling (Phelps, Herford, Cazamian), some chiefly his method of expression (Saintsbury). None succeeds in constructing a formula that is both inapplicable to classical works and completely applicable to all the Romantics.

Attempts to Find the Originator of Romanticism.—A similar state of chaos is seen in the efforts to explain Romanticism by tracing it to a chief originator. Among the suggested founders are:

Joseph Warton (*Gosse*)—cf., above, p. 17.

Rousseau (*Lasserre, Babbitt, et al.*)—because he is [mistakenly] alleged to advocate an extreme form of naturalism, primitivism, and democracy.

Kant (*Santayana, Bertrand Russell, et al.*)—because of his transcendental idealism.

Mlle. de Scudéry (*Ker*)—because of her heroic romances.

Sir Philip Sidney (*Ker*) —because of his *Arcadia*.

Bacon (*Babbitt*) —because of his practical and anti-Aristotelian tendency.

St. Paul (*Grierson*) —because of his introduction of Christian mysticism into Greek civilization.

Christ (*Heine:* "Romanticism is a passion flower blooming from the blood of Christ"; *Victor Hugo; Olwen W. Campbell; etc.*) .

Plato (*Grierson*) .

Homer (*Whibley*) —because of the *Odyssey*.

The Serpent in the Garden of Eden (*Whibley*) —because he was the first inciter to rebellion against law and order.

The unlikelihood that personalities as incongruous as these should have originated one and the same movement is too obvious to require demonstration. In the search for a "father," as in that for a formula, one comes up against an impasse.

Inability to Define, No Proof of Unreality.—Prosaic logicians have analyzed Romanticism into fragments, some of which do not neatly fit into one another; and they suppose that thereby they have proved the meaninglessness of the term. What they actually have shown is that the varieties, and the aberrations, of Romanticism are many; but not that among the varieties there is no basic unity at all. There are other vitally important concepts, such as Democracy and Christianity, that are too comprehensive and complex to be satisfactorily summed up in the oversimple brevity of a dictionary definition; nevertheless such concepts correspond to realities which can be set forth in ampler forms of discourse. The unity amid the variety of romantic works has been felt for generations by readers with literary and imaginative sensibility. Those who in the preceding chapters have studied the sixteen leading Romantics will have observed that there was much similarity among their views, despite surface differences; and that their attitudes toward God, Man, and Nature were essentially in harmony, as well as their principles of art and literature.

Romanticism and Classicism.—The main characteristics of a literary movement are best discerned in its historical development, and in the hostile forces that arise to attack it. The dominance of Romanticism was assailed by the middle of the nineteenth century; its Everlasting Yeas were called into question. Matthew Arnold, for example, occasionally raised doubts about the romantic faith in Nature, and wrote:

> Nature is cruel, man is sick of blood . . .
> Nature and Man can never be fast friends.

But, as we shall see, the chief opposition which Romanticism was to encounter did not arise from any form of feeling, taste, or thought that can fairly be termed classical. For that reason, among others, it seems doubtful whether there is any *essential* difference (whatever differences of relative emphasis may exist) between the spirit of great classical literature and that of great romantic literature. Even as Christianity stands toward the "paganism" of Plato and Aristotle not in a relation of opposition so much as in one of fulfillment, so Shakspeare, Milton, and the Romantics stand in relation to Homer, Pindar, Aeschylus, and Virgil. In this opinion, "Grecians" like Coleridge, Shelley, and De Quincey, would agree.

Romantic Beliefs.—The Romantics were keenly conscious of the difference between two worlds. One was the world of ideal truth, goodness, and beauty: this was eternal, infinite, and absolutely real. The other was the world of actual appearances, which to common sense was the only world, and which to the idealist was so obviously full of untruth, ignorance, evil, ugliness, and wretchedness, as to compel him to dejection or indignation. This state of the romantic mind was brilliantly expressed by Byron, and all the Romantics passed through it at times. Most of them, however, passed onward to a faith that the ideal world and the actual world were not so dissevered as mere common sense or an abstract and escapist kind of idealism assumed. Man was gifted with a higher reason, called the imagination, which enabled him to see that the good, the true, and the beautiful were not removed to a sphere unattainable to him in this life, but were interwoven with his human existence and earthly environment. It was the highest function of literature and art to portray man and his world in such a way that the presence of the infinite within the finite, of the ideal within the actual, would be revealed in all its beauty. Hence, although a smug acceptance of things as they were was fatuous, we should overcome despair, and by sympathizing with certain aspects of nature, and with certain characteristics of man, achieve fortitude and wisdom. In short, most of the Romantics, after passing through the Slough of Despond, found somewhere the possibility of happiness. Wordsworth found it in nature and in the moral nobility of the simple life; Lamb, in the delightful variety of individual characters and in the amenities of urban existence; Scott and Landor, in historical epochs and traditional types of character; Coleridge, in the revelation of the Eternal in literature; Keats, in Universal Love as manifested in nature, friendship, and art; Carlyle, in the working out of one's individual ideal for one's fellowmen; and Shelley, in contemplating the glorious future of humanity. Different as these means of seeking happiness were (it is their endless diversity that frustrates definition), all rested on the assumption that our universe is rich in ideal blessings and therefore not inhospitable to the better nature of man.

The Opposition.—The real opposition and distinction is between Romanticism on the one hand, and, on the other, materialism, mechanistic science, secularism, and "common sense" in the baser meaning of the term. The most hostile anti-romantic writers, including the "Humanists" and the "New Critics," have assumed that modern science made it rationally impossible to maintain the romantic beliefs about Nature and

Man. Romanticism, said Paul Elmer More, is "the illusion of beholding the infinite within the stream of nature itself, instead of apart from that stream." He and the other anti-romantics assumed without question that this was an "illusion," because they supposed that science had failed to find any indications of a spiritual or ideal purpose in the flux of natural phenomena. In the second half of the nineteenth century that assumption seemed to rationalists an inevitable one.

The Doubts Raised by Darwinism.—The first serious threat against fundamental romantic beliefs arose out of interpretations of Darwin's *Origin of Species* (1859). His theory of evolution was misrepresented by its adherents, and misunderstood by its opponents. It was supposed to prove that the processes of nature did not manifest anything that indicated purposiveness. All that happened was by chance; there was no directive tendency, no foresight, nothing like moral governance or an ultimate tendency towards righteousness. The widespread, though ill-founded, notion that Darwin had refuted all evidence of design in the universe is at the bottom of that modern doubt which presently grew into the tragic conviction of the utter meaninglessness of human life. The Darwinians emphasized everything that showed Nature wasteful and cruelly savage. Huxley, their champion, declared: "The animal world is on about the same level as a gladiator's show." Those who survived in the brutish struggle for existence were the fittest only in the sense that they were the most selfish, aggressive, rapacious, physically strong, and mentally keen.

Philosophers of this school accumulated more and more data which seemed to them to prove that the universe is nothing but colorless, soundless, scentless masses, wholly unbeautiful, describing aimless orbits through infinite space and time in obedience to mechanical laws and indifferent to all human aspirations. "Man," said Bertrand Russell as recently as 1925, "is the product of causes which had no prevision of the end they were achieving; his origin, his growth, his hopes and fears, his loves and beliefs, are but the outcome of accidental collocations of atoms." Man is merely a product of matter. Psychology is wholly a branch of physiology. Man has no free will. He is a prisoner under a life sentence in a horrible prison house. His art and literature and religion are merely pleasant narcotics enabling him to escape from the brutal facts into false dreaming. He learns the truth only when he studies natural and human history by strictly scientific methods, i.e., on mechanistic and deterministic assumptions. The only real knower is the scientist, and his imitator in the humanities. The Romantics were dreamers: the beauty of Nature was an illusion; its moral value was nothingness. In such a modern world the Romantic became, like Keats's lover.

> a wretched wight,
> Alone and palely loitering;
> The sedge is withered from the lake,
> And no birds sing.

The triumph of this materialistic philosophy was followed, in the field of action, by two devastating world wars; and in the field of imagination by the dominance of pessimistic literature, frenetic art, and cacophonous music. It seemed as if Man, having been scientifically assured that his cosmos was an infernal Chaos, had tried to make his own little world as nearly hell-like and inhuman as his limited powers of deviltry would permit.

The Rehabilitation of Romanticism.—During the 1920's and even earlier, in physics, zoology, biology, psychology, and other sciences, many phenomena attracted attention that could not be satisfactorily explained on the materialistic hypotheses. The progress of knowledge imperatively called for a radical revision in the philosophy of nature. In works of the highest scientific or philosophical importance—by Lloyd Morgan, A. N. Whitehead, Sir Arthur Eddington, J. D. Haldane, John Oman, Jan Christian Smuts, and many others—there was no longer that contempt for romantic ideas about Nature and Man which has ruled for two generations. Since the rise of Einstein, Rutherford, and Heisenberg, the notion that Science (and Science only) would be able to reduce all nature to the definitely knowable and fully predictable has been abandoned. The new school admits that there are limits to what can be ascertained through scientific methods; and henceforth those other fields of human experience and other methods of inquiry which the Romantics believed in are reassuming their former dignity. To continue to talk of the sciences as alone giving real truths, and of the humanities, art, and literature, as giving only imperfect truths or mere dreams, has in the twentieth century again become indefensible. For the guidance of human life, humane culture, as the Romantics insisted, is at least as important as scientific knowledge.

When the evolution of nature and man was re-examined by the science of today, truths emerged which were neglected by the Pseudo-Darwinians. The process appears far less revolting. Struggle, agony, and death have played their grim roles; but not, as was formerly implied, the chief ones. There is no special amorality, or cruelty, in nature that is not found on the human level, though on the latter the possibilities of high moral achievements are present. Of great significance are the abundant manifestations of mutual helpfulness, or symbiosis, in flora and fauna; it is a vast system of beneficent interrelationships. As for survival, it has not usually been the lone wolves, the savage, the predatory, who have been most successful; but rather the adaptable, the responsive, the cooperative, and those who have developed enough imagination and intelligence to learn by experience.

The emergence of new life phenomena in evolution (what we call progress) has not been the result only of savage struggle. Struggle educates some needed traits; but it does not inaugurate creative originality; to talk, like the Fascists or Communists, about "creative strife," whether on the physical or psychic level, is to talk in ignorance of evolutionary history. The emergence of new life phenomena is the consequence of freedom, of liberty for fuller and more complex development.

Phenomena which the Pseudo-Darwinians either did not explain at all or assumed to be due to mere chance—phenomena like the structure of the eye, or the intricate mechanism of flight, or symbiotic cooperation among plants and animals—cannot have developed step by step accidentally; their appearance required simultaneous and correlated modifications of many factors. Modern science and philosophy recognize in such natural processes a coordinating "holistic" principle or design, as Smuts calls it; or, in Bergson's phrase, an *élan vital*, a creative evolution. The Gestalt psychology, insisting that "perceptual wholes are more than the sum of their parts," exhibits similar tendencies of thought, and, militating against mechanization and fragmentation, lays new foundations for the romantic philosophy.

Nineteenth-century materialism drew man's attention to his base origin; twentieth-century science and philosophy point to the advances that all living creatures have made. They dwell upon the upward gradations in the evolution of beings from their lowest forms—from rudimentary reflexes through more and more amazing development of instincts toward the gradual achievement of real intelligence and imaginative foresight. At the lowest stages of life there was between existences a bare relatedness; subsequently came a progressive development of sexual and social life from instinctively formed communities up to higher stages where fully developed individuals, having increased in sensitiveness and having developed through the discipline of suffering the beginnings of imaginative sympathy, consciously and voluntarily form social groups which in the course of time enter into wider and wider relationships. Crescent throughout the evolution of man have been freedom, reason, imagination, and love. Each has been intermittent and imperfect, but has nevertheless groped and stumbled toward perfection. The capacity to improve, and the will to aspire, have been manifested again and again. Evolution has always shown an urge toward the prolific creation of freer and freer and more highly individual personalities, and toward their voluntary association in societies with the intention of protecting and fostering the progress of such free individuals. The advance has often been retarded by convulsions of nature, or by man's own follies and crimes. But it is manifestly a process which Man, the vanguard of evolution, can partly direct and accelerate toward higher stages of individual and social well-being. The account which modern science gives of evolution is not so preoccupied as it was in the nineteenth century with the *descent* of man from the ape. It gives at least equal importance to man's occasional *ascent* into the genius, the hero, or the saint.

As W. Macneile Dixon says in *The Human Situation,* a scholarly and eloquent work undeservedly neglected by students of Romanticism:

> By her own methods nature has brought us into being, raised us above the organic world, and conferred upon us a primacy in the organic. By

her own methods she has elevated us to intellectual heights whence at least other heights can be discerned . . . The astonishing and least comprehensible thing about Man is his range of vision; his lonely passion for ideas and ideals far removed from his material surroundings and animal activities, and in no way suggested by them, yet for which, such is his affection, he is willing to endure toils and privations, to sacrifice pleasures, to disdain griefs and frustrations, for which, rating them in value above his own life, he will stand until he dies, the profound conviction he entertains being that if nothing be worth dying for nothing is worth living for.[1]

Those are the words of a man of letters and philosopher; but the conviction that in Man Nature comes into consciousness of its possibilities, and of its freedom to attain them, is shared by as strictly scientific a mind as that of Julian Huxley, who writes:

The new history has a basis of hope. Biological evolution has been appallingly slow and wasteful. . . . It has led life up innumerable blind alleys. But in spite of this it has achieved progress. . . . The evolution of the human brain at one bound altered the perspective of evolution. Experience could now be handed down from generation to generation. . . . In man evolution could become conscious.

Past human history represents but the tiniest portion of the time man has before him . . . His setbacks are as natural as the tumbles of a child learning to walk. . . . The potentialities of progress which are revealed, once his eyes have opened to the evolutionary vista, are unlimited. . . . At last we have an optimistic instead of a pessimistic theory of this world and our life upon it. . . . Perhaps we had better call it a melioristic rather than optimistic view; but at least it preaches hope and inspires to action.[2]

Such is the attitude of science today. It is an almost complete reversal of the nineteenth-century attitude, and it destroys the supposedly scientific foundations for that materialistic philosophy which temporarily had made Romanticism seem an unbelievable faith.

The Effect of the Scientific Revolution upon the Status of Romanticism.—Romanticism is a faith, or system of beliefs, expressible only through a symbolical and emotional art such as literature. Its truths are chiefly discerned by the imagination, and it is chiefly to the imagination that they appeal for acceptance.[3] The truths of Romanticism are neither "proved" nor "disproved" by the methods of science. What the revolution in scientific opinion in our day has done is, so to speak, to make Romanticism an intellectually respectable faith, which for a time it had ceased to be. Coleridge always maintained that the genuine Imagination did not contradict Reason, although it was an independent pathway to higher truths. The Romantic believes in "the evidence of

---

[1] W. Macneile Dixon, *The Human Situation,* pp. 431, 207, 190–191.
[2] *I Believe,* ed. Fadiman (1940) , p. 132.
[3] Imagination is of such crucial importance in Romanticism that a separate chapter is devoted to it below, Chapter 20.

things not seen"; [4] and the modern scientist does not deny the possibility that such visions may be revelatory. Says Albert Einstein:

> The most beautiful thing we can experience is the mysterious. It is the source of all true art and science. He to whom the emotion is a stranger, who can no longer pause to wonder and stand wrapped in awe, is as good as dead; his eyes are closed. The insight into the mystery of life, coupled though it be with fear has also given rise to religion. To know that what is impenetrable to us really exists, manifesting itself as the highest wisdom and the most radiant beauty, which our dull faculties can comprehend only in their most primitive forms, this feeling is at the center of true religiousness. . . . It is enough for me to contemplate the mystery of conscious life perpetuating itself through all eternity, to reflect upon the marvelous structure of the universe we can dimly perceive, and to try humbly to comprehend even an infinitesimal part of the intelligence manifested in Nature.

Thus today the scientist and the Romantic pursue their different paths in the same spirit toward the same goal.

On philosophies of Nature, and on their changing relationship to Romanticism, see especially Charles E. Raven, *Science, Religion, and the Future* (1943), to which I am much indebted both for facts and for phraseology; A. N. Whitehead, *Science and the Modern World* (1925); and W. Macneile Dixon's Gifford Lectures, *The Human Situation* (1937).

Among other works which may help the inquirer into this problem are the following, which differ from one another in purpose, method, and value:

William Temple	*Nature, Man, and God* (1900)
Henri Bergson	*Creative Evolution* (1907)
	The Two Sources of Morality and Religion (1932)
C. Lloyd Morgan	*Emergent Evolution* (1923)
	Life, Mind, and Spirit (1926)
E. A. Burtt	*The Metaphysical Foundations of Modern Science* (1925)
Jan Smuts	*Holism and Evolution* (1926)
A. S. Eddington	*The Nature of the Physical World* (1928)
John W. Oman	*The Natural and the Supernatural* (1931)
James Jeans	*The Mysterious Universe* (1930; rev., 1932)
	Physics and Philosophy (1943)
Charles Sherrington	*Man on His Nature* (1940)
Julian Huxley	*Evolution: The Modern Synthesis* (1942)
Lecomte Du Noüy	*Human Destiny* (1947)
	The Road to Reason (1948)

---

[4] "For the invisible things of him from the creation of the world are clearly seen, being understood by the things that are made, even his eternal power and Godhead" (*Romans*, 1: 20). This is one of the texts cited to show that St. Paul was a Romantic.

SELECTED BIBLIOGRAPHY OF THE
ROMANTIC MOVEMENT

Subdivisions

  I. The History of the Romantic Movement
 II. The Romantic Movement in Germany, France, etc.
III. The Nature and the Value of Romanticism
  Attempts to Define the Nature
  The Value
    The Attack by "Humanism," and the Defense
    The Attack by the "New Criticism," and the Defense
    The Appreciative Enthusiasts
    Miscellaneous Criticisms

 IV. Anthologies and Miscellanies

  V. Background: Political, Economic, Social

 VI. Bibliographies

I. THE HISTORY OF THE ROMANTIC MOVEMENT

For introductory purposes, the most useful of the works listed below, besides the general *Symposium* (1940), probably are: Herford (1897), Legouis and Cazamian (1924), Sherwood (1935), Colum (1937), Bush (1937), Evans (1939), and Bate (1946).

Gilfillan, George; *Gallery of Literary Portraits,* 3 vols., 1845–1855; rptd. in Everyman's Library, 1909. — Historically interesting as one of the first Victorian accounts of the chief Romantics.

Taine, H. A.; *History of English Literature,* [in French] 1863; transl. 1871. — Shows the hostility of the materialistic school. Only Byron admired.

Brandes, Georg; *Main Currents in Nineteenth Century Literature,* [Danish] 1871 ff.; transl. 1901 ff. — Likewise of the materialistic school. Makes political radicalism a principal test of merit. Valuable for interrelationships between English and continental Romantics.

Saintsbury, George; *A History of Nineteenth Century Literature,* 1896. — Interprets the Romantic Movement as the outcome of such forces as medieval and foreign literatures, the French Revolution, the usual ebb and flow of the world spirit, and mere accident — resulting in a renewed exploration of all history, art, and literature.

Herford, C. H.; *The Age of Wordsworth,* 1897. — For many years the most useful brief introductory treatment. Includes sketches of the economists, theologians, historians, and many of the minor authors. Chief sources of the movement seen in the revolutionary naturalism of Rousseau and the transcendentalism of German philosophers.

Beers, H. A.; *A History of English Romanticism in the Nineteenth Century,* 1901. — Confined to the revival of medieval, and of some value on that aspect; but almost entirely omits Wordsworth, Byron, and Shelley.

Courthope, W. J.; *A History of English Poetry,* vols. v-vi, 1903–05. — Unsympathetic. Romantic Movement frustrate and destructive; ultimately turning away from national life into artistic monasticism.

Bradley, A. C.; *English Poetry and German Philosophy in the Age of Wordsworth* (Univ. of Manchester), 1909; rptd. in *A Miscellany* (Macmillan), 1929. — Cf. below, Stokoe, 1926, and Stockley, 1929.

Saintsbury, George; *History of English Prose Rhythm*, 1912.

Elton, Oliver; *A Survey of English Literature: 1780–1830*, vols. I and II, 1912. — Conception of history of Romanticism much like Herford's (above, 1897), but pays little attention to historical causes. Thorough accounts of individual authors; especially valuable on effects of the new ideas on the old forms.

Richardson, S. F.; "A Neglected Aspect of the English Romantic Revolt," *Univ. of Cal. Publ. Mod. Philol.*, III, 1915. — Emphasizes economic, political, and social movements.

Pierce, Frederick E.; *Currents and Eddies in the English Romantic Generation*, 1918. — Good on the subdivisions of the movement, their differences from one another. and the influences of the various group environments.

Havens, Raymond D.; *The Influence of Milton on English Poetry*, 1922.

White, Newman I.; "The English Romantic Writers as Dramatists," *Sewanee Review*, April, 1922.

Lehman, B. H.; "The Doctrine of Leadership in the Greater Romantic Poets," PMLA, XXXVII, 639; 1922.

Brinton, Crane C.; *Political Ideas of the English Romanticists*, 1926. — Cf. Walter Graham, PMLA, XXXVI, 60; 1921.

Legouis, Emile, and Cazamian, Louis; *A History of English Literature* [French ed., 1924], 1926, rev. 1947. — Interprets the movement as a renaissance of emotion consummated in a renaissance of the imagination. One of the best introductions to the subject.

Stokoe, F. W.; *German Influence in the English Romantic Period: 1788–1818*, 1926. — Believes the influence exaggerated. Cf. above, Bradley, 1909; and below, Stockley, 1929.

Inge, William R.; *The Platonic Tradition in English Religious Thought*, 1926. — Influence on Wordsworth, etc.

Bernbaum, Ernest; "The Views of the Great Critics on the Historical Novel," PMLA, XLI, 424; 1926. — The lack of a romantic aesthetics of historical fiction; the realistic reaction against Scott; etc.

Viatte, Auguste; *Les Sources Occultes du Romantisme: Illuminisme-Théosophie, 1770–1820;* Paris, 2 vols., 1928. — Secretive heresies, black arts, spiritualism, etc. Cf. below, Saurat, 1930.

Stockley, V.; *German Literature as Known in England: 1750–1830*, 1929. — Cf. above, Bradley, 1909, and Stokoe, 1926. See also in the Bibliography of Coleridge. "The German Influence"; and Logan, *Wordsworthian Criticism*, p. 124 n.

Saurat, Denis; *Literature and Occult Tradition: Studies in Philosophical Poetry*, 1930. — Blake, Shelley, etc. — Cf. below, Hungerford, 1941.

Nicoll, Allardyce; *A History of Early Nineteenth Century Drama: 1800 to 1850*, 2 vols.; 1930. — Charges Romantics with aloofness from theatre; see TLS, Jan. 1, 1931. — Cf. J. F. Bagster-Collins; *George Colman the Younger*, 1946.

Fairchild, Hoxie N.; *The Romantic Quest*, 1931. — An account of naturalism, medievalism, and transcendentalism, combining in an "illusioned view of the universe and of human life."

Wellek, René; *Immanuel Kant in England: 1793–1838*, 1931. — Represents the Romantics (except H. C. Robinson) as misinterpreting Kant. Critical of the religious beliefs of Coleridge, etc. — Cf. Edgar F. Carritt; "Addison, Kant, and Wordsworth," *Essays and Studies by Members of the Engl. Asso.*, XXII; 1937.

Levin, Harry; *The Broken Column: A Study in Romantic Hellenism*, 1932. — Holds that the Romantics gave a too sentimental interpretation of ancient Greece. Cf. below, Larrabee, 1942.

Erhardt-Siebold, Erika von; "Some Inventions of the Pre-Romantic Period," ES, LXVI, 347; 1932. — Camera obscura, color organ, Aeolian harp.

Moraud, Marcel; *Le Romantisme Français en Angleterre: 1814–1848*, 1933. — French Romantics were usually reinterpreted to conform with English tendencies.

Bradbury, Ronald; *The Romantic Theories of Architecture of the Nineteenth Century in Germany, England, and France*, 1934. — Cf. Warren H. Smith, *Architecture in English Fiction*, 1934; Agnes Addison, *Romanticism and the Gothic Revival*, 1938 (sketchy, but has useful bibliography of architectural studies) ; and Sacheverell Sitwell, *British Architects and Craftsmen: A Survey of Taste, Design, and Style: 1600–1830*, 1946 (brilliant). — Cf. TLS, July 15, 1946, and the many discussions, beginning March 23, 1946, of Baroque, Rococo, and Romantic, as terms of art criticism. — René Wellek, "The Parallelism Between Literature and the Arts," *Engl. Institute Annual: 1941*, 1942, warns against superficial "analogizing between the arts"; see also his "The Concept of Baroque in Literary Scholarship," *Journal of Aesthetics*, Dec., 1946.

Abrams, Meyer H.; *The Milk of Paradise: The Effect of Opium Visions on the Works of De Quincey, Crabbe, Francis Thompson, and Coleridge*, 1934. — Cf. Elisabeth W. Schneider's important corrections in "The 'Dream' of Kubla Khan," PMLA, LX, 784; 1945.

Baker, Ernest A.; *The History of the English Novel*, VI, 1935 (Scott, etc.). — Cf. W. H. Rogers, "The Reaction Against Melodramatic Sensibility in the English Novel: 1796–1830," PMLA, XLIX, 98; 1934; and John T. Taylor, *Early Opposition to the English Novel: 1760–1830*, 1943.

Sherwood, Margaret; *Undercurrents of Influence in English Romantic Poetry*, 1935. — Emphasizes the development of "the organic idea" of the universe as a living and developing whole.

Law, Marie Hamilton; *The English Familiar Essay in the Early Nineteenth Century*, 1935. — Lamb, Hazlitt, Hunt. Cf. Melvin R. Watson; "The Spectator Tradition and the Development of the Familiar Essay," ELH, XIII, 189; 1946.

Lovejoy, Arthur O., ed.; *Documentary History of Primitivism and Related Ideas*, 1935. — George Boas; *Essays on Primitivism, etc. in the Middle Ages*, 1948.

Winwar, Frances; *The Romantic Rebels*, 1935. — Lives of Byron, Keats, and Shelley; emotional and overdramatic.

Lovejoy, Arthur O.; *The Great Chain of Being*, 1936. — A scholarly history of the idea of Oneness developing into the idea of Diversity within the Oneness — the change of emphasis from the uniform, static, or typical toward the variegated, growing, and individual.

Beach, Joseph W.; *The Concept of Nature in Nineteenth-Century English Poetry*, 1936. — Important, though rather unfavorable, interpretation of the romantic attitude toward Nature, especially in eighteenth-century poets, and in Coleridge, Wordsworth, and Shelley. — Cf. Ernest Bernbaum; "Is Wordsworth's Nature-Poetry Antiquated?" ELH, VII, 333; 1940.

Wicks, Margaret C. W.; *The Italian Exiles in London: 1816–1848*, 1937.

Colum, Mary M.; *From These Roots: The Ideas That Have Made Modern Literature*, 1937. — Has wide scope — German (Lessing and Herder) , French, Russian, as well as English and American. Focuses on the stimulus given by Romanticism to interpretation of *all* aspects and conditions of life. Fervent.

Bush, Douglas; *Mythology and the Romantic Tradition in English Poetry*, 1937. — More than a factual record of the use of classical myths. Shows how they were recreated by Wordsworth, Keats, Shelley, etc., and given modern significance and high poetical values. Creative historical criticism.

Gill, Fred C.; *The Romantic Movement and Methodism*, 1937. — Juxtaposes them, without really clarifying their relationship.

Dutt, Sukumar; *The Supernatural in English Romantic Poetry: 1780–1830*, 1938. — From Collins and the Ballads to Keats and Shelley.

Tinker, Chauncey B.; *Painter and Poet*, 1939. — Reynolds, Gainsborough, Blake, Wilson, Turner, Constable. Admirable. — Cf. William Gaunt, *Bandits in a Landscape: A Study of Romantic Painting from Caravaggio to Delacroix*, 1937.

Gilbert, Katherine E., and Kuhn, Helmet; *A History of Aesthetics*, 1939. — Ch. 13 deals with some of the chief Romantics, but neglects Hazlitt and De Quincey.

Evans, B. Ifor; *Tradition and Romanticism: Chaucer to Yeats*, 1939. — The history of foreign literatures may show sharp distinctions between Classicism and Romanticism, but in English literature continuity and compromise has persisted. The so-called age of reason encouraged sentiments which burst forth in the romantic revival; and Wordsworth admired Pope more than "Ossian."

Irvine, Magnus; *The Unceasing Quest*, 1940. — The search for perfection, especially by Coleridge, Hazlitt, Byron, Shelley, and Carlyle.

Welker, John J.; "The Position of the Quarterlies on Some Classical Dogmas," SP, xxxvii, 542; 1940. — They were not quite so hostile to Romanticism as is sometimes supposed. Cf. below, Peyre, 1944.

Rudman, Harry W.; *Italian Nationalism and English Letters*, 1940.

Fairchild, Hoxie N., Nitchie, Elizabeth, et al.; "Romanticism: A Symposium," PMLA, lv, 1; 1940. — Brief surveys of the Romantic Movement in Germany, France, England, Italy, and Spain, by leading specialists. As an attempt to set forth the interrelationships of the several national movements it is not entirely successful; but as a learned introduction to the separate parts of the field this is praiseworthy and useful.

Hungerford, Edward B.; *Shores of Darkness*, 1941. — A study of the forgotten books of the "speculative mythologists" who tried to find in ancient myths hidden historical or pseudo-scientific meanings, and may have influenced Blake, Keats, Shelley, etc. Jumps too readily to conclusions.

Larrabee, Stephen A.; *English Bards and Grecian Marbles: The Relationship Between Sculpture and Poetry, Especially in the Romantic Period*, 1942. — The tendency in the Romantics away from mere descriptions of statues toward interpretation of their inner meanings. Cf. above, Levin, 1932.

Miles, Josephine; *Pathetic Fallacy in the Nineteenth Century*, 1942. — Statistically proves that the "fallacy" was more frequently used before Ruskin attacked it in 1856 than afterwards. Cf. below, Miles, *Vocabulary of Poetry*, 1946.

Dykes, Eva B.; *The Negro in English Romantic Thought; or, A Study of Sympathy for the Oppressed*, 1942.

Barzun, Jacques; *Romanticism and the Modern Ego*, 1943. — Refutation of the allegedly widespread belief that Nazism was an outgrowth of the Romantic Movement — a belief not held by scholars. The main thesis is factitious, but there are some valuable digressions. Entertaining; journalistic. Cf. Robert B. Heilman, "On Diatribe as Definition," *Quart. Rev. Lit.* (Chapel Hill) , 1, 288; 1944.

Baldensperger, Fernand; "1793–1794: Climacteric Times for 'Romantic' Tendencies in English Ideology," JHI, v, 3; 1944. — The picturesque, the Gothic, the horrific, the Asiatic, the pseudo-scientific, the prophetic, etc.

Peyre, Henri; *Writers and Their Critics: A Study of Misunderstanding,* 1944.— Ch. 1 deals with the failure of contemporaries to understand the Romantics.— Cf. William S. Ward, "Some Aspects of the Conservative Attitude Toward Poetry in English Criticism: 1798–1820," PMLA, LX, 386; 1945.

Gugler, Ilse; *Das Problem der Fragmentarischen Dichtung in der Englischen Romantik,* Schweizer-Anglistische Arbeiten, xv, Bern, 1944.

Liljegren, S. B.; *Essence and Attitude in English Romanticism,* 1945.— Misleading title; actually deals with affectation in manners and attire — self-display, attitudinizing, and public melancholy, in Sterne, Byron, etc. Ignores whatever does not fit into a narrow concept of Romanticism.

Ullmann, Stephen de; "Romanticism and Synaesthesia: A Comparative Study of Sense Transfer in Keats and Byron," PMLA, LX, 811; 1945.

McKeehan, Irene P.; "The Vocabulary of Landscape Description among the Early Romanticists," *Univ. of Colorado Studies in the Humanities,* 1945.— "Majestic," "grand," "sublime."

Miles, Josephine; *The Vocabulary of Poetry: Three Studies,* Univ. of Cal. Press, 1946.— (1) "Wordsworth and the Vocabulary of Emotion," (2) "Pathetic Fallacy in the Nineteenth Century, A Study of a Changing Relationship Between Object and Emotion," (3) "Major Adjectives in English Poetry from Wyatt to Auden."— Cf. Dr. Miles's "From Good to Bright," PMLA, LX, 766; 1945; the thesis of which is that the more frequent use of "bright" signifies "a declining interest in human relation and thence ethical judgment."

Bate, Walter J.; *From Classic to Romantic: Premises of Taste in Eighteenth-Century England,* 1946.— Change from neo-classic intellectualism toward intuitional assimilation of experience and romantic expression thereof. Basically important.

Skard, Sigmund; *The Use of Color in Literature: A Survey of Research* (Proceedings of the American Philosophical Society, XC), 1946.

II. THE ROMANTIC MOVEMENT IN GERMANY, FRANCE, ETC.

Brief introductory surveys and bibliographies in "Romanticism: A Symposium," PMLA, LV, 1; 1940.— Germany, France, England, Italy, and Spain. Closer to literary history than the next item.

"Symposium on Romanticism," JH I, II, 257; 1941.— Contributions to a discussion of the Romantic Movement in Europe, including A. O. Lovejoy, "The Meaning of Romanticism for the Historian of Ideas"; E. A. Anderson, "German Romanticism as an Ideology of a Cultural Crisis"; Jacques Barzun, "Romantic Historiography as a Political Force in France"; H. N. Fairchild, "Romanticism and the Religious Revival in England." Good in parts, not satisfactory as a synthesis.

Van Tieghem, Paul; *Le Romantisme dans la Littérature Européenne,* Paris, 1948 — An attempt by a veteran in the field of comparative literature to survey in one 560-page volume the chief romantic works in English, German, French, Italian, Spanish, Portuguese, Scandinavian, and Slavic.

Knowlton, Edgar C.; *An Outline of World Literature from Homer to the Present Day,* 1929.

Vaughan, Charles E.; *The Romantic Revolt,* 1900.

Omond, Thomas S.; *The Romantic Triumph,* 1900.

Mowat, R. B.; *The Romantic Age: Europe in the Early Nineteenth Century,* 1937. European literary and political history, c. 1789–1848.

Béguin, Albert; *L'Ame Romantique et la Rêve,* 2 vols., Paris, 1937.— Relation of German Romanticism to French Poetry; reverie as the source of poetry of nature.

Strich, Fritz; *Goethe und die Weltliteratur*, Bern, Switzerland, 1946. — On the originator of the term "world literature," English influence on him, and his influence on English literature.

Roubiczek, Paul; *The Misinterpretation of Man*, 1947. — Kant, Goethe, Hegel, Marx, etc. The "misinterpretations" are perversions of Romanticism.

Willoughby, L. A.; *The Romantic Movement in Germany*, 1930.

Benz, Richard; *Die Deutsche Romantik: Geschichte einer Geistigen Bewegung*, 1937.

Petersen, Julius; *Die Wesensbestimmung der Romantik*, 1926.

Price, Lawrence M.; *The Reception of English Literature in Germany*, 1932.

Lasserre, Pierre; *Le Romantisme Français*, 1907. — Cf. Selim Ezban, "Les Débats Littéraires de Lasserre," PMLA, LXII, 1108; 1947.

Clement, N. H.; *Romanticism in France*, 1938.

Giraud, Jean; *L'Ecole Romantique Française*, 2nd ed., 1931.

Bray, René; *Chronologie du Romantisme: 1804–1830*, 1932.

Souriau, Maurice; *Histoire du Romantisme en France*, 3 vols., 1927.

Finch, M. B., and Peers, E. Allison; *The Origins of French Romanticism*, 1920. — For the eighteenth century.

Partridge, Eric; *The French Romantics' Knowledge of English Literature*, 1924.

Moraud, Marcel; *Le Romantisme Français en Angleterre: 1814–1848*, 1933.

Farinelli, Arturo; *Il Romantismo nel Mondo Latino*, 3 vols., 1927. — For the movement in Italy.

Peers, E. Allison; *History of the Romantic Movement in Spain*, 2 vols., 1939.

III. THE NATURE AND THE VALUE OF ROMANTICISM

ATTEMPTS TO DEFINE THE NATURE OF ROMANTICISM

(The main purpose is to define, to analyze, to subdivide, or to discriminate Romanticism from other kinds of literature, such as classicism and realism.)

Pater, Walter; "Romanticism" (1876), in *Appreciations*, 1889. — Classicism is "order in beauty"; Romanticism, "addition of strangeness to beauty."

Watts-Dunton, Theodore; "The Renascence of Wonder in Poetry," in *Chambers's Cyclopædia of English Literature*, III, 1; 1903. — The title (the phrase was first used in his novel *Aylwin*) is better known than the essay, but the essay is still worth reading.

MacClintock, W. D.; *Some Paradoxes of the English Romantic Movement*, 1903. — An early protest against too rigid definition.

Neilson, William A.; *Essentials of Poetry*, 1913.

Lovejoy, Arthur O.;
  "The Meaning of Romantic in Early German Romanticism," MLN, XXXI, 1916; cf. XXXII, 1917.
  "Schiller and the Genesis of Romanticism," MLN, XXXV, 1; 1920.
  "On the Discriminations of Romanticisms," PMLA, XXXIX, 229; 1924.

"Nature as Aesthetic Norm," MLN, XLII, 444; 1927.

"Optimism and Romanticism," PMLA, XLII, 921; 1927.

"The Meaning of Romanticism for the Historian of Ideas," JHI, 2; 1941. Elaborate analyses of many kinds of Romanticism (German, French, English, etc.) , with a denial of any unity among them; "there are many Romanticisms." So-called "romantic" ideas are "heterogenous, logically independent, and sometimes essentially antithetic," have no one connection in actual literary history, and are therefore not reducible to any one term and definition having objective validity.

For a refutation of the philosophical assumptions underlying these studies, see Bernard Phillips, "Logical Positivism and the Function of Reason," *Philosophy*, XXIII, 346; 1948; and cf. below, Wellek, 1948.

Deutschbein, Max; *Das Wesen des Romantischen*, 1921. — Discriminates between "romantic" and "romanesque," proposing the latter term for those Romantics who, like Byron, emphasize discords rather than harmony.

Frye, P. H.; "The Terms Classic and Romantic," in *Romance and Tragedy*, 1922.

Grierson, H. J. C.; "Classical and Romantic," 1923; rptd. in *The Background of English Literature*, 1925. — Classic and romantic "the systole and disastole of the human heart."

Smith, Logan Pearsall; *Four Words: Romantic, Originality, Creative, Genius*, 1924; rptd. in *Words and Idioms*, 1925. Good historical sketch of the meanings of the words.

Robertson, J. S.; "The Reconciliation of Classic and Romantic," *Publ. Mod. Hum. Research Asso.*, 1925. — Attacked by R. S. Crane, PQ, V, 351; 1926.

Kaufman, Paul; "Defining Romanticism," MLN, XL, April, 1925. — Advocates continuation of attempts to define it.

Petersen, Julius; *Die Wesensbestimmung der Deutschen Romantik*, 1926. — Romantic and classic not diametrically opposed.

Pierce, F. E.; "Romanticism and Other Isms," JEGP, March, 1926. — Four tendencies, two bad (sentimentality and aestheticism) and two good (exploratory and mystical-ethical) .

Abercrombie, Lascelles; *Romanticism*, 1926. — The real distinction is not between romantic and classic, but between romantic and realistic.

Butt, John, Ustick, W. E., et al.; "Romantic," TLS, Aug. 3, Dec. 21, 1933; Jan. 4, April 8, 1934. — Early occurrences of the word.

Lucas, F. L.; *The Decline and Fall of the Romantic Ideal*, 1936. — The revolt of the unconscious. Quotes many definitions by others.

Baldensperger, Fernand; " 'Romantique,' ses Analogues et ses Equivalents: Tableau Synoptique de 1650 à 1810," *Harvard Studies and Notes*, XV, 13; 1937.

Borgerhoff, E. B. O.; "Réalisme and Kindred Words: Their Use as a Term of Literary Criticism in the First Half of the Nineteenth Century," PMLA, LIII, 837; 1938. — "Objective" Romanticism.

Ash, David; "Creative Romanticism," *College English*, IV, 100; 1942. — A medieval renaissance, abortive because premature. Discusses previous definitions.

Zeydel, E. H.; "The Concepts of 'Classic' and 'Romantic' "; GR, XIX, 161; 1944.

"Rococo to Romanticism," TLS, March 23, 1946. — Primarily about terms in architecture, but has literary implications. Cf. the correspondence on Baroque, Rococo, etc., TLS, Aug. 18, Sept. 8, 1945; April 20, 1946; and on Art Terms, June 8, 1946.

Weisinger, Herbert; "English Treatment of the Classical-Romantic Problem," MLQ, VII, 477; 1946. — Discussions of the distinction by Coleridge, Hazlitt, and De Quincey.

Wellek, René; "In Defense of the Term Romanticism" (Read at the MLA meeting, Dec., 1947; to be published in the new journal, *Comparative Literature,* Univ. of Oregon). — Refutes the nominalism of Lovejoy (above, 1916 ff.), and reasserts the objectivity and coherence of the movement, especially in its attitudes to nature, the imagination, and symbolism.

THE VALUE OF ROMANTICISM

(The main purpose of these works is not historical but critical. They condemn, or praise, or — in fewer instances — judiciously weigh and consider. My subdivisions are not meant to indicate sharp divisions between the groups, but may help to bring some order into an apparently chaotic mass of criticism, and thereby help in planning courses of reading. The subdivisions are:

The Attack by "Humanism," and the Defense

The Attack by "The New Criticism," and the Defense

The Appreciative Enthusiasts

Miscellaneous

The last designation is not intended to be derogatory: the fourth subdivision includes some works as important as any in the first three categories.)

The Attack by "Humanism," and the Defense

More, Paul Elmer; "The Drift of Romanticism," *Shelburne Essays,* VIII, 1913.

Babbitt, Irving; *Rousseau and Romanticism,* 1919. — Romanticism the glorification of an uncritical, aesthetic, centrifugal imagination — egotistic, unbridled, optimistic, and generally lacking in reason and good sense. — Reviewed by A. O. Lovejoy, MLN, XXXV, May; 1920.

Babbitt, Irving; "Schiller and Romanticism," MLN, XXXVII; May, 1922. — Cf. Lovejoy, "Reply to Professor Babbitt," ibid., a refutation.

Herford, C. H.; "Romanticism in the Modern World," *Engl. Asso. Essays and Studies,* VIII, 109; 1922. — Similarity between More's and Babbitt's attitudes and those of Gifford and Croker, the neo-classic critics contemporaneous with the Romantics. Discusses "the inner check."

Foerster, Norman; *Humanism and America,* 1929.

Knickerbocker, W. S.; "Humanism and Scholarship," *Sewanee Review,* XXXVIII; Jan., 1930. — Good introduction to the then state of the controversy.

Draper, John W.; "The Summa of Romanticism," *The Colonnade,* 1928. — A reply to Babbitt.

Tresnon, Jeanette; "The Paradox of Rousseau," PMLA, XLIII, 1010; 1928. — Cf. G. R. Havens' reply, PMLA, XLIV, 939; 1929. — The question as to what Rousseau actually maintained is of fundamental importance.

Fausset, Hugh I'A.; *The Proving of Psyche,* 1929. — Part II, "The New Humanism Disputed," is one of the best replies to Babbitt on psychological, ethical, and aesthetic grounds.

Bernbaum, Ernest; "The Practical Results of the Humanistic Theories," EJ, XX, 103; 1931. — Humanism condemns most of the great authors — a *reductio ad absurdum.*

Hyde, Lawrence; *The Prospects of Humanism,* 1931. — Humanism erects too sharp an opposition between moral and natural elements in man, and is too anti-religious.

Munson, Gorham; "Humanism and Modern Writers," EJ, XX, 531; 1931.

Babbitt, Irving; *On Being Creative, and Other Essays,* 1932. — Attacks on the "primitivism" of Wordsworth, etc.

Jones, Richard E.; "Romanticism Reconsidered: Humanism and Romantic Poetry," *Sewanee Review,* XLI, 396; 1933.

Beach, J. W.; *A Romantic View of Poetry*, 1944.— Against Humanism, as a moral strait jacket. Good appreciations of poems which "enable us to realize the satisfaction that we take in living." This is, however, a hedonistic view, rather than a romantic one, since it lacks faith in mystical vision.

Guerard, Albert, Jr.; "Romanticism and the Aeolian Lyre," YR, xxxiii, 482; 1944. — Romantic beliefs are "myths," including the belief in a harmony between Man and Nature.

The Attack by the "New Criticism," and the Defense

(This school is indebted to the Humanists. — For introductory surveys of its attitude toward the Romantics, see Richard H. Fogle, "Romantic Bards and Metaphysical Reviewers," ELH, xii, 221; 1945; and his "A Recent Attack Upon Romanticism," CE, ix, 356; 1948.)

Eliot, T. S.; *The Sacred Wood*, 1920; and *The Use of Poetry and Criticism*, 1933. — Romanticism fails to present the heterogeneity of life. A widely influential doctrine. In *The Use*, see especially "Shelley and Keats" (they are considered immature) .

Hulme, T. E.; *Speculations*, 1924. — "I object even to the best of the Romantics." — Cf. Michael Roberts, *T. E. Hulme*, 1938; Anon., "A Lost Defender of Tradition," TLS, June 4, 1938; and F. O. Matthiessen, *The Achievement of T. S. Eliot*, 1939.

Richards, I. A.; *Principles of Literary Criticism*, 1924. — Modern psychology in the service of "appentencies" which are hostile to Romanticism. On the absurdity of Richards' system of values ("satisfactions") , see C. S. Lewis, *The Abolition of Man*, 1947, p. 22, n2.
Richards, I. A.; *Coleridge on Imagination*, 1934. — Coleridge emphasized synthesis too much; what is real is the discordant. On the impoverishment and perversions of Coleridge's principles, see the rev. TLS, April 4, 1935.

Ogden, C. K., Richards, I. A., and Wood, J.; *The Foundations of Aesthetics*, 1925.

Cabell, James Branch; *Beyond Life*, 1925. — The theory of escape: all good literature is "romantic" because it is unlike life.

Empson, William; *Seven Types of Ambiguity*, 1930. New and rev. ed., 1947 [new Introduction added]. — All the Romantics escapist or childish; see especially pp. 26–27, and (on "Tintern Abbey") pp. 191–194. — On Empson's "critical silliness" see R. S. Crane, MP, xlv, 239; 1948.

Wilson, Edmund; *Axel's Castle: A Study in the Imaginative Literature of 1870–1930*, 1931. — Especially the essay on T. S. Eliot.

Riding, Laura, Graves, Robert, and Reeves, James; *Epilogue: A Critical Summary*, 1936. — The Romantics tradition-ridden, or "spiritually hermaphroditic," or "predominantly sexual," etc.

Hamilton, G. Rostrevor; *Poetry and Contemplation*, 1937. — Attack on the "new" critics, especially on I. A. Richards and the notion that "the function of the arts is to increase the activity and promote the health of the nervous system."

James, D. J.; *Scepticism and Poetry: an Essay on the Poetic Imagination*, 1937. — Important defense of the poetics of Wordsworth, Coleridge, and Keats. Refutes Richards' interpretation of Coleridge.

Anon.; "Romanticism in the Dock: A Plea for a Reprieve," TLS, Jan. 8, 1938. — Against both humanists and "new" critics.

Ransom, John Crowe; *The World's Body*, 1938. — "The modern poet has performed a work of dissociation and purified his art." Cf. his *The New Criticism*, 1941.

Brooks, Cleanth; *Modern Poetry and the Tradition*, 1939. — Systematic exposition of the New Criticism, combined with disparagement of the Romantics.

Brooks, Cleanth; *The Well-Wrought Urn*, 1947. — The requisites of good poetry are tension, paradox, or irony. — Cf. his "Irony," CE, IX, 231; 1948.
On his narrowing down of the literary principles of Romanticism, see below, R. S. Crane, 1948.

Burke, Kenneth; *The Philosophy of Literary Form*, 1941. — See Stoll, 1948.

Tate, Allen; *Reason in Madness*, 1941. — Condemns "the poetry of communication" of intelligible sentiments and ideas; prefers "perfect inutility." Assails Coleridge as the source of all bad modern criticism — psychological and historical; cf. Alice D. Snyder in ELH, IX, 11; 1942.

Tate, Allen, ed.; *The Language of Poetry*, 1942. — Various viewpoints; see especially Philip Wheelwright's.

Abel, Darel; "Intellectual Criticism," AS, XII, 414; 1943. — Against the "new" school. — Cf. Cleanth Brooks; "The New Criticism: A Brief for the Defense," Do., XIII, 285; 1944.

Bentley, Eric R.; "Romanticism: A Re-Evaluation," *Antioch Review*, IV, 6; 1944. — A pragmatist defends the Romantics for their encouragement of individualism and their sense of historical development; opposes Eliot and Tate, "Grand Inquisitors," for their addiction to rigidity and dogmatism.

Reynolds, Lorna; "In Defense of Romanticism," *Dublin Magazine*, XXI, 24–34; 1946. — Against T. S. Eliot; uses Wordsworth as exemplar.

Stoll, E. E.; "Symbolism in Coleridge," PMLA, LXIII, 214; 1948. — Trenchant attack on misinterpretations of romantic works by New Critics, especially by Kenneth Burke and R. P. Warren.

Crane, R. S.; "Cleanth Brooks; or, The Bankruptcy of Critical Monism," MP, XLV, 226; 1948. — Exposure of the basic unsoundness of the New Criticism's theories; their shallowness and narrowness contrasted with the depth and comprehensiveness of Coleridge's philosophy of literature. (By "monism" is meant the reduction of all criteria to one merely rhetorical concept.)

The Appreciative Enthusiasts

(Distinguished by unusually sympathetic insight into the spirit and purposes of the Romantics, also by religious, mystical, or highly — sometimes excessively — imaginative tendencies.)

Symons, Arthur; *The Romantic Movement in English Poetry*, 1909; 4th ed., 1924. — Deals little with historical influences. Deprecates distinctions between classic and romantic — "the great poets of every age are romantic."

Campbell, Olwen Ward; "Some Suggestions on the Romantic Revival and Its Effects," *Shelley and the Unromantics*, ch. 9, 1924. — Positive convictions about the nature and importance of the Romantic Movement and its faith in the inherent greatness of man's soul. Intense admiration for its highest qualities and achievements combined with frank recognition of its weaknesses and failures.

Murry, J. Middleton;
Keats and Shakespeare, 1925.
Heroes of Thought, 1938. — Heroes, despite faults, who were devoted to religion (not necessarily to a church) and to democracy, especially Wordsworth and Shelley, with some discussion of Godwin, Blake, and Keats.

Fausset, Hugh I'A.; *The Proving of Psyche*, 1929. — Part I, "The New Romanticism," is an interpretation and defense from the standpoint of a liberal Christianity. On Part II, see above, section on Humanism. — See also his *Studies in Idealism*, 1923.

Williams, Charles; *The English Poetic Mind*, 1932. — How the souls of poets grow through experience, and are threatened by disillusionment (Shakspeare, Milton, Wordsworth, Keats, etc.) .

Knight, G. Wilson;
   The Christian Renaissance, 1933. — The religious foundations of his criticism — a kind of Hellenized Christianity welcoming Eros.
   The Burning Oracle: Studies in the Poetry of Action, 1939. — The high and adventurous seriousness of Byron. — Fervent appreciation for those emotional and imaginative audacities in poetry which rationalistic and prosaic criticism shies away from.
   The Starlit Dome: Studies in the Poetry of Vision, 1941. — The profundities of Wordsworth, Coleridge, Keats, and Shelley, prophetic revelations expressible only through paradox and symbolism. — Cf. the review in TLS, Jan. 3, 1942, which is of independent importance.

Dawson, Christopher; "The Origins of the Romantic Tradition," in *Medieval Religion and Other Essays,* 1934.

De la Mare, Walter; "Dream and Imagination," Preface of *Behold, This Dreamer!* 1939.

Du Bos, Charles; *What Is Literature?* 1940. — Based on the philosophy of Thomas Aquinas, the answer is "Beauty is the body of essence," — "life becoming conscious of itself." The three greatest poets: Shakspeare, Dante, and Keats.

Earnest, Ernest; "Infinity in the palm of Your Hand: A Study of the Romantic Temper," *College English,* II, 347; 1941.

Sayers, Dorothy; *The Mind of the Maker,* 1941. — An amateur in theology tries to draw a parallel between the Creator's work and that of the poets. Cf. her *Unpopular Opinions,* 1946.

Sitwell, Edith; *A Poet's Notebook,* 1942. — (Especially Blake, Wordsworth, and Byron.)

Miscellaneous Criticisms

   (Some of the best and most judicious criticisms are found in this subdivision.)

Mordell, Albert; *The Erotic Motive in Literature,* 1919. — Like Praz (1930), studies extreme development of some features of Romanticism. Sees Freudian libido in Keats, Shelley, etc.

Prescott, F. C.; *The Poetic Mind,* 1922. — Interested in theories of dreams and the unconscious mind, but takes a sane and broad view.

Powell, Annie E. (Mrs. A. E. Dodds); *The Romantic Theory of Poetry: An Examination in the Light of Croce's Aesthetic,* 1926. — Good survey of the theories of Blake, Coleridge, Wordsworth, Shelley, and De Quincey.

Inge, William R.; "Romanticism," in *Lay Thoughts of a Dean,* 1926. — The Christian tradition flowing from *Morte d'Arthur* to the Romantics.

Buck, Philo M., Jr.; *Literary Criticism: A Study of Values in Literature,* 1930. — The values often illustrated by quotations from the Romantics.

Praz, Mario; *The Romantic Agony,* (Ital., 1931), transl., 1933. — Erudite accumulation of exotic, erotic, Satanic, and pathological excesses growing out of the Romantic Movement in European literature. Unintentionally suggests that Romanticism necessarily leads to the perverse and frenetic.

Brightfield, Myron F.; *The Issue in Literary Criticism,* 1932. — Radical attack in the name of "scientific method."

Leavis, F. R.; *Revaluation: Tradition and Development in English Poetry,* 1936. — Admires aesthetic and moral sensibility when united with critical intelligence. Observant, and usually judicious (but aberrant as to Milton and Shelley). Undervalues Coleridge; but, so far as his secularism permits, appreciates Wordsworth and especially Keats.

Lucas, F. L.; *The Decline and Fall of the Romantic Ideal,* 1936. — On the whole anti-romantic, especially anti-Coleridgean; and chiefly concerned with emotional and sensational extremes of the movement ("the crocodiles of the unconscious"). Lively style.

Bronowski, J.; *The Poet's Defence,* 1939. — Thinks the Romantics' confidence in the value of poetry has been lost today, because faith in a transcendental ideal world has faded away.

Burgum, E. B.; "Romanticism," KR, III, 479; 1941. — Economic interpretation of Romanticism as expressing "antagonisms between the middle and lower classes."

Lamont, Corliss; "Naturalism and the Appreciation of Nature," *Journal of Philosophy,* XLIV, 597; 1947. — The importance of the romantic appreciation of nature in a philosophy of naturalism.

IV. ANTHOLOGIES AND MISCELLANIES

Woods, George B.; *English Poetry and Prose of the Romantic Movement,* 1916.

Campbell, O. J., Pyre, J. F. A., and Weaver, B.; *Poetry and Criticism of the Romantic Movement,* 1932.

De la Mare, Walter; *Behold, This Dreamer!* 1939. — Passages on Dreams, Imagination, the Unconscious, the Artist, and other themes of importance in Romanticism.

Grigson, Geoffrey; *The Romantics,* 1942.

Andrews, C. E., and Percival, M. O.; *Romantic Poetry,* 1924.

Milford, H. S.; *The Oxford Book of Regency Verse: 1798–1837,* 1928.

Stephens, James, Beck, E. L., and Snow, R. H.; *English Romantic Poets,* 1934.

Spender, Stephen; *A Choice of English Romantic Poetry,* 1947. — Too erratic in choices to be representative.

MacIntyre, C. F., and Ewing, M.; *English Prose of the Romantic Period,* 1938.

Stevenson, E.; *Early Reviews of English Poets: 1786–1832,* 1890.

Haney, John L.; *Early Reviews of English Poets: 1757–1885,* 1904.

Johnson, R. Brimley; *Famous Reviews,* 1914.

Alden, R. M.; *Critical Essays of the Early Nineteenth Century,* 1921.

Bald, R. C.; *Literary Friendships in the Age of Wordsworth: An Anthology,* 1932. — "What the Romantics said to or about one another."

Morley, Edith J.; *Blake, Coleridge, Wordsworth, Lamb, etc., Being Selections from the Remains of Henry Crabb Robinson,* 1933.

V. BACKGROUND: POLITICAL, ECONOMIC, SOCIAL

Fisher, H. A. L.; *A History of Europe* (1939), vols. II and III.

Mowat, R. B.; *The Romantic Age: Europe in the Early Nineteenth Century,* 1937. — Literary and political history.

Bryant, Arthur; *The Years of Endurance: 1793–1802,* 1942.

Bryant, Arthur; *The Years of Victory: 1802–1812,* 1944.

Thompson, J. M.; *The French Revolution,* 1945.

Oman, Carola; *Britain Against Napoleon,* 1942.

Ffrench, Yvonne, ed.; *News from the Past: 1805–1887;* 1934. — Contemporaneous accounts from newspapers, etc., with illustrations.

Cole, G. D. H., and Postgate, Raymond; *The British Common People*, 1939, chs. 5–21. — Economic history.

Trevelyan, George M.; *English Social History*, 1942, chs. 11–16. — Brilliant, and of outstanding importance for the student of literature.

Quinlan, Maurice; *Victorian Prelude: English Manners, 1700–1830*, 1941.

Edwards, Maldwyn; *Methodism and England*, 1943.

Rosebery (Earl of); *Pitt* (Twelve English Statesmen), 1893.

Guedalla, Philip; *Wellington*, 1931.

Fulford, Roger; *George IV*, 1935.

Cecil (Lord), David; *The Young Melbourne*, 1939.

Marriott, J. A. R.; *Castlereagh*, 1936.

Webster, Charles K.; *The Foreign Policy of Castlereagh*, 2nd ed., 1934.

Temperley, Harold; *The Foreign Policy of Canning*, 1925.

Griggs, Earl Leslie; *Thomas Clarkson: The Friend of Slaves*, 1936.

VI. BIBLIOGRAPHIES

Bateson, F. W., ed.; *Cambridge Bibliography of English Literature*, especially II and III (1941). — Important for individual authors as well as for the general movement. Rev. in ELH, IX, 3; 1942.

Modern Humanities Research Asso., *Annual Bibliography of English Language and Literature*, 1920 ff. — Full lists, including references to the learned reviews of the books.

The Romantic Movement: A Selective and Critical Bibliography, annually, beginning in March, 1937, in ELH. — Indispensable as a record of the more important current books and articles, with scholarly comments on them.

Boas, Frederick S., ed.; *The Year's Work in English Studies* (The English Association, London), annually 1919 ff. — Critical survey of new studies.

For the Pre-Romantic period (also for Blake) see *English Literature, 1660–1800*, annually in PQ.

CHAPTER 20

THE IMAGINATION: ROMANTIC CONCEPTS OF ITS NATURE, FUNCTIONS, AND POWERS

The quintessence of Romanticism is perhaps best revealed by setting forth its concepts of the Imagination—what it is, what it is not, how it functions, and why it is of the greatest importance in human life. To those Romantics who, like Coleridge, sought metaphysical foundations for their beliefs, the Imagination was a superior kind of Reason, a power to discover basic or general or unifying truths in philosophy, or on the higher levels of scientific and mathematical speculation, as well as a power to create literature and art; but here I am endeavoring to clarify only those aspects of the romantic beliefs concerning the Imagination which have a direct bearing upon literature.

What the Imagination Is Not.—It is not vagrant reverie, indulging in wishful illusions, however pleasing. It is not merely emotional self-expression, in which self-consciousness is all that matters and the non-ego is of no interest. It is not observation in the service of the practical purposes of the individual self, or in the service of greed or ambition, or in the service of any economic or political power. It is not self-expression, or self-service, but self-surrender.

What the Imagination Is.—It is a feeling, a sensibility, an intuition, immediate and intense, by which the ego apprehends the character of something outside itself. It is concentrated upon that external object. It is thus rooted in experiences of the senses, though it may rise above its primary source. In this activity of the human consciousness, all the human powers are integrated; the whole personality is alert. The Imagination is not a function of "the mind" or "the heart" abstracted from the rest of man's nature. Even the terms "mental life" or "conscious life" are too narrow. In Imagination there may be cooperatively involved the subconscious and conscious feelings, the will, the memory; every emotional, intellectual, and spiritual experience and power may be integrated. The recollections of the individual's past may be focused upon his present sensations and reactions toward the object he is trying to comprehend. The feelings, the states of vivid awareness, are the bases of the thoughts which are later phases of that experience; the Imagination elevates the senses to their full powers and fruition. Coleridge admired Milton's statement that poetry was superior to rhetoric because it was more *sensuous,* for he believed that Milton thereby meant that in poetry the sense-experience had been imaginatively realized, had been transcended without being lost. When Wordsworth and Coleridge read in a prosy book the assertion that Milton was one of those who "wrote from the head rather than the heart," they wrote in the margin: "Milton wrote chiefly from the Imagination, which you may place where you like, in head, heart, liver, or veins."

The comprehensiveness and profundity of the romantic doctrine of the Imagination is illustrated in the following passage from *The Prelude* (II, 232–265; *Anth.*, 247):

> Blest the infant babe,
> (For with my best conjecture I would trace
> Our being's earthly progress,) blest the babe,
> Nursed in his mother's arms, who sinks to sleep,
> Rocked on his mother's breast; who with his soul
> Drinks in the feelings of his mother's eye!
> For him, in one dear presence, there exists
> A virtue which irradiates and exalts
> Objects through widest intercourse of sense.
> No outcast he, bewildered and depressed:
> Along his infant veins are interfused
> The gravitation and the filial bond
> Of nature that connect him with the world.
> Is there a flower, to which he points with hand
> Too weak to gather it, already love
> Drawn from love's purest earthly fount for him
> Hath beautified that flower; already shades
> Of pity cast from inward tenderness
> Do fall around him upon aught that bears
> Unsightly marks of violence or harm.
> Emphatically such a being lives,
> Frail creature as he is, helpless as frail,
> An inmate of this active universe:
> For feeling has to him imparted power
> That through the growing faculties of sense
> Doth like an agent of the one great mind
> Create, creator and receiver both,
> Working but in alliance with the works
> Which it beholds.—Such, verily, is the first
> Poetic spirit of our human life,
> By uniform control of after years,
> In most, abated or suppressed; in some,
> Through every change of growth and of decay,
> Pre-eminent till death.

There we have an attempt to describe the birth of the functions of the Imagination, a process obscure but magically potent.

In the helpless infant the first stirrings of conscious mental life arise out of the separate sensations, repeated day after day, for weeks and months, separate sensations of smoothness of touch, of warmth, of nourishment, sensations again and again associated. The child's first exercise of its imaginative power, after its feelings of those separate sensations have been associated sufficiently often, is to combine the parts of this experience into the apprehension of a single whole—a person, his mother—with emotional associations of peace and security and abiding love. To what was separate, unrelated, the imagination now gives coherence. What was mere sensibility becomes a rudimentary creative sensibility; but it creates not something fanciful or nonexistent; it creates true knowledge of an actual person, an actual reality. The separateness of the experiences was appearance; their organic unity is truth and reality. As experiences increase in the child's life, as other objects and persons enter it, sensibility grows keener and more versatile; apprehensive habitude is developed; the powers of creative sensibility, of imagination, are, or may be, strengthened; and larger and larger tracts of his experience are envisioned as interrelated to himself and to one another. The child, the adolescent, the adult—if the growth of his personality is normal and wholesome—both receives and gives, and progressively finds himself, by means of his imagination, in his enlarging world. Other conscious powers also contribute to the adjustment—including haphazard experimentation and purely logical inferences—but unless imagination is kept alive, the world will be only imperfectly or mistakenly apprehended. In many lives, the processes of sensation become merely passive or mechanical; there is nothing but what the Romantics call "vulgar sense," yielding only a knowledge of superficial appearances; there is lacking the creative intuition which gives contact with beauty, truth, and reality.

Out of their own psychological experiences, the great Romantics testified that the habitude of apprehensive sensibility, in ways partly intelligible and partly mysterious, develops the power of direct intuition of objects and persons in their essential reality and relationships—of seeing things as they truly are, not in meaningless separateness but in relationship to one another and ultimately to a universal Oneness. A yellow primrose becomes more than a yellow primrose without losing its individual concreteness, and without being misrepresented. The process is confessedly mysterious. It is intermittent. But whenever it is operative it is overpoweringly impressive, convincing, and delightful. Creative sensibility may be a fleeting joy, but it is a higher joy.

Imagination is a natural and general endowment of every sane mind— a capacity rudimentarily present in every human being, potentially exercisable by everyone. Historically it has proved one of the strongest forces in human life upon beliefs, and therefore upon actions. It is not wholly and constantly controllable by the will. It is affected by subconscious forces, external circumstances and accidents, and by inner addictions and habits. It is much more highly developed in some than in others. It is strong in childhood. It may be dulled by experience, encumbered by repression and censorship, or impaired by wrong kinds of education; but it can be developed and strengthened by liberal culture. The dread of the loss of imaginative power has often worried poets and artists; that fear was felt by Coleridge, Wordsworth, Keats, and Shelley, also perhaps by Milton and Shakspeare. The shrines of man's spirit are frail. Imagination is fostered by freedom from "mind-forged manacles," by untrammeled contact with all important aspects of life, by great art and literature, by familiarity with nature, by communion with noble characters, by self-dedication to magnanimous purposes, and, most of all, by humility of spirit, childlikeness, and unworldliness. Yet Imagination itself confesses that, even when such beneficent influences are present, it also depends upon inspiration from a transcendental realm.

The Function of the Imagination in Relation to Its Object.—The romantic doctrine of the Imagination does not consist of separate, loosely related beliefs about the ego and the non-ego; it is a coherent theory about the *vital and reciprocal relationship* that may and should exist between the individual and the world. To understand it one must therefore turn back and forth, even at the risk of some repetition, from the individual, who up to this point has been the chief consideration, to the objective world which he imaginatively contemplates. The Romantics believed that it was through the proper exercise of the imagination that the soundest and most fruitful relationship between the ego and the non-ego was achieved. There is, they maintained, no genuine consciousness without objectivity, and self-realization at its best requires an harmonious relationship with the non-self. The Imagination is pursuing its proper task when it is engaged in a free search for significant meanings in the world, when it tries to penetrate beneath the appearances which deceive the "vulgar sense." This it can achieve only when, so to speak, it loses itself; then it becomes identified with the innermost or essential nature and meaning of the object it contemplates. Imagination, thus functioning (sometimes termed "sympathetic," sometimes "empathic") senses the *real* life or nature of the object, the processes of its existence and growth, the endless varieties in what is apparently a static thing or static human being, the ebb and flow of feelings, how one passion is affected and modified by the rise of another—all the complex processes in nature and in human life, of composition, metabolism, and decomposition. Imagination fathoms depths of individual personality which are not apparent to science and purely logical rationalizing. It has a cognitive function of the highest importance, and is an independent pathway to genuine reality. Through his revelatory imagination, man, though dwelling in a finite world, has the power to discern and experience the infinite and absolute. He is an organic and conscious being, and by the force of his creative imagination the natural and the unconscious in the world take on their forms and meanings. Thus all life and being becomes, as it were, conscious of itself. The Imagination, seeking truth, finds beauty, the embodiment of the true essences of all things and all beings. Thus the Imagination, as the Romantics knew it in their own lives and reduced it to theory, began in the humblest kind of sense experiences, though it might ultimately rise to the almost incomprehensible exaltations of mystical union with the eternal verities.

The Belief in Inspiration.—Although, as indicated above, men could create for themselves, or by good fortune fall into, ways of life that were favorable to the activity of the Imagination, the Romantics did not regard it as a power that was wholly of human origin or wholly within human control. At its highest, and in its sublimest creative moments, Imagination was inspired by more than human, by preternatural, forces. "The definition of genius," said Hazlitt, "is that it acts unconsciously; and those who have produced immortal works, have done so without knowing how or why; the greatest power operates unseen." "The mind in creation," Shelley testified, "is as a fading coal, which some invisible influence, like an inconstant wind, awakens to transitory brightness . . . the conscious portions of our natures are unprophetic either of its approach or its departure." Since what this inspired Imagination disclosed was *truth* about man and his world, the underlying assumption, usually tacit, was that the universe willed, so to speak, to reveal, at least in part, its essential nature and its eternal purposes to man. Indeed this assumption of an "external world fitted to the mind of man," even as the mind is reciprocally fitted to the eternal world, is one of the most important of all the romantic points of faith. Whence came the inspiration? From Nature, some of the Romantics assumed; others said, from the Spirit that created and sustains the whole universe. Thus Wordsworth gives thanks to the

> Power Supreme
> Who send'st thyself into this breathing world
> Through Nature and through every kind of life,
> And mak'st man what he is, creature divine.
> *The Prelude* (1805–06), x, 386–389

The Consequences of Faith in Imagination.—Although, as was said in Chapter 19, the romantic philosophy is not irreconcilable with doctrines based on scientific evidence and on logical reasoning, its deepest foundations rest upon faith in the Imagination as a revealer of the highest realities. That faith is implicit in all the masterpieces of romantic literature, in poetry and in prose. *The Prelude* is an imaginative autobiography of the progress toward truth by means of the growth of sound imagination in a poet's mind; and its intent is the awakening of imagination in the reader, and of confidence in its guidance. Shelley's *Defense of Poetry* is a eulogy of Imagination, maintaining that the cultural forces which it creates have been the chief means of man's intermittent progress toward civilization in the past, and must be his chief aid if he is to reach his goal of justice and peace in the future.[1] The theme of *The Ancient Mariner* would be unconvincing to Reason unallied with Imagination—the theme of the exaltation of the oneness of all life, a sacred oneness which the mariner violates, whence his bitter sorrow and repentance. The sublimest vision of the Romantics arose not out of mere reasoning upon phenomena but out of imaginative insight—out of the vision of a universe which is an organic unity; a universe in which, despite obvious conflicts and dissonances, harmony predominates, in which Justice and Love are indestructible and unifying powers, ulti-mately to prevail; a universe, therefore, in which the spirit of man need not live as an alien. It was confidence in Imagination which made Romanticism a saving gospel of this transcendental integration.

Imagination was the source of what was distinctive in the ethics of Romanticism. These express themselves in romantic literature, not in the form of moral maxims, but in a consistent attitude with a definite moral effect. As ethical theory they are perhaps best expounded in that too much neglected treatise, William Hazlitt's *Principles of Human Action* (1805), which influenced, among others, John Keats. Arguing against Hobbes's doctrine of self-love as the basic motive, Hazlitt insists that virtuous conduct arises out of *imaginative* sympathy, out of our identifying ourselves with our fellowmen. The likewise imaginative vision of a universe under the reign of law also inspires a willing and glad acceptance of our duty to others. Thus we are freed from the evil forces which unimaginative and short-sighted concentration upon practi-cal objectives entails — freed from greed, fear, and pride. The ethics of Romanticism placed a high value on the individual, but it did not justify an unrestrained individualism of selfish competition such as Nietzsche was later to encourage. Since Romanticism recognized the unity of the universe, a community of spiritual forces, the individual would find his true self-realization in willing and happy cooperation and unselfishness. Duty, in other words, was not blind obedience to an ex-ternally imposed and arbitrary commandment, but a willing acceptance of the law of love. This ethical doctrine and criterion is the most magnanimous that has ever been propounded, as well as the one that is in closest accord with human nature in its highest development. Im-aginative sympathy has been the motive in many of the most noble and generous deeds in human history; for it not merely enlightens the mind but also impels the will toward self-sacrifice.[2] Thus, as Wordsworth says, Imagination becomes

> subservient to moral purposes,
> Auxiliary to divine.

---

[1] For an application of this doctrine to our own times, see Ernest Bernbaum, "The Unsought Springs of Civilization," PMLA, LXII, 1197; 1948.

[2] In later times the liberal ethics of Romanticism were "restated in a more con-sistent manner by such thinkers as Bergson and Croce and by their many followers" (Stallknecht, *Strange Seas*, p. 238).

This concept of the Imagination is central in the philosophy of Romanticism. It underlies the Romantics' psychology, epistomology, cosmogony, ethics, and aesthetics, as well as its creative art and literature. Particularly important is the interdependence of their faith in Imagination and their faith in the one harmonious universe. If the latter belief is a delusion, Imagination as they conceived it must be judged a deceiver. On the other hand, if the Imagination does not have the marvelous powers and functions which the Romantics believed it has, we cannot trust its testimony as to the reality of an harmonious universe and the validity of an altruistic ethics. The romantic concepts of the mind of man and of the universe stand or fall together.

For many of the various points in this chapter, I am indebted to the books and articles of the authors named below; but for the general plan of the exposition, and for any errors in the interpretations, I alone am responsible. The titles will be found under the following names and dates in the Bibliographies at the ends of Chapters 4, 5, 7, and 19.

Chapter 4: Coleridge	C. D. Thorpe (1937–44)
	N. P. Stallknecht (1945)
Chapter 5: Wordsworth	Francis Christensen (1946, under *The Prelude*)
Chapter 7: Hazlitt	J. M. Bullitt (1945)
Chapter 19: History of Romanticism	W. J. Bate (1946)
Chapter 19: Value of Romanticism	H. I'A Fausset (1929)
	D. J. James (1937)
	Charles Williams (1932)
	G. Wilson Knight (1933–41)
	Charles Du Bos (1940)
	J. Bronowski (1939)

For the opposition to the romantic concept of Imagination, see the New Critics listed in the Bibliography of Chapter 19 — Eliot, Richards, Empson, Brooks, Tate, etc.

CHAPTER 21

WHAT KINDS OF MODERN PROSE FICTION WOULD THE ROMANTICS ADMIRE?

(AN ESSAY IN SPECULATIVE CRITICISM)

In most of this chapter I relinquish the historical method, because I believe that those characteristics of Romanticism which are of the highest value today may best be illustrated by trying to apply its principles to the modern novel, the most popular of contemporary genres. If the Romantics could read the prose fiction of our times, they would no doubt express themselves vigorously either for or against it. Would they be vigorous in admiration or in disgust? that is the question. Unfortunately they have left us no systematic exposition of their principles of prose fiction, nothing which does in that field what was so extensively done in the fields of poetry, and of literature in general, by Coleridge's *Biographia Literaria,* Wordsworth's *Prefaces,* and Shelley's *Defense of Poetry.* Not even Hazlitt, who says more on this subject than any other Romantic, gives us anything approaching a comprehensive treatise. Nevertheless the Romantics occasionally expressed opinions regarding prose fictions; and though the data are widely dispersed and apparently not related to one another, by piecing together some of their literary practices, their preferences, and their *obiter dicta,* one may perhaps discover therein an approximately coherent pattern.

To begin with, we know what fictions they successfully wrote—most important being of course the Waverley Novels, to which we should not forget to add, even though significant in lesser degree, Beckford's little classic, *Vathek;* Lamb's *Dream Children: A Reverie;* the dream visions of De Quincey, sometimes masquerading as merely autobiographical; and the young Carlyle's *Sartor Resartus,* definitely of the Romantic School in its interest in symbolism, its contrast between the shows of things and things themselves, and its denunciation of conventional worldlings who will not hearken to the voice of The Everlasting Yea. Other pregnant hints concerning romantic tastes in prose fiction may be found in their many masterpieces of narrative verse, from *The Ancient Mariner* to *Don Juan.* As to the latter, it may be maintained that Byron's superb and sulphurous prose would have been an even better medium than the verse of *Don Juan* for its infinite variety of impassioned or satiric moods. What a superb satirical romance it would have been! What a vital fusion of ardent romance, ferocious realism, and mocking disillusionment!

Turning from the creative works to the critical, we find significant comments in Lamb and Coleridge. The former, in *The Sanity of True Genius,* describes the popular novels of his day in a phrase which Philip Wylie might like to borrow, viz., as "the scanty intellectual viands of the whole female reading public," fictions which "instead of turning dreams into sobrieties" (as Coleridge and De Quincey could do) "turned life into a dream," novels crammed with "impossible events, incoherent incidents and the inconsistent characters or no-characters of some third-rate love intrigue." Complementing this testimony from "gentle" Charles, we have Coleridge's reviews of two best sellers—Mrs. Radcliffe's *The Italian* and Lewis' *The Monk.* They are condemned, in spite of the fact that what interested Coleridge most was, in his words, "the eternal mystery of the interpenetration throughout universal life of spirit and matter, of good and evil," because they attempted to please "by what is unnatural," by a departure from "the observance of real life," and, worst of all, by fantastic characterizations. A novelist, in Coleridge's view, should have great freedom in the invention of fictitious actions, but he must never falsify human character.

To indicate what the Romantics liked to praise in prose fiction (besides the human and historical values in the Waverley novels),[1] nothing is more revelatory than Carlyle's essay on Jean Paul Richter (*Anth.,* 1038), the author of those astounding philosophical, humorous, and sentimental fantasies, *Hesperus, Titan,* and *Levana.* From Carlyle's geyser of eulogy I draw the following fervid phrases, which exemplify what most of the Romantics admired in an author's personality, themes, and manner. Richter, says Carlyle, is a man who dares to be original to the verge of rashness, whose intellect is vehement, and whose spirit is that of a dreamer, lover, and mystic. In inanimate Nature he, like his friend Herder, senses a mysterious Presence. His themes are not petty or commonplace; his Imagination is of extraordinary force and compass, wandering through Infinitude with a sober magnificence of speculation, and evoking shapes of brilliancy, solemnity, or terror. He unfolds a variegated scene, full of astonishing products, sometimes crude, but often sublime or benignant. In his eyes, incidents of the humblest life may have dignity through their relationship to transcendental realities. A humorist, he holds Man "to be forever laughed at, and forever loved." "Every gentle and generous affection, every thrill of mercy, awakens in his bosom a response." "His delight and best endeavors are with all that is beautiful and tender and mysteriously sublime, in the fate or history of Man." It may be acknowledged that Richter is at times extravagant, even grotesque; his style is difficult, a stone of stumbling; his too frequent digressions irritate: but the irregular form suits the author's vehemence; and in the minds of his faithful readers his apparent confusion more

---

[1] See, above, p. 144.—Coleridge was among the assiduous readers of Scott, but his remarks on the novels were marred by personal irritations, as pointed out in the excellent discussion in TLS, Sept. 19, 1936. For his comments on Galt, see TLS, Sept. 25, 1930; and on Defoe, TLS, Feb. 1, 1936.

and more unfolds itself into the semblance of order. There, then, is one kind of prose fiction the Romantics welcomed.

What the Romantics appreciated in prose fiction is further shown in their attitudes toward three works of much greater value than Richter's. They regarded highly Goethe's philosophical novel, *Wilhelm Meister,* chiefly because it focused attention upon the steps in a sensitive youth's intellectual and moral education through trials and errors—was, in short, a kind of prose *Prelude.* A more surprising fact is that the English Romantics were among the first to appreciate Rabelais at his true value. Before their time Rabelais was looked down upon as a disgusting buffoon. Coleridge was among those who descried, behind the farce and nonsense, a learned genius who hated pedantry and formalism and reveled in the joys of life, liberty, and enlightenment.

It is even more indicative that the Romantics did much to elevate the fame, and disclose the true nature, of *Don Quixote,* which they loved and admired more than any other novel. With its spirit they stood in real affinity. They liked the atmosphere of idealism which permeated it, the penetrative wisdom, the unerring discernment of character traits, the brave acceptance of human grandeurs and human follies. They admired its characters, who were not merely odd in a lifelike manner, but also of profound and general significance. They loved the Knight of the Doleful Countenance not solely because he was engagingly foolish, but because he was so in the service of magnanimous enthusiasms. They relished Sancho Panza because he personified their arch-opponent and oppressor, the world-that-is-too-much-with-us, the practical man with no taste (as Emerson said, Sancho Panza, like Panurge, was "good Wall Street"). Sancho Panza was so self-satisfied, so short-sightedly shrewd, so self-deceived in his sophistication, so narrow in his interests, so unerringly vulgar, so censoriously certain that art and literature should consist of clichés and moralizings and half-true proverbs, so scornful of his master's notion that Imagination might be the source of truth and wisdom. Sancho could not understand what Don Quixote meant when he spoke of Poetry and History as "sacred things," because "Truth is essential thereto; and where Truth is, there God himself is, so far as truth is concerned,—notwithstanding which there are those who concoct books and toss them into the world as if they were fritters!" On the one hand, the books wherein Truth is, wherein there is a touch of something of the divine, in other words, the Literature of Power; and on the other hand, the books concocted like fritters, the Literature of mere Knowledge— there was a distinction which the Romantics could appreciate. Even more significant to them than the Knight and his Squire was Cervantes himself—he who could live imaginatively in each of those characters, yet rise with romantic irony above them both, who could comprehend the world as a whole in this ever-recurring tragi-comic conflict between idealism and pseudo-realism, who could weep and laugh thereover, and rejoice in the painful and hilarious fact that God had made such men in such a world. And the boldest among them wondered whether even as Cervantes transcended their prototypes in his fictional world, mankind in the future could perhaps some day transcend in reality both its Don Quixotes and its Sancho Panzas.

In gathering together these data about the Romantics' attitudes toward prose fiction, I have touched upon some of their chief principles and literary tastes—their antagonism to worldliness, their fondness for original characters who are individual human beings but have affinities with eternal forces, their confidence in life and its ultimate improvement, their love of Nature, and their trust in freedom within and without, both in substance and in form. Their judgments on fiction confirm what has previously been said (in Chapter 20) concerning their concept of the Imagination as the prime creative force in all good art and literature, and of its magical power to penetrate beneath the surfaces of all things and beings, to discover their essential nature, and to reveal those inter-relationships which bind the universe together. If literature, including prose fiction, was thus imaginatively inspired, it was the truest possible revelation of God, Nature, and Man. Romanticism did not discourage concreteness or objectivity; what it would not countenance was the failure to discern beneath the concrete appearances the inner realities, or beneath the superficial aspects of human nature any indications of its possible harmony with the spirit of the universe. The Romantics would have applauded the critic who recently said:

> In some of the greatest novels of the world, the Russian, we find, not economic man, but man who is a spirit, celebrated; there we find the soul, the eternal aspirant to things beyond earth, the things which if they exist at all, have a life transcendent of the flesh. That is the chief message of the great Russian novels—that man is unhappy because he is a spirit.

To which the Romantics would have added that whenever man is most happy it is because his *spirit* has found joy or peace.[2]

Nearly all the well known prose fictions since the 1920's would be condemned by the Romantics. Most of them were written by cynics, hedonists, journalists, or propagandists; some, by plain simpletons. From the romantic point of view the evil in the so-called realistic novels is not their unrestrained frankness, but their materialism and defeatism. They imply that Man finds himself in an alien, hostile universe; that he is the helpless product of evil heredity and degrading environment, that his ideas are not his own but are wholly determined by the economic class to which he happens to belong, that transcendental ideals are sentimental illusions, and that only a stupid or insincere novelist could describe life as anything better than an agonizing or tiresome flux without meaning, purpose, or value. Some of the authors remind one of the judge at the trial of Conrad's Lord Jim, who was concerned "not about the funda-

---

[2] Contrast this quotation with one of the half-true proverbs that the Sancho Panzas admire, "All sorrows are bearable if there is *bread*."

mental *why,* but the superficial *how* of the affair." They cannot rise above the level of clever reportage; theirs is a fiction of sensory impressions. When perchance they attempt interpretation, it is shallow; they accept the first plausible explanation of human conduct that would occur to a mediocre unimaginative mind. The hedonists among them, like Somerset Maugham, who enjoy the surface values of civilization, do not appreciate the principles on which they are based. Perspective is lacking —distance, and depth, and elevation. The historical novel gives no sense of any spiritual or ethical significance in the past; and the novel of the contemporaneous finds life today either silly or revolting. In twenty-seven volumes, verbosely documented, all the "Men of Good Will" are shown frustrated or disintegrated. In Longfellow's day, his cousin, Tom Appleton, remarked that "Mankind fell in Adam, had been falling ever since, but had never touched bottom until it got to Henry Ward Beecher." He did not foresee the far lower depths that have been reached in most of the fiction of our time—the allegedly human creatures, "herds of flurried automata," the merely political or economic robots—anemic, corrupt, either apathetic or neurotic, interested in what they miscall love "only in its contactual aspects," jittering crazily around in a hard stereotyped world, trying to find content in pipe dreams, and themselves reaching the conclusion that their lives mean nothing at all. Hence the novelistic themes are trivial, and the plots end in a whimper. It is a world so empty of fully human characters and problems that when Cleanth Brooks and Robert Penn Warren compile a lengthy book about it entitled *Understanding Fiction* they can find almost nothing to understand except mechanical devices of narration. And those bemused reviewers who, week in and week out, praise such novels remind us of that unfortunate heretic whom the Spanish Inquisition condemned to sleep on blunt spikes for fifteen years—and who afterwards couldn't sleep on anything else.

In reaction against this subhuman drift there has arisen a movement which is called the New Romanticism, but so far it has borne fruits in criticism and in poetry rather than in prose fiction. Before it can produce great romantic novels, we must have novelists who will turn away from the current worldly ways of authorship, from commercialization and Book Clubs and Book Weeks and Best Seller Lists, and all kinds of Nobel and ignoble prizes and self-elected academies, and all that artificially engendered fame by which the author's soul is lured away from his solitude and independence. The romantic ideal must be restored— the ideal of the Man of Letters as a Messenger-from-on-High and a Servant and Leader of Mankind, a more enlightened and inspired leader than the dunderheaded politicians, soapy racketeers, and fatuous economists whose greed and fear have brought us to the brink of ruin. Genuine men of letters, hierophants of humane civilization, can give us the romantic fiction we long for, which will interpret life as Imagination truly discloses it—Imagination the begetter of *all* creation—fiction afire with spontaneity and forthrightness that will re-illumine those truths that "everybody knows and nobody realizes." Such romantic fiction may be pungently realistic, but it will also be compassionate. It will infuse the world of fact with values. It will reach below the surface appearances to those profundities of individual personality which are not fathomable by scientific analysis, and will express truths about the creative purposefulness of life which no abstract philosophizing can render convincing. It will help us to raise from the depths of our consciousness those thoughts and feelings we have not fully understood, make us spread them out in the sunlight, learn the meaning of them—and thereby know ourselves.

The romantic novel will characterize man as in part and potentially a spiritual being, capable of the virtues of intellectual and moral honesty, of courage, and of good will. It will restore belief in the dignity of ordinary human life, and disclose the mysterious worth that hides behind the deceptive veil of appearances. It will re-endow man with a sense of moral responsibility, and thereby with a power to fulfill his destiny. It will instill a sense of life triumphant—of man's spirit as a power capable of overcoming the follies and wickedness of our modern world, which is deluding itself by supposing it can gain ideal ends cheaply, by crooked means. The Romantics of the future as of the past will renew our trust in life, in one another, in man's future, and in the governance of the Universe—a faith, as Justice Holmes said, "in a universe not measured by our fears."

Our times have not yet produced a really great work of prose fiction in which the romantic spirit rules from the beginning to the end. Recently, however, romantic passages have burst forth in novels which on the whole are not of that school. I shall quote three passages of that kind, but shall not name the authors, for to do so might distract attention from the main point. In each of these passages the speaker is either the hero or some other person with whom the author is in sympathy. First we hear a character protesting against skepticism, as follows:

> The essence of all faith . . . is that man's life can be, and will be, better; that man's greatest enemies, in the forms in which they now exist —the forms we see on every hand—of fear, hatred, slavery, cruelty, poverty, and need—can be conquered and destroyed!

Secondly, in a cruder style, a wayside preacher is groping toward religion:

> "I figgered about the Holy Sperit and the Jesus road. I figgered 'Why do we got to hang it on God or Jesus?' 'May be,' I figgered, 'maybe it's all men and women we love; maybe that's the Holy Sperit—the human spirit —the whole shebang. Maybe all men got one big soul ever'body's part of.' Now I set thinkin it, an' all of a suddent—I knew it. I knew it so deep down that it was true, and I still know it!"

In my third quotation, a thirteen-year-old girl, sensitive and imaginative, is speaking to her sister:

"And even if there isn't a war, it is just the same," she said. "There are *always* hurt people, and starved people, and beaten people, and misery."

"And there are always the people who don't care," said Bea.

"Well, I care really. I *have* to," said Harriet.

There are three unmistakably romantic notes. But as is too often the case, they fade away; Chaos and old Night return. In a few modern instances, a genuinely romantic feeling is woven into the whole texture of the novel, and brief quotation is therefore not feasible; but such instances are few in comparison with the overwhelming numbers of either brutally realistic or fatuously sentimental productions. Perhaps Romanticism will, as I believe, arise again in prose fiction. But for the time being, we must usually say of the novelists who momentarily fall into a romantic vein, what Winston Churchill said about that blunderer Stanley Baldwin, "He occasionally stumbles over the truth, but always hastily picks himself up and hurries on as if nothing had happened."

CHAPTER 22

THE HISTORY OF THE STUDY OF THE SUBJECT

The History of the Subject from c. 1890 to 1930.[1]—In an article entitled "Graduate Study in English Literature,"[2] I mentioned the Romantic Movement as one illustration of the principle that the study of periods of literary history becomes more vitally interesting when we realize how modern the best interpretation of them is. The following sketch tries to set forth, in the broadest outlines, and without pausing to discuss the finer shades and intricacies of a very complex subject, the ways in which scholars of this generation have enabled us to arrive at a more accurate and sound appreciation of the Romantic Movement.

Forty years ago it was difficult or impossible to obtain reliable and even approximately complete editions of the works and letters of many important authors of the romantic period. To this day certain authors remain deplorably ill-edited—notably Coleridge. But in 1890 we were almost as badly off with respect to many others; in the case of Wordsworth, for instance, as Professor Knight's successor, Professor De Selincourt, remarks, it was still "the reign of Chaos and old (K) night." Since 1890 the patient labors of our scholars have given us much more nearly correct and complete editions—of Scott in 1892, of Wordsworth in 1895, of Burns in 1896, of Byron's letters in 1903 and 1922, of Hazlitt in 1902, of Lamb in 1903, of Blake in 1905 and 1925, of Campbell in 1907, of Southey in 1909, and of Landor and Shelley in 1928. Our time has been an unusually brilliant period in the history of editorship; and it is owing to the arduous and too little recognized work of textual scholars of the present generation that we now at last have access (with a few exceptions only) to reliable texts of all the essential documents of the Romantic Movement.

Concurrently, there has taken place a radical change in the general conception of the romantic authors. If a student of today who has gained his impression of them from only the best recent accounts were to turn back to the accounts that passed current in about 1890, he would be amazed at the meagerness and incorrectness of the older sketches. And strangely enough this limited vision characterized the friends as well as the enemies of the Romantic Movement. What the friends and admirers —largely under pre-Raphaelite influence—went into ecstasies over was almost entirely the style and tone of some of the poets. Even academic

---

[1] Except for a few slight alterations, this part of this chapter has been left as it stood in 1930, since it may be instructive to indicate how the history of the subject appeared at that stage of its development.

[2] The English Journal, XXVII, 33; 1928.

studies focused on their technique; a typical dissertation of 1898 is entirely devoted to the subject "The Use of Color in the Verse of the Romantic Poets." Even ardent devotees at that time were impercipient as to their profound themes, their imaginative intuitions, or their ethical axioms; in short, they slighted some of the most essential values and chief problems.

As for the enemies of the Romantics, those materialists who felt and dreaded their messages or intimations, they dominated criticism and did all they could to dim the glory of the romantic galaxy. Taine, whose *History of English Literature* was still powerfully influential, appreciated only Byron and dismissed Wordsworth and Coleridge as writers who tried to be natural but failed. His ally Georg Brandes asserted that their wisdom was dullness. He valued Shelley and the rest only in so far as they expressed the spirit of political revolt, and he achieved a triumph in disproportion when on that ground he gave to Thomas Moore thirty pages and to Sir Walter Scott only thirty lines.

Subsequently—and strangely enough long after the real scholars had begun to understand the movement—this attitude of the Dark Ages was continued, especially in France and America, by the so-called "Humanists." Paul Elmer More and Irving Babbitt accepted the pre-Raphaelite critics' interpretation of the Romantics at its face value. They accepted their false interpretation that the Romantics were merely beautiful singers of misty impressions and emotional yearnings; but instead of reckoning it to their credit, they thought it spelled their doom. As the "Humanists" justly said, there never had been any kind of truly great literature that answered such a description. It could therefore be neither great nor good; it must be pernicious. Their indignation against the idea of poetry as achieving greatness without moral stamina or mental vigor was the one good quality of their criticism. Blinded by fear and zeal, they could see in Wordsworth, Keats, and Shelley only those passages which might be tortured into commendation of primitivism, imbecile reverie, and emotional unrestraint; and they interpreted their lives, characters, doctrines, and styles as expressions of folly and depravity. Though some of the most violent of these neo-neo-classic denunciations were published as late as 1919, the interpretations had been conceived some twenty years earlier; and by 1919 they were already so out of accord with scholarly knowledge that they seemed antediluvian in their ignorance.

To turn to the constructive achievements of true scholarship in the subject. Concurrently, there were reconstructed three large and complex subjects: (1) the general history of the period from 1798 to 1838, (2) the history of Pre-Romanticism, and (3) one by one, the biographical and critical interpretations of most of the romantic masters. With respect to the first, comparison of typical general histories of forty years ago with those of today shows the former altogether too simple. About all that the romantic revolution amounted to in the accounts of 1890 was a sudden change in the fashion of poetic diction and verse forms, the creation of the historical novel, and a much greater love for nature and for the common man. How indescribably richer, more extensive, and more varied the change is now discerned to have really been! We see "the one spirit's plastic stress" affecting not only two or three literary types and tendencies but every type and every subject, from ode to essay, and from theology and historiography to rhetorical theory or journalistic reviewing. In fact, it is the richness of its manifoldness, not a lack of unity in its essential inner nature, which has baffled those who, for the sake of sweet simplicity, wish to translate the fruitful vitality of its historical manifestations into the rigid deadness of one abstract definition (clear enough for the simplest undergraduate mind to grasp and to apply without effort).

The older histories of Pre-Romanticism were likewise too simple and meager. They misunderstood their study of the anticipations because they did not fully understand the full-blown thing itself. In the Dark Ages, the cataclysmic theory had been assumed; we were told that in the days of Pope everybody was preoccupied with town life, conventions, and common sense, and the heroic couplet was the only poetry; Milton, Spenser, and Shakspeare were totally neglected. Then came a sudden revolution—a lyrical and democratic outcry that the peasantry were your only true men, that ballads, sonnets, and naïvely crude diction were your only poesy, and that medieval subjects were your best themes. A new age was, we were told, thus suddenly born, in which Milton's early verse was for the first time appreciated. The progress from the cataclysmic theory to the evolutionary has been a painful and laborious one; but, little by little, we have witnessed a great accumulation of pre-romantic works and ideas formerly neglected. Not only the French and English medieval, but the Oriental, Celtic, and Scandinavian, have been dragged forth; and one eighteenth-century theme after another has been heaped upon the pre-romantic pile—the literature of gloom and graveyard, of noble savage and savage noble, of Gothic castle and cottage garden. It has been pretty well proved that the Augustans loved everything in life and literature, from moonlight to Milton, that formerly they were declared to have ignored or detested. Indeed it has at times been made to seem as if they were more addicted to romantic materials and ideas than the Romantics themselves! In all this there was, of course, some lack of measure. There is little literary or artistic sense in the assumption that a crude and ugly expression of a half-baked idea is a genuine anticipation of the beautiful expression of a complex masterpiece which contains that idea as merely one element. And it is with some justice that Professor Oliver Elton, in his very conservative history of the period from 1730 to 1780, refuses to attach much literary or historical importance to some discoveries in Pre-Romanticism.

Yet the general result of the many researches has been of fundamental value. The sum and substance of them all seems this: The Romantic Movement before its coming to fullness, greatness, and self-consciousness in the nineteenth century, was prepared for by an infinite number of intellectual and aesthetic impulses—was, in other words, an evolution not a revolution; and the difference in emphasis and method between it and Classicism was not a sudden or consistent break but the occasional stirring and reawakening of tendencies never in any previous age quite unrepresented. It has also been made clear that the history of pre-romantic ideas is more important than that of forms and topics, the choice of which was finally determined by the nature of the ideas.

To turn from the general movements to the individual leaders, I shall grant that, in the instances of a few of the greater romantic poets, there has been little progress in knowledge. In Scott's case, the painstaking work of the late Professor Emerson has corrected numerous errors of fact in Lockhart, but there has been nothing of revolutionary importance. As for Byron, he has long been understood as one who led an abnormally wayward life and whom remorse and exile stimulated to great poetry. Since 1922 we feel less uncertain of the precise nature of one of his abnormalities, but the Melbourne letters have not seriously modified our understanding of his poetry. The chief change in the accounts of Byron has been that we tend more than formerly to appreciate that he was one of the greatest masters of epistolary and other prose and, also, that not until *Don Juan* did his fullest powers find really adequate expression.

It is with respect to Blake, Coleridge, Wordsworth, Keats, and Shelley that changes of the highest importance have occurred. Blake, once neglected, is now almost worshiped. As recently as 1906 a Shelburne essay on him, which repeated many of the picturesque and false old anecdotes, condescendingly dismissed him as a self-deceiver who finally went insane. From 1907 onward the biographies of him have been steadily improving; and in 1924 the most elaborate attempt was made to understand and interpret his allegorical system.

Wordsworth was represented in the Dark Ages as a second Lady of Christ's, passionless, and chiefly remarkable for an effeminate affection for gentle scenes and country folk. In Arnold's view his poetry had "no philosophy"—a variant of which error was the allegation that when, especially in his later years, he did try to philosophize he ceased to be a poet. Since then the true Wordsworth has at last risen from the dead. At Princeton and at Paris the legend of the passionless prig was destroyed by biographical research; at Oxford his great contributions to the history of political thought and of liberty were disclosed; and at Wisconsin there was revealed the richness and profundity of his ethics, psychology, and cultural theories, as well as some of the origins thereof. It has come to be realized that some of Wordsworth's early lyrics, in which he illustrated youthful phases of human development, have been overemphasized and misunderstood, and that they were not meant to advocate that we should be guided by inexperience. It has become clearer that to be a Wordsworthian in the true sense means something more than loving simple verses or idiot boys—means, indeed, a discipleship in a most arduous moral and mental effort persevered in throughout the three ages of man's life. The importance, to the seeker after wisdom, of Wordsworth's later poems has become evident. Even of *The Excursion,* at last rightly apprehended, we no longer say "This will not do," but rather that it is we who cannot do without it.

The character and the creative ways of Coleridge have emerged from the shadows. No longer will a Leslie Stephen misrepresent him as one who may have talked like an angel but who lived like an opium-slave. After the recent disclosures of his true love, and its connection with his poetry, we can look into his heart as never before and perceive the relation of some of his best poems to his deepest experiences. His intellectual history has likewise become clearer and clearer. Much of his reading has been traced, and the supposedly desultory idler over books has become the omnivorous, purposeful explorer of not merely *belles-lettres* but of many sciences, natural history, travels, history, and theology—the mind that ingeniously tried to harmonize the thoughts of the English neo-Platonists with the terminology of the German Idealists—the searcher everywhere for the ideal unity underlying the multitudinous variety of experience and of literature. The process by which his *Ancient Mariner* grew—the part which conscious memory, subconscious brooding, and deliberate purpose, cooperatively played in creation—has been traced more fully than in the case of any other English poem ever written. Furthermore, the neo-neo-classic conception of Coleridge as a capricious dreamer of purely fanciful notions, and an advocate of unchecked reverie, has been shattered by closer scrutiny of his criticism, which recommends the rational power that "controls, determines, and modifies" the "phantasmal chaos of association." Indeed, Coleridge uses the very term "check" which his enemies suppose him to have despised, and says that both fancy and inspiration need the check of the senses and of the reason; otherwise art becomes, in his words, "delirium or mania."

As for Shelley and Keats, after reading their latest biographies, we feel that, as in the case of Wordsworth, about the only privacy left to them is a privacy of glorious light. Though Miss Lowell's biography is somewhat weakened by the pre-Raphaelite critical tradition that Keats cared only for art for art's sake, his life and character can surely no longer be misrepresented as that of a mawkish cockney who had a knack for writing merely sensuous verse, which is the misinterpretation of him given twenty years ago by the greater of the "humanistic" Dioscuri. Closer and closer scrutiny of Keats's letters in chronological relation to his poems, more careful study of the meaning he intended his phrases to bear, such as the unfortunately ambiguous "O for a life of sensations rather than of thoughts!" have disclosed a character gallantly struggling toward the light, a thinker anxious to take account of all the problems of humanity, and an artist eager to learn from Shakspeare, Milton, and Wordsworth.

Even so with Shelley. Arnold, Symonds, and Stephen looked askance at him; and Dowden tried to exalt him by ignoring the earthy facts of his career. The more candid critics believed him given, in actual life, to hallucinations, and in his poetry from first to last to a fatuous Godwinian Utopia, his harmonies and rhythms alone giving value to his work. Biographical research has disclosed that the manly, generous, and sensible traits of Shelley's character were much more significant and directive in his life than his caprices and follies. His intellectual curiosity in science and all manner of learning has been perceived; his youthful sentiments and hasty opinions in politics and religion have no longer been permitted to obscure his truer and maturer social and political views, which were Spinozan and neo-Platonic rather than Godwinian. His so-called Utopianism is disclosed as a hopeful liberalism—very optimistic, to be sure, but with no touch of madness. Indeed, the higher social philosophy of all the romantic poets in their greater works now appears essentially the same, amid all their varied manner of expressing it, and despite their quarrels over the petty politics of the moment.

I do not know of a greater source of intellectual pleasure and of pride in the intellectual life of today than to follow this gradual disclosure by our contemporary scholars of the true lives, characters, themes, purposes, and literary traits of the great romantic authors. They spoke to their own times, but it is by us of today that at last they are clearly heard.

They are understood not only because the facts have been more accurately gathered but also because the weighing of the facts has been more judicious and tolerant and courageous. We no longer shrink, like Matthew Arnold, from admitting the fact that great and beautiful poetry and prose may be created by men who at times commit evil or folly. Not only in Byron's case but in Coleridge's and Shelley's and Wordsworth's and others', we grant that in the course of their lives they fell into temptation, were torn by evil passions, or deluded by vain conceits, or in their feebler moments descended into vulgarity, meanness, or dullness, and nevertheless remained in their best works the hierophants of beauty and of truth. Today we would not wish it otherwise. We now realize that humanity would be in a worse case if the creation of literature were a monopoly of morally impeccable and unearthly beings. The truth again has set us free. We rejoice to discover that, even as the sublimest mystery of religion is the incarnation of the divine in the truly human, so the greatest mystery of art is the incarnation of artistic genius in beings fundamentally like unto our frail selves.

There is one other aspect in which the progress of this scholarship may have effects far beyond the special field of its study. Soon the knowledge of the Romantic Movement will have reached a point where its study will become more illuminating than that of any other period of English literary history. In making this assertion, I am assuming that the study of a period is pursued not merely to become acquainted with that period but also to observe how great literary masterpieces have been created. Study of the later-nineteenth-century period is not so certainly profitable, inasmuch as the permanent intrinsic value of those authors is not yet quite so assured. The chief rivals of the great Romantics are, from this point of view, Chaucer, Shakspeare, Milton, and possibly Spenser. But even if it were granted that those older classics are still greater than Scott, Wordsworth, Coleridge, Byron, Keats, and Shelley, there will always remain serious obstacles to learning by a study of them the processes and conditions of creative imagination. Never can we hope to ascertain concerning Chaucer, Shakspeare, and Milton, their lives and personal characters, the development of their inward intellectual and aesthetic life through their reading, their use of their sources, their theories of art, their philosophical assumptions, their social and political environment, with that precision and that fullness with which such matters are being ascertained concerning the romantic group.

Imagine what it would mean to the study of Shakspeare or of Milton if we had in their cases such reading lists as we have of Scott and Coleridge, or such great contemporaneous critics as Lamb and Hazlitt; or if we had so many personal letters as we have of Shelley, Byron, and Keats, documents revealing their personalities as tested by a thousand and one contacts with everyday life, stating the purpose of their works, and exhibiting the significant aspects of their emotions, minds, and souls. In short, the scholars who are making our knowledge of the Romantic Movement more rich, more precise, and more accessible are not merely achieving that worthy end itself but will soon enable the student of English literature to study almost the entire process by which a great and varied group of literary masterpieces were composed—and no essential factor in that process will be unobservable, because oblivion happens to have covered it. It should be the most illuminating literary discipline the world has ever known.

The History of the Subject from 1930 to the Present.—A critical survey of recent scholarly works on the Romantic Movement and its chief authors, is now in preparation under the editorship of Professor Thomas M. Raysor. The several chapters on the general history, and on Coleridge, Wordsworth, Byron, Shelley, Keats, etc., are being written by specialists. The book is expected to appear in 1949–50. Therefore it seems futile to present here a detailed account of the matter, for it would be superseded almost as soon as it was published. Accordingly I confine myself to a brief statement about the most outstanding new developments.

As an inspection of the Bibliographies in this *Guide*, with attention to the dates, will show, there has been during the last fifteen or twenty years a large increase of interest in Romanticism, and a great accumulation of facts and materials—bibliographical, biographical, historical, and critical. But there have been no such radical changes in the general interpretation of the Romantic Movement as took place before 1930; nor have there been revolutionary changes of opinion regarding the chief individual characteristics of the Romantics.

We have a more accurate knowledge of the works owing to the scholarly editions that have appeared, especially of Coleridge (his criticisms), Wordsworth (*The Prelude*), Scott (Letters and Journals), Keats, etc. We have fuller and more reliable biographies of Coleridge, Hazlitt, Scott, Landor, and Shelley. We have more precise and detailed analyses of the philosophical and critical principles of Wordsworth, Keats, Shelley, and the young Carlyle. And in the movement as a whole there have been valuable contributions on such topics as the treatment of mythology by the Romantics, their interpretation of Nature, their relation to the history of art, and their aesthetics, craftsmanship, and symbolism.

The cultivation of knowledge concerning Romanticism, and of understanding and due appreciation of its masterpieces, has been mainly owing to the devoted labors of academic scholars. Despite the efforts of nominalists arguing that, because Romanticism could not be briefly defined, it must be a chaotic absurdity; despite the "humanists" who feared that it was ethically too liberal, and the "new critics" who scorn its faith as too optimistic and its manner of expression as too harmonious, the works of the Romantics have more and more been acclaimed by the learned as among our greatest classics. Scholars have remained devoted to the study of these authors during a period when the nonacademic world grew indifferent or hostile, when current literature was dominated by cynicism and despair, and when political events were misguided toward world catastrophe by anti-romantic and materialistic ideologies. Even in so unpropitious a present, the learned literary world has turned to the Romantics as among the brightest glories of the past and the strongest hope for the future. Their influence

like a star
Beacons from the abode where the Eternal are.

CHRONOLOGICAL TABLE OF THE
CHIEF ROMANTIC WORKS

For the Pre-Romantic works, see the chronological table given above, page 6.

1783	Blake	Poetical Sketches
1789	Blake	Songs of Innocence
1789	Blake	The Book of Thel
1791	Blake	The French Revolution
c. 1793	Blake	The Marriage of Heaven and Hell
c. 1793	Blake	A Song of Liberty
1793	Blake	Visions of the Daughters of Albion
1793	Blake	America: A Prophecy
1793	Wordsworth	An Evening Walk
1793	Wordsworth	Descriptive Sketches
1794	Blake	Songs of Experience
1794	Coleridge	La Fayette
1794	Coleridge	Koskiusko
1794	Coleridge	To the Reverend W. L. Bowles
1794 (?)	Coleridge	To the Author of "The Robbers"
1794	Coleridge	To a Young Ass
1794	Coleridge	Lewti
1796	Coleridge	Religious Musings
1796	Coleridge	The Eolian Harp
1796	Coleridge	Reflections on Having Left a Place of Retirement
1796	Coleridge	Ode on the Departing Year
1797	Coleridge	This Lime-Tree Bower My Prison
1797	Blake	The Four Zoas
1798	Coleridge	The Ancient Mariner
1798	Coleridge	France: An Ode
1798	Coleridge	Frost at Midnight
1798	Coleridge	Fears in Solitude
1798	Coleridge	The Nightingale
1798	Coleridge	The Ballad of the Dark Ladie
1798	Wordsworth and Coleridge	Lyrical Ballads
1798	Wordsworth	Lines Composed a Few Miles Above Tintern Abbey
1798	Lamb	Rosamund Gray
1798	Landor	Gebir
1799	Coleridge	The Devil's Thoughts
1799	Coleridge	Love
1799	Campbell	The Pleasures of Hope
1800	Wordsworth	The Old Cumberland Beggar
1800	Wordsworth	Ruth
1800	Wordsworth	The Fountain
1800	Wordsworth	Michael
1800	Wordsworth	The Danish Boy
1800	Wordsworth	Preface, Lyrical Ballads, 2nd ed.
1800	Moore	Odes of Anacreon
c. 1801	Blake	To Tirzah
1801	Scott	Ballads
1801	Southey	Thalaba the Destroyer

1801	Campbell	Ye Mariners of England
1802	Coleridge	Dejection: An Ode
1802	Coleridge	Hymn Before Sunrise, in the Vale of Chamouni
1802	Lamb	John Woodvil
1802	Campbell	Hohenlinden
1802	Campbell	Lochiel's Warning
1802–03	Scott	The Minstrelsy of the Scottish Border
wr. c. 1803	Blake	The Mental Traveller
wr. c. 1803	Blake	Auguries of Innocence
1804–08	Blake	Milton
1804–20	Blake	Jerusalem
1805	Hazlitt	Principles of Human Action
1805	Scott	The Lay of the Last Minstrel
1805	Southey	Madoc
1807	Wordsworth	Poems
1807	Lamb	Tales from Shakspeare
1807–34	Moore	Irish Melodies
1808	Lamb	Specimens of English Dramatic Poets
1808	Scott	Marmion
1808	Hunt	The Examiner
1808–18	Coleridge	Lectures (delivered)
1809	Wordsworth	On the Convention of Cintra
1809	Campbell	Gertrude of Wyoming
1809	Campbell	The Battle of the Baltic
1809	Byron	English Bards and Scotch Reviewers
1809–10	Coleridge	The Friend (revised 1818)
1810	Scott	The Lady of the Lake
1810	Southey	The Curse of Kehama
1811	Landor	Count Julian
1811	Lamb	On the Tragedies of Shakspeare
1812	Byron	Childe Harold, I-II
1813	Scott	Rokeby
1813	Southey	The Life of Nelson
1813	Shelley	Queen Mab
1813–14	Byron	Turkish Tales (The Giaour, The Corsair, etc.)
1814	Wordsworth	The Excursion
1814	Scott	Waverley
1814	Southey	Ode During Negotiations with Napoleon
1814	Southey	Roderick
1815	Wordsworth	Poems
1815	Scott	Guy Mannering
1815	Byron	Hebrew Melodies
1816	Coleridge	Christabel
1816	Coleridge	Kubla Khan
1816	Scott	The Antiquary
1816	Scott	Old Mortality
1816	Byron	The Dream
1816	Byron	Childe Harold, III-IV
1816	Byron	The Prisoner of Chillon
1816	Shelley	Alastor
1816	Hunt	The Story of Rimini
1817	Coleridge	Biographia Literaria
1817	Hazlitt	Characters of Shakspeare's Plays
1817	Hazlitt	The Round Table
1817	Shelley, Mary	Frankenstein, or the Modern Prometheus
1817	Moore	Lalla Rookh
1817	Byron	Manfred

1817	Keats	Poems
1817	Shelley	Laon and Cythna (= Revolt of Islam, 1818)
c. 1818	Blake	The Everlasting Gospel
1818	Hazlitt	The English Poets
1818	Hazlitt	The English Comic Writers
1818	Scott	Rob Roy
1818	Scott	The Heart of Midlothian
1818	Byron	Beppo
1818	Keats	Endymion
1818	Hunt	The Nymphs
1818–33	De Quincey	Essays on Kant
1819	Scott	The Legend of Montrose
1819	Byron	Mazeppa
1819	Byron	Don Juan, I-II (1821, III-V; 1823, VI-XIV; 1824, XV-XVI)
wr. 1819	Keats	The Fall of Hyperion (publ. 1856)
1819	Shelley	Lines Written Among the Euganean Hills
1819–21	Hunt	The Indicator
1820	Shelley	The Cenci
1820	Shelley	The Witch of Atlas
1820	Shelley	Prometheus Unbound
1820	Hazlitt	Dramatic Literature of the Age of Elizabeth
1820	Scott	Ivanhoe
1820	Southey	The Life of Wesley
1820	Keats	Lamia, Isabella, Eve of St. Agnes, Hyperion, etc.
1820–23	Lamb	Essays of Elia
1821	Scott	Kenilworth
1821	Hazlitt	Elizabethan Literature
1821	Byron	Sardanapalus
1821	Byron	Cain
1821	Shelley	Epipsychidion
1821	Shelley	Adonais
wr. 1821	Shelley	A Defense of Poetry (publ. 1840)
1821	De Quincey	Confessions of an English Opium-Eater
1822	Wordsworth	Ecclesiastical Sonnets
1822	Lamb	Dream Children
1822	Lamb	A Dissertation Upon Roast Pig
1822	Scott	The Fortunes of Nigel
1822	Scott	The Pirate
1822	Byron	The Vision of Judgment
1822	Shelley	Hellas
1822	Hunt	The Liberal
1823	Southey	The History of the Peninsular War
1823	Lamb	Old China
1823	Hazlitt	Liber Amoris
1823	Scott	Quentin Durward
1823	Campbell	The Last Man
1823	Byron	Heaven and Earth
1823	Byron	The Island
1823	Byron	Don Juan, VI-XIV; 1824, XV-XVI
1823	De Quincey	On the Knocking at the Gate in "Macbeth"
1823	De Quincey	Letters to a Young Man Whose Education Has Been Neglected
1823	Carlyle	Schiller
1824	Scott	Redgauntlet
1824	Shelley	The Triumph of Life
1824	Shelley	Posthumous Poems
1824–53	Landor	Imaginary Conversations

1824	Carlyle	Translation of "Wilhelm Meister"
1825	Coleridge	Aids to Reflection
1825	Hazlitt	Spirit of the Age
1825	Scott	The Talisman
1825	Scott	Lives of the Novelists
1826	Lamb	Sanity of True Genius
1826	Hazlitt	The Plain Speaker
1826	Scott	Woodstock
1827	Scott	Life of Napoleon
1827	Moore	The Epicurean
1827	De Quincey	Murder as One of the Fine Arts
1828	Scott	The Fair Maid of Perth
1828	Hunt	Lord Byron and Some of His Contemporaries
1828	Carlyle	Goethe, Burns, etc.
1828	Carlyle	Richter
1828–30	Hazlitt	Life of Napoleon
1829	Scott	Anne of Geierstein
1829	Southey	Colloquies on Society
1829	Carlyle	Signs of the Times
1829	Carlyle	Novalis
1830	Scott	Letters on Demonology and Witchcraft
1830	Moore	Life of Byron
1830	Carlyle	On History
1832	Hunt	Christianism (The Religion of the Heart)
1832	Carlyle	Boswell's Johnson
1832	Carlyle	Death of Goethe
1832	Carlyle	Biography
1833	Lamb	Last Essays of Elia
1833–34	Carlyle	Sartor Resartus
1834	Landor	The Examination of Shakspeare
1834–47	Southey	The Doctor
1834–53	De Quincey	Autobiography
1835	Wordsworth	Yarrow Revisited and Other Poems
1835	Wordsworth	On the Power of Sound
1836	Landor	Pericles and Aspasia
1837	Lockhart	Life of Scott
1837	Landor	Pentameron
1837	De Quincey	The Revolt of a Tartar Tribe
1837	Carlyle	The French Revolution
1838	Carlyle	Sir Walter Scott
1841	Carlyle	Heroes and Hero-Worship
1843	Carlyle	Past and Present
1844	Hunt	Imagination and Fancy
1845	De Quincey	Suspiria De Profundis
1845	De Quincey	Levana and Our Ladies of Sorrow
1845	De Quincey	The Palimpsest of the Human Brain
1846	Hunt	Wit and Humor
1846	Landor	The Hamadryad
1847	Landor	Hellenics
1847	Hunt	Men, Women, and Books
1847	De Quincey	Joan of Arc
1848	De Quincey	The Literature of Knowledge and the Literature of Power
1849	De Quincey	The English Mail Coach
1850	Wordsworth	The Prelude; or The Growth of a Poet's Mind
1850	Hunt	Autobiography
1859	Hunt	Selections from the English Poets

KEY TO ABBREVIATIONS

Anth.   Bernbaum, *Anthology of Romanticism,* Third Edition
CE   *College English*
DR   *Dublin Review*
EJ   *English Journal*
ELH   *Journal of English Literary History*
ESt   *English Studies* (Amsterdam)
EXP   *The Explicator*
GRM   *Germanisch-romanische Monatsschrift*
HJ   *Hibbert Journal*
JEGP   *Journal of English and Germanic Philology*
JHI   *Journal of the History of Ideas*
KR   *Kenyon Review*
MLN   *Modern Language Notes*
MLQ   *Modern Language Quarterly*
MLR   *Modern Language Review*
MP   *Modern Philology*
N&Q   *Notes and Queries*
NYT   *New York Times Book Review*
PMLA *Publications of the Modern Language Association*
PQ   *Philological Quarterly*
RES   *Review of English Studies*
RLC   *Revue de Littérature Comparée*
SAQ   *South Atlantic Quarterly*
SP   *Studies in Philology*
SR   *Sewanee Review*
TLS   *Times Literary Supplement*
UTQ   *University of Toronto Quarterly*

INDEX OF CHIEF AUTHORS AND TOPICS